Public Opinion, Crime, and Criminal Justice

CRIME & SOCIETY
Series Editor John Hagan
University of Toronto

EDITORIAL ADVISORY BOARD
John Braithwaite, Robert J. Bursik, Kathleen Daly,
Malcolm M. Feeley, Jack Katz, Martha A. Myers,
Robert J. Sampson, and Wesley G. Skogan

Public Opinion, Crime, and Criminal Justice,
Julian V. Roberts and Loretta J. Stalans

Poverty, Ethnicity, and Violent Crime, James F. Short, Jr.

Great Pretenders: Pursuits and Careers of Persistent Thieves,
Neal Shover

Crime and Public Policy: Putting Theory to Work,
edited by Hugh D. Barlow

Control Balance: Toward a General Theory of Deviance,
Charles R. Tittle

Rape and Society: Readings on the Problems of Sexual Assault,
edited by Patricia Searles and Ronald J. Berger

FORTHCOMING:

Women's Careers in Violent Crime: Casualties of Community Disorder,
Deborah R. Baskin and Ira B. Sommers

Public Opinion, Crime, and Criminal Justice

Julian V. Roberts
and Loretta J. Stalans

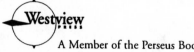

A Member of the Perseus Books Group

Crime & Society

Copyright © 2000 by Westview Press, A Member of the Perseus Books Group

Published in 2000 in the United States of America by Westview Press, 5500 Central Avenue, Boulder, Colorado 80301-2877, and in the United Kingdom by Westview Press, 12 Hid's Copse Road, Cumnor Hill, Oxford OX2 9JJ

Library of Congress Cataloging-in-Publication Data
Roberts, Julian V.
   Public opinion, crime, and criminal justice / Julian V. Roberts
and Loretta J. Stalans.
      p.   cm.—(Crime and society)
   Includes bibliographical references.
   ISBN 0-8133-2318-5 (hc)   ISBN 0-8133-6793-X (pbk).
   1. Crime—United States—Public opinion.   2. Crime—Great Britain—
Public opinion.   3. Criminal justice, Administration of—United
States—Public opinion.   4. Criminal justice, Administration of—
Great Britain—Public opinion.   5. Criminal statistics—United
States.   6. Criminal statistics—Great Britain.   7. Public opinion—
United States.   8. Public opinion—Great Britain.   I. Stalans,
Loretta J. (Loretta Jane)   II. Title.   III. Series: Crime & society
(Boulder, Colo.)
HV6789.R63   1997
364.973—dc21   97-15795
                                                                                                    CIP

To Kay Roberts and the teachers in my life
— Julian V. Roberts

To Raymond B. and Diane T. Stalans for
their strongly held opinions and their love
— Loretta J. Stalans

Contents

Acknowledgments

The preparation of this book was aided by the research assistance of Pao Yang and the Department of Criminal Justice at Loyola University, who provided support for a research assistant. The authors extend their gratitude to Sylvie Chiasson from the University of Ottawa for her assistance in preparing the manuscript. Loretta Stalans also is grateful for the patient and loving support of her husband, Paul Yarnold.

Julian V. Roberts
Loretta J. Stalans

Public Opinion, Crime, and Criminal Justice

1

Introduction and Overview:
Crime in the Public Eye

To the public, crime seems to be everywhere, from the boardrooms to the bedrooms of the nation, in peoples' homes and on their television screens. Americans worry about criminal victimization, are concerned about the proliferation of illegal drugs, and the transformation of many urban centres into "no-go" areas. But it is not just crime that engages the public's attention: The criminal justice response is equally interesting. Most Americans have seen footage of the assault on Rodney King in what became the most well-known amateur video since Zapruder's footage of the Kennedy assassination. The ensuing trials of the officers involved in the Rodney King case also fascinated the public. Rodney King, William Kennedy Smith, the Menendez brothers—all these cases attracted prime time media coverage. Riveting though they were for the public, none have attracted the degree of media coverage or public interest than the Simpson murder trial which in 1995 attracted more media attention than any other news story in America. Well over one hundred million Americans watched television in anticipation of the verdict in that case. Millions more followed the case in other countries.

Public Concern About Crime

An indication of the degree of public concern about the crime issue can be found by examining poll data. In 1994, crime was identified as the number one problem confronting America (Maguire and Pastore, 1994). Fully 37 percent of the public endorsed this view, a much higher percentage than any other social problem, including unemployment or the economy.

Examination of the historical record shows that concern over crime is greater now—and by a substantial degree—than ever before. In 1993 only 9 percent, and in 1992 only 5 percent of Americans identified crime as the number one national problem. In fact, this statistic had never been in excess of 10 percent since the question was first posed in 1980. The results are the same whether people are asked about the whole country or their own specific communities. When respondents were given a list of fifteen neighborhood problems, crime was identified more frequently than any other issue, including unemployment (Maguire *et al.*, 1993). In a poll published by Gallup as the U.S. Crime Bill passed in 1994, over 80 percent of Americans surveyed thought that crime was the most serious threat to individual rights and freedoms in America. Only 41 percent of respondents identified lack of economic opportunity as the most serious threat in this respect.

Another indication of the concern of Americans regarding the crime problem is to be found in their willingness to pay for additional criminal justice expenditures. Even though the justice system costs almost the country seventy-five billion dollars a year, fully three-quarters of the American public believe that too little is being spent to combat crime (Maguire and Pastore, 1995). This attitude has not changed appreciably in the past fifteen years: In 1980, 69 percent of the public held this opinion (Maguire and Pastore, 1995). Finally, it is important to note that the uneven distribution of criminal victimization means that fear or concern is also distributed differentially across the country. For example, Asian Americans are significantly more likely than African-Americans to identify crime as the most important problem facing their community (Maguire and Pastore, 1994).

This widespread public concern over crime in America is accompanied by a highly negative view of the criminal justice response. Here too, there has been a shift in public opinion. The last few years have witnessed a significant decline in public support for the criminal justice system. When Americans were asked in 1994 how much confidence they had in various institutions, the criminal justice system received the lowest ratings. Over half the sample said that they had "a great deal" or "quite a lot" of confidence in the U.S. military and the Church, while only 20 percent expressed a similar degree of confidence in the criminal justice system. Over 40 percent of respondents acknowledged that they had very little or no confidence in the justice system (Maguire and Pastore, 1995). Only one quarter of Americans believe that equal justice exists all or most of the time (Keeva, 1994).

Most people view the criminal justice system as excessively lenient and tilted towards protecting the offender at the expense of the rights of the individual victim, or society in general. In fact, one of the ironies in the field is that the public perceive the criminal justice system itself as a cause of crime. When asked to state the cause of increased crime rates, leniency by the courts and the prison system were identified by more respondents than any other possible cause (Maguire and Pastore, 1995). Over 41 percent identified the law enforcement system or the courts and the prison system as the part of society that is most to blame for the increase in crime. Although no stage of the criminal justice system escapes criticism, the public are far more critical of the courts and correctional authorities than the police. Thus almost two-thirds of the American public rate the police in their community as being excellent or good. Ratings of prosecutors are less positive (48 percent), as are ratings of judges (45 percent). It is the authorities responsible for parole who receives the most negative evaluation: Fewer than one in four Americans perceives them to be doing a good job (Maguire *et al.*, 1993).

Prime-Time Crime

Media coverage of crime stories explains much of the public's interest in criminal justice, as well as the limited extent of their knowledge of the criminal justice system. The news media pay a great deal of attention to crime, whether in the form of fictionalized dramas or news programs. People who watch a lot of television or who read a lot of newspapers will be exposed to a steady diet of crime stories. The information conveyed, however, will not necessarily reflect the true nature of crime as recorded in official crime statistics or victimization surveys. The same can be said for news media coverage of the criminal justice response to crime. Here too, media coverage presents a distorted view of reality, one that stresses the leniency of the system. Finally, with the possible exception of research on the effectiveness of capital punishment, the results of systematic research in the field of criminology are seldom transmitted to the public via the media.

Criminal cases involve conflict, between individuals, or between individuals and the state. Conflict lies at the heart of all drama, so crime stories are inherently dramatic. This is particularly true of the criminal cases that attract the attention of the news media. They almost always involve conflict, at the time of the crime and in subsequent judicial proceedings. There is frequently a degree of mystery: What really happened? In a murder trial, only one person, (the accused) may know the truth, and he or she is not obliged to say anything either before or during the trial. There is also a sense of curiosity too, when a trial unfolds with two sides providing contradictory accounts of events. The model of procedural justice employed in America (the common law system), heightens the drama. Courtroom events follow an adversarial model: Two theoretically equal adversaries representing opposing sides in the dispute. The inquisitorial model,[1] followed in many European jurisdictions such as France, is from the perspective of the public less compelling, and this may explain in part, Americans' fascination with crime and justice.

The link between criminal justice and the public is also closer in America than other nations. One reason for this is the presence of television cameras in courtrooms. Americans are able to participate (passively at least) in every major trial, as though they were jurors. In theory they have access to same amount of information as jurors. It is interesting to compare the media coverage and public interest in major criminal cases in different countries. The trial of the boys charged with killing Jamie Bulger in England received a significant amount of media attention, but almost exclusively in the newspapers. Television cameras were excluded from all stages of the judicial proceedings.

Although attitudes are formed and modified by direct and indirect experiences, in the area of crime and justice, the news media are predominant. Polls in the area of sentencing illustrate the point well. A nation-wide survey in Canada found that 96 percent of the public cited the news media as their source for information about the punishment of offenders. Most people have only very limited direct experience with the criminal justice issues that generate most controversy. For example, many people have strong views on what prison life is like, and what it should be like, yet how many people have actually spent time inside a prison, or visited inmates often enough to understand what goes on behind bars? We rely on the media, through factual and fictional representations, to provide us with information about crime and justice. Our perceptions of offenders are based on what we see on the screen not what we see in the streets.

In Canada, cameras are restricted to the steps of the courthouse, and not permitted inside the court room. In fact, in the most notorious criminal case in recent years, the news media were effectively gagged from reporting anything other than the verdict.[2] In contrast, Americans interested in following any of the major trials in recent years needed only a television and the time to watch to have access to all the information provided to the actual courtroom participants and witnesses.

The most dramatic crime stories evoke—indeed compel—public attention in a way that can be matched by no other issue. The Simpson trial generated more public interest than any other single event in recent memory. Media coverage of crime stories has always been extensive, or excessive, depending on one's perspective. The trial of Bruno Hauptmann, who was accused of killing the son of aviator Charles Lindbergh received a great deal of coverage in the 1930s. However, in the absence of television, there was a limit to how much—and how quickly—the public could learn of developments in the case. The only source of information for the public in those days was the print medium or newsreels that played in movie theatres. Today, over 96 percent of American households contain at least one television set. This means that almost every American could have followed the Simpson trial on a daily basis. Crime is brought to the public in a way that was simply not possible prior to the advent of television. Live television coverage of the trials of O.J. Simpson or the Menendez brothers has brought criminal justice news to the public to a degree unknown to this time. Even trials without the national profile of the Simpson case are brought to the public through edited summaries on programs such as "Inside America's Courts." If people miss these television programs, they can now retrieve from the Internet complete transcripts of high profile cases.

The media have also made criminal justice a truly international issue. High-profile cases such as the assault on Rodney King or the Simpson murder trial are covered by the international news media, and followed by the public in several countries, not just in America. Concern over the ten-year olds convicted of murdering a toddler in a Liverpool suburb was not restricted to people in Britain. Cases such as this, and the mass murders that occurred in Gloucester have become, through the news media, international crime stories. In this sense much as changed over the past thirty years. The "Moors" murders in the early 1960s in England (in which a couple were convicted of torturing and killing children) attracted considerable attention in Britain, but not elsewhere.

Crime, then, is in many ways a social issue like no other. Clearly the public have opinions, sometimes strong ones, on other questions such as whether the U.S. should intervene militarily in the world's hot spots, or what to do about the economy or the health care system. But criminal justice engages our attention and stirs our emotions on many different levels. We respond viscerally to images of urban violence projected by the news media. We feel a more detached sense of outrage when we learn of corruption by senior public officials, or of offenders who commit serious crimes and yet who escape with derisory penalties.

Public Opinion and Criminal Justice Policy-Making

No other people on Earth expect as much from their justice system as Americans do. When we feel we've been wronged, we expect the law and courts to set things right. When we feel threatened—by crime, hatred or intolerance—we expect law enforcement, the corrections system and the courts to restore a semblance of safety and calm. (Keeva, 1994, p. 46)

Considering crime and criminal justice naturally leads to debates over crime control policies. Such debates have become ever more heated in recent years, as one solution after another has been adopted or rejected, sometimes adopted then rejected. The war on illegal drugs, violent crime in the inner cities, insider trading, illegal immigration—all these and many other problems have generated seemingly endless debates over crime policies. Should we build more prisons and pass harsher sentencing legislation, or invest in crime prevention through social development? Do we need more police, or more social workers? Should we abolish capital punishment or simply work harder to ensure that it is not applied in a discriminatory manner? Are more rigorous gun controls necessary or simply harsher (or mandatory) sentences for offenders who commit crimes with a firearm? Is it wrong to execute offenders who were juveniles when they committed the crimes that landed them on death row? The vigorous discussion around the 1994 Crime Bill attests to the high degree of public interest in the policy questions surrounding crime.

Public opinion plays an important role in criminal justice policy-making. This too, sets it apart from many other social issues. It is true that policy-makers involved in foreign affairs frequently consult public opinion surveys, but public views in the area of criminal justice are more directly engaged. American judges who have to face re-election are more responsive than their counterparts in other countries who are appointed to the bench for life. Politicians at the state and federal level listen to the views of the public. Law and order has consistently emerged as a key issue during elections. The case of Willie Horton is now well-documented. Horton was a murderer who killed a second time while on furlough. His case played a key role in the defeat of democratic candidate Michael Dukakis (see Tonry, 1995). Law and order has played a similar role in elections in other countries as well. The "Three strikes" sentencing laws in America (such as the one contained in the Violent Crime Control and Law Enforcement Act of 1994) were passed, in large part, as a result of public pressure for governments to do something about violent, recidivist crime. And finally, the issue of community values has played an important role in several Supreme Court decisions relating to criminal justice cases.

All too often legislators and policy-makers and newspaper editorialists use public opinion to advance their own criminal justice policy agendas. "This is what the people want," we are told, as politicians attempt to peddle their pet criminal justice policy. For example, appeals to public opinion have been used to bolster proposals to toughen juvenile offender legislation in Canada (Bala, 1994) as well as the U.S. (see Schwartz, Guo and Kerbs, 1993). Advocates in many different areas of criminal justice have claimed that the public is on their side. These claims, however, are almost never accompanied by public opinion data. At best, they cite letters to the editor, readership surveys and similarly unsystematic measures of public opinion. When the results of public opinion surveys have been cited, the results are often surprising. In this book we shall identify issues where policy-makers, politicians or Supreme Court judges have drawn conclusions about public opinion which do not stand up in light of actual survey results.

Going Beyond the Results of Polls

In order to understand public views of crime and criminal justice we need to explore more than just the results of surveys. We need to know about the ways in which people process information, and how our views relate to previously-existing beliefs and attitudes. Whether you believe that Anita Hill was an innocent victim of predatory male sexuality may well depend upon your view of gender relations in society. Whether you feel that William Kennedy Smith committed the crime of rape may well depend upon what kinds of conduct you believe to be acceptable between men and women. As for the Rodney King case, people with a strong law and order orientation and who identify with the police may well "see" a different event as they watch the videotape of the assault on Mr. King. Was Bernard Goetz exercising his legitimate right to defend himself when he shot three black youths in the New York subway? Or was he committing the crime of attempted murder? People's positions may well be determined by whether they have been victimized. And finally, opinions about the verdict in the Simpson trial are related to the race of the respondent: Polls have demonstrated a strong racial difference in reactions to the verdict. African-Americans were significantly more likely to believe that the accused was not guilty.

This book is about crime, criminal justice and the public. Since the 1960s, crime has been the focus of a great deal of polling and public opinion research. Pollsters have surveyed the public on almost every topic relating to criminal justice. Some issues—such as capital punishment—have been addressed so often that a significant historical analysis is now possible. We now know a great deal about the ways in which people select, assimilate and respond to news about crime and criminal justice. We shall review research upon this issue. Throughout this book we shall attempt to go beyond the results of public opinion polls. For example, approximately two-thirds of the public in America, Canada and Great Britain support the use of the death penalty for offenders convicted of murder. But this is the beginning, not the end, of the story. This bald empirical fact does not tell us *why* the public endorse capital punishment, what kinds of cases they have in mind or whether they have considered alternative punishments such as life in prison without the possibility of parole. Nor does it tell us what they know about the administration of the death penalty, or its effectiveness (relative to life imprisonment) as a general deterrent to murder.

Simple polls also fail to tell us what underlies the attitude, whether it is founded upon bedrock support for harsh, retributive punishment or perhaps a more malleable (and mistaken) belief in the deterrent efficacy of the death penalty. The same argument applies to many other issues in the area of criminal justice. Some of these questions can be (and have been) resolved by additional research, but others require knowledge of material from several fields of inquiry including social psychology, criminology and the study of the law. Our plan is to convey an understanding of public views of crime and criminal justice, rather than simply provide an inventory of findings from surveys on criminal justice topics.[3]

We also aim to highlight areas in which the public have significant misperceptions about crime, offenders or criminal justice. It is important to know whether a particular attitude is founded upon faulty knowledge, or some fundamental value. Whenever possible, we contrast the opinions of the public (as reflected in the results of representative surveys) with the results of systematic research from the field of criminology. We shall show, for example, that the public systematically over-estimate critical statistics such as criminal recidivism rates and crime rates. At the same time, they under-estimate the severity of the justice system. Many of these misper- ceptions feed into, and sustain a general public ideology with regard to crime and punishment. This view is that crime is a phenomenon committed by a small, identifiable group of people, and that crime can be prevented or offenders deterred if the system would simply impose harsher penalties.

It is important to note that the public are far from monolithic in their attitudes. People from different backgrounds and life experiences do not always share the same views about criminal justice. This is particularly true when demographic characteristics relate to involvement in crime or contact with the criminal justice system. Perhaps the most obvious example of this is that of race. Michael Tonry has demonstrated that incarceration rates for Black Americans are approximately seven to eight times higher than for whites (Tonry, 1995, p. 4). For this reason, it is perhaps not surprising that African-Americans and Caucasian Americans have different views about criminal justice policies. To take just one example, when Bernard Goetz (the so-called "Subway Vigilante") was acquitted of charges arising from the shooting of several black youths in the New York subway, public opinion surveys showed a deep racial split: 83 percent of Caucasian-Americans supported the verdict compared to only 45 percent of African-Americans (Fletcher, 1990). A similar racial split emerged after the verdict in the Simpson trial was announced: A significantly higher percentage of African- Americans believed that Simpson was not guilty. Throughout the book, we shall point out subjects which provoke very different responses from different groups in American society.

The principal focus in this book is upon Americans' knowledge of, and attitudes toward crime and criminal justice. However, we also draw upon polls and research conducted in other countries, principally Canada, the United Kingdom and Australia. While there are obviously differences between these countries in terms of their crime rates and criminal justice systems, there are also important common attributes. The differences in crime rates tend to be ones of degree. For example, the percentage of crime involving violence is fairly constant in all these nations, although the actual rates of violent crime vary considerably. The same can be said for public attitudes towards criminal justice issues. Americans share many of the same concerns faced by Britons, Canadians and Australians. As well, there are basic problems and processes that are common to residents of all these countries.

Some restrictions upon the breadth of issues covered in this book have been necessary, and should be made explicit at this point. First, for the most part, only polls or research conducted in English have been reviewed. (For research pertaining to other jurisdictions, see, for example, Makela, 1966 (Finland); Podgorecki, Kaupen, Van Houtte, Vincke and Kutchinsky, 1973 (Scandinavia); van Dijk, 1978 (Holland); Ocqueteau and Perez Diaz, 1990 (France); Zimmerman, Jeangros, Hausser and Zeugin, 1991 (Switzerland); Sebba, 1983 (Israel)). Thus few cross-cultural comparisons will be made. Second, the extensive literature on public fear of crime is not addressed here as it has already been the object of previous publications (see for example, Stinchcombe *et al.*, 1980). Finally, beyond the brief discussion provided in this introductory chapter, we shall not discuss methodological issues in great length. Several monographs already exist for the reader interested in knowing more about the way that polls are conducted.

Plan of the Book

The rest of this introductory chapter is devoted to articulating the concepts that guide the subsequent discussion. Pollsters, researchers and indeed the general public use terms such as "attitude," "belief" and "opinion" in different ways. While we try to avoid being dogmatic, we shall at least try to lay down a conceptual framework and terminology to guide the reader through the rest of the volume. After this conceptual framework has been elaborated, we shall provide a brief description of the principal methodologies employed in the study of public opinion.

Chapter 2 explores public knowledge of crime rates and the characteristics of offenders. The next chapter (3) examines public awareness of legal reforms and the criminal justice response to crime. This chapter reviews research on public knowledge of crime and critical criminal justice statistics such as sentencing trends and recidivism rates. We also review public knowledge of important criminal justice policies and legislation. In these two chapters dealing with knowledge rather than opinion, we argue that what the public thinks about crime and criminal justice can only be understood in light of what they know about the issues.

Chapter 4 examines research on public perceptions of the seriousness of crime as a social problem: How serious does crime seem when compared to other important social problems such as health care or the economy? This chapter also reviews research on public perceptions of the relative seriousness of different crimes. How much consensus is there regarding the crimes that are most serious and which accordingly should be punished most harshly?

Chapter 5 is devoted to information processing by the public. People do not simply absorb information like computers: We are highly selective in the information that we acquire, and the ways in which we use this knowledge. This chapter reviews the social psychological literature dealing with the way that people assimilate and process information about crime and criminal justice. We address questions such as the following: Do the public change their views when they receive additional information, or are attitudes quite immutable? As we shall see, while some beliefs are highly resistant to change, others shift more easily.

Public theories of crime and perceptions of offenders are the subject of discussion in Chapter 6. We examine lay explanations of delinquency, which obviously have an important bearing upon public support for various criminal justice policies: How we respond to delinquency reflects our conceptions of what (or who) is responsible for crime. We all have theories of criminal behavior. Some theories stress concepts of personal responsibility, others lay emphasis on social factors such as unemployment and discrimination. Chapter 6 explores these theories and the ways in which they relate to reactions to crime.

Chapter 7 explores public evaluations of the ethical standards and the procedural fairness of the police and courts, and the role of direct experience in shaping public support for these institutions.

In Chapter 8, we review data pertaining to public perceptions of the way the police handle cases, and the correctness and competence of decisions made about arrest. This chapter also explores public evaluations of the courts. Chapter 8 also explores the question of whether community sentiment about crime is consistent with legislative definitions of crimes.

Chapter 9 examines public reaction to two corner-stones of the western legal tradition: The adversarial system and the jury. Are both of these institutions central to public conceptions of justice?

Sentencing and parole attract more attention (and criticism) than any other topic in criminal justice. Notions of punishment are central to our conceptions of justice, and this issue has generated more surveys and research than any other. In Chapter 10, we review research on questions such as the following: Which sentencing aims are favored by the public? Are the public harsher than the judiciary towards offenders? Is there a gap between public opinion and the perceptions of public views held by politicians?

Chapter 11 deals with the ultimate punishment. The death penalty has been the subject of more debate (and more opinion polls) than any other single topic in criminal justice. As well, the U.S. Supreme Court has cited public opinion research in several of its judgements relating to the constitutionality of capital punishment. The chapter concludes with a discussion of social science measures of community sentiment and the Supreme Court's use of social science evidence.

Chapter 12 explores the ways in which public opinion is used to define central concepts in constitutional law such as obscenity and privacy. Supreme Court Justices have explicitly recognized the importance of community sentiment in these areas.

The proliferation of firearms has become a source of public concern as well as legislative activity in several countries. Many proposals have been advanced, and several laws passed in western nations to restrict access to guns, particularly handguns. Where do the public stand on the issue of gun control? Chapter 13 reviews the data on this topic.

Youth crime is another priority for criminal justice systems in America, Great Britain as well as Canada. The public believe that crime rates by young offenders have escalated dramatically in recent years, and that lenient youth justice legislation is in large measure responsible. This chapter (14) takes a close look at public sentiment regarding crime by the young, and solutions that have been proposed.

Finally, in the last chapter (15), we draw some conclusions about public attitudes to crime and justice and suggest a number of steps that need to be taken to advance the field. Although there has been a steady accretion of opinion polls over the past few decades, a number of topics have been overlooked, including, for example, the ways in which public attitudes towards criminal justice are predictive of public behavior vis-a-vis crime. We conclude by addressing the question of whether public opinion should play a formal role in the criminal justice system.

Before turning to some methodological matters, we now describe some basic conceptual distinctions that are relevant to the material that follows.

Crime Control Versus Due Process Models of Justice

Herbert Packer has outlined two competing models of criminal justice. According to the due process model, the justice system should incorporate numerous safeguards to protect the rights of the suspect or the accused. For example, a police officer is obliged, when making an arrest, to provide a clear statement to the suspect of his or her rights under the law. Likewise, when gathering evidence, the police cannot just search any premises; they must first obtain permission from the owner or a search warrant from a judge. Evidence obtained without these precautions will probably be ruled inadmissible, even if it points clearly to the guilt of the accused. These due process safeguards have the effect of making it harder for the state to secure a conviction. For this reason, some people oppose them. Critics of the due process model favor an alternative, which is known as the crime control model. According to this perspective, the prevention of crime and the punishment of offenders should take precedence over other concerns. Protecting the rights of the accused is less important. Advocates of the crime control model endorse the use of extensive police powers, few rights of appeal and limited accountability of criminal justice professionals.

It is easy to see how the two models can be in conflict with one another. Advocates of the crime control model would argue that what is important is whether the evidence obtained points to the guilt of the accused, not the manner in which it was acquired. Consider the case of a man charged with first degree murder who confesses to police as soon as they begin questioning him in custody. The confession is videotaped. Later, the man recants the confession and asserts his innocence. His attorney notes that he was not given the standard Miranda warning about his rights prior to making the confession. Crime control advocates would consider the confession (witnessed by several officers) to be a legitimate piece of evidence. Due process supporters would argue that the confession should be ruled inadmissible, and that the jury should not be made aware of its existence. Where do the public stand regarding this dichotomy? Are they due process supporters or advocates of crime control? As we shall see, they tend to endorse elements of both models, and are not consistently on one side of the debate.

Consensus Versus Conflict

Another important dichotomy of relevance to the issue of public opinion concerns the nature of criminal justice itself. There are two principal opposing conceptions of justice: consensus and conflict. According to the consensus view, the laws and the administration of justice reflect agreement throughout society regarding subjects such as the relative seriousness of crimes. Consider the issue of sentencing. The consensus view argues that the legal system punishes some crimes more severely than others because this is what society as a whole believes should be done. There is agreement in society that street crimes of violence are more serious than white collar crimes, and the sentencing trends merely reflect this degree of consensus. Laws and criminal justice policies emerge from a social consensus about the nature of criminal law and how it should be administered. On the other hand, the conflict perspective stresses an absence of consensus. Following this logic, conflict theorists assert that certain crimes are punished more severely than others because the dominant social class has been able to impose its view upon the system. Throughout this book we shall see how the views of the public follow these two perspectives on criminal justice.

Information Processing by the Public

Research in the field of social and cognitive psychology has shown that people do not always use information in a rational, scientific manner. The way in which we respond to information depends on a number of factors, including our prior attitudes. This fact has important consequences for attitudes to crime and justice since for many issues information plays a critical role. Capital punishment is perhaps the classic example. Although there is an obvious moral dimension to the question of whether we should execute offenders convicted of murder, information also plays a critical role in determining public attitudes. For a significant number of people, the deterrent effect of capital punishment is central to their pro-death penalty position.

The literature on public opinion generates two images of the public. One is that of a "lazy cognitive miser" who is apathetic and uninformed about justice topics. Supporters of this perspective suggest that laypersons should play a very circumscribed role in criminal justice policy and should have only limited participation in the decisions made in the criminal justice system. In support of the lazy cognitive miser view, these critics of public participation point to research that shows that people use cognitive shortcuts to arrive at opinions (e.g., Converse, 1964; Kahneman, Slovic, and Tversky, 1982). These critics also note that people change their opinion when the decision-making context changes. For example, research has found that prior questions affect responses to subsequent questions in surveys, and that the specificity of a crime story determines the punitiveness of the public's response (e.g., Doob and Roberts, 1984; Doble, 1987; Stalans and Diamond, 1990; Tourangeau and Rasinski, 1988).

An alternative view to the lazy cognitive miser perspective is the image of a pragmatic social thinker who is interested in justice issues and conserves energy for the most difficult topics (Stalans and Lurigio, 1996). The pragmatic social perspective suggests that people may not make optimal decisions, but they may often make decisions that are in some significant sense "good enough" for the task at hand (Fiske, 1992). Even professionals use cognitive shortcuts and prior beliefs to make decisions; it is not the reliance on these processes that determines the quality of the decision. To determine whether decisions are "good enough," researchers must know the beliefs, perceptions, and values on which people based their judgments. Cognitive shortcuts do not automatically produce biased decisions; it depends on whether the perceptions driving the decisions are unrepresentative or are irrelevant to the issue. In this book, we attempt where possible to highlight the underlying meaning of opinions expressed in public opinion polls. By examining the concerns underlying an opinion, we are better able to understand the relativity, validity, and stability of expressed views.

At this point we provide some information on methodologies in the area of public opinion research.

Research Methodologies

The following material is provided to give the reader an idea of research methods employed in the area, but it is not intended to be anything more than an overview. For further information about survey methods, the reader is directed towards several excellent texts on the subject (e.g., Hoinville *et al.*, 1978). Research on public opinion falls into one of three principal methodological categories: quantitative analyses of representative samples of the public; qualitative analyses of much smaller "focus groups;" studies employing non-representative "purposive" samples, usually college students. Attitudes and opinions have been measured or explored in other ways (e.g., Sarat, 1977; Shoemaker and South, 1978; Webb, Campbell, Schwartz, and Sechrest, 1981) but these alternate measures account for few studies in the field.

Representative Surveys

Along with the penetration of television into modern society, we have also witnessed a proliferation of public opinion polls. Surveys are conducted daily on a national or state-wide level, dealing with almost every conceivable social issue. Crime is frequently one of the issues addressed. As well, public opinion polls have become more sophisticated and are now capable of rendering accurate estimates of population trends on the basis of relatively small samples of respondents. Surveys of representative samples of the public account for most contemporary research. (See Durham, 1993, for a discussion of earlier polling work).

There is no substitute for a well-conducted representative poll. Research on the jury illustrates this. As we shall document later in this volume, the public are strong supporters of trial by jury. However, this finding does not necessarily emerge if the poll is not representative of the population from which it was drawn. When readers of a national magazine were asked to respond to a question about the jury, four-fifths stated that they would like to scrap the jury system entirely (cited in Antieu, 1996). Representative surveys reveal a very different result.

Surveys are typically conducted by major polling companies (e.g., Louis Harris, Gallup) either as an independent survey for a specific client or as part of monthly or annual surveys; recently there has been an increase in the number of polls conducted by university-based polling centers. In addition to mail surveys, both telephone and in-person interviews have been used, although researchers show a preference for the former, as they cost less and result in comparable accuracy (Klecka and Tuchfarber, 1978; Quinn, Gutek, and Walsh, 1980).

National and state-wide surveys all use a probability sampling procedure which ensures a final sample that conforms to the characteristics of the population from which the sample was drawn. This entails over-sampling respondents in certain categories that would be under-represented by a simple "sweep" survey in which interviews are conducted with whoever happens to be at home when the interviewer calls. Different polling companies employ different sample sizes. The critical issue common to all is sampling error, which refers to divergences between results obtained from the sample, and results that would have been obtained had a census of the population been conducted. Consider a poll using a sample of 1,000 respondents with a margin of error of plus or minus 4 percent that finds 33 percent of respondents favor the abolition of parole. This means that the actual percentage of the population (from which the sample was drawn) that favor parole abolition lies somewhere between 29 percent and 37 percent, although 33 percent is more likely to be correct than a statistic located at the extremes. For most criminal justice issues, this degree of precision is probably adequate; whether the percentage favoring parole abolition is 30 percent or 34 percent is not a critical difference. In this respect, polls are a more useful tool to criminologists than to political scientists, who require greater precision. After all, a 5 percent difference in voting patterns can, when converted to parliamentary seats, mean a change in government.

In recent years the representative survey has evolved in some interesting ways, principally to incorporate the advantages of small-scale surveys. The general idea is to increase (and sometimes manipulate) the amount of information and the manner in which that information is conveyed. Two techniques in particular have proved fruitful. One is known as the factorial survey, and was pioneered by Peter Rossi and his colleagues (see Rossi and Anderson, 1982; Rossi and Nock, 1982; Rossi, Simpson and Miller, 1985). This technique permits researchers to explore the independent (and interactive) effects of several variables simultaneously. The simultaneous manipulation of multiple independent variables would typically be reserved for factorial experiments conducted in a laboratory using college students as subjects.

In a factorial survey, computer-generated vignettes are presented to a large number of subjects in a way that ensures the statistical properties of a randomized factorial experiment. For example, Rossi, Simpson, and Miller (1985) explored the effects of several offense and offender characteristics on ratings of crime seriousness and punishment severity. Using this technique, researchers can see how different crimes (and different offender characteristics) affect judgments of the appropriate penalty in the case. The benefits of a factorial survey are clear: The design permits the researcher to run complex experiments with large numbers of subjects; the technique has become increasingly popular (e.g., Applegate, Cullen, Link, Richards, and Lanza-Kaduce, 1996; Miller, Rossi and Simpson, 1986; Roberts and White, 1986; Thurman, 1989).

A second survey innovation is known as Computer-assisted telephone interviewing (CATI). This is a computerized opinion poll which has several advantages in terms of cost-saving and efficiency, but it also permits greater flexibility in the nature of the questions posed. Specifically, CATI permits the researcher to manipulate variables such as the wording of the question, or the nature of the information that precedes the question. For example, in a survey about capital punishment, half the respondents may be given a small amount of information about the case, while the other half would be given a more complete account of the case. Both groups would then be asked to respond to the same question (e.g., "Is the death penalty appropriate in this case?"). This means that a randomized experiment is possible, using a representative survey of respondents. Of course the technique can also go much further than this. The computer can easily provide further information to respondents, the exact nature of the information being contingent upon the respondent's response to the preliminary question. Innovations of this kind will have considerable application in criminal justice, where to date, polls have employed more traditional techniques (see Cantril, 1980; Bradburn and Sudman, 1988, for further information).

Focus Groups

This kind of study is a relatively recent innovation in public opinion research, although the idea of intensive discussion, or "focused interviews" goes back many years (see Merton, 1987, Krueger, 1988, for discussion of the historical antecedents of focus groups). The concept arose from dissatisfaction (see Bertrand, 1982; Himmelfarb, 1990) with polls in which the interviewer poses questions that require answers within seconds, usually entailing a simple choice among a small number of alternatives. Focus groups generate an environment in which respondents have the opportunity to reflect upon the question posed, and can then discuss their reflections with other participants. These groups are designed to go beyond the reflexive (but far from reflective) responses elicited by surveys posing simplistic questions such as "Are you in favor of, or opposed to, the use of the death penalty?"

Generally speaking, focus group studies consist of small numbers of people (usually ten-fifteen) selected to represent major demographic categories (to the extent that this is possible with so small a number). Several groups are conducted in different cities, with an attempt made at the end to synthesize the findings. In short, focus groups are a kind of public opinion jury, in which the task is not to render a verdict (in this case a single unanimous opinion), but to generate qualitative material which is recorded and later summarized for publication. Unlike juries, there is usually a moderator present who directs the discussion and who, in some cases, is responsible for introducing material to which group discussants are asked to respond. The focus group approach has become popular in North America; reports of recent studies employing this approach can be found in Doble (1987); Doble and Klein (1989) and Environics Research Group (1989a).

What exactly do focus groups add to the information derived from a large-scale, representative public opinion poll? They clearly generate material that cannot be derived from an opinion survey, but how far should such qualitative data be trusted, and to what extent are they a reflection of public opinion rather than the views of a particular moderator (or of the person who happens to summarize the group's discussion for publication)? Some empirical research into the way in which focus groups are conducted, with direct comparisons with other methodologies would be informative; unfortunately none appears to be available at the present. At the very least, focus groups offer researchers an opportunity to explore the phenomenology of responses to questions posed on large-scale surveys. Thus a focus group discussion of the death penalty would quickly uncover the fact that many proponents of capital punishment have specific offenders in mind, and are in fact prepared to rule out capital punishment for many kinds of offenders.

Focus groups also provide researchers with an opportunity to test the strength of attitudes by providing discussants with relevant information, counter-arguments and so on. This function of a focus group was explored with considerable success in a recent analysis of public attitudes towards punishing offenders in Alabama (Doble and Klein, 1989). Focus group participants were asked to sentence several offenders described in vignettes. At a later point the moderators provided information about alternative dispositions and asked discussants to re-sentence the offenders. The sentencing preferences of the group shifted significantly once they were made aware of the alternative sanctions. This kind of technique is less feasible in a large-scale survey.

This measure of public opinion is open to criticism on several method-ological grounds. In a study such as the sentence-re-sentence study in Alabama (Doble and Klein, 1989), the "manipulation" must be apparent to subjects. This can lead to the presence of "demand characteristics," cues inadvertently given which then permit subjects to guess the hypothesis being tested. In some cases, the subjects then respond in ways to confirm the hypothesis they perceive is being tested. This phenomenon must be considered as a plausible alternative explanation of the findings. Subjects may have felt compelled to use the alternative sanctions simply because the moderator introduced them. And issues of external validity must also be addressed when one is attempting to make general statements about the residents of a state on the basis of a non-representative sample of (in this case) 420 focus group participants. As long as broad generalizations are not made (and to date authors of reports based on focus group discussions have been scrupulous in setting the limits beyond which their data cannot be stretched), the focus group approach constitutes a valuable adjunct to surveys using larger, representative samples.

Experimental Research with Convenience Samples

This final category of research has proved to be at least as useful as the others. It includes all experimental, quasi-experimental and correlational research, usually conducted on a university campus, but sometimes using more heterogeneous samples of subjects than university students. While precluding generalization to national, state, provincial or county popula-tions, these studies have permitted researchers to examine the effects of various experimental manipulations which cannot be used on representa-tive surveys. Examples of this approach can be found in: Vidmar and Dittenhoffer (1981); Doob and Roberts (1983); Higginbottom and Zamble

(1988) and Hilton (1989). In the study by Doob and Roberts for instance, a sample of 115 members of the general public were randomly assigned to read either the newspaper description of a sentencing hearing, or a description of the same hearing but based upon the actual court documents. Thus the sentence imposed was the same in both cases. The purpose of the study was to see if subjects would rate the sentence differently depending upon whether they read the news media account or an account based on court documents. A representative survey was not necessary to test this hypothesis. Estimating population values was not the goal of the study. What was at issue was whether the two groups, statistically equivalent before the study began (due to random assignment) would react differently.

The distinction between large-scale traditional opinion polls, and a more recent techniques such as focus groups or Deliberative Polling (see below) reflects the distinction proposed by Yankelovich (1991) between mass opinion and public judgment. According to Yankelovich, top-of-the-head responses to simple polls reflect mass opinion; they tend to be volatile, have little internal consistency and indicate the respondent may be giving a response without accepting (or even considering) the consequences of the view. On the other hand, public judgment is characterized by acceptance of the consequences of the opinion, by firmness (indicating the view changes little over time) and by the degree of consistency between this view and others held by the respondent.

To cite a concrete example, when people are asked "Are you in favor of, or opposed to alternatives to incarceration?", they frequently express opposition. This reflects mass opinion more than public judgment. Why? Because the percentage opposing alternative measures frequently varies from poll to poll, and because responses change dramatically when the consequences are made clear to respondents. To date, surveys in criminal justice have all too often reflected mass opinion rather than public judgment. Developments such as CATI and Focus groups are a definite step towards establishing the true nature of public opinion in the field. The most recent innovation combines elements of the focus group approach with the advantages of a representative survey, with the goal of uncovering the true nature of public opinion.

Deliberative Polls

This hybrid methodology is known as a Deliberative poll (see Fishkin, 1995). A random sample of the public is contacted and asked to respond to a series of questions. From this original sample, a sub-set of several hundred participants are brought together for an entire week-end. Over the course of this period, participants are encouraged to reflect on the issues, discuss their ideas with other individuals and in small groups and even to pose questions to panels of experts in the field as well as politicians. At the end of the week-end, participants complete the questionnaire a second time. The differences between their opinions on the first and second occasions reflect the difference between public opinion and informed public judgment. To date, the only deliberative poll on crime was conducted in England in 1994.[4]

Significant shifts of opinion emerged, for some issues at least. For example, before the week-end sessions, a third of the group was opposed to sending first-time burglars to prison. This percentage rose to half the sample at the second administration of the questionnaire. Statistically significant shifts also emerged for other issues such as the right of suspects to remain silent under questioning by the police. Comparisons of the original large sample, and the smaller subset who actually participated in the experiment indicated that these shifts were not due to certain kinds of individuals self-selecting themselves to participate. The second sample was representative of the sample originally contacted. No significant shifts emerged for some issues. For example, there was no change in the percentage of participants/respondents who thought that the death penalty is the most appropriate sentence for some crimes, or the percentage who agreed with the statement that "Prison life is too soft" (see Fishkin, 1995, pp. 177-181).

It is too early to conclude that deliberative polling is the wave of the future in terms of public opinion research. One obvious impediment to its widespread application is the cost of assembling the participants. In the future, this may be circumvented by electronic "meetings." As well, there is as yet no scholarly literature on the topic. Questions remain: To what extent are the shifts in opinion dependent on the information provided to the participants? Is there a danger that deliberative polls can be manipulated by the choice of "experts" that participate? To what extent are the shifts in opinion a function of the fact that on the first administration the surveys were completed in respondents' homes, while on the second occasion they were completed in the presence of others? Without scrupulous attention to balancing the material on controversial issues such as the use of imprisonment and the rights of defendants, the outcome of deliberative polls may reflect more the agenda of the organizers than informed public judgement.

Conclusions

Responding to crime has become a priority for the public in all western nations. In America, the percentage of Americans concerned about crime is currently at an all-time high. The public have a keen interest in criminal justice issues, and awareness of some specific cases is widespread. For this the media are largely responsible. Crime news captures the attention of the public like no other topic. This is particularly true for dramatic, individual cases such as the Simpson murder trial in America, the Bernardo trial in Canada and the serial murders committed in Gloucester in Great Britain. As the debate continues as to the best way to respond to the crime problem, politicians and policy-makers appeal to the public for support. Judges, too, are sensitive to public reaction to the sentences that they impose. For these reasons, it is important to have an accurate understanding of public opinion in the area. This entails going beyond a surface reading of public opinion poll findings.

A comprehensive picture of public knowledge and opinion in the area of criminal justice can only be obtained by a multi-method approach. Representative opinion polls are necessary to set the approximate bounds on public attitudes and in order to identify issues requiring greater public education (Margarita and Parisi, 1979). Focus groups are needed in order to evaluate the depth of a particular opinion, and laboratory-based research is essential to test experimental hypotheses. In this volume we shall discuss research drawing upon all these methods, although we draw most heavily upon the findings of surveys using samples of respondents that are representative of the populations from which they are drawn.

Notes

1. Under the inquisitorial system, judges take over many of the functions of the defense and prosecution.

2. This did not prevent details of the case from leaking out. The judicial "gag" of news media applied only to publications within Canada. Accordingly, Canadians with access to American television or certain American publications could learn about the case. In fact, notwithstanding the restraining order, within six months, a poll showed that one-third of the residents of Ontario (where the case occurred), were aware of some aspects of the case.

3. For readers wishing to consult polls regarding crime and justice, the annual "Sourcebook of Criminal Justice Statistics" which goes back many years now, contains a section summarizing the results of national surveys in the U.S. The Sourcebook is published by the U.S. Department of Justice. In this volume we draw upon material from the most recent Sourcebook (1995) available at the time this book went to press in 1997.

4. A two-hour videotape of the British Deliberative Poll on Crime is available from Channel Four in London.

2

Public Knowledge of Crime:
Myths and Realities

Almost every day the news media confront us with policy questions relating to sentencing, gun control, drugs and crime, violent offenders, young offenders, parole and many other criminal justice issues. In England, the government has proposed abolishing the right of a suspect to remain silent under interrogation by the police. What are the likely consequences of this reform? Offenders convicted of first degree murder in Canada receive a mandatory life sentence, with no possibility of parole before twenty-five years have been served in prison. However, under a little known provision of the Canadian *Criminal Code*, these life prisoners may have their cases reviewed by a jury at the fifteen-year mark. The jury has the power to end the inmate's period of parole ineligibility, and to allow him to apply for parole, notwithstanding the original sentence. Should this provision of the *Code* be repealed? How often is it successfully invoked?

We all have opinions about what is being done about the crime problem, and what should be done (for most people the two are almost never the same), yet how much do we actually know about the issues? Politicians are quick to note public support or opposition to various policies. To take just one current example in America, there has been widespread public enthusiasm for the "Three Strikes and You're Out" sentencing provision. Support for such a provision has now spread to other countries such as Canada and the United Kingdom (see Roberts, 1996). But is the enthusiasm for this proposal based upon a realistic appreciation of the nature of criminal recidivism, and the consequences of such a draconian solution? Do people understand the costs of the provision, and the likely benefits in terms of crime control? Or is it more a case of "it seemed like a good idea at the time?" Public views about crime control policies can only be understood by knowing about public knowledge in this area. Accordingly, in this chapter and the next we review research that has explored not what the public *feel*, but rather what they *know* about the phenomenon of crime, criminal justice statistics or the nature of the criminal justice system. Empirical research has been accumulating for decades now in the field of criminology. How much of this research has reached the general public?

Public criticism is not restricted to criminal justice policies. As well, people form strong opinions regarding the decisions in individual cases. Frequently these opinions are founded upon little more than a few media stories and informal discussions about the case. Many people were critical of the sentences imposed on Ivan Boesky for insider trading, and Leona Helmsley for tax evasion, but how much do the public know about penalties for these crimes imposed in other cases?

Researchers have generally neglected public knowledge of the problem of crime, and the nature of the criminal justice response, tending to focus almost exclusively on public attitudes. Pollsters usually ask whether respondents are for or against the death penalty, not how much they know about the costs and benefits of capital punishment. We estimate that surveys examining public *knowledge* represent less than 2 percent of all polls that have been published. It is curious that public knowledge in this area has been researched far less extensively than public opinion,[1] for as the criminologist Richard Quinney noted "Reaction to all that is associated with crime rests initially upon knowledge about crime" (1975, p. 176).

When politicians talk about popular support for abolition of the insanity defense, the "Three Strikes" proposal or any other crime policy, we must bear in mind the limited amount of information that the public have about some of these criminal justice issues. Clearly we should be careful when interpreting the results of opinion surveys showing public support for, or opposition to, some criminal justice policy or procedure. The public may be basing their views on misinformation. An important aim then of survey research should be to document gaps in public knowledge. The public can only make an informed judgment about justice policies when they have a reasonably accurate idea about the true nature and extent of crime and the criminal justice response to crime.

There are other reasons for wanting to have information about public knowledge of the criminal justice system. Some of these concern the effectiveness of the criminal justice system: General deterrence is a good example. People can only be deterred from offending if they are aware of the severity of penalties which may follow a conviction. No matter how severe the penalty, it will have no deterrent effect if people are unaware of it, or if they believe it is never imposed. As well, many reforms of the criminal justice system are dependent upon a change in public awareness. Consider rape reform legislation.

Legal reforms in many American states and Canada (see Marsh, Geist and Caplan, 1982; Roberts and Mohr, 1994) have attempted to stress the aggressive rather than the sexual nature of crimes of sexual aggression. Thus offenses of rape and indecent assault were replaced by crimes of sexual aggression, or criminal sexual conduct. One of the aims of these reforms was to increase the proportion of victims of sexual assault who report to the police. In the past, research had demonstrated that victims of sexual aggression were reluctant to report crimes to the police on account (in part) of the stigma associated with being a victim of a sexual crime. But legislative changes of this kind can only be effective if the public become aware of them. An important reason for conducting knowledge surveys then, is to find out whether the public have learned about important legislative reforms, a subject we shall address in the following chapter.

In the course of Chapters 2 and 3 we shall document gaps in public knowledge, or areas in which public perceptions conflict with the findings of systematic research into crime and criminal justice. Such an exercise can only be preliminary in nature, for two reasons. First, because we are limited to studying issues upon which pollsters have explored public knowledge. And second, because there is not always a great deal of research to demonstrate the exact nature of "reality." Throughout this discussion we shall stay close to public misperceptions that have been documented by representative surveys. In this sense we distinguish between a misperception that can be documented (for example the proportion of reported crime that involves violence) and a crime myth, which while appearing to be widespread, has not been the subject of a public opinion survey. (For further discussion of myths about crime and criminal justice, see Kappeler, Blumberg and Potter, 1996; Bohm, 1987; Wilbanks, 1987).

This chapter examines public knowledge of crime rates, the nature of crime and certain characteristics of offenders. Chapter 3 explores public awareness of some important criminal justice trends and laws. It will be seen that some areas of criminal justice have been well-explored, while others have been almost totally ignored by pollsters. A number of important criminal justice issues such as prostitution, pornography and so on are not examined here simply because no survey has explored public *knowledge* of these issues. A fair amount of this research draws upon surveys of the public in other countries such as Canada and Great Britain. However, comparisons suggest that public misperceptions of crime and criminal justice are at least as great in the United States. Finally, we omit coverage of public knowledge of juvenile justice as this will be dealt with in a separate chapter. The focus here is exclusively on adult offending.

Crime Rates and Patterns[2]

Crime rates are of paramount concern to the public who, as we document elsewhere in this book, subscribe to a crime control model (rather than a due process model) of criminal justice. If crime rates are rising dramatically, then the criminal justice system has failed in its primary function, to reduce or at least slow the increase in offending. There are two principal sources of statistical information regarding the incidence of crime: reports of crimes recorded by the police (e.g., the Uniform Crime Reporting survey) and victimization surveys (e.g., the International Crime Survey). We shall review public perceptions in light of both data sources, beginning with the official crime statistics. The general finding emerging from different questions posed in a number of jurisdictions is that while crime rates vary considerably, there is a misperception common to many countries that the situation is worse than it really is.

Changes in Crime Rates

Surveys in the U.S., Canada and Australia have consistently found that the public hold several misperceptions about crime rates. These include the view that crime rates are always rising and that a high percentage of crimes involves violence. The following are some examples of misperceptions relating to crime statistics that are derived from national and state surveys conducted in the United States (e.g., Knowles, 1984, 1987), Canada (e.g., Doob and Roberts, 1982) and Australia (e.g., O'Connor, 1978; Indermaur, 1987). Many Americans over-estimate the victimization rate for violent crime. For example, when the annual rate of violent crime was fewer than four incidents per 100 residents in Ohio, only one citizen in twenty perceived the rate to be that low (Knowles, 1984). Earlier research in the same state found that one-third of the respondents provided an estimate of the violent crime rate that was at least six times higher than the actual rate. In fact, only one citizen in five provided an estimate of the violent crime rate which was anywhere near accurate (Knowles, 1982).

As well, whenever polls have asked people about changes in crime rates, most people respond that crime rates have been increasing rapidly. This response has generally been independent of actual changes in the crime rate, whether measured by official statistics or victimization surveys. For example, although victimization rates declined in the 1980s (Bureau of Justice Statistics, 1987), polls still found that the public believed rates were rising inexorably. The results of several surveys conducted in Ohio shed important light upon public misperceptions of crime rates. All five polls conducted in the 1980s found that almost 80 percent of Ohio residents believed that the crime rate had increased over the previous three years, when in fact it had not (see Knowles).

Data from the national level make the point. In 1993 a Harris poll asked Americans whether they thought that the crime rate had increased, decreased or remained the same. Over half the respondents believed that it had increased (Maguire and Pastore, 1995). However, national arrest rates do not confirm a pattern of ever-increasing crime rates. Property crime rates declined over the period 1990-1993 by 9 percent. Significant declines were observed in motor vehicle theft, larceny-theft, burglary. Several other crimes of concern to the public, such as forcible rape demonstrated either stability over the period or modest declines. The murder rate was stable (9.5 arrests per 100,000 inhabitants) and there was a small increase in the overall violent crime rate (see Maguire and Pastore, 1995, Table 4.2).

Crime rates are generally lower in Canada than the United States. Nevertheless, Canadians share with their neighbors a perception of high (and rising) crime rates. When asked to compare the crime problem in Canada with the United States, most Canadians believed that the Canadian crime problem in their country was comparable to, or worse than, the crime problem in America (Doob and Roberts, 1982). In 1995, over half the polled public believed that the violent crime rate had increased a great deal (Macleans, 1995). In reality, police statistics for the period 1994-1995 revealed the largest decline in violent crime since the government began collecting crime statistics in 1962 (Hendrick, 1996). Violent crime rates declined 8 percent over the period 1992-1995, while crime rates in general declined 13 percent over the same period.

The results of an Australian survey led O'Connor to conclude that "When citizens' estimates of the numbers of thefts, violent crimes, rapes and acts of vandalism, prostitution and fraud (both committed and convicted) were compared with official figures, it was found that estimates were higher than the official crime rates" (1978, p.64). Similar, though less pronounced misperceptions were found with regard to the rates of property crimes committed.

Victimization Rates in Canada. An alternate portrait of crime emerges from other sources of information about crime patterns, such as victimization surveys. The periodic victimization surveys conducted in Canada provide an illustration of this. The most recent Canadian data show that from 1991 to 1992, there was a very modest (2 percent) increase in the rate of violent crimes reported to the police (Canadian Centre for Justice Statistics, 1994). Nevertheless, the public perception is different, and has been so for some years now. The most recent nation-wide poll (Angus Reid, 1994a) found that two-thirds of Canadians believed that there had been an overall increase in crime over the past five years. Yet how does this public perception square with findings from victimization surveys?

The General Social Survey was conducted in 1988 and five years later in 1993. Accordingly, researchers have been able to explore changes in victimization over the five year period. Victimization rates were stable over this period: 24 percent of the population experienced at least one instance of criminal victimization in 1988 and 1993 (Gartner and Doob, 1994). As well, the victimization rates of offenses of great concern to the public changed little: The assault rate, for example, was 68 per 1,000 population in 1988 and 67 per 1,000 population five years later. There were even significant decreases in rates of robbery and personal theft from 1988 to 1993 (Gartner and Doob, 1994).

After reviewing the findings from the survey, Gartner and Doob concluded:

> Canadians are not at a higher risk than they were five years earlier, overall. There is almost no evidence to support the [public] view that Canadians 15 years and older were more at risk of being victims of any of the crimes examined in this survey in 1993 than they were in 1988. The likelihood of a person being the victim of an assault, robbery, personal theft, and the likelihood of a household being victimized by way of a break and enter, motor vehicle theft, theft of household property, or vandalism, has either decreased or not changed. (Gartner and Doob, 1994, p. 19)

Rates of Specific Offenses. Canadians' apprehension about rising crime rates does not encompass all offenses; some crimes obviously provoke greater concern than others. The gap between public knowledge and reality in this area is that the offenses the public believe to be rising at the fastest rate are not necessarily the ones that have shown the greatest increases. Canadians' perceptions of trends in homicide rates illustrate the point well. Although crime rates vary for many reasons, the homicide statistics are good indicators of the level of violence in society. The official statistics for many crimes such as assault or rape are highly influenced by victims' reactions to the criminal justice system. Changes in attitudes towards reporting to the police will have an impact on the number of crimes recorded, independent of any changes in rates of actual offending. In addition, for some offenses, many crimes will never enter official crime statistics. In contrast, "official" homicide statistics are far more reliable indicators of the true incidence of murder in society. Almost all homicides will eventually come to the attention of the police. For this reason, the homicide statistics provide a relatively stable indicator of the level of violence in society.

A perception common to the public in several countries is that the homicide rate has been escalating dramatically in recent years, even though this is not the case. Over the decade 1978-1987, the average rate of homicide in Canada was 2.6 per 100,000 population (Canadian Centre for Justice

Statistics, 1989). In the most recent year for which data are currently available, the rate was 1.98 per 100,000 (Hendrick, 1996). This is the lowest rate since 1969 (Ogrodnik, 1994). Although the homicide rate rose significantly in the 1960s and 1970s, over the decade 1983-1992, there was a 3 percent decline in the homicide rate, and over the year 1994-1995 there was a 3 percent decline (Ogrodnik, 1994). The trend for attempted murder in Canada follows the same pattern. How do these trends compare to public knowledge? In 1989, a survey found that the Canadian public believed that murder was increasing at a faster rate than any other crime. Once again there are international parallels. David Indermaur (1987) found similar results with his sample of Australians: Three-quarters erroneously believed that the murder rate in Western Australia had increased over the previous decade.

One of the major reasons that the public in Canada support the restoration of capital punishment is that they perceive the abolition of the death penalty to have increased the homicide rate. This is the corollary of a public belief (held in many countries, not just Canada) that people intending to commit murder are more effectively deterred by capital punishment than life imprisonment. In 1982, over two-thirds of the public believed that the homicide rate had increased since the abolition of capital punishment in 1976. But in fact the homicide rate in Canada *has actually declined* since the death penalty was abolished. In the first year after abolition, the homicide rate was 3.06 per 100,000 population. As noted, by 1992, the homicide rate had declined to 2.7 incidents per 100,000 population (Ogrodnik, 1994).

Similar misperceptions relate to another crime that causes considerable public concern in Canada and elsewhere: burglary. A nation-wide poll found that Canadians were more concerned about burglary than any other offense (see Moore, 1985). Four years later another poll found that 57 percent of the public believed that burglary rates were increasing, but in reality the opposite is true. There were 26 incidents of break and enter (per 1,000 households) reported to the police across Canada in 1980. A decade later, the rate had declined to 22 reports per 1,000 households (Fedorowycz, 1992b). Similar trends emerge from victimization survey data, which show a decline in the incidence of burglary of 7 percent over the period 1988 to 1993 (Gartner and Doob, 1994).

Percentage of Crime Involving Violence. Public concern about crime focuses upon violent crime. When most people think of serious crimes, they are thinking of crimes of violence. Not surprisingly perhaps, the public appear to have a distorted view of the amount of crime that involves violence. Research by Doob and Roberts (1982) found that three-quarters of a representative sample of the Canadian public over-estimated by a considerable margin the percentage of crimes that involve violence. In fact the proportion of recorded crime that involves violence does not vary a great deal: Recent statistics show that it is approximately 5 percent in Holland, 4 percent in Australia, and 11 percent in Canada (Canadian Centre for Justice Statistics, 1996). It is likely that the public in most western countries over-estimate this statistic. In Australia, Indermaur (1987) found that fully three-quarters of the sampled public provided a large over-estimate of the proportion of crimes involving violence.

This finding is significant, because it implies that the public have an erroneous perception of crime as involving more harmful behavior than is in fact the case. It helps to explain public support for very punitive sentencing practices, since the public may feel that a harsh reaction is necessary to respond to a very serious crime problem. The reality is that much of what is recorded as criminal behavior is not very serious, although the small minority of cases involving violence are of course very costly in terms of the impact on the victim and society.

It would be an over-simplification to say however that the public are always wrong about crime rates. Some research has in fact demonstrated that they are occasionally accurate in their beliefs. Mark Warr (1980; 1982) has shown that the public are aware, for example, of the gender ratio in offending patterns. As well, the public are right in thinking that over a long-term period—say thirty years—the crime rate is higher today. The preponderance of evidence however suggests that the public have a view of crime rates that differs from the official statistics or victimization surveys. Moreover, the public knowledge tends to reflect a more negative view of the crime rates than is warranted by the crime statistics. Simply put, to most members of the public, crime generally involves violence.

Criminal Recidivism Rates

Public misperceptions about offenders include the extent to which they re-offend. When members of the public were asked to estimate the percentage of first-time offenders that would be re-convicted within five years of release, they over-estimated the recidivism rates of property offenders and offenders convicted of crimes involving violence. Thus 60 percent of respondents over-estimated the recidivism rate for property offenders, while 79 percent over-estimated the figure for violent offenders (Doob and Roberts, 1983). Public estimates of the violent offender recidivism rates were particularly high, relative to the actual figures. As well, there was little demographic variation on these questions (Roberts and White, 1986). Canadians are also inclined to believe that recidivism rates are as high in Canada as in the United States, when in fact the Canadian rates of re-offending are lower.[3] These results have now been replicated in other countries. For example, a study of public perceptions in Spain found comparable results. Although the actual recidivism rate was 35 percent, the public estimated this figure to be 75 percent (Redondo, Luque and Funes, 1996). Finally, as we shall see in a subsequent chapter, the public also over-estimate the percentage of offenders released on parole who commit further crimes before the elapse of their parole period.

Further evidence of stereotyping offenders can also be seen in public estimates of recidivism rates of different offender categories. The probability of further offending increases as a direct function of the number of previous convictions. Thus ex-offenders with five prior convictions are more likely to be re-convicted than offenders with only one prior offense. However, this is not how the public see things. When asked to estimate the recidivism rate of first, second and third time offenders, the public estimates of recidivism risk were the same for all three categories (see Roberts and White, 1986). This result may seem counter-intuitive at first. After all, would it not be reasonable to expect a higher re-offending rate for someone who has repeatedly offended in the past, than someone does not have a history of repetitive delinquency? Yes, but not if one has a simple two-way classification scheme comprising offenders and non-offenders.

Members of the public appear to categorize offenders as people with a certain temperament and disposition. The public are making an internal attribution: What caused an individual to offend is not external circumstances (such as provocation, drunkenness, loss of a job) but the personality attributes of the individual, which are less likely to change than the external circumstances, hence the public's expectation of further offending. In short, the public seem to subscribe to the view that "Once an offender, always an offender." This perception is likely to affect large numbers of people. Few members of the public are aware of the large numbers of people with criminal records: In America, state information systems carry criminal record information on fifty million individuals. In Great Britain, fully one-third of males in their thirties have a criminal record, while in Canada almost three million people have records (Roberts, 1997).

Finally, the public have very concrete perceptions about the nature of re-offending. They see a high degree of consistency across episodes of offending. Thus the public predicted that sex offenders would commit further sex offenses, violent offenders further violent offenses and property offenders additional crimes against property. The official data on re-conviction show a very different pattern: In the U.S., and in Canada, there is little criminal specialization of this kind. Data from the state of Washington for example show that violent offenders were more likely to have a nonviolent than a violent previous conviction. Of all violent sex offenders, only 6 percent had a similar prior offense (Washington State

Sentencing Guidelines Commission, 1992, Table 8). Similar results emerge elsewhere. In England, Bottomley and Pease show that when reconviction occurred, it was more likely to be for a different offense than the first conviction (Bottomley and Pease, 1986, p. 108). Canadian data show that over two-thirds of recidivists were re-convicted of an offense in a different category. Offenders released from prison after serving time for a crime of violence were more likely to be re-convicted of a crime against property than another violent crime (see Campbell, 1993; Roberts, 1997).

These findings regarding public estimates of recidivism are important because they help to explain why the public have a negative view of sentencing (to be discussed in a later chapter). The public are likely to interpret the recidivism statistics (or their perceptions of the recidivism statistics) as evidence that the sentencing system has failed to deter or reform convicted offenders. The statistics also suggest that negative public attitudes towards offenders and ex-offenders arise as a result of an overly-pessimistic view of the proportion of these individuals who re-offend.

Conclusions

Most people have a great deal of interest in crime and justice. However, this does not mean that they are necessarily that well-informed about the issues. It would be naive to expect the public to have accurate views of all aspects of crime and justice. A theme that is heard in many countries is that the public believe the crime problem is much worse now than in the past. At some points in time, they may be correct, but the perception appears to exist independent of actual changes in rates. Linked to the perception that things are constantly getting worse is an attribution of declining moral standards. This perception appears to be shared with criminal justice professionals such as the police (see Levi and Jones, 1987). The findings of opinion surveys in a number of countries demonstrate that the public have a poor idea of the nature or prevalence of crime. We should bear this in mind when evaluating crime control policies in terms of public support. It is only when the public have a realistic perception of crime and justice that an informed public debate over crime control policies can take place.

The misperceptions of the public are neither random nor unrelated. For the most part, they reflect a cohesive, although distorted world of crime and criminal justice. It is a world in which crime rates are escalating dramatically, particularly rates of violent crime. In addition, a high percentage of crime is violent in nature. These crimes are committed by a relatively small and easily identifiable group of people. Table 2.1 summarizes some public misperceptions of crime-related statistics.

TABLE 2.1   Examples of Public Misperceptions of Crime-related Statistics

Public Misperception	Reality
Crime rates constantly increasing	Crime rates decline or stable over period 1990-1995
Violent crime rate increasing faster than any other kind of crime	Violent crime rate increasing no faster than property crime
Murder rate increasing	Murder rate stable or declining in Canada, Australia and U.S.
The murder rate increased in Canada after abolition of death penalty	Murder rate has declined since abolition of death penalty
Violent crime accounts for approximately half all crime recorded by the police	Violent crime accounts for approximately 10 percent of crimes recorded by police; smaller percent of all crimes committed
Crime committed by a small, easily identifiable part of population	Crime committed by a wide range of offender
Most offenders re-offend, and commit same kind of crime over and over again	Most offenders not re-convicted. Little specialization in terms of criminal careers
Most offenders on parole re-offend	Most parolees do not re-offend
Burglary rates increasing faster than other crimes	Burglary rates stable or declining

Summaries are by nature over-generalizations. As Mark Warr observes, "only a cynic would maintain that *all* public beliefs about crime are irrational or uninformed" (Warr, 1982, p. 199). No-one subscribes to *all* the views we have outlined in this chapter, and some of these misperceptions of crime are further from the truth than others. Nevertheless, they do seem to characterize the views of the public not just in America but in the other countries included in our review. These misperceptions help to explain the public desire for a more repressive response to crime. After all, if escalating crime rates are associated, in the public mind, with lenient sentencing and parole practices, then a harsher response should lead to lower crime rates. The public have accepted an attractive but false syllogism of punishment. In the next chapter, we review research which has examined public knowledge of the law as well as the structure and function of the criminal justice system.

Notes

1. The heavy emphasis on public attitudes rather than public knowledge of crime and justice is reflected in the contents of the annual "Sourcebook of Criminal Justice Statistics" (U.S. Department of Justice, Bureau of Justice Statistics) which contains a great deal of public opinion data but almost no surveys about public knowledge.

2. Public misperceptions are not restricted to statistical issues such as crime rates or the costs of different forms of offending. They also extend to what we might term myths about victimization. For example, Ewing and Aubrey (1987) conducted a survey of the general public and found that "many subjects... appeared to endorse the myths that a battered woman is at least partially responsible for her battering and is masochistic if she remains in a battering relationship. Moreover, a clear majority of subjects appeared to subscribe to the myth that a battered woman can simply leave her batterer" (p. 261). Professionals working with spousal abuse cases are well aware of the dangerous inaccuracy of such opinions. As with other myths, these views may have consequences for the legal system. Jurors in cases of spousal homicide where the accused has killed her batterer-husband may be guided by such myths, and this would tend to undermine claims of self-defense by the accused.

3. The most recent research in Canada found that 35 percent of those who had an opportunity to re-offend were reconvicted of a subsequent offense (Canadian Centre for Justice Statistics, 1993).

3

Legal Reforms and Criminal Justice Statistics: What Does the Public Really Know?

In this chapter we continue to pursue the issue of public awareness of criminal justice. We explore the extent of people's knowledge of the legal system and the criminal justice system. A diversity of issues is included because research has not systematically examined every stage of the criminal justice process. Our focus in this chapter is upon adults' knowledge of the criminal law and the criminal justice system. It is worth noting that research using younger subjects (i.e., children and adolescents) shows widespread ignorance of the law (see Peterson-Badali and Abramovitch, 1992 for a review). The results of surveys at the adult level show that many misconceptions about the criminal process persist into adulthood, suggesting that public legal education is a priority for adults as well as adolescents. Before turning to the results of surveys dealing with specific issues, we note the findings from surveys which have posed a series of questions on a diversity of criminal justice topics. For example, Cumberland and Zamble (1992) posed a series of knowledge questions to a sample of Canadian residents. Scores on this test of criminal justice knowledge could range to a maximum of 100 points. The mean score of the sample was forty-four. Thus the average response of the group was a failing grade on criminal justice knowledge.

Knowledge of the Law and Legal Rights

Residents of several U.S. states have been surveyed about their legal rights, and related issues such as police powers. Knowledge tends to be poor, particularly, as Sarat, 1977, points out, for civil issues, rather than criminal justice, but even for the latter, members of the public appear to know little (see California Assembly Committee on Criminal Procedure, 1975; Michigan Law Review, 1973; Williams and Hall, 1972). For example, Americans were asked if the following statement was correct: "In a criminal trial, it is up to the person who is accused of the crime to prove his innocence." Only a bare majority (56 percent) were aware of the presumption of innocence and the obligation on the district attorney to prove an accused guilty beyond a reasonable doubt (Parisi, Gottfredson, Hindelang and Flanagan, 1979).

I must inform you that anything you say will be taken down and may be used against you...

We have all seen many television dramas or movies in which, prior to an arrest, a police officer uses a phrase along these lines to inform a suspect of his or her rights. The frequency with which these lines are enacted would suggest that almost everyone must be aware of the right to remain silent at arrest. Nevertheless, almost a third of the Canadian public were not aware of the nature of this legal protection (Moore, 1985). Earlier research by Sarat (1975) is an exception to the trends described in this chapter. For example, he found that almost all respondents were aware of the necessity to issue a Miranda warning. Not all questions generated such high rates of knowledge. Fewer than 75 percent of the public were aware that it is up to this state to prove a criminal case against a defendant. Finally, White and Roberts (1985) found that most people were not aware of the law concerning intent. That is, the public did not know that the State has to prove (for most offenses) both that the accused committed the act (the *actus reus)* and that he intended to commit the act (the *mens rea).*

At the heart of the common law system of justice is the accused's right to remain silent at trial: In a criminal proceeding, the onus is on the crown to establish the case against the accused without the benefit of his or her testimony. Yet when a sample of Canadians were asked "When someone is charged with a criminal offence, is that person required to testify in court or does that person have a right to remain silent?", only a minority of respondents knew that accused persons are not compelled to testify. These rights—the presumption of innocence; the right to remain silent and the burden of proof necessary to convict a person—are frequently alluded to in news media stories about crime and justice. If over half the public are unaware of rights as central to our system of justice as these, it is unlikely that they will be familiar with other, lesser rights that receive less attention from the news media.

Public awareness of the powers of the state is not any greater than awareness of the rights of the individual. When a sample of Americans was asked: "If someone is found innocent of a crime, the state can appeal the case. Is this true or false?" less than a third responded correctly (McGarrell and Flanagan, 1985; Table 2.62). People were also asked if it were true that decisions taken by a state court could be reversed by the U.S. Supreme Court. Only 10 percent were correct on this question (McGarrell and Flanagan, 1985, Table 2.66). This suggests the existence of serious misperceptions about the powers of the Supreme Court, and, by inference, the very nature of the U.S. constitution. A national survey conducted by the National Center for State Courts in 1978 found that almost half the respondents incorrectly believed that the onus is upon a person accused of a crime to prove his or her innocence (National Center for State Courts, 1978). Demographic variables were related to levels of awareness. Thus African-Americans, respondents with lower levels of education and lower self-reported incomes were more likely to be incorrect. In fact, over a series of items, the percentages of respondents with limited knowledge of the law were twice as high for African-Americans and Hispanics than for Caucasians.

Legal Aid provides a telling illustration of the extent to which the public lack adequate knowledge of the legal system. A survey in Great Britain found that half the respondents gave the wrong answer, or failed to answer, the simple question "Can people who don't have much money get free legal advice?" When asked specifically about the Legal Aid scheme functioning in their community, three-quarters of respondents did not know about the program (Abel-Smith, Zander and Brooke, 1973). More recently, in Canada, two-thirds of respondents to a nation-wide poll were unsure of the nature of Legal Aid (Environics Research, 1987). Most disquieting of all, awareness of Legal Aid tends to be poorest among those for whom the program was created: Individuals without sufficient resources to obtain legal representation.

This result has been found with other justice programs: Williams and Hall (1972) found that low-income groups performed only at chance level on a test of factual questions dealing with the law. In Canada, the federal Department of Justice conducted a national survey and found that two-thirds of the public stated that they were not familiar with the legal aid plan in their province (Department of Justice, 1988). Increasing public awareness of the law, and particularly important programs such as legal aid, is clearly a priority if universal access to justice is to be achieved.

Knowledge of Specific Laws

If the public hold inaccurate perceptions about crime rates, and criminal justice trends, how much do they know about specific pieces of legislation? The answer is probably not a great deal, even for well-publicized legal reforms, as the following case histories show. Few studies have addressed Americans' knowledge of specific laws but those that have provide little evidence of widespread legal awareness. An early survey in Texas posed a series of questions about thirty important laws. Scores were significantly lower for lower income respondents, who correctly identified, on average, only twelve out of thirty laws. In fact, this group performed no better than chance on the legal knowledge test.

More disturbingly, though were false perceptions: Over half the sample believed that "under Texas law, a person, because of his color or nationality can be prohibited from living where he wants" (Williams and Hall, 1972). It seems unlikely that this particular misperception persists today, but in all likelihood legal knowledge is still poor, especially among certain demographic groups. Similar results emerged in Michigan. Members of the public correctly answered only nine out of twenty-six questions relating to criminal law, and there were significant misperceptions. More than half the sample were unaware that homeowners must allow a police officer to search their homes if the officer is pursuing a suspect.

Edwards (1987) reports the findings of a telephone survey that addressed the Domestic Violence Prevention program established in New Jersey several years earlier. Results indicated that only 40 percent of the public (including, presumably, many victims of domestic violence) knew that there was a state law regarding domestic violence; fully one-third were not aware of any services available for the victims of violence. Although legal matters, and in particular criminal law issues, are of great general interest, public legal knowledge is very sketchy, and reflects little understanding of the structure and function of the law. An example of this is the fact that a significant minority of Canadians have trouble distinguishing between civil and criminal law. In 1994, a poll found that fully one third of the sample were unsure of the distinction, even after having received a brief explanation from the survey interviewer (Insight Canada, 1994). Similarly, O'Barr and Conley (1988) found that some civil plaintiffs approach civil trials with expectations that the burden of proof and the standard of proof were the same as in criminal trials. These trends may have changed following the widespread news coverage of the criminal and civil cases involving O.J. Simpson.

In Canada, most members of the public do not know which level of government is responsible for criminal justice. According to a 1992 poll, almost two-thirds of the public believed that the federal government had the primary responsibility for the administration of criminal justice, when in fact provincial governments hold this responsibility (see Decima, 1993).[1]

The absence of public awareness extends to victims' rights as well. A survey in Canada found that fewer than one-third of respondents were aware of the criminal injuries compensation program in their province. Half the sample had never heard of the existence of such programs. Even fewer respondents were aware of similar programs which provide assistance to victims immediately after having reported the crime to the justice system (Department of Justice Canada, 1988).

In 1990, the Ohio legislature passed, after considerable debate, what was described as "one of the most significant pieces of drug legislation in the State's history" (Schroot, 1990, p. 17). A central aim of this legislation was to crack down on illegal drug use by increasing the penalties for drug crimes; the seriousness values of all drug offenses were inflated, with a corresponding increase in the severity of penalties. A survey conducted shortly afterwards found that nine out of ten residents of Ohio (including, presumably, many illegal drug users) had not heard anything about the new law (Schroot, 1990). This lack of awareness was not due to an absence of interest in drug issues in general, for the same survey found that Ohio residents had generally accurate perceptions of several substance abuse issues. Similar findings emerge from another state. In 1985, new legislation passed in Colorado doubled the presumptive sentencing ranges for a number of offenses. This obviously had an important impact on sentence lengths served in that state. And yet public surveys three years later showed that the legislation had had no effects on public knowledge of sentencing (Mande and English, 1989).

In 1985, significant amendments were introduced to Canadian law relating to drinking and driving offenses, including substantial increases in the severity of penalties. These statutory reforms were the target of a significant public legal education initiative by the federal Department of Justice. But when the Department of Justice carried out opinion polling two years after the reforms were introduced, people knew very little beyond the fact that the law relating to impaired driving had changed (Department of Justice, 1988). Thus less than half the sample were able to identify a fine and a driving prohibition as the penalties for a first impaired driving conviction.

Over three-quarters of the public surveyed in 1987 responded "don't know" when asked to state the minimum penalty for impaired driving. Less than half the public were aware that the impaired driving legislation also applies to people driving under the influence of drugs (Department of Justice, 1988). The national survey on drinking and driving (which was carried out in 1988) found that only about half the respondents were aware that there was a mandatory license suspension for first offenders convicted of impaired driving. Only half of the respondents knew about the mandatory minimum fines for individuals convicted of impaired driving (see Beirness, Simpson and Mayhew, 1993).

As in America, gun control legislation has been at the center of public debates over criminal justice reforms. Several important amendments have been introduced since the massacre of fourteen students at a technical college in Montreal in 1989. In 1992, a Decima poll asked respondents to state how familiar they were with gun control legislation. Only 9 percent responded that they were very familiar. A further 37 percent were "somewhat familiar," while over half said that they were not very or not at all familiar with the legislation (Decima, 1993). As with other areas of legislative activity reviewed in this chapter, awareness did not correspond to accurate knowledge of specific provisions. In fact, one quarter of the respondents who had heard about the new gun laws could not identify any specific reforms introduced by the laws (Insight Canada, 1994). Gun owners were better informed about the legislation than the general public.

This pattern seems to emerge from a number of surveys, and suggests that people do not wish, perhaps for reasons of self-presentation, to admit that they are unaware of a particular law. In the late 1970s, there was considerable debate about the death penalty in Canada's Parliament, as the legislature grappled with the decision to abolish capital punishment. Accordingly, this issue received a great deal of media attention. Nevertheless, a year after capital punishment was abolished in Canada, less than half the public knew that there had been a change. More tellingly, only 14 percent of the sample were able to identify the exact decision that had been taken by Parliament (Bertrand, 1982).

Comparable results emerged from a British study. Walker and Argyle (1964) found that a year after attempted suicide was de-criminalized, fully three-quarters of the population still believed it to be a crime. Fewer than one in five respondents even knew that suicide had been decriminalized. Finally, it is worth noting that these trends are consistent with research in other countries. Podgorecki, Kaupen, Van Houtte, Vinke, and Kutchinsky (1973) reviewed findings from a number of other European countries and came to the general conclusion that "public knowledge concerning legal topics is considerably poorer than presumed by the legal authorities and by many scholars" (p. 105).[2]

This gap between legislative reform and public awareness of the reforms is counter-productive. After all, legislation is frequently introduced for instrumental purposes that concern the attitudes and behavior of the public. Awareness of new laws, or amendments to existing laws may not occur overnight, but if the public remain ignorant of such changes, many of the goals of law reform will prove unattainable.

Knowledge of Legal Defenses: Guilty and Insane

Little research has been conducted on public awareness of the defenses available to people charged with crimes. However, some research on the insanity defense provides a good example of how the public hold strong views which are nevertheless founded on a poor knowledge base. In a later chapter we shall explore public attitudes to the defense; for the present we restrict our attention to public knowledge of the way that the defense functions in America.

In 1982, John Hinckley Jr. attempted to assassinate the President. Hinckley was charged but subsequently acquitted through a verdict of not guilty by reason of insanity. This verdict came as a surprise to many Americans. After all, the attempted assassination had involved considerable planning on Hinckley's part, and people felt that such premeditation was inconsistent with somebody who was criminally insane. Shortly after the verdict was made public, a survey found that almost 90 percent of Americans disapproved of the insanity defense in general, not just the specific verdict in the Hinckley case. However, at the same time, another question on the same poll revealed that a similarly high percentage of respondents were unable to generate even an approximation of the legal definition of insanity. In fact, only one out of 434 respondents provided anything which came close to the legal definition (Hans and Slater, 1985). The public don't know what insanity is; they just know Hinckley wasn't insane. Steadman and Cocozza (1977) report similar findings. They asked people to identify individuals that had been classified as criminally insane. High-profile offenders such as Lee Harvey Oswald and Sirhan Sirhan were cited, but there was not a single criminally insane person on the list of individuals identified by the public (see also Hans and Slater, 1983). More recent data confirm these findings. Hans (1986) found that almost all respondents in her survey agreed with the statement that "the insanity plea is a loophole that allows too many guilty people to go free." This was not a sudden concern precipitated by the Hinckley verdict. Surveys conducted before the Hinckley case found the same result (see Pasewark and Seidenzahl, 1979).

These perceptions are at odds with reality. Silver, Cirincione and Steadman (1994) collected data on almost one million felony indictments from eight states to obtain data on the almost 9,000 defendants who had entered an insanity plea. They compared the use of the insanity plea, the acquittal rate, and the length of confinement with data from public surveys reported by Hans (1986). While the public think accused murderers are the defendants most likely to plead not guilty by reason of insanity, in reality only 14 percent of insanity pleas came from individuals charged with murder. The public estimated that over one-third of defendants use the insanity plea whereas in reality the statistic is less than 1 percent. As well, the public over-estimate the percentage of acquittals that result in the release of the defendant. At the same time they under-estimate the length of confinement imposed on persons found not guilty by reason of insanity. Presumably, high-profile media stories have fostered these misperceptions. So when we learn that two-thirds of the American public favor abolition of the insanity defense (ABC News, 1993), this result should be considered in the context of the absence of public knowledge of the defense.

Knowledge of the Criminal Justice System

Although it would be interesting to know the extent of public knowledge about all phases of the criminal justice process, unfortunately researchers have yet to systematically evaluate public awareness of police, courts and corrections. We do have information about public knowledge of sentencing and parole, and we shall review that research momentarily. First it is worth noting the findings from the one study that did explore public knowledge of the three principal stages in the criminal justice process. Fagan (1987) sent a mail questionnaire to members of the public, as well as a sample of criminal justice professionals in the state of Washington. Respondents were asked a series of questions about police, courts and corrections. The results indicated that the public (and the criminal justice professionals) were most knowledgeable about the correctional system, followed by the courts and then the police. However, since there were only four items asked about each branch of the system, the study is far from definitive.[3] Not surprisingly, the professionals were more knowledgeable than the public. More interestingly, demographic variables were relatively unimportant in terms of predicting knowledge.

The most comprehensive portrait of public awareness of court structures in America emerges from a national survey conducted for the National Center for States Courts in 1978. Members of the public were asked about various levels of courts. By their own admission, the public knew very little: Three out of four respondents admitted that they knew very little or nothing at all about state and local courts. Their self-perception was correct. The public were clearly misinformed about several topics relating to court jurisdiction, powers and procedures. For example, almost three-quarters believed (incorrectly) that the Supreme Court has the constitutional authority to reverse any decision made by a state court. In addition to ignorance of court structure and powers, very few people knew about court reforms. The Task Force report notes that "Recent court reforms have gone largely unnoticed by the public. Citizens of states which have recently introduced rather sweeping court reforms are no more aware of changes in the complexion of courts than those who live in states which have not introduced significant changes" (National Center for State Courts, 1978, p. 5). The public were aware of some issues. Most respondents were aware that trial courts exist in every state.

Paradoxically, a finding that emerged from this study as well as others is that the more knowledgeable respondents were also more critical of the administration of justice. The explanation for this would appear to be that those with more knowledge were also those with more direct experience, and this contact promoted both awareness and criticism. It also led respondents to be more likely to perceive a need for reform. Thus almost six out of ten respondents with court experience perceived a great need for court reform, whereas only 40 percent of those without direct experience had this view (National Center for State Courts, 1978, Table 1.7).

Knowledge of the Sentencing Process

The issue of sentencing is at the heart of public conceptions of criminal justice. This may well explain why most of the research on public knowledge of the criminal justice system has focused upon sentencing and corrections. A subsequent chapter in this book will address public evaluations of the sentencing process. At this point, we review public knowledge of the sentencing structure and sentencing practices.

Public Knowledge of Penalties and the Penalty Structure

Maximum and minimum penalties are supposed to serve a number of functions relating to the public. For example, they may help members of the public gauge the relative seriousness of different crimes. Rape, for example, is a more serious crime than theft or assault, and this is reflected by the fact that it carries a higher maximum penalty. When legislatures increase the penalty for a particular crime, one of the aims is usually to convey a message to the public that the offense in question is more serious than people have hitherto realized. Minimum penalties are created for the same reason, but sometimes there is an additional message, one of deterrence. Mandatory minimum penalties for committing an offense with a firearm are intended to deter potential offenders from carrying guns. In both cases—crime seriousness and deterrence—it is important that potential offenders and society in general are aware of the statutory penalties. However, it is clear that significant discrepancies exist between the true state of the sentencing system and public knowledge. This seems to be true in all western nations.

Research in America has consistently found little public awareness of statutory penalties. An early study in California found that up to half the sample had no idea whatsoever about the maximum penalties for a series of common crimes (Assembly Committee on Criminal Procedure (California), 1975). When people did generate an estimate of a particular maximum penalty, they tended to under-estimate the severity of the penalty. For example, two-thirds of the general population under-estimated the penalty for rape. Even though the state legislature had recently increased the minimum penalties for certain crimes, this fact had escaped the attention of fully 80 percent of the population (Assembly Committee on Criminal Procedure (California), 1975). Williams, Gibbs and Erickson conducted a similar survey in Arizona and concluded that "the overwhelming majority of respondents were unaware of the statutory maximums for all penalties and all crimes" (1980, p. 115). In light of the widespread ignorance of the maximum penalties, it is not surprising that there were very few differences as a function of demographic characteristics such as age, sex, ethnicity or education (see Williams and Erickson, 1982).

Canadian trends are strikingly similar. Although the maximum penalty for theft over $1,000 is ten years imprisonment, over two-thirds of the public estimated the maximum to be much lower (Doob and Roberts, 1983). The public also have little idea of the minimum penalties prescribed by the Criminal Code of Canada: When asked to identify one of the offenses carrying a mandatory minimum penalty, only 16 percent of the public were able to do so (Canadian Sentencing Commission, 1987). More recently, Douglas and Ogloff (1996) found that public perceptions of maximum lengths of imprisonment were inaccurate. The public over-estimated the maximum penalties for crimes against the person and under-estimated the maxima for crimes involving property.

Sentencing Practices

If the public know little about the sentencing structure, they also have a very imprecise idea of the severity of penalties actually imposed. In a later chapter we shall explore the public attitude or opinion that sentences are too lenient. For the present we simply note that the public in all western countries share the view that the severity of penalties is not commensurate with the seriousness of the crimes for which they are imposed. This opinion has been documented by opinion polls for well over twenty years now (Roberts, 1992). Moreover, this issue generates strong emotions among members of the public. The question we address in this chapter is the following: How accurate are people in estimating the severity of sentences imposed in their local courts?

We have often tried the following informal experiment on acquaintances or students. First we have asked them whether they think sentences are too harsh, too lenient or about right. Since surveys show that four-fifths of the North American public hold the view that sentences are not harsh enough, there is a high probability that the answer will be "too lenient." Then we have posed a subsequent question about actual sentencing trends. For example, we have asked them to estimate the incarceration rate or the average sentence for a crime like manslaughter. Usually the "subject" in this experiment has no idea about the severity of sentences actually imposed. So once again we have a strong negative *perception* of the sentencing process founded on little more than a hazy recollection of a lenient sentence reported in the news media. Moreover, as we point out elsewhere, this perception is held with a great deal of confidence by members of the public. As Leslie Wilkins noted: "[I]n criminal justice matters, the degree of confidence with which views are expressed tends to be inversely proportional to the quality of knowledge" (quoted in Flanagan, 1988, p. 116).

But it is not just that the public have little idea about sentencing practices, there is a bias to this misperception. When asked to estimate incarceration rates or average sentences, people consistently *under*-estimate the severity of the sentencing process. This result has emerged from surveys in the United States, the United Kingdom and Canada. The British Crime Survey found that most people under-estimated the severity of penalties imposed upon offenders convicted of burglary (see Hough and Mayhew, 1985; Hough and Moxon, 1988). According to Canadian sentencing statistics (Turner, 1993), approximately 90 percent of offenders convicted of robbery are sent to prison. However, fully three-quarters of the public estimated the incarceration rate for this crime to be under 60 percent (Canadian Sentencing Commission, 1987). Similar results emerged for other offenses as well. Over twenty years ago, Gibbons, Jones and Garabedian (1972) conducted surveys of residents in Portland and San Francisco and found that many people estimated prison terms to be shorter than they actually are. Finally, a 1986 survey in Ohio found that even though in reality sentences had become more severe, almost 90 percent of Ohio residents polled believed that sentences had become more lenient (Knowles, 1987).

Knowledge of the Effects of Harsher Sentencing Policies

Why punish? The debate over the purposes of sentencing has been going for centuries. Some people feel that the sentencing process should be concerned with simply inflicting punishment, others advocate a rehabilitation-oriented approach towards convicted offenders. To some degree this becomes a matter of personal philosophy or inclination, the way some people support the Dodgers, others the Yankees. Research alone cannot resolve the issue of what the sentencing process *should* be doing; there may well always be a diversity of opinion on this issue. However, criminologists can say something about what the sentencing process can be reasonably expected to achieve in terms of crime prevention. Many people believe that increasing the severity of penalties will lower crime rates. This finding has emerged in a number of different ways in several polls. When the public are asked, for example, to explain increases in crime rates at the adult or juvenile level, they frequently cite a lenient criminal justice system. Thus in a poll in Canada, over three-quarters of the sample agreed with the statement that "There is a great deal of crime because sentences are not severe enough" (Brillon, Louis-Guerin, and Lamarche, 1984). In America, when respondents were asked to explain increases in crimes rates, almost half the sample identified the criminal justice system, and specifically the court system (Maguire and Pastore, 1995).[4]

The reality is that such a small percentage of offenders are actually sentenced that the ability of the sentencing process to affect crime rates is very limited. This point has been made repeatedly in the sentencing literature. We regard it as one of the central public misperceptions in the field of crime control. Speaking of British findings, a major sentencing scholar points out that sentencers probably deal with no more than 3 percent of the offenses actually committed. He concludes: "It should be clear that, if criminal justice policy expects sentencing to perform a major preventive function, it is looking in the wrong direction" (Ashworth, 1992, p. 23).

The explanation for this paradox is the fact that only a small percentage of all crimes result in the imposition of a sentence. Thus not all crimes are reported to the police, not all reports are deemed by the police to be "founded," not all "founded" incidents result in the laying of a criminal charge, not all charges are brought to court and not all cases end in the conviction and subsequent sentencing of an accused. Canadian statistics on sexual assault illustrate the problem. In 1992, there were 38,337 reports of sexual assault made to the police in Canada (Canadian Centre for Justice Statistics, 1992). Assuming a reporting rate of 6 percent (Canadian Centre for Justice Statistics, 1993), a rough estimate of the number of sexual assaults occurring across Canada would be 600,000. In the year after, there were approximately 2,000 sentences imposed for sexual assault (Roberts, 1994). Thus a sentence was imposed in approximately one case in 300.

With statistics like these, even doubling the average sentence for rape would have very little impact upon the overall incidence of rape.[5] Clearly then, there are important limitations upon the ability of the sentencing system to reduce the crime rates through specific deterrence or incapacitation. The widespread public enthusiasm for harsher penalties as a solution to rising crime rates suggests that people are probably unaware of this constraint upon the sentencing process. This should be recalled when interpreting polls which examine public sentencing preferences.

Knowledge of Alternatives to Incarceration

Many jurisdictions, including America, Canada and England and Wales, have attempted to reduce the use of incarceration as a sanction. Canada has the third highest incarceration rate in the western world (Mihorean and Lipinski, 1992). This has led to the passage of specific law reforms that have proscribed the use of imprisonment except for offenders convicted of serious crimes. The 1991 Criminal Justice Act of England and Wales had similar ambitions. According to this Act, a custodial sentence could only be imposed under one of two conditions: When the offense was so serious that only imprisonment could be justified, or where the offense is a violent or sexual offense and only incarceration would be adequate to protect the public from serious harm (Wasik and Taylor, 1992). An argument against initiatives aimed at reducing the use of imprisonment has repeatedly been that the public are opposed to any increase in the use of alternative sanctions. But what do the public actually know about alternatives to imprisonment?

When most members of the public think of sentencing, they tend to think of prison. To members of the public, criminal justice consists of an equation with crime seriousness on one side and sentence length on the other. One reason for this is that the public are more likely to read about sentences of imprisonment than any other disposition. Another explanation for the fact that the public equate *sentencing* with *incarcerating* is that they are unaware of the alternative sanctions available to a sentencing judge in Canada. This fact can be demonstrated in a number of ways.

First, the public have difficulty identifying sentencing options *other* than imprisonment. The Canadian Sentencing Commission found that people could identify the correct definition for community service, but otherwise they knew little about other non-custodial sanctions such as probation (Canadian Sentencing Commission, 1987). A second way of showing the absence of familiarity with community-based sanctions is the following. When people are asked to "sentence" offenders having been given a list of possible alternatives, including incarceration, the proportion favoring imprisonment is much lower than if subjects are simply asked to sentence an offender in the absence of information about alternatives (Galaway, 1984). This suggests that the public do not spontaneously think of alternative dispositions when they consider sentencing options.

People also favor the use of incarceration because they under-estimate the cost of imprisoning an offender, and over-estimate the costs associated with administering non-custodial sanctions. Few people are aware of exactly how expensive imprisonment can be. The latest Canadian data (Correctional Services Canada, 1993) show that it costs $47,760 to keep an offender in a Canadian penitentiary for one year. However, fewer than 20 percent of respondents to a national poll were able to accurately estimate this cost.

Although little research has been conducted on the topic, it is clear that public lack of knowledge of sentencing matters springs from the media. As already noted, almost all (96 percent) Canadians cited the news media as their source of information about sentencing and parole.[6] What then do they learn from the news media regarding this topic? A systematic content analysis of the newspapers in Canada found that fully 70 percent of sentences reported were terms of imprisonment (Roberts, 1995). In reality, prison sentences account for only one sentence in four in Canada (Canadian Centre for Justice Statistics, 1993).

If the public read about imprisonment more often than any other sentence, it is not surprising that they know little about alternative sanctions. The newspaper stories that described sentencing hearings contained almost no reference to the purposes of sentencing. Information about the structure of the sentencing system was also conspicuous by its absence: The maximum penalty was mentioned in only twenty-three out of almost 800 stories. Not a single story made reference to the average sentence for a particular offense, thus making it very hard for the reader to know whether the sentence imposed was in line with other sentences imposed for the same crime. Small wonder then that the public know little about the sentencing process.

Prison Life

Many people feel that an inmate's life is an easy one; they are not aware of the privations and difficulties confronting incarcerated offenders. Nor are they aware of the high rates of homicide, suicide, physical and sexual assault in correctional institutions (see for example, Burtch and Ericson, 1979; Roberts and Jackson, 1991). One Canadian survey conducted in 1991 found that half the respondents felt that conditions in penal institutions were "too liberal," although fewer than 5 percent had first-hand experience of a correctional institution. Another survey conducted a few years earlier found that over half the sample believed that the treatment accorded inmates in Canada was "too soft," and almost 60 percent of respondents agreed with the statement that "prisons are veritable hotels" (Gallup

Canada, 1984). The responses of people in other countries are the same. In the U.S., several polls find widespread support for the view that prison "was not a harsh experience" (e.g., Mande and Butler, 1982). Two-thirds of a sample of Britons thought that prisoners had "much too easy a time" (Dowds, 1995). Likewise, Banks, Maloney and Willcocks (1975) found that the British public was poorly informed about prisons and prison life. Once again we see that public perception is founded upon second-hand information. Most people "know" that imprisonment is too "easy" for offenders, and yet almost no-one who holds this view has ever been inside a correctional institution.

These stereotypes of prison life may have several negative consequences for the system; they may bring the image of the system into disrepute. After all, many people believe that prison should be a severe punishment, and if it is not perceived that way, dissatisfaction with the correctional system will increase. There may well be a more negative consequence as well. If a prison term is not an onerous a punishment, then perhaps sentences should be longer; the result could be an inflation of punishment preferences by members of the public. In fact, research has shown that a preference for harsher sentencing patterns is directly related to the perception that prisons are soft on criminals (Brillon, 1984).

Knowledge of Parole Statistics

The correctional issue that generates most public criticism concerns early release from prison. According to a 1988 survey, over three-quarters of the public in Canada said that they had little or no faith in the Canadian system of granting parole (Gallup, 1988). Most Canadians feel that too many inmates get released too early in their terms of imprisonment. This view is to a large degree based upon a misperception of the functioning of the parole system. Let us begin with public knowledge of different early release mechanisms.

Research by the Canadian Sentencing Commission (1987) found that when provided with three incorrect definitions of parole and one correct definition, only 15 percent of the public were able to identify the correct answer. Although most people have a negative view of parole, few are aware of what conditional release from prison actually entails. A subsequent poll found that only one person in four knew what proportion of a prison sentence must be served before the inmate becomes eligible to apply for parole (Canadian Criminal Justice Association, 1989).

There are two principal public misperceptions in this domain: (1) that full parole grant rates have been increasing (Roberts, 1988a); (2) that parole rates are over 50 percent (Canadian Criminal Justice Association, 1987). In this latter survey, half the respondents over-estimated the parole rate. Both these misperceptions feed the widespread opinion that the parole system is lenient. The most recent statistics show that the parole grant rate in Canada was 34 percent (see Hewer and Birkenmayer, 1994). It has remained at, or under one-third over the past decade (see Hann and Harman, 1986). Therefore the public view that parole boards have become more lenient in recent years is simply incorrect.

In 1990, a study found that 87 percent of the respondents believed that the number of violent offenders released on parole was too high (Zamble, 1990). It is ironic that so many people have such a definite opinion on this issue without having any idea how many violent offenders are in fact released, or even what the release rate is for inmates serving sentences for crimes of violence. As with the perception that sentences have become more lenient, the view that parole boards have been getting more lenient also cuts across international boundaries. An Ohio poll found that three-quarters of the public were unaware that the parole board had become tougher in its releasing decisions. Over half the sample held the view that parole had in fact become easier to obtain (Knowles, 1987).

Parole Success Rates and Recidivism Rates

The gap between public perception and reality is probably greater for this issue than any other in criminal justice. We shall illustrate the point drawing upon Canadian data. The public tend to believe that a significant percentage of parolees commit further offenses. Doob and Roberts (1982) found that over 60 percent of the public estimated the parole recidivism rate to be between 40 and 100 percent while in reality only 13 percent of inmates released on parole were re-convicted of a violent crime at the time the public survey was conducted. Research conducted in 1987 (Canadian Criminal Justice Association, 1987) found that only 10 percent of respondents were able to accurately estimate parole success rates. Moreover, to members of the public, parole revocation means fresh offending, whereas the majority of revocations occur because the parolee failed to abide by some condition of parole. Between 1978 and 1988, almost three-quarters of inmates released on parole were successful in completing their terms in the community without incident. Only 12 percent were revoked for new offenses (Correctional Services Canada, 1994; Nouwens, Motiuk and Boe, 1993). David Indermaur (1987) replicated this finding in an Australian survey: Over two-thirds of the respondents under-estimated the percentage of parole releases that ended successfully. Public misperceptions regarding parole recidivism may also fuel public antipathy towards the early release of inmates serving terms of imprisonment for crimes of violence.

Costs of Parole Supervision

Just as the public *under*-estimate the costs of incarceration (see above), they also *over*-estimate the cost of supervising an offender in the community. The average annual cost of supervising an offender on parole in Canada today is $9,422, which is approximately one fifth the cost of incarceration (Correctional Services Canada, 1994). When members of the public were asked to estimate the annual cost of parole supervision, a third estimated a figure in excess of $20,000.

If the public know little about critical statistics relating to sentencing and corrections, they are also poorly informed about important changes in the nature of the correctional environment. The Alabama public appeared unaware of the recent, drastic increase in that state's prison population (only 14 percent of respondents to a state-wide poll were accurate in their perceptions of the change in inmate populations—see Doble and Klein, 1989). Britons are equally in the dark about correctional trends: An early survey found that "less than 2% had even the haziest idea of the number of people in prison" (Silvey, 1961). Gibbons (1963) found little awareness of correctional programs or procedures[7] (see also Banks, Maloney and Willcocks, 1975).

Conclusions

Awareness of the structure, function and powers of various criminal justice institutions is far from widespread.[8] It is hard to make direct comparisons between public knowledge in the area of criminal justice and other areas such as politics or the economy, as surveys tend to focus on one issue or the other, but not both. However, it would appear that the public are less knowledgeable about criminal justice than other domains. Carpini and Keeter (1992) reviewed a series of surveys of public knowledge of politics and concluded that "a solid majority of the public has some familiarity with the basic institutions and procedures of U.S. government" (p. 24). We are not so positive about public awareness of criminal justice issues.[9]

The misperceptions of the public in terms of the functioning of the criminal justice system are clear. People tend to believe that offenders escape punishment by taking advantage of a criminal justice system hobbled by too many due process safeguards designed to protect the rights of the accused. Even those offenders who are prosecuted and punished receive sentences that fail (in the eyes of the public) to adequately reflect the seriousness of the crimes for which they were imposed. From the perspective of the public, the system lacks efficiency, effectiveness and proportionality. And, as we have seen, for certain topics such as the insanity defense, and the sentencing process, people have strong views that are founded upon a very poor knowledge base. These results should be borne in mind as we proceed through the research that has explored public opinion, rather than public knowledge of crime and justice.

Notes

1. Unlike the U.S., Canada does not have federal and provincial criminal courts.

2. To take just one example, these authors cite a survey of Danish adult Danes found that only 3 percent gave the correct answer to the question "Who passes laws?"

3. With only four items it is hard to correct for level of difficulty across the three areas.

4. Thirty-three percent identified the courts and the prison system, and a further 8 percent the law enforcement system. This is much higher than the percentage that identified the next most frequently chosen option, "home and schools" (27 percent; see Maguire and Pastore, 1995).

5. Harsher sentencing might have an impact by means of general deterrence, but here too, there is little conclusive evidence that demonstrates that potential offenders are deterred by sentences imposed on other offenders (e.g., Beyleveld, 1992).

6. Indermaur (1990) reports a remarkably similar figure (97 percent) using a sample of Australian respondents.

7. Gibbons found that the public were well aware of correctional issues likely to be covered by the media. For example, almost all respondents knew that executions were carried out at San Quentin. On the other hand few members of the public could identify the authority responsible for parole decisions, or the location of specific correction facilities (see Gibbons, 1963, pp. 140-141).

8. Public confusion and misinformation about criminal justice issues can be explained in part by the complexity of the system itself. Understanding the system is not easy even for criminal justice professionals. The public appear aware of this. Over three-quarters of respondents to a survey in Canada agreed with the statement that "The justice system is so complicated [that] it's impossible to understand it" (Brillon, Louis-Guerin, and Lamarche, 1984).

9. In one of the few exceptions to the pattern of misperception, Schroot (1990) reports that Ohio residents held generally accurate perceptions of substance abuse issues. However, even for these items, significant numbers of the public were incorrect. For example, 41 percent thought (erroneously) that the following statement is true: "Crack cocaine is responsible for more deaths than alcohol or any other drug."

4

Crime Seriousness

In this chapter we turn to a concept which is central to the criminal law, and also to public understanding of punishment: Crime seriousness. We examine two aspects of the issue. First, we evaluate public perceptions of the seriousness of crime as a social problem, relative to other social problems. Are members of the public in America and elsewhere more concerned about crime than other pressing issues such as unemployment? How serious, in the eyes of the public, is the crime problem compared to the crisis in health care, for example? These questions are important because government policy is to a degree determined by public priorities. Afterwards, we examine the relative seriousness of different crimes.

There is a complex, and perhaps issue-specific relationship between public priorities and government policy initiatives. Do governments set priorities in areas such as health care or the economy and then attempt to convince the public that the gravity of these problems warrants the attention of the government and hence the expenditure of public funds? Or do governments discern the tenor of public sentiment and then set their policy agendas accordingly? When do the two (the public and their government) have concerns of mutual interest? All relations are clearly possible; it is a question for political scientists more than criminologists to resolve. In the area of criminal justice policy, there is evidence that public perceptions of the seriousness of the crime problem, or certain aspects of the crime problem, are determined, (some might say manipulated) by opinion leaders such as the head of state. For example, in a recent work, Margaret Beckett has argued that the so-called "War on Drugs" in America, which now has the support of a substantial proportion of Americans, is an example of a major criminal justice policy initiative which reflects neither the magnitude of the problem nor any deep-seated public disapproval of illegal drug use, but rather the interests of a specific federal administration. The present (and previous) administrations have taken the opportunity to pass very punitive drug-related sentencing laws, which, it now appears, have had a disastrous effect upon African-Americans (see Tonry, 1994).

Seriousness of Crime as a Social Problem

For many years now, pollsters in several countries have asked members of the public to rate the importance of crime as a social problem in comparison to other social issues. Until recently, when placed in the context of other major public policy problems, crime has not assumed a very high profile in America, Great Britain or Canada. Responses to the question: "What is the most important problem facing the nation today?" show little variation over the 1970s and 1980s. (Reactions have been somewhat different when people were asked a slightly different question which ties the issue to their local community rather than the nation as a whole. Most people in America have always agreed with the statement that crime is an important problem in their community.)

Over the decade 1984 to 1993, the percentage choosing crime as the number one *national* problem in America did not vary: 5 percent of respondents in 1984 and the same percentage in 1993 identified crime as the most important social problem facing the country (Maguire, Pastore and Flanagan, 1993). This figure is low compared to other issues. In 1992, fully one-quarter of respondents identified unemployment as the number one problem; 42 percent identified the economy in general. When the same question has been asked of residents of Canada, and Great Britain, the results have been quite similar. Concern over crime is widespread, but pales in significance when compared to other social issues. Until 1994, then, the public appeared to believe that crime was an important social problem, but not necessarily *the* most important. They were more concerned about employment and medicare than crime in the streets.

More recently there has been a significant change in the responses of Americans and Canadians to the question about crime as a major social problem. In America, the percentage identifying crime as the Number one problem rose to 9 percent, and in 1994 there was a dramatic jump: Fully 37 percent of respondents shared this view. In fact, the degree of concern was greater for crime than for any other social issue.[1] A *Time* magazine poll found that twice as many Americans were worried about crime than the state of the economy, while concern over crime exceeded concern over the federal budget deficit by a factor of four (cited in Kappeler, Blumberg and Potter, 1996). Differences in responding as a function of demographic variables such as race and age were minimal (Maguire and Pastore, 1995). This increase in concern over crime was matched by a corresponding decline in the percentage identifying unemployment as the major issue confronting the country. Over the decade 1985-1994, crime was never identified as the country's top problem by more than 2 percent of the population. In 1995, a survey found that crime had risen to the rank of the third most important social problem (Macleans, 1995). Similar results emerge when the public are asked to identify social problems on which more money should be spent. Halting the rising crime rates was cited by three-quarters of Americans as a problem that was receiving insufficient government funds. In contrast, only 31 percent felt that improving the conditions of blacks was receiving insufficient funds (Maguire and Pastore, 1995).

Why public concern about crime should have arisen to this extent is unclear. Rising crime statistics cannot account for the change in views: In fact, crime rates declined somewhat over the two-year period preceding this survey. Nor was there any evidence that employment figures had shown a dramatic recovery, although they were marginally better than in the period of the post 1980s' recession. These statistics seem to attest to the importance of the media and the influence of politicians in setting the nation's agenda.

Earlier research by the National Center for States Courts lends some further precision to the issue of public concern about the crime problem. A representative sample of Americans were asked to rate the seriousness of a list of social problems, including both criminal justice and other problems such as inflation, pollution and unemployment. However, rather than simply asking about "crime," respondents were given a series of options, such as drugs and white collar crimes. Consistent with other polls, a criminal justice issue topped the list: 88 percent rated "Street crimes" as a very serious, or serious problem. White collar crimes were rated as being very serious by less than half the sample (National Center for State Courts, 1978). It is clear then, that when Americans talk about the seriousness of crime as a social problem, they have in mind street crimes.[2]

The increase in public concern over crime as a social problem has led to an increase in support for more punitive criminal justice policies. For example, although most polls in America have for years shown that the public believes sentencing should be harsher, the percentages have risen recently. In Canada, too, the growth in concern over crime has provoked an interest in more punitive measures. Thus in 1994 a poll revealed 70 percent of the public favored a tightening of parole, 77 percent supported making it easier to transfer young offenders to adult court and 68 percent favored the use of detention centers where young offenders would have to perform manual labor (Angus Reid, 1994).

Perceptions of the Relative Seriousness
of Different Crimes

In the second part of this chapter we review the extensive literature on how the public evaluate the relative and absolute seriousness of different crimes. Before reviewing this material, however, we might reasonably ask why this topic is important. Surely determining the seriousness of a particular crime is a matter for judges, who must impose a sentence the severity of which reflects the level of seriousness? This is true, but there is a strong public interest for a number of reasons. First, if the public have a very different view of crime seriousness, they are going to respond negatively to sentences imposed by judges. Sentences for crimes of sexual aggression are illustrative of this point. It is often said that judges (most of whom are men) do not appreciate the seriousness of crimes such as rape. This leads judges to impose sentences that are inappropriately lenient in light of the harm inflicted on victims of sexual assault (most of whom are women). These sentences are then criticized by members of the public, but the reason for the discrepant views of the sentence is not necessarily a difference in punitiveness, but rather a difference between judges and the public in terms of the perceived seriousness of the crime.[3]

Another reason for wanting to explore this issue is that judges themselves frequently attempt to reconcile their sentencing practices with the views of the public (or what judges perceive the views of the public to be). If judges believe that a particular crime is now viewed as being less serious than in the past, they are likely to impose less severe sanctions on offenders convicted of this crime. One of the reasons that judges in many western nations have tended to impose lenient sentences on persons convicted of possessing small amounts of "soft" drugs, is that mere possession is no longer regarded as a serious crime by most members of the public. This was probably not the case in the 1950s and 1960s, when drug use was concentrated in a narrowly defined sector of the public, and when many people believed that smoking marijuana would inevitably lead to drug abuse involving "hard" drugs, such as heroin.

We are also interested in the subject of crime seriousness because criminal justice policy, or more specifically the punishment response focuses on street crimes of violence. The reason for this is that public fear street crimes such as robbery and homicide more than other forms of criminality such as white collar crimes. In this respect, public reaction does not necessarily reflect an objective assessment of the harm to society. Estimates of the magnitude of the problem vary but statistics show that annually approximately 100,000 workers die from accidents and diseases contracted as a result of violations of health and safety codes (Kramer, 1984). The perception that white collar crimes are relatively benign is part of the mythology of crime and criminal justice (see Kappeler, Blumberg and Potter, 1993). It is important, then, to understand public perceptions of the relative harm associated with different forms of criminality.

The government should also have an interest in whether societal members agree on the perceived seriousness of crimes, and whether the public's views of crime seriousness accord with legislative statutes which define the seriousness of criminal acts by associating them with penalties of varying severity. In order to secure compliance with these laws, the public must believe the laws are legitimate (Robinson and Darley, 1995). Moreover, in order to punish offenders justly, public views on crime seriousness are needed to calculate equitable punishment for different offenses. Punishments that exceed community sentiment regarding the seriousness of the crime may be perceived as violating the eighth amendment of the U.S. Constitution which prohibits cruel and unusual punishment (Finkel, Maloney, Valbuena, and Groscup, 1995). Furthermore, from the standpoint of efficiency, prosecutors can use public views on crime seriousness to allocate resources to those offenses that are seen as being more serious (Miethe, 1984).

All of these purposes, however, require that societal members hold the same values and can agree on the acts that constitute the most serious threats to these values compared to other acts. People may hold the same values, but may prioritize these values differently, which then leaves the government with the problem of choosing which group's priorities should take precedence. As the purposes outlined above illustrate, decisions by the government made in the face of conflicting values or priorities among different ethnic and cultural groups can have negative consequences such as noncompliance with laws and distrust of the system.

Scholars have long recognized the importance of understanding whether people perceive criminal acts in a similar way. Durkheim (1964) and other supporters of the consensual model proposed that criminal laws reflect the "collective consciousness of society," and criminal laws are made to protect consensual community values through enforcement and punishment. Marxist and other "radical" criminologists have challenged this view of criminal law, and proposed the conflict model, which states that people from different social classes and ethnicities disagree about which acts should be criminalized and punished. As noted in Chapter 1, according to the conflict model, criminal laws serve to protect the interest of the powerful members by being enforced primarily against the less powerful members of society such as the poor, women, and ethnic minorities.

In this part of this chapter we attempt to answer the following questions (among others): How much consensus is there among different demographic groups regarding ratings of crime seriousness? Are there cross-cultural differences in these perceptions? That is, do Americans share the views of people from other countries regarding which crimes are most serious? Are perceptions of seriousness affected by sentencing laws or by media coverage of crime? Do members of the public and criminal justice professionals (such as judges) see eye-to-eye regarding crime seriousness?

Consider the following three crimes of violence: armed bank robbery, assault, and rape. Which of these offenses is the most serious? Few readers would hesitate in identifying rape as the most serious offense, and would justify this evaluation by citing the long-lasting harm, or the high degree of personal violation that rape entails. But this is a relatively clear-cut comparison. What about two other crimes: manslaughter and attempted murder. Which of these is more serious? At first glance, we might be tempted to regard manslaughter as the most serious crime. After all, a life has been taken. With attempted murder, there is no loss of life, and if the victim is fortunate, the physical injuries may be only transitory. But let us examine these two crimes more carefully, by considering a couple of real cases.

The first crime is a typical case of manslaughter. A man goes to a bar, gets very drunk, and in the course of a fight, slashes at his opponent with a broken bottle. The other individual subsequently dies. Since the accused did not intend to kill, he is convicted of manslaughter. Now let's turn to the attempted murder. In this case, a jumbo jet, loaded with passengers, is at the ramp awaiting permission to take off. Airport security then receives an anonymous call telling them that there is a bomb aboard the jet. The pilot returns the jet to the departure gate and the passengers and crew disembark. A search of the plane reveals a package of semtex explosive. Eventually the police apprehend a suspect (not the man who made the last-minute call). The accused pleads not guilty, but after a trial is convicted of attempt murder. No physical or psychological harm came to the passengers, beyond a four hour delay in their travel plans. In fact they were never aware of the true cause of their delayed departure. However, the threat of harm was immense. Had the warning call not been made (or not been believed), 568 persons would have perished.

This comparison illustrates the fact that the criminal law is concerned not just with the harm *inflicted*, but also with the harm *threatened*. A man who walks into a bank and fires a gun wounding a bank employee commits a serious crime. But so does the man who walks through a crowded shopping mall brandishing a loaded firearm, but without actually firing the weapon. So which of these two crimes—the manslaughter or the attempted murder—was the more serious offense? Do we still believe that the manslaughter was the more serious? The problem of crime seriousness is clearly quite complicated, and involves some comparison of offenses along the dimension of harm, whether actually inflicted or simply threatened.

Methodological Issues

Perhaps the most important problem confronting researchers is that members of the public have unrealistic perceptions of the consequences (one of the components of seriousness) of different crimes. We are all aware of the harm inflicted on victims of rape, or the families of murder victims. But how many among us really comprehend the consequences of a crime that receives almost no coverage from the media, such as perjury? Few people perceive perjury to be a serious crime that is worthy of a severe response from the sentencing process. That is because we cannot readily understand the potential cost for the administration of justice. In fact, the consequences of perjury can be very serious indeed.

When witnesses perjure themselves, two judicial mistakes become more probable. The system becomes more likely to acquit the guilty and to convict the innocent. Systematic research on false convictions in American courts has found that perjured testimony plays a key role in generating erroneous verdicts. People who have seen Errol Thompson's film "The Thin Blue Line" will recall that an innocent man who spent years in prison for a crime of which he was innocent, was convicted in large part as a result of testimony by eye-witnesses who were lying under oath. Cases like this explain why perjury carries a very high maximum penalty.[4]

For these reasons, researchers frequently give subjects clear definitions of crimes, and examples of actual incidents when exploring public perceptions of offense seriousness. This is only a partial solution, however, and this fact must be considered when evaluating comparisons between public and professional perceptions of crime seriousness. It means that differences between the two populations may reflect knowledge of the true nature of criminal behavior, rather than basic differences in terms of perceptions of crime seriousness. Public perceptions of crime seriousness reflect stereotypical conceptions of crimes and their consequences, just as perceptions of individual offenders are influenced by what the public think a typical offender is like.

Most research has used a paradigm which requires respondents to read brief descriptions of criminal acts which lack information about the offenders' and victims' characteristics, degree of intentionality, and culpability. Respondents are simply asked to rate the "seriousness" of the behavior in each description. This approach leaves the term "serious" undefined and assumes that people have a common and simple understanding of seriousness as amount of harm inflicted (Miethe, 1982; Forgas, 1980; Howe, 1988; Parton, Hansel, and Stratton, 1991; Warr, 1989).[5] Contrary to this assumption, studies employing scaling techniques suggest that seriousness has multiple meanings. Respondents use either harmfulness or wrongfulness to rate seriousness depending on which one is most salient in a particular crime description (Warr, 1989).

Although an evaluative dimension determines how people judge and categorize crimes, this dimension consists of several facets such as seriousness, deserved punishment, moral wrongfulness, the likelihood of conviction, the offender's dangerousness and the likelihood of injury (Howe, 1988). These studies find multiple meanings are associated with these concepts, but this does not seriously threaten the assumption that people distinguish crimes primarily using the amount of harm inflicted and the wrongfulness of the act. These studies, however, do not provide a fair test of alternative meanings such as intentionality, culpability, and status of offender or victim because all excluded scales of intentionality and presented descriptions void of information about the offender or victim.

Research on public perceptions of crime seriousness goes back many decades. However, Sellin's and Wolfgang's (1964) classic study initiated the bulk of research in the field. Studies before Sellin's and Wolfgang's study focused more on methodological issues (e.g., Coombs, 1967; Thurstone, 1927a,b) than on the substantive and applied issues pertaining to perceptions of crime seriousness. Sellin and Wolfgang (1964) believed that a scale of crime seriousness based on public perceptions could be used to define the seriousness of different offenses in criminal law, which then could inform police, prosecutorial and judicial responses to crime.

These researchers asked samples of students, police officers, and juvenile court judges to rate the seriousness of each crime story in a set of 141 crimes. The crime stories were extremely brief and by Sellin's and Wolfgang's choosing, focused on the act committed. Characteristics of the offender and victim were not provided, with the exception that the offender was always referred to as a male and his age was indicated as thirteen, seventeen, twenty-seven or left unspecified. These researchers found that respondents consistently agreed about the relative seriousness of the crimes. Violent crimes were perceived as more serious than property crimes which were perceived as more serious than public order and victimless crimes. In addition to this widespread consensus on the relative seriousness of different crimes, Sellin and Wolfgang found that the degree of physical harm or the value of the property stolen determined perceived seriousness. The age of the offender as well as several characteristics of the offense such as whether the offender was legally or illegally at the place from which property was taken, or used violence after entry, used a specific type of weapon (e.g., gun, knife, blunted object), or stole an unlocked or locked car, did not influence perceptions of seriousness.

An important test of the consensus theory involves the perceptions of offenders versus non-offenders. It might be argued that convicted, imprisoned offenders are likely to have very different perceptions of the seriousness of crimes. After all, offenders have direct, first-hand experience with crime as well as a great deal more indirect experience (conversations with other offenders, contact with criminal justice professionals and so forth) than the average member of the public. As well, there is an element of personal involvement for offenders; they may seek to downplay the seriousness of crimes similar to those for which they are currently being punished. Robert Figlio (1975) compared the seriousness ratings derived from a sample of incarcerated adult and juvenile offenders with ratings of the same crimes provided by middle-class sociology students. Once again, qualified support for the consensus perspective emerged. There was substantial agreement between the two samples regarding the ordering of offenses along the dimension of seriousness. However, some differences did arise in terms of the absolute value of the harm inflicted in each of the crimes. Across a range of offenses, seriousness ratings provided by offenders were on average lower than those derived from a sample of the public. Offenders may have become hardened by their direct and indirect exposure to crimes.

Is Intent a Component of Perceived Crime Seriousness?

The issue of intent is critical for the criminal law. In order to obtain a conviction, the prosecution must prove that the accused intended to commit the act.[6] As well, evidence of a great deal of premeditation is frequently an aggravating factor, resulting in a harsher penalty than when the accused intended to commit the crime, but only formed the intention on the spur of the moment. The issues of intent and premeditation, then, relate to the culpability of the offender, and determine whether he will be convicted, as well as the magnitude of any penalty imposed. Does the issue of intent also affect public perceptions of the seriousness of the crime? The answer would appear to be that intent does have an influence over public views, although this result has not emerged from every study that has examined the question.

Riedel (1975), for example, found that intent did not influence seriousness ratings, but the design of the study contained several flaws.[7] Respondents in another study read crimes that varied in four levels of intent and used intent in making seriousness judgments (Sebba, 1980). When intent was left unspecified, respondents assumed offenders of ordinary street crimes intended to commit the offense, but assumed offenders who committed regulatory offenses acted recklessly (see also Blum-West, 1985). In another study, students read six stories about drunk driving incidents in which the researchers had manipulated three variables: whether personal or property damage was involved, whether the property was replaceable, the amount of damage and whether the offender was arrested. When offenders escaped arrest, personal damage was perceived as more serious than property damage. When offenders were arrested, personal damage and property damage had similar seriousness ratings. Offenders who escaped compared to those arrested were seen as acting with a greater degree of intent. Ratings of perceived intent and seriousness were moderately related (Gebotys and Dasgupta, 1987).

Studies that asked respondents to rate the similarity of different pairs of crimes also provide evidence that intentionality is one of the dimensions along which people naturally distinguish between crimes. Sherman and Dowdle (1974) discovered that four dimensions were used to classify crimes: whether the victim was an individual or an institution, whether the crime was committed openly; the extent to which the victim may have precipitated the crime; and the degree of premeditation involved. Although ratings of seriousness were closely related to the classification of crimes, seriousness was not related to any of these dimensions. Forgas (1980) found that people used intentionality as well as the violent nature and the frequency of the offense to classify different crimes; moreover, only violence was related to seriousness ratings. Sherman and Dowdle provide a concise summary of these studies: "[W]hen subjects' attention is drawn to seriousness alone, as in past studies, a well-ordered seriousness scale is obtained. When subjects are left to their own predilections, however, they judge crimes along several dimensions, no one of which is highly associated with seriousness" (p. 124). Moreover, it is clear that intent as well as harm done are central features when people are allowed to categorize the crimes along the dimensions that they see as relevant.

Cross-Cultural Perceptions of Crime Seriousness

One of the most interesting areas of research concerns the existence of cross-cultural differences in perceptions of crime seriousness. In many ways, this takes us to the heart of definitions of crime itself. Is the concept of harm, which underlies perceptions of crime seriousness, culturally relative, or are there certain basic human values (such as a prohibition against the taking of human life), the transgression of which strikes people from all cultures as equally reprehensible, equally serious?

For a number of reasons, it is hard to make adequate comparisons between cultures. First, different cultures define crimes in different ways. To take just one example, it would be hard to compare Canadians' and Americans' perceptions of the seriousness of crimes of sexual aggression, because the crimes are defined differently in the two countries. In Canada, the offense of rape was abolished in 1983, and replaced with three crimes of sexual assault. The physical act defined in some American states as rape could be classified as any of the three levels of sexual assault in the Canadian Criminal Code, depending upon characteristics of the incident.[8] In order to get around this problem, researchers have to provide respondents with fairly general descriptions of crimes, that do not reflect any particular statutory definition.

The limited research literature on this issue suggests that there is a significant degree of agreement across countries in terms of the relative seriousness of different crimes. This consensus suggests that there may be an almost universal element to the concept of harm, which underlies offense seriousness, although variation may exist for crimes that have a particular significance for one culture or another. The fact that residents of countries as diverse as Canada and Kuwait all see intentional homicide as the most serious of crimes, and that they also agree on the relative seriousness of lesser crimes is evidence of this.

Sellin's and Wolfgang's study stimulated many researchers to examine how well these findings generalized across time and across different groups within the same country as well as held in comparisons of citizens from different countries. Using respondents from Canada (Akman, Normandeau, and Turner, 1967), Puerto-Rico (Valez-Diaz and Megargee, 1971) and the United States (Filigio, 1975; Wellford and Wiatrowski, 1975; Wolfgang, Figlio, Tracy, and Singer, 1985), studies have repeatedly found that the rank order of seriousness in Sellin's and Wolfgang's data and the rank order of seriousness in data from their respondents are highly related. Men and women (Hsu, 1973; Rossi, Waite, Bose, and Berk, 1974), and people from different ethnicities and social classes (Rossi *et al.*, 1974), as well as victims and non-victims of crimes (Rossi *et al.*, 1974) agree on the relative seriousness of different crimes. Educational level, however, is related to agreement with the group. Those with less education tend to deviate more from overall group ratings (Rossi *et al.*, 1974), and tend to place importance on attributions about sexual acts and the privacy of the act (Hanzel, 1987).

Comparisons across different countries reveal that people in Great Britain, Canada, Denmark, Finland, Holland, Kuwait, Norway and the United States generally agree about which crimes are more serious than other crimes (e.g., Hsu, 1973; Newman, 1976; Scott and Al-Thakeb, 1977; Evans and Scott, 1984b). A few exceptions, however, are worth noting. Kuwaitis and Americans perceive rape to be more serious than the violent crimes of robbery or aggravated assault whereas respondents from Scandinavian countries and from Great Britain perceive these offenses to have the same seriousness level. Kuwaitis considered selling heroin or marijuana to be more serious than any other offense except murder whereas respondents from other countries do not rank drug offenses as serious as other violent crimes (Scott and Al-Thakeb, 1977).[9] Kuwaiti students also perceived victimless crimes which violate moral codes to be much more serious than did United States students. This would appear to be due to differences in the relative importance of religion in the two countries (Evans and Scott, 1984b).

Where cultures appear to differ is in terms of the other half of the crime-punishment equation. That is, although there is a high degree of consensus about the relative *seriousness* of different crimes, there is more variability in terms of the *magnitude* of the appropriate punishment. Although Americans and Swedish people may agree that murder is the most serious crime, they differ in terms of their preferences for the appropriate punishment. Americans are more likely to demand life sentences or the death penalty for offenders convicted of murder. Sentences for murder vary in the U.S., but they are usually in excess of ten years. Sometimes they can mean natural life behind bars, or execution. In Sweden, the usual sentence for murder is ten years, but release on parole occurs in the fifth year of incarceration (Jareborg, 1993).

Some recent data suggest that college and high school students in the U.S. perceive victimless crimes as harmful to society and to the participants and their families. Veneziano and Veneziano (1993) manipulated three dimensions in brief hypothetical vignettes of drug crime, pornography, prostitution, and gambling: (1) the frequency of involvement (occasional or excessive); (2) the extent of involvement (mild was defined as marijuana user or seller; adult pornography, prostitution without sadistic acts, and gambling for small amounts whereas severe was defined as heroin user or seller, child pornography, prostitution with sadistic acts, and gambling for large amounts); (3) nature of involvement (purchaser or supplier).

Respondents read and rated one randomly assigned vignette on the harmfulness to participant, the participant's family, and to society. They were also asked whether the act should be decriminalized. Severe acts and providers of these vices were rated as significantly more harmful to society. Compared to selling, simple drug use was perceived as more harmful to the participant and the participant's family. Frequency of involvement did not affect perceptions of harm. The majority of respondents for all these acts except gambling were opposed to decriminalization. For gambling, between 36 and 55 percent were opposed, depending on the scenario that they read. Research using a sample of United States adults, however, has found that most were indifferent to prostitution and uninformed about alternative strategies for handling it (McCaghy and Cernkovich, 1991).

Historical Variation in Perceptions of Crime Seriousness

Related to the issue of variation across cultures is the question of variation in perceptions over time, but within a single culture. Here too, the research speaks to an issue at the heart of criminology. If perceptions of seriousness reflect some basic dimension of harm, they are unlikely to change in a generation. Comparisons over time have revealed some interesting changes in public views of crime seriousness, but also considerable stability in perceptions of the overall relative seriousness of different crimes. Coombs (1967) compared Thurstone's (1927a) data to his own 1966 findings and discovered an important change had occurred across these forty years. Whereas rape was viewed as the most serious crime in the 1920s, by the 1960s, murder was viewed as more serious than rape. Since this time, studies generally find that murder is seen as the most serious crime. There has also been a shift in public views of white collar crimes and drug crimes. In 1974, respondents in Scandinavian countries, Great Britain and Kuwait perceived white collar crimes to be as serious as index property offenses whereas United State respondents perceived index property crimes to be more serious than white collar crimes (Scott and Al-Thakeb, 1977).

Once again, the general results appear to be that crimes at the extremes of seriousness do not generate different reactions over time. In 1967, offenses against the person were judged to be more serious than had been the case forty years earlier. There was also a tendency for the ratings of property crimes to receive less serious ratings from subjects in the replication. The most recent research now shows that growing public awareness of the extent, and true nature of white-collar crimes has resulted in enhanced seriousness ratings of these crimes, although they do not approach crimes against the person in severity in the eyes of the public (see Cullen, Link and Polanzi, 1982). Similar trends have been observed in other countries such as Australia (see Grabosky, Braithwaite and Wilson, 1987). The conclusion then would appear to be that public perceptions of crime seriousness are far from unchanging, except perhaps for the most serious crimes.

Rossi *et al.* (1974) found that a sample of Baltimore residents in 1972 ranked white collar crime as less serious than violent, property, victimless, and drug crimes. A study comparing this 1972 sample to a sample of Illinois residents in 1979 found that the Illinois sample ranked white collar crime as more serious than crimes against the police, less serious property crimes, and victimless crimes (Cullen, Link, and Polawzi, 1982). White collar crimes resulting in physical injuries and corporate price fixing changed the most in perceived seriousness whereas income tax fraud, government corruption, and employee embezzlement remained stable. Whereas white collar crime increased in serious, this study found that selling and using drugs significantly decreased in perceived seriousness.

Questioning the Empirical Verification and Meaning of Consensus

Studies in the 1980s began to question the adequacy of the conceptual definition and empirical measurement of consensus. To that point, research had focused on correlations between group means across offenses, and had not examined an obvious measure of disagreement, the variance around the mean (Miethe, 1982). Several researchers (Rossi and Henry, 1980; Miethe, 1984) have also noted that prior studies generally focused on consensus across the entire set of offenses (i.e., global consensus), and ignored whether people agreed about the perceived seriousness of different acts of a subcategory of crimes (e.g., violent, property, white collar); this latter consensus is labeled local consensus. Miethe (1984) also suggested another dimension of consensus that varied in prior studies: the metric of the comparison.

Whereas most prior studies examined whether people agreed about which crimes were more serious relative to other crimes (i.e., relative consensus), absolute consensus sometimes was considered. Absolute consensus "refers to cases in which the ordering of items and the numerical scores assigned to each item are similar across and within groups" (Miethe, 1984, p. 462). The variability around the means and the extent to which demographic variables influence ratings of crime seriousness indicate the degree of absolute consensus. High absolute consensus requires small variances and requires that demographic variables do not systematically relate to seriousness ratings (Miethe, 1984) or to the errors made in making seriousness judgments (Rauma, 1991).[10]

Relative Consensus Within Crime Categories

Categories of crimes such as violent, white collar, property, public disorder, and victimless consist of a vast array of different acts. For example, victimless crimes include such offenses as illegal drug use, selling illegal drugs, prostitution, pornography, and gambling. White collar crimes include auto repair fraud, bribery, oil price fixing, negligent drug manufacturing and distribution, illegal land acquisition and disposition, false advertising regarding reduction in costs, false advertising concerning quality of product, and income tax evasion. Respondents in eight countries (United States, Great Britain, Finland, Sweden, Denmark, Netherlands, and Kuwait) agreed on the ordering of these eight white collar crimes with negligent drug manufacturing and oil price fixing rated as most serious and auto repair fraud and income tax fraud rated as least serious (Scott and Al-Thakeb, 1977). Miethe (1984) found that African-Americans and Caucasian-Americans had similar orderings for acts within violent, white collar and public disorder categories. Men and women in the United States (Rauma, 1991), in Canada (Akman and Turner, 1967; Hsu, 1973), and in England (Walker, 1978) agreed that murder is more serious than rape.[11]

People within the same culture can disagree about the relative seriousness of different acts representing a category of crime (e.g., property). Cullen, Link, Travis, and Wozniak (1985) found that United States respondents demonstrated high consensus about the seriousness of the most serious violent crimes and of crimes against police officers, but considerably less consensus about the ordering of acts *within* the categories of white collar, victimless, and minor property offenses (see also Carlson and Williams, 1993). Compared to the agreement among Caucasian-Americans, African-Americans agreed less with each other about the relative seriousness of different property acts and white collar acts (Meithe, 1984).

Different perspectives about crime and attitudes toward government may result in diminishing consensus about the ordering of crimes. Carlson and Williams (1993) found that individuals in their sample could be categorized into one of four perspectives about crime. Some individuals agreed with the conflict model and perceived crimes committed by powerful members of society (e.g., white collar crimes) as being more serious and victimless crimes as not very serious at all. Another group perceived victimless crimes which violated moral codes (e.g., prostitution, statutory rape, drug selling), as very serious. The third group had more sympathy for business than individuals who are victims of property crimes. The fourth perspective perceived misconduct by government as very serious.

Absolute Consensus Across and Within Crime Categories

Although relative local and global consensus may be informative and sufficient for allocating police and prosecutorial resources, absolute consensus is needed to evaluate sufficiently the merits of the conflict model and to inform legislative and judicial policies on legal punishments (Miethe, 1984). Several studies have discovered that people from different backgrounds provide disparate overall average ratings across all crimes. African-Americans rate criminal acts as more serious than do Caucasian-Americans (Miethe, 1984; Rauma, 1991). Individuals with less formal education and those living in smaller communities (e.g., rural areas and small towns) assign higher average seriousness scores across crimes (Cullen, Link, Travis, and Wozniak, 1985); these two individual characteristics explained 21 percent of the variability in perceived seriousness.

Other studies (Rossi *et al.*, 1974; Rauma, 1991) also have also found that educational achievement influences perceived crime seriousness. Individuals with less education may make crime seriousness judgments on emotional grounds and may be more supportive of crime control than due process rights of defendants. Few studies have examined either of these hypotheses. One study found that those with less intellectual sophistication emphasized the private and sexual aspects of crimes (Hanzel, 1987). Rauma (1991) found that conservatives rated crimes as being more serious than did liberals. In summary, several studies suggest that there is significant global dissension about the overall seriousness of crimes.

Which crime categories are the sources of this global dissension? People from different backgrounds appear to have similar views regarding the relative seriousness of different acts of violence (Miethe, 1984; Cullen, Link, Travis, and Wozniak, 1985) with the exception of murder and rape. Men compared to women in England (Walker, 1978) and Canada (Akman, Normandeau, and Turner, 1967; Hsu, 1973) perceived murder as more serious. In these same studies, women compared to men judged rape to be more serious. For example, men in Lampe's research rated murder as the most serious crime, rape as the second most serious offense. Women, however rated these two offenses in the reverse order. Otherwise, sex differences in crime seriousness judgements tend to be minimal, both in the U.S. and elsewhere (e.g., Wilson, Walker and Mukherjee, 1986).

Effects of Criminal Record on Perceptions of Crime Seriousness

Many crimes are committed by people with previous convictions. Does the nature of the criminal record affect perceptions of crime seriousness? In theory, it should not. A sexual assault is no more serious because the offender has committed the crime twice in the past. However, public perceptions of crime seriousness are affected by the offender's criminal history. This has been demonstrated by research in which respondents are asked to rate the seriousness of crimes committed either by offenders with previous convictions or without previous convictions. The general finding is that when the offender is a recidivist, the crime receives elevated seriousness ratings. For example Hilton (1993) found that when an offender was a recidivist, ratings of crime seriousness were higher than when he was a first offender (see also Higginbottom and Zamble, 1988; Klein, Newman, Weis and Bobner (1983).

Studies which examine the influence of offenders' criminal histories also demonstrate the importance of intent in seriousness judgments. Previous convictions can be seen as being relevant to intentionality: If the offender has four previous convictions for assault, his claim to have lacked intent for an assault will be seen as rather implausible. Hilton (1993) varied whether the victim was a stranger or wife and whether the batterer was a first-time offender or recidivist in hypothetical stories. She found that for both stranger and wife battery, respondents perceived incidents involving first-time offenders as less serious and as less likely to be repeated compared to incidents involving recidivists.

Another study found that American students considered an offender's arrest record in judging the seriousness of some crimes (violent and property crimes), but not others, such as drug or public disorder offenses. For violent and property crimes, respondents rated crimes involving offenders with a prior arrest for assault as most serious, those with a prior arrest for a non-assault offense as moderately serious, and those with no prior arrest as least serious (Klein, Newman, Weis, and Bobner, 1983). Similarly, ratings of the seriousness of homicide cases were affected by the criminal history of the offender (Higginbottom and Zamble, 1988). Thus, across several studies and different offenses, the prior record of an offender shapes perceived seriousness ratings either through perceptions of intent or the likelihood of recidivism. This finding may well explain why the public favor harsher sentences for recidivist offenders. Crimes by repeat offenders are seen as being more serious, and the public accordingly favors harsher sentences.

These findings are important, for they help to explain the punitive attitudes towards recidivists which result in public support for "Three Strikes" legislation. The public want to punish recidivists not just because they believe additional punishment will deter these offenders, but also because the public finds crime by recidivists to be inherently more serious, independent of the question of future offending (see Roberts 1996, for a discussion).

Role of the Media

An area that has been insufficiently explored concerns the influence of the news media on our perceptions of the absolute seriousness of crimes. Content analyses have demonstrated that serious crimes of violence are disproportionately represented in news stories. Gordon and Heath (1981) found that one front-page story in five across the U.S. death with violent crime. Similar results emerge from content analyses of Canadian news media. Sacco and Fair (1988) report that homicide accounted for 40 percent of crime stories, while Doob (1985) found that over half the crime stories in his sample involved violence. These trends should come as no surprise: Violent crime, particularly murder is dramatic and newsworthy. Property crimes are far less interesting. This over-representation of violent crime explains in large part the public perception that a significant amount of crime involves violence (see Chapter 2). Some studies suggest that the news media may also have an effect on perceptions of crime seriousness.

The first study tested two competing hypotheses. It is possible that a steady diet of violence on television will de-sensitize people to the seriousness of crimes. After all, if we see serious crime all the time, it may seem banal and less serious than if we just encounter it occasionally. This might be termed the *de-sensitization* hypothesis. Alternatively, the opposite effect may occur: Serious, violent crime may act as anchor, inflating our perceptions of the seriousness of other, unrelated crimes. This might be termed the *anchoring* hypothesis. In one study, subjects were asked two general sets of questions. First, they were asked how often they were exposed to the news media. Second, they were asked to rate the seriousness of a number of crimes. The predictions are clear: If the de-sensitization hypothesis is correct, there would be a *negative* correlation between frequency of media use, and seriousness ratings: People who watch a lot of news would rate crimes as being less serious than would people who were seldom exposed to the news. The anchoring hypothesis predicts a *positive* relationship, and this in fact is what emerged from the analyses. Seriousness ratings of a number of crimes were significantly higher for people who were high media users (Gebotys, Roberts and Dasgupta, 1988).

The problem with this study is that it is correlational in nature. We cannot be sure that the news media had the effect predicted, or whether it is simply a coincidence that people who watch a lot of news programmes also regard crimes as being more serious than do low-media consumers. Fortunately, several research studies using the experimental approach have confirmed the anchoring hypothesis. The basic structure of these studies consists of providing subjects with descriptions of crimes, some of which are very serious, some of which are of low seriousness. The dependent variable in the experiment is the rating of seriousness provided by subjects when they are asked to read a second crime description unrelated to the first story. Results of studies along these lines show that subjects who have just read about very serious crimes such as murder and rape provide higher seriousness ratings than subjects who have not read about serious crimes (e.g., Roberts and Edwards, 1989; Pepitone and Dinubile, 1976). These results suggest another negative effect of the news media emphasis on very serious violent crime. In addition to distorting public perceptions of the amount of violent crime, the media may well also be changing our perceptions of the seriousness of crimes. This in turn may feed into the demand for harsher sentencing which will be explored in a later chapter of this book. If, over time, we see crimes in a more serious light, we may well demand ever harsher penalties than those that are currently imposed.

Do members of the public and criminal justice professionals hold similar views about the relative seriousness of different crimes? Research suggests that officers and citizens agree on the seriousness of some crimes, but disagree about others (e.g., Levi and Jones, 1985; Sellin and Wolfgang, 1964). Sellin and Wolfgang found that police officers, judges, and members of the public generally had similar perceptions of crime seriousness. Subsequent research has examined whether the public and police officers agree about the absolute seriousness of certain crimes, such as white collar crimes. Levi and Jones (1985) for example, asked laypersons and police officers in England to rate the seriousness of fourteen different crimes. These researchers found that the two groups of subjects agreed that violent crimes were the most serious. The police sample, however, ranked residential burglary as being more seriousness than did members of the public.

In terms of absolute seriousness, police ratings of all violent crimes were higher than seriousness ratings derived from citizens.[12] The public ratings of the seriousness of white collar crimes (such as tampering with a car's odometer) were higher than police officers' ratings. The public provided higher seriousness ratings of statutory rape (i.e., sex with a minor) than did the police. In general, then, there was considerable agreement, although the police placed priority on street crimes such as assault and robbery. The public rated these offenses as very serious as well, although white collar crimes also attracted the attention of the public.

Conclusions

Americans have become increasingly concerned about the seriousness of crime as a social problem. Most recently, there has been a significant increase in the percentage of people identifying crime as the number one problem facing the nation. This growth in concern over crime seems to have occurred independently of any increase in crimes rates, or the percentage of crime involving violence.

What does the research on crime seriousness tell us about the conflict and consensus models outlined in Chapter 1? Neither model provides a perfect accounting of the research findings in the area of social perceptions. Nevertheless, the consensus model would appear to have the edge: For most crimes, particularly for the ones with which we are most familiar, there would appear to be more consensus than disagreement about rankings of seriousness. There also appears to be a fair degree of concordance across different countries in terms of crime seriousness rankings.

The research on public perceptions of crime seriousness shows that a significant degree of consensus exists across different groups in society regarding the relative seriousness of most common crimes (e.g., Coombs, 1967; Wellford and Wiatrowski, 1975; Thomas, Cage and Foster, 1976; Turner, 1978; Rossi and Henry, 1980; Miethe, 1982; Indermaur, 1990). Not surprisingly, perhaps, crimes of violence received the highest seriousness ratings. It is clear that the greatest degree of social consensus exists for crimes at the extremes of seriousness. This makes sense: We can all agree that murder is the most serious crime and that shoplifting or jay-walking are relatively trivial offenses. However, there is far less agreement among people about crimes in between these two extremes.

In this respect, there is probably little difference between the public and judges: Some offenses consistently generate a higher degree of disparity than others. This suggests that judges agree on the seriousness of some crimes, but less so on others (see Austin and Williams, 1977; Palys and Divorski, 1986). As well, there appears to be more agreement than disagreement about crime seriousness ratings derived from different societies. Since the first crime seriousness study was conducted in 1927, it has been possible to compare perceptions of crime seriousness over a seventy-year period. Once again, it would seem that crimes at the extremes of the seriousness dimension generate similar reactions over time. There has however been some shifting in public perceptions of crimes at the intermediate level of seriousness. In addition, white collar crimes are now perceived by the public to be more serious than in the past.

Notes

1. The response does not change when the wording of the question is modified. Thus when asked to identify the "two most important issues for the government to address," crime emerged along with health care as one of the issues (Maguire and Pastore, 1995).

2. After street crimes, the social problems identified as very serious were: drugs (83 percent); inflation (79 percent) and unemployment 67 percent).

3. Public perceptions of crime seriousness also relate to the issue of proportionality in sentencing (von Hirsch, 1985, 1986). Most people endorse the principle that the severity of punishments should reflect the seriousness of crimes. This suggests that we need to know about the public's perception of crime seriousness if we want to understand their perceptions of sentencing decisions.

4. For example, in Canada, the most serious form of perjury carries a maximum penalty of life imprisonment.

5. One study (Travis, Link, Cullen, and Wozniak, 1986) examined whether the word "crime" in the instructions typically given in serious study biased respondents' ratings. They compared three groups who were instructed differently. Groups were instructed either to rate "crimes," "behaviors" or "deviant behaviors." They found that instructional differences did not affect seriousness ratings. Sheley (1980) found that one crime per page compared to the full array on the page did not affect seriousness ratings, and the insertion of a shoplifting crime early, in the middle, or at the end of the array did not affect ratings on this item. Sheley (1980) found limited support for whether the context of the array (mostly severe items; or mostly severe and less severe items) shaped ratings.

6. Most legal systems contain a limited number of usually less serious, regulatory offenses in which the prosecution only has to prove that the accused committed the act, not that he actually intended to break the law. These are known as offenses of strict liability.

7. Sebba (1980) notes that intent was inferred from a set of circumstances provided in the instructions, but not connected with the event when respondents were rating seriousness. Parton *et al.*, (1991) notes that Riedel (1975) manipulated intent across subjects, but manipulated harmfulness of acts within subjects. Moreover, Riedel (1975) found support that intent affected absolute ratings of the seriousness of murder.

8. For example, if a weapon was used to accomplish the assault, the incident would be classified and prosecuted as sexual assault level II, which is the intermediate level of seriousness.

9. This research used a scale of punishment as a proxy for perceived seriousness.

10. Rossi and Berk (1985) provide an excellent extensive discussion on different models of consensus. Several researchers have discussed more sophisticated statistical tools for assessing the degree of consensus such as Q-sort technique (Carlson and Williams, 1993), intra-class correlations (Cullen, Link, Travis, and Woznick, (1985), and extended regression model (Rauma, 1991). Crime seriousness studies have used magnitude estimation, categorical ratings, and pair comparison techniques. Studies comparing these different methodologies find that they tend to yield similar results (e.g., Cullen *et al.*, 1985; Sellin and Wolfgang, 1964; Walker, 1978).

11. One study has documented that Chinese women perceive rape as more serious than murder whereas Chinese men perceive murder as more serious than rape; the cultural requirement that women who were sexually molested should commit suicide may account for this finding (Hsu, 1973).

12. Curiously, assaulting a police officer was the exception to this rule. This may be explained by the fact that police officers have direct experience with this offense, and are aware that most crimes of this category result in less harm being inflicted than citizen-to-citizen assaults.

5

Beyond Public Responses:
The Hidden Effects of Context,
Recall, and Stereotypes

Sometimes mass media stories stimulate ordinary people to think about the nature and solutions to specific crimes, even though they have given little prior consideration to a particular topic. For example, on December 22, 1984, a white New Yorker named Bernard Goetz made the evening news. It was reported that several African-American youths, riding the New York subway, had accosted Goetz and attempted to rob him. Goetz's response was to pull a gun from his coat pocket and fire several shots, wounding the youths. Goetz argued that he had acted in self-defense. In January 1985, a survey revealed that 75 percent of New Yorkers agreed with Goetz. There were no racial differences in the responses of the public, but this inter-ethnic agreement and the perceptions of both groups was to change over time as additional information became public.

News media stories over the next three months informed the public that Goetz had made statements that he would do it again to protect himself from "punks" like the three young men. The stories also revealed that one youth was shot in the back as he was running away, and that Goetz had shot one youth twice. This information changed some people's perceptions about the legitimacy of Goetz's actions. By March, only 55 percent of New Yorkers felt that Goetz had acted in legitimate self-defense (Alderman, 1984). The additional information persuaded many who had approved earlier of his actions but now disapproved: 25 percent disapproved because of Goetz's recent statements, 9 percent mentioned his shooting twice at one youth, and 5 percent mentioned shooting at some of the youths' backs (Alderman, 1984). A significant minority (16 percent) indicated that their first opinion was based on little thought and that, upon reflection, they had decided it was wrong. This group clearly illustrated how opinion polls sometimes may capture ephemeral opinions based on little reflection or incomplete information.

As this example illustrates, the amount (and nature) of information underlying opinions and attitudes is central to evaluating the stability and validity of public views of criminal justice. In this chapter, we examine some key concepts about how people process information and form judgments and attitudes. Wherever available, we use applied research in the legal system to illustrate a concept and its implications for public opinion about crime and justice. When prior research has not directly tested the applicability of a concept in the area of crime and justice, we illustrate its potential explanatory power using a hypothetical example. It is a daunting task to summarize research on how people process information and to apply it to attitudes about crime and justice. This literature often tests assumptions and distinctions that are irrelevant to an adequate understanding of what people want from the justice system. Thus, in this chapter we attempt to highlight only the most pertinent distinctions and processes for an understanding of public opinion about crime and justice.

Context

One of the most fundamental distinctions that provides insight into changes of public opinion over time, surveys, and geographical areas is that the context surrounding the decision making task matters a great deal (Fiske and Neuberg, 1990; Stalans, 1993). Thus, we organize this chapter around two main sections that highlight different decision-making contexts. The first section discusses two heuristics or mental shortcuts that people frequently use in responding to questions in national opinion polls. The next section examines the question of whether lack of interest and motivation makes people express attitudes based on scant and atypical information recalled from their memory. In the third major section, we examine the ways in which people form opinions when the task allows sufficient time to make decisions. This section demonstrates how prior expectations and stereotypic knowledge can shape interpretations of information. This section also discusses the kind of data researchers that must gather to determine whether cognitive heuristics result in biased opinions or lead to efficient "good-enough" decision making (Fiske, 1992). We conclude with a summary of what research has shown about information processing by the public and what issues research should address in the future.

Time Pressure and Answers to General Questions

When people are asked questions in national opinion polls, the decision task has many features that lead people to use shortcuts in forming a response. Respondents feel time pressure as questions are asked one after another in rapid succession. This leads people to believe that they must respond quickly. As well, respondents may have recently been exposed to atypical and exaggerated media stories on the topic of the survey. They may be uninterested in the topic of the survey or they may have inaccurate prior knowledge about the topic. Given the limitations of the decision context, people often respond with opinions which are either fleeting or do not represent their true views. In this section, we will discuss two shortcuts (called cognitive heuristics) that people use to form responses: the availability heuristic and the representativeness heuristic.

Availability Heuristic or Accessibility Bias

When people form responses based on information about the topic that is easily recalled, they use what is known as an availability heuristic (Tversky and Kahneman, 1973) or accessibility bias (Taylor, 1982; Tourangeau and Rasinski, 1988). This heuristic is perhaps the most widely examined heuristic in opinion polling. A concrete example illustrates the concept. Many Gallup polls have asked respondents "Do you think the courts are too lenient, about right, or too harsh?" Most people choose the 'too lenient' response option. However, researchers have discovered that people say "too lenient" because they rely on atypical information which is easily recalled. For example, Doob and Roberts (1984) found that when answering this question, most people recalled violent offenders, and based their opinions of leniency on cases involving these offenders who constitute a small, unrepresentative minority of all criminals. In a similar way, Stalans and Diamond (1990) found that respondents who had concluded that judges were too lenient towards offenders convicted of burglary often recalled an atypical stereotype of burglary that involved burglars who carried weapons and ransacked homes. In other words, people are not thinking of sentences in general, but sentences imposed in the worst case scenario.

These studies used survey data collected only at one point in time. Survey data, however, cannot disentangle which opinion came first: whether the recall of crime images influenced opinions about criminal sentencing or whether the recall of crime images merely justified a decision that occurred prior to recalling the images. Stalans (1993) used experimental manipulations to test whether biased recall fueled demands for harsher punishment found in public opinion polls. By randomly assigning subjects to experimental condition, she was able to control for the possibility that prior attitudes to punishment determined the kinds of stories that are recalled. This experiment provided additional and more convincing evidence that an accessibility bias underlies how people form punishment preferences to global questions asked in telephone surveys.

Representativeness Heuristic and Generalizations About a Group

When people answer general questions about a group of cases, they will attempt to recall information about the topic. For example, respondents may be asked what percentage of parolees commit violent crimes when they are released on parole. Searching their memory they might quickly recall Willie Horton (the inmate paroled in New Hampshire who raped a girl while on parole) or similar cases reported by the media. Once these images are brought to mind, people make a judgment about how similar or representative they are of all parolees. This judgment of similarity is called a representativeness heuristic. Respondents may overestimate the percentage of parolees who will commit another violent crime because they conclude that the parolees that they recalled are similar to most parolees.

This use of a representativeness heuristic shows that people deviate from sampling theory, and believe that a small sample is generally representative of the population. Sampling theory guarantees that large samples will have a higher probability than smaller samples of being representative of the population from which they are drawn. However, people do not adhere to scientific principles, have too much confidence in the representativeness of small samples and are quite willing to generalize from the small sample to the population (Tversky and Kahneman, 1982b).

Respondents also use a representativeness heuristic to respond to attitudinal statements. For example, respondents in a survey might be asked their reaction to the following statement: "Most police officers abuse their power and use excessive force with suspects." People then search their memory for incidents in which officers abused their power. One respondent, George, generally believes that officers generally do not abuse their power. However, George recalls officer "X," one of the four officers who used excessive force on Rodney King because a talk show that he watched the night before featured officer "X." George concludes that officer "X" is somewhat similar to most officers and agrees with the statement. This influence of the context results in what is known as a "carryover effect"—the evaluation about the category is shifted toward the evaluation of the recalled exemplar. If George had not recalled officer "X," he would have expressed disagreement with the statement. Other respondents, however, may recall officer "X" from last night's media show and judge officer "X" to be dissimilar to most police officers.

What happens if people recall an extremely atypical exemplar (e.g., officer "X"), but exclude this exemplar from the category of police officer because they conclude that the exemplar is irrelevant to the task or is unrepresentative of police officers? One possibility is that their true opinion on the topic would be expressed. Frequently, respondents are still affected by the recalled atypical exemplar even though they judged it as irrelevant and excluded from the representation of police officers that they created before answering the question. The exclusion causes people to evaluate the police more positively than if they had not thought about officer "X." When the subsequent evaluation is in the opposite direction to the evaluation associated with the exemplar that came to mind, researchers call this a "contrast effect."

The contrast effect can be caused either through excluding the image from the representation of the whole group or creating a standard of comparison based on the extreme image (see Schwarz and Bless (1992) for relevant research and further information on the model). "Whether the information that comes to mind results in assimilation (carryover) or contrast effects depends on how it is categorized" (Schwarz and Bless, 1992, p. 218). Thus, when respondents categorize a recalled exemplar as atypical or irrelevant, contrast effects occur and when respondents categorize an exemplar as typical or similar to the group, carryover effects occur.

These two heuristics, availability and representativeness, can produce answers to questions which distort respondents' true opinions about crime and justice. The amount of distortion, however, depends on whether the recalled information is atypical or irrelevant to the topic. People also use several other heuristics to form judgments about crime and justice, which we will describe in later sections. Before examining this material, the next section addresses the question of why people resort to heuristics in forming judgments: is it due to laziness or pragmatism? The next section also provides a more detailed understanding of how different characteristics of an attitude influence how susceptible people are to changes in the context of the decision task.

Are People "Lazy Cognitive Misers" or "Pragmatically Involved Individuals?" Systematic research suggests that several irrelevant aspects of the decision-making context influence public opinion. For example, prior questions affect responses to subsequent questions in surveys (for review see Tourangeau and Rasinski, 1988). Media stories about vivid violent crimes affect peoples' judgments about the severity of sentencing (Doob and Roberts, 1984). The specificity of the crime story determines the punitiveness of the public's response (Roberts and Doob, 1990; Stalans and Diamond, 1990; Thomson and Ragona, 1987). Moreover, people easily change their opinion about topics such as community-based sentences, and the insanity defense when given additional information (e.g., Doble, 1987; Thomson and Ragona, 1987). These effects of the decision-making context on expressed opinions raise questions about whether people actually have *prior* opinions before researchers asked the questions. As Durham (1993) notes:

> There are several important reasons to be concerned about whether the responses elicited in surveys of public views of appropriate punishment really indicate the existence of discrete opinions on appropriate punishment. The survey time constraints imposed on respondents, the likely unfamiliarity of the specific circumstances respondents are asked to evaluate, the complexity of the highly detailed vignettes, the fact that citizens sometimes offer views on matters about which they have given no thought (even fictitious matters), . . . are all consistent with the proposition that public sentiment regarding appropriate sentences for crime is an illusion. (p. 8-9)

Topics such as police competence, definitions of crimes, parole, the insanity defense, police searches and seizures also are affected by the context of the decision task and are subject to the criticism that people may express opinions even though they have given little prior thought to a particular topic.

Cognitive Miser Explanation. Why are individuals so easily influenced by the context of the decision task? Two models of how people make decisions provide different answers to this question. The *cognitive miser* perspective proposes that people use cognitive heuristics because they are apathetic about most criminal justice topics. This perspective assumes that people rarely think about crime and justice and when they are asked to respond, they use as little thought as possible to provide answers. In short, according to this view, people employ cognitive shortcuts because they are simply lazy and uninterested participants in a democratic society (e.g., Converse, 1964).

This image of the public also fuels skepticism among legal professionals about the lay public's ability to provide fair and informed verdicts in criminal cases, and to assist the court in settling disputes (see Zemans, 1995). Obviously, the cognitive miser perspective questions the value of research on public opinion, and whether lay persons can make a meaningful contribution to improving the administration of justice. This perspective also assumes that susceptibility to irrelevant contextual features derives from laziness and an inability to make rational decisions. On account of this indolence, people often make erroneous decisions and express fleeting opinions. Research has shown that the amount of importance a person places on an attitude determines how resistant they are to attempts at changing their attitude or to the influence of irrelevant contextual pressures (for a review see Eagly and Chaiken, 1993).

If accepted fully, the lazy cognitive miser view would question whether the State should operate on democratic principles which encourage public participation in government business. After all, it would be imprudent of governments to base their criminal justice policies on the momentary, vacuous opinions of an uninvolved and lazy citizenry. The cognitive miser perspective, however, is overly pessimistic about the contribution that the public can make to criminal justice and the extent to which people are interested in criminal justice issues. Moreover, motivation is a necessary, but not sufficient condition to insulate people from the influence of contextual information.

The cognitive miser view cannot explain three other research findings. First, it is not just those who are uninterested who are influenced by context. People who are involved and interested in the topic also are influenced by the context (Tourangeau and Rasinski, 1989a). Second, although views do change, many people hold fast to their opinions about some topics such as the death penalty and abortion (Lord and Lepper, 1979; Scott, 1989). Finally, many people use several criteria to judge how fairly they were treated by authorities and to make decisions about the verdict and sentencing of specific cases (e.g., Finkel, Hurabiell, and Hughes, 1993; Lind, MacCoun *et al.*, 1990; Stalans, 1994; Stalans and Henry, 1994).

The Public as Pragmatic Decisionmaker

An alternative explanation can account for these additional research findings. According to the pragmatically social perspective, people may use cognitive heuristics (Fiske and Taylor, 1991), but this conservation of cognitive energy derives from concerns of efficiency and practicality not mere laziness (e.g., Macrae, Milne, and Bodenhausen, 1994; Fiske, 1992; Swann, 1984). Most people are pragmatic social thinkers who are interested in justice issues and "conserve" cognitive energy for the most difficult topics. Because they are interested and motivated citizens, they form beliefs about crimes and criminals from all sources of information including media stories, conversations, community awareness programs, and personal experience. Thus, the pragmatically social perspective suggests that campaigns to educate the public about the court system or about the nature of crime can indeed be successful. If people obtain representative information about a topic, they can form more representative stereotypes and make "good enough" decisions even when they employ stereotypes (Fiske, 1992). As pragmatic thinkers, people pay attention to the context of the decision task to determine whether it is wise to rely on their prior beliefs. Individuals make decisions based on expectations when the information fits a preexisting category, but attend more to presented information about a case when information in the situation indicates that their prior expectations are not applicable to the case (Stalans, 1994).

This perspective attributes fleeting opinions and influences of irrelevant contextual features to inappropriate research designs rather than to the fact that people are lazy and uninformed. The public often provide uninformed opinions or opinions that misrepresent their true views because the research design affects their responses to research questions. Some people also are uninterested about crime and justice. Instead of attributing laziness to the entire public, researchers should use questions to determine the degree of involvement and interest in a topic. The pragmatically social perspective suggests that attention to both changes in the context and to the information underlying the public's attitude can uncover the public's real perception of justice. In the next section, we discuss the structure of an attitude in memory and then turn to the question of why involved decisionmakers are influenced by changes in the context. We then discuss which decision-makers will be influenced by the contextual changes.

Associative Network and Spreading Activation in Attitude Formation

An attitude is an association between an evaluation and an issue, object, or event which resides in long-term memory (Fazio and Williams, 1986; Fazio, 1989). The structure of an attitude in memory is important for understanding the context-dependency, stability, relativity, and value-based nature of an expressed attitude. Attitudes are associated in memory with other relevant beliefs, values, images, emotions, personal experiences, and visual images; an associative network has been used as an analogy to represent the proposed interconnections among these beliefs (Anderson, 1983; Fazio and Williams, 1986; Tourangeau and Rasinski, 1988).[1]

For example, an individual who supports the death penalty, but holds some reservations about its actual application may have a detailed associative network. This network can be compared to a bicycle wheel. The center hub is the concept labeled "death penalty," and extending away from this hub are spokes that connect the concept 'death penalty' to experiences and personal beliefs. Our hypothetical person may have "spokes" that connect the hub to memories that support the death penalty (such as an image of Charles Manson, anger about brutal murders, or an attitude favoring retribution as a goal for sentencing). This same person may also have spokes connecting the hub to beliefs which oppose the death penalty—such as a belief that it is unfair to execute all murderers, to a belief that if the death penalty is used too widely, society is promoting violence, and to the belief that the system applies the death penalty in a discriminatory manner.

Our hypothetical person clearly has given a great deal of thought to the issue of the death penalty. Her attitudinal structure can serve to illustrate four structural features which will be highlighted in our review: (1) consistency of beliefs; (2) complexity; (3) value connection; and (4) value conflict. The attitudinal structure is inconsistent (i.e., having both beliefs that support and oppose the death penalty) rather than evaluatively-consistent (i.e., having beliefs that either only support the death penalty or only oppose the death penalty), and is more complex (has several dimensions) than simple. Another feature of this structure is its embeddedness with other beliefs, values and attitudes (Scott, 1969). To understand the principle-based nature of expressed attitudes, we must determine if attitudes are connected to values, which are our important objectives or goals. Our hypothetical person has "value-connection," but also has value conflict (i.e., two values that cannot be both met are connected to the concept of the death penalty).

Using the image of an associative network, researchers have proposed that when one belief is assessed, its activation will cause beliefs, images, values, or other attitudes connected to it to be recalled more easily; this is known as "spreading activation" (Tesser and Shaver, 1990). Supporting the idea of spreading activation, respondents who first answered questions about the equal rights amendment responded more quickly to a related issue of women's right to abortion, but did not respond more quickly to an unrelated issue such as the freeze on nuclear weapons. Moreover, respondents who first answered questions about gun control gave more extreme responses to capital punishment than did respondents who first answered the capital punishment question. This finding was not due to a directional shift toward either opposing or favoring capital punishment, and did not depend on subjects' attitude toward gun control. Presumably, this finding occurred because attitudes about gun control were linked in memory to attitudes about capital punishment and the activation of the gun control attitude spread and activated attitudes about capital punishment (Judd, Drake, Downing, and Krosnick, 1991).

Three assumptions underlie the "spreading activation" theory: (1) people generate answers at the time the questions measuring attitudes are asked; (2) answers are based on a quick sampling of their relevant beliefs, experiences, images, and feelings; and (3) beliefs and images that are most accessible at the time of questioning will be over-represented in the sample (Tourangeau, Rasinski, and Bradburn, 1989a). This spreading activation theory suggests that people who believe an issue is important and have thought a great deal about the issue may also be sensitive to the context in which relevant questions are asked. The importance of attitudes (Tesser and

Leone, 1977) alone does not insulate people from context-dependency. How much the context influences a person to change their opinion is also determined by the complexity of their attitude structure, the consistency of their beliefs, and whether their attitude is connected to values and whether all these values can be achieved. We now turn to research on how these dimensions of an attitude determine how irrelevant contextual characteristics shape people's opinions.

The Vulnerability of Naive Decisionmakers Compared to Informed Decisionmakers

The number of dimensions in people's knowledge structures about a topic is an indication of the complexity of the structure. People who have less complex structures are often those who are less informed about a topic. The simplicity of their prior knowledge leaves them vulnerable to being influenced by contextual pressures. For example, people who have less well-developed beliefs about a topic are more likely to change their minds if they are required to think about their reasons for an attitude. In contrast, people who have more developed knowledge about a topic are more immune to shifts as a result of thought about the reasons behind their attitudes. Wilson, Kraft, and Dunn (1989) found this difference between individuals with more simple belief structures and those with more complex structures about a topic when they examined undergraduates' attitudes toward a presidential candidate. Students with less developed belief systems were more likely to generate both positive and negative reasons for voting than were those with more developed belief systems; because evaluatively inconsistent beliefs were recalled, less informed individuals were more susceptible to change due to more focused thought. The phenomenon that people with less developed belief systems change their attitude when they examine their reasons also relates to changes in opinion when researchers provide respondents with additional information. Doble (1987), for example, found that people were much more supportive of community-based sanctions after they were told about the cost associated with keeping an offender in prison.

People with simple structures also may be more impressionable when forming beliefs about the procedures of an unknown legal arena or process. Stalans (1994b) conducted interviews with randomly selected taxpayers to examine how people form beliefs about an unknown arena such as a tax audit. For people who had been audited in the past, prior positive experiences led to more positive views of the fairness and neutrality of tax auditors, whereas exposure to media stories led to more negative views. In contrast, naive taxpayers (i.e., those without prior audit experience) concluded that tax auditors were biased and unfair because they generalized from previous loosely-related, but irrelevant negative experiences in traffic court and unfavorable conversations about police officers. This study suggests that generalizing from irrelevant, but loosely-related experiences is limited to those who have less developed knowledge about a domain.

Involved Decisionmakers with Inconsistent Beliefs

Susceptibility to context also depends on whether people hold mixed beliefs about the issue or hold evaluatively consistent beliefs. Two studies have found that people who have mixed beliefs and believe the issue is an important one are *most* susceptible to context effects. In one study (Tourangeau, Rasinski, Bradburn, and D'Andrade, 1989a), respondents were asked the following question: "Do you think that the Supreme Court has gone too far in protecting the rights of people accused of crimes or do you think it has generally done what is necessary to see that the accused are fairly treated?" Respondents answered in one of three contexts. One group first answered neutral, unrelated questions. Another group first answered questions about civil liberties. The third group answered questions about fear of crime before answering this question.

Fewer respondents who first answered questions about civil liberties (33 percent) indicated that the courts had gone too far compared to those who answered neutral questions (43 percent). This difference between groups shows a "carryover effect" where the valuative nature of the prior context led to more responses on the relevant questions that were evaluatively consistent with this prior context. Respondents who first answered fear of crime questions disapproved as often (40 percent) as the neutral group (43 percent), perhaps because people in the neutral group used the word "criminal" to guide their search in memory and more easily recalled violent criminals going free because police officers had violated their constitutionally-protected rights.

Prior context, however, did not have the same effect upon all respondents. Respondents who indicated that the issue was important to them, but that they had mixed views[2] showed the largest context effects (a 19 percent change compared to a 10 percent change for uninvolved people with evaluatively consistent beliefs). This greater susceptibility of the involved group who had conflicted beliefs cannot be explained with the image of a 'lazy cognitive miser'.[3] Tourageau *et al.*, (1989a) also note that the greater carryover effect for the important, but conflicted group also may explain why prior studies (e.g., Krosnick and Schuman, 1988) have found that those who had "crystallized" or central attitudes also were susceptible to context effects.

This finding was also independent of whether respondents agreed or disagreed with the context questions. The shift toward the valuative nature of the prior context was not accompanied by stronger correlations between responses to the context items and the relevant question. These null findings suggest that respondents' desire to be consistent in their responses to survey questions is an insufficient explanation for the carryover effect. Nor does familiarity with the issue constrain the effect; stronger carryover effects are found for those with important, but conflicted beliefs on both unfamiliar and familiar issues.

Carryover effects in surveys, however, are weaker or eliminated when a set of neutral buffer items are inserted between two related sets of items or when the related set of questions are scattered throughout the survey rather than presented as a single block of questions (Tourageau *et al.*, 1989a). Does the passage of time (a few minutes) also serve to weaken the effect of media portrayals of vivid and severe crimes? The research we reviewed earlier (Doob and Roberts, 1984; Stalans and Diamond, 1990) suggests not. Moreover, other survey research shows that attention to media stories is related to perceptions that crimes are more serious (Gebotys, Roberts, and Dasgupta, 1988). Gebotys *et al.* concluded that:

> This result is consistent with recent work suggesting media presentations of crime have an anchoring effect: by emphasizing high serious crimes such as homicide, the news media appear to affect perceptions of the seriousness of other, less serious and unrelated offences. (1988, p. 3)

Thus, it is important to consider the issue of what determines accessibility of beliefs within neutral survey contexts. We will turn to this issue in the section on the sources of accessible beliefs for creative storymakers.

Involved Decisionmakers with Conflicting Values

Some people care deeply about an issue, but their values regarding an issue both support their opinion and contradict their opinion. For the sake of clarity, we will call this group "decisionmakers with conflicting values." This group of decisionmakers is quite interesting because they believe the topic is important and they clearly have been exposed to, and have accepted, information from at least two opposing perspectives. For example, consider the topic of abortion. The pro-choice camp argues that women should have the right to choose whether and when to terminate a pregnancy. On the other side, pro-life supporters argue that society has a moral obligation to protect life and that human life begins at the point of conception. The pro-life camp then, considers abortion a crime of murder. Decisionmakers who hold values which are inconsistent with their opinion about the issue of abortion believe the issue is very important, and believe that both sides have valid arguments; generally these decisionmakers support a woman's right to choose, but believe that such a choice may be immoral and thus they could not *personally* choose abortion.

Can changes in the wording of questions about abortion or changes in questions which precede abortion questions influence the responses given by decisionmakers who hold conflicting values? We have already discussed research that shows involved decisionmakers with inconsistent beliefs give responses which are shaped by the context of the survey. By contrast, two studies demonstrate that involved decisionmakers who hold conflicting values gave the same opinion irrespective of the questions that preceded the abortion questions. These decisionmakers have stable opinions which are insulated from changes in the survey design—when a pro-choice stance rests on personal moral doubt people are less sensitive to irrelevant information within the survey context (Tourangeau *et al.*, 1989a, b).

People may be less susceptible to context effects in the measurement of their attitudes toward legalization of abortion because the conflicting views represent a prior choice between two values which they support, but which cannot both be achieved through social policy. Some research supports this idea (Chaiken and Yates, 1985; Scott, 1989). Scott (1989) found that respondents who supported pro-choice favored legal abortion even though many of them held reservations that it was morally wrong whereas pro-life supporters were more "absolute and rule-bound in their moral stance."

Scott (1989), however, did not directly test susceptibility to context. Two laboratory studies have examined how additional thought about the topic of the attitude being measured changes the attitude. Chaiken and Yates (1985) found that individuals who held values consistent with their attitude compared to those who held values inconsistent with their attitude expressed more extreme attitudes after they were induced to write an essay on the topic. These findings emerged for attitudes towards capital punishment as well as opinions regarding censorship. Why did polarization occur for those who held consistent values, but not for those who had conflicting values? Respondents who had consistent values were more likely to reinterpret information inconsistent with their values by discounting it or by assigning less importance to information which was inconsistent with their value (Chaiken and Yates, 1985). For example, an individual who values using the death penalty to deter potential murderers may discount information showing that the death penalty is not an effective deterrent and may assign less importance to information suggesting that the death penalty is inhumane.

Liberman and Chaiken (1991) provide direct support for the idea that people who hold conflicting values about a topic will be less susceptible to context than those who hold consistent values. Respondents were asked their opinion about a privacy issue: Should the CIA have the authority to open mail belonging to United States residents?. Value conflict was measured by whether respondents judged national security and individual freedom as equally important objectives, and value consistency was indicated if respondents assigned more importance to one of these issues. After subjects thought about this topic, respondents who held conflicting values did not polarize their opinion, but those who held consistent beliefs did. Individuals who held consistent values polarized their attitude because they recalled primarily evaluatively consistent beliefs whereas those who held conflicting values recalled both evaluatively consistent and inconsistent beliefs.

People who have conflicting values for an attitude may be less susceptible to context effects in overall attitude measurement because they have thought more about the issue and have made a prior judgment about the overall balance between these two conflicting values. For example, women who support the pro-choice position, but who nevertheless have moral reservations about abortion, say it is wrong for them, but other women should have the right to choose. These women have balanced the value conflict by determining which value should take precedence over the other in specific circumstances. The value in human life and the related belief that abortion takes human life wins in their personal situation whereas the value of individual freedom wins in the social policy realm. Similarly, some people who support capital punishment have made a choice between the importance they assign to retributive justice and the value to oppose what they believe is a system that applies the death penalty in a discriminatory fashion against African-Americans. They have reconciled the conflicting values of retributive justice and discriminatory treatment toward African-Americans by attributing blame to the offenders: African-Americans who commit murder know that it is wrong and know that the system will treat them more harshly than Caucasian-Americans.

People are susceptible to changes in context because when asked a question, respondents first recall beliefs related to the topic and then reconstruct their opinion on the topic. The context of the survey makes certain beliefs more easily recalled than other beliefs about the topic—hence when the context changes the beliefs that they recall also change. This then leads respondents to express different opinions. Involved decisionmakers who hold conflicting values about a topic may not reconstruct their opinion. Instead, they may recall their overall position on the issue because they have given much thought to the topic before the interviewer posed the question. Because the overall evaluation is highly accessible for this group they are less susceptible to context effects when related attitudes or beliefs are assessed. Research should more directly test the process underlying resistance to context effects for involved decisionmakers who hold conflicting values. This research is especially relevant to attitudes toward capital punishment, privacy, punishment preferences, gun control, and self-defense of property or life, for it is here that the Supreme Court must often balance competing values such as an individual's rights to privacy and society's need to obtain evidence to convict guilty offenders.

People as Creative Storymakers

Researchers often ask the public to make judgments about detailed description of offenses. In their role as jurors, members of the public directly create and evaluate the plausibility of alternative stories to deal with the frequently conflicting information they receive during a trial (Pennington and Hastie, 1986). Stories are not simply interpreted or judged, but constructed and made more coherent by adding information from prior knowledge. What prior knowledge and processes do people use to interpret and construct stories? In this section we first examine how prior expectations and attitudes shape information processing and decisions about detailed stories. We then turn to the conditions under which people generate alternative stories and how knowing that a story ends with a negative outcome makes this outcome seem more predictable. This section thus illustrates that people use both images of criminals and crimes in their memory as well as images of crimes that they generate with their imagination at the time they face making a decision.

As earlier material illustrated, people hold an array of knowledge about crimes, about human motives, about social interactions, and about social roles that can be brought to bear to understand a detailed story about a crime that contains ambiguous and conflicting information. For example, people have schemata about criminal events that exist at all levels of abstraction from concrete specific episodes, to subtypes of crimes, to abstract stories about categories of offenders. Before knowledge structures can guide and assist in the interpretation of information, they must be activated.

How do people recall schemata about crimes and social interactions? When asked to evaluate the guilt of a defendant, information about the case reminds them of the prior knowledge that they have which relates to the topic. For example, jurors in the Rodney King trial presumably had prior knowledge about police officers. Jurors may have recalled their beliefs that officers are unbiased and reluctant to use force and that suspects are often uncooperative and quite dangerous. In watching the videotape, the uniform of the officers cued the knowledge about police and based on this knowledge jurors interpreted the struggles of the suspect as evidence that he was resisting arrest and trying to harm the officers.

Concrete vivid instances such as the videotape of the police officers or a vivid description of the officers' behavior are more successful at activating prior knowledge than are abstract or dull descriptions. Actions central to a story also more easily activate prior knowledge than do peripheral actions. The officers' call for assistance activates the plot of handling a difficult suspect and the goal of the officers to restrain the suspect rather than harm the suspect. With these prior knowledge structures activated, other information such as King's pleas may be selectively ignored or discounted. In addition to concrete and central actions serving as an initiators of prior knowledge structures, distinctive characteristics will automatically activate knowledge structures (Black *et al.*, 1984). For example, when people read the statement "a drive-by shooting took place in a housing project," they may automatically think of a gang-related shooting. Drive-by shootings have rather distinctive characteristics belonging to gang-related crimes.

To summarize, the information activated in memory is a result of complex interactions between the goals of the perceiver, the concreteness, centrality, and distinctiveness of the story elements, and the frequency and recency of category activation. In addition, categories that are frequently used may become chronically accessible and have an advantage over recently activated categories (Higgins and King, 1981).

Using Prior Knowledge to Make Inferences About Detailed Stories

People can complete stories by filling in missing links in the presented information and resolving inconsistencies by inferring from their prior knowledge (Black *et al.*, 1984; Fiske and Taylor, 1991). In this section, we provide examples of how prior knowledge shapes inferences in three different decision tasks. At trial, jurors are presented with competing stories about what happened. Jury verdicts provide an indirect gauge of where community sentiment stands on certain constitutional and legal issues. To understand whether community views are consistent with defining certain acts as crimes, researchers must delve deeper into the reasons and inferences behind these verdicts. Community sentiment about active euthanasia provides an example. By looking at the reasons underlying their verdict choices, Finkel *et al.*, (1993) demonstrated that many respondents either found the accused not guilty or guilty of a less serious offense for reasons that were outside of the law (such as the reason that it is a private matter). These reasons reveal quite clearly that jurors use their values and concepts of crimes to make legal decisions in a specific situation.

An understanding of inferences is also necessary to assess the public's preferences for sentencing offenders. A study comparing the sentencing preferences of the public to a sample of criminal justice professionals suggests that differences in prior knowledge may have shaped the public's more punitive stance (Tremblay, Cordeau, and Ouimet, 1994). Laypersons, for example, perceived information that the offender had no prior record to be of neutral value in assessing blameworthiness whereas court personnel believed that the absence of previous convictions reduced an offender's blameworthiness. The authors speculate that the public perceives the absence of a criminal record to be of neutral value because they compare the first-time offender to the average honest person, whereas criminal justice professionals compare the first-time offender to the average offender. This makes them more inclined to be lenient towards first offenders.

An understanding of how prior knowledge shapes inferences is also relevant in comparing public preferences to legal statutes. For example, a study employing short stories illustrates how story features can shape inferences and determine sentencing preferences (Stalans and Henry, 1994). A sample of the public inferred that abused juveniles had less intent to kill and less understanding of the wrongfulness of violence than did juveniles without a history of abuse. The inferences about intention and understanding of the wrongfulness of violence for abused juveniles probably derived from prior knowledge about battered children. Based on these inferences, the vast majority of respondents (77 percent) preferred juvenile trials for abused juveniles accused of murdering their fathers whereas half (49 percent) of the respondents preferred juvenile court for nonabused juveniles who killed their fathers.

Using Prior Knowledge to Filter and Remember

Are we more likely to recall information that supports our views rather than material that contradicts our opinions? This question has provoked a great research going back many decades now (Roberts, 1983). It is related to another question which is whether we pay closer attention to supportive information. If we are selective in what we learn or remember, this may help to explain why some attitudes change very slowly, or not at all. One reason why some people are strongly in favor of capital punishment is that they are unaware of the research literature that shows that the death penalty is no better a deterrent to murder than life imprisonment. The reason why they are unaware of this research may be that they avoid it, or if confronted with the research (in a newspaper article, for example), do not learn the material well. Although a great deal of research has addressed the mechanisms of selective learning and memory, the results cannot easily be summarized.

Sometimes people may ignore information that is inconsistent with their prior beliefs, whereas at other times people may attempt to reconcile the discrepancy between their prior knowledge and the discrepant information by engaging in more extensive and deeper processing. Novel information requires the most processing to reconcile it with an existing prior knowledge structure (Black *et al.*, 1984). Evidence for selective attention is based in part on research findings that people recall more information congruent with their prior knowledge, make guesses (false memories) consistent with their prior knowledge, and have more difficulty correctly recognizing whether novel information was presented. This pattern of findings supports selective attention because novel information should be less well recognized if it is ignored or "filtered" into a schema (Stangor and McMillan, 1992). If, however, novel information is deeply and extensively processed it should be better recalled and recognized based on the associations that deeper processing makes between novel information and schematic information in memory.

Based on a meta-analysis of studies examining congruency and incongruency effects in memory, Stangor and McMillan (1992) found no overall tendency to filter incongruent information. Both the recall and the recognition-sensitivity data showed better recall and recognition of novel information. This finding accords with an earlier meta-analysis of the selective recall literature (Roberts, 1985). Stangor and McMillan (1992), however, found that both personal and task characteristics determined when people recalled more congruent information. The readers' goals determined whether people recalled congruent information better than novel information. Stangor and McMillan (1992) note that:

> Perceivers who are attempting to form or maintain coherent, well structured evaluative impressions are least likely to engage in inconsistency resolution processes and most likely to ignore, filter, or distort the incongruent information. (p. 57)

People with well-developed expectations about crime (e.g., expectations derived from direct experience and interpersonal conversations) also may recall more information congruent with their expectations than may people with less developed expectations about crime (see Stangor and McMillan, 1992). In addition to these personal characteristics, task characteristics also determine the amount of selective recall. People recalled more congruent information when the information consisted of traits, perhaps because the abstractness and uncertainty of this information made novel trait information easy to discount. This finding has direct implications for the maintenance of unrepresentative stereotyped knowledge about crimes and criminals. Subjective states such as an offender's intent, understanding of wrongfulness, and future dangerousness as well as beliefs about the causes of crime should be relatively resistant to change because novel information is discounted and stored separately in memory.

Stangor and McMillan (1992) also found that some task characteristics lead people to process novel information more deeply and elaborately. When the set of materials contained fewer items of novel information, people were more likely to recall novel information. This finding accords with Stalans's (1993) finding that crime stories containing distinctive, but less severe harm were better recalled than were crime stories about severe harm that may have been more congruent with their expectations. Individuals who are trying to form an impression or have less developed expectations recall more incongruent information than congruent information (Stangor and McMillan, 1992). To summarize, the literature shows that listeners' goals and the structure of their prior beliefs as well as task characteristics determine when people will deeply process novel information.

Discounting and Explaining Away Inconsistent Information

In our discussion of how people encode and explain stories, we will distinguish between perception and attribution. Perception is the stage where people encode information and assign meaning to it whereas attribution is the stage where people interpret why an event occurred. The police response to the Los Angeles riots provoked by the not guilty verdicts of three police officers who beat Rodney King illustrates this distinction.

> An overwhelming number of residents—80 percent—thought that the police reacted too slowly when violence broke out April 29. Asked why they thought the police response was slow, a plurality of Blacks said they believed that the delay was deliberate while a plurality of Whites and Hispanics said the police simply were not prepared for the massive outbreak. (Clifford and Ferrell, 1992, p. 7)

Here most respondents encoded the delay in the police response and concluded it was too slow, but attributed this slowness to different sources. Sometimes people may see the same event, but explain it differently.

People often are exposed to information that is inconsistent with their existing attitudes in the course of everyday life. For example, the public may watch television coverage of a violent confrontation between police and student rioters. The news report may attribute the fault to the actions of the police or to the actions of student rioters. How do individuals who have pro-police attitudes interpret a news story that claims the police acted improperly and caused the violent confrontation? Similarly, how do individuals who hold pro-student attitudes interpret a story that claims the students acted improperly and caused the violent confrontation? Zanna, Kloson and Darley (1976) addressed these questions using an experimental manipulation to vary whether students or police were blamed in a television news report on a violent confrontation between students and police. Respondents who viewed a news report that conflicted with their prior attitudes (e.g., pro-police respondents watched report attributing blame to the police) perceived the newscast as less objective, and perceived the reporter as less credible and as being partisan to the political position consistent with the newscast. Respondents who were exposed to information inconsistent with their attitudes discounted the information by concluding that the media were biased and hostile toward the view of the other side.

Who is more likely to discount information that is inconsistent with their prior attitudes? The answer is based in part on the structure and accessibility of the attitude. When attitudes are based on principles or values, respondents are more likely to discount the position of the opposite side (Chaiken and Yates, 1985). Respondents with more accessible attitudes about capital punishment discounted research reports on the effectiveness of the death penalty more than did those who held weaker attitudes (Houston and Fazio, 1989). Lord, Lepper and Preston (1984), however, reduced discounting by asking subjects to consider whether they would have made the same judgments about studies testing the deterrent effect of the death penalty if the studies had found the opposite effect. Simply asking subjects to be unbiased in their judgments, however, did not reduce discounting. These researchers concluded, consistent with the pragmatically social perspective, that "these findings are generally congruent with the proposition that many biases of social judgment are the result of inadequate cognitive strategies rather than inadequate motivation" (p. 1239).

Representativeness Heuristic: Making Judgments of Similarity and Difference

When people are motivated to understand evidence and arrive at a verdict, they will give much thought and attention to the evidence and attempt to create a coherent story (e.g., Fiske and Neuberg, 1990; Pennington and Hastie, 1988; Stangor and McMillan, 1992). Involved decision-makers with the goal of reaching a decision do not ignore evidence or readily discount it, but instead attempt to reconcile any information inconsistent with their activated prior knowledge (Black *et al.*, 1984). Once a schema is activated, people may abandon it if they discover it fails to explain the data and will construct a story that is more coherent based on the available evidence. Schema theory assumes that laypersons are flexible decisionmakers who switch to other promising schemata when the data suggest that the activated schema is a poor interpretation of the current event (see Stalans and Lurigio, 1990, p. 335).

In their attempts to determine the fit of the evidence with their prior knowledge about topics related to the case, people make judgments about how similar a case is to the exemplars and stereotypes that they have recalled. The judgment of similarity is an efficient cognitive tool called the representativeness heuristic (Bar-Hillel, 1982; Tversky and Kahneman, 1982c). As we noted in the first section of this chapter, the representativeness heuristic affects judgments about groups or expressions of attitudes about groups; it also affects judgments about actual interactions with a group member or decisions about a specific defendant or convicted criminal. The representativeness heuristic can produce "contrast effects" where an offender appears different based on the standard of comparison recalled from prior knowledge. For example, previous studies in the area of crime and punishment (Pepitone and DiNubile, 1976; Roberts and Edwards, 1989) manipulated expectations by changing the context of the judgment. Respondents who read about a theft case judged an assault case to be more serious and assigned more punished than people who first read about a murder case; this finding represents a contrast effect. Stalans (1988) also found that the severity of punishment assigned was moderately related to the judged similarity between the targeted offender and the contextual offender, which provides direct support for the representativeness heuristic.

These studies, however, did not directly assess prior knowledge about crimes and criminals. An innovative study, however, has employed a technique called "concept mapping" to measure the underlying structure and content of people's attitudes toward social policies such as capital punishment and welfare and provides a test of how the representativeness heuristic produces contrast effects when comparisons are made to prior knowledge (Lord, Desforges, Fein, Pagh and Lepper, 1994). When concept mapping, respondents draw a map that links the concept (e.g., capital punishment) to beliefs, experiences, and values associated with it. Students had three general "nodes" connected to the concept of capital punishment: person nodes such as Bundy (the serial killer), principle nodes such as the immorality of the death penalty, and general information nodes such as information relating to methods of execution. Proponents of capital punishment used person nodes more extensively and earlier than did opponents, and also had deeper associations (more connections) from the central person node than did opponents. Opponents and supporters, however, did not differ in terms of the total number of nodes (i.e., the complexity) or on their use of principle nodes. The centrality and depth of the person node in the welfare concept were similar for supporters and opponents of welfare.

Having discovered differences in respondents' knowledge structures of welfare and capital punishment, Lord *et al.*, (1994) presented undergraduates with moderately detailed written descriptions of two murderers. They found that proponents supported the death sentence more for specific cases that were typical of the exemplar in memory than for specific cases judged to be atypical, whereas opponents did not distinguish between typical and atypical specific murderers. For opponents of capital punishment, similarity of a specific case to an exemplar was irrelevant because they based their attitude on values.

Though Lord *et al.*, (1994) did not test actual jurors, their findings probably generalize to the way in which jurors in real life make decisions about the life or death of a defendant. For example, jurors in a death penalty case may recall John Wayne Gacy's serial murders and their evaluation that death is what Gacy deserved. This evaluation links the image of Gacy to the decision about death for the current case, Tom C. If Tom C. killed two people during a burglary and had no prior record, he will look quite different from Gacy. This judgment of similarity/difference determines whether Tom C. will be contrasted away from the image of Gacy or assimilated toward Gacy. To the extent that jurors perceive Tom C. as different from Gacy, they will be more likely to sentence Tom C. to life imprisonment. This example shows that the contrast effects reviewed in the earlier section may also occur in real life decisions about actual cases. The contrast effect occurs because respondents may use Gacy as a standard of comparison. Extreme cases that are recalled serve as standards of comparison only when the extreme case is linked to the judgment (e.g., the appropriateness of life or death) (Schwarz and Bless, 1992).

Research on taxpayers' evaluations of their treatment by the auditor also illustrates the contrast effect, and shows how prior expectations can shape judgements of authorities even when people recognize that their expectations are unsupported by the authorities' actions. Stalans (1994a) measured taxpayers' expectations about auditors in a pre-audit interview and then in a post audit interview measured respondents' evaluations of the fairness of their auditor. Taxpayers who expected unfair and rude treatment, but perceived fair and polite treatment judged the tax auditor as less concerned with the amount of money obtained for the government than did taxpayers who expected fair and polite treatment and perceived fair and polite treatment. When taxpayers who expected to receive a rude and unfair response were confronted with unambiguously polite behavior such as apologizing for repeatedly auditing the taxpayer, these taxpayers judged the auditor as differing from their expectations. When individuals judged their expectation as incorrect, they paid more attention to the actual features of the audit. In support of this conclusion, taxpayers who displayed contrast effects mentioned more features about the audit than did those with assimilation effects. Though they paid more attention and remembered more features, their expectation served as a standard of comparison and displaced their attributions away from the initial attribution. These attributions mediated the effect of expectations on evaluations of the fairness of the tax audit procedures.

Hindsight Bias

Respondents read the following short story in a study by Smith (1991):

Ben and his business partner, Terry, were standing on a train platform when Terry told Ben he had used company money to pay his gambling debts, and they were bankrupt. Ben had invested everything in the business. Enraged, he grabbed Terry and held him over the edge of the platform. A train was rapidly approaching the station, and Terry was afraid Ben would let go. Ben knew Terry had a heart condition and that stress would kill him, but he didn't care. Ben pulled him back onto the platform just as the trained roared by. (p. 872)

How does the story end? Many people will imagine several possibilities: Terry promises to pay Ben the money; Ben threatens to sue Terry, and Terry threatens to sue Ben; Ben punches Terry; and so forth. Though few people will predict that Terry will die of a heart attack after being set on the platform, once told, many people will think that "they knew it all along" (Fischoff, 1975) that Terry would have a heart attack. When people learn of an outcome and project this knowledge on what they concluded about the probability an outcome in foresight, this effect is called a "hindsight bias" (Fischoff, 1975). Hawkins and Hastie (1990) note that "The hindsight bias does not refer to all retrospective increases in the probabilities assigned to events. The hindsight bias is a projection of new knowledge into the past accompanied by a denial that the outcome information has influenced judgment" (p. 311).

Several processes may produce the hindsight bias (for a review see Hawkins and Hastie, 1990). One of the most frequent and interesting processes is that people attempt to create a coherent story by integrating the evidence and learned outcome through filling in missing information that makes it seem logical. When an outcome is learned, people find it easier to create stories consistent with the outcome than to think of stories that end with a different outcome (such as Terry lives and pays Ben back the money). As story interpreters, people complete the sparse details of what caused the outcome (Fischoff, 1975). For example, in the story about Terry and Ben, Smith (1991) tells story-readers that: "Terry clutched his chest and died of a heart attack" (p. 872). Some people will attempt to make sense of Terry's actions that could have been otherwise (i.e., taking the money). They may infer that Terry violated a business loyalty and provoked Ben into holding Terry over the platform, and in this moment of anger Ben didn't care, but did not intend to kill Terry. They may fault Terry for creating the stress that killed him. Other individuals may conclude that because Ben and Terry were business partners, Ben knew that Terry had a heart condition and held Terry over the platform with the foreknowledge that the stress could kill him. Thus, people may judge the responsibility and actions of Ben and Terry by completing the vignette in a way that makes it plausible and coherent with the outcome. Moreover, people in foresight can easily imagine endings in which Terry lives and may perceive a heart attack as an unlikely event, but people using hindsight judgment believe the outcome was more foreseeable because they rewrite the story to make it more coherent.

Smith (1991) found that many people (33 percent) concluded that Ben was not guilty of first degree murder even though the story explicitly stated that Ben knowingly acted in a manner that put Terry's life in danger. One interpretation of this finding is that people have misconceptions about the necessary and sufficient information needed to convict someone of murder, and often confuse manslaughter with murder (Smith, 1991). Another possibility is that people as story writers used hindsight judgment and concluded that the facts support the interpretation that Terry provoked Ben and created the stress that put his life in danger. The difference between these interpretations is important. The first interpretation assumes that people hold misconceptions in memory about the defining features of murder which conflict with substantive law and jury instructions.

The second interpretation assumes that the not guilty verdicts are not created from misconceptions about murder, but from the filling in of missing information that makes the story whole. Smith (1991) notes "the facts were presented in a straightforward, coherent, and internally consistent manner; subjects did not have to interpret or make inferences about the evidence to generate a plausible representation of the facts" (p. 869). Subjects are automatically stimulated to make inferences because the story does not provide enough background detail, provides only loose causal connections between statements, and provides actions that could have been otherwise. Why was Ben enraged enough to hold Terry over the platform? Was it because Terry stated he took the money and Ben could not prove that it was his money? Did Ben have reasons not to care beyond the passion of the moment? Coherence of the story is determined by the causal linkages between statements and the goals of the actors (Black, Glambos, and Read, 1984). In this story, neither the goals of the actors are clear nor is the causal linkage between Ben's actions and Terry's death. As active processors, people will attempt to infer the goals of the actors and make causal linkages between the concrete novel information by filling in background and contextual information (Black *et al.*, 1984).

The hindsight bias has been demonstrated in judgments of civil liability suits (Casper, Benedict and Perry, 1989), judgments of a co-resident's right to consent to a police search of the common areas of a home (Kagehiro, Taylor, Kaufer, and Harland, 1991), and blaming victims of rape (e.g., Janoff-Bulman, Timko, and Carli, 1985). In the area of community sentiment about unreasonable searches and seizures, researchers (Kagehiro *et al.*, 1991) asked subjects to read a story in which the police asked the co-resident for consent to search the common area of the home when the targeted person was either present and protesting or absent. The group that read that the police found incriminating evidence against the targeted suspect believed the co-resident had more of a right to consent than did the group who read that no incriminating evidence was found. Perceptions about what is a reasonable search and seizure thus are affected by outcome information due to a hindsight bias.

To assess the role that hindsight bias plays in victim blaming, undergraduates read a detailed story about a heterosexual date. One group read the story with an ending that the man took the woman home, and the other group read the same story except the story ended with the man raping the woman. Respondents who learned about the rape concluded it was more likely to occur than did respondents who learned that the man took the woman home, even though the two groups read about the same behaviors and were told to answer as if they did not know the outcome. Respondents who read about the rape attributed more blame to the woman's behavior than did those who read about a neutral outcome. In a third study, Janoff-Bulman *et al.*, (1985) found that the more likely respondents judged the rape to be, the more they held the woman responsible. The researchers attempted to reduce the hindsight bias by having respondents imagine and explain an alternative outcome (i.e., the man took her home). This intervention, however, did not reduce the hindsight bias, perhaps because rape is a vivid outcome and has a disproportionate influence on respondents' inferences (Janoff-Bulman *et al.*, 1985).

Simulation Heuristic and Counterfactual Thought

The hindsight bias—thinking one knew it all along and denying the influence that learning about the outcome had on perceptions of its likelihood in foresight—occurs because people are good editors of documentaries and good writers of fiction. An additional process underlying the hindsight bias is that people think about alternative scenarios such as "if only" the victim had acted differently (e.g., Janoff-Bulman *et al.*, 1985). People mentally "undo" the actions to assess whether the outcome could have occurred through additional routes. Because it is easier to undo actions than to undo failures to act (Kahneman and Tversky, 1982), people are more likely to fault the victim for what she did than for what she failed to do. For example, people may conclude that a rape victim could have acted otherwise when she went to the boyfriend's home and fault her because of the mental ease of undoing the action, and conclude from the ease of running simulations of alternative courses that the victim should have foreseen the probable outcome of rape. Controlling for prior beliefs about rape victims, people will be less likely to conclude that a rape victim should have resisted because it is more difficult to imagine undoing of failures to act than her actions.

The hindsight bias may occur from editing and completing a documentary so that it is more coherent and plausible, but it also may occur through a simulation heuristic, which is "an assessment of the ease with which the model could produce different outcomes, given its initial conditions and operations parameters" (Kahneman and Tversky, 1982, p. 201). Kahneman and Tversky (1982) note that people employing a simulation heuristic do not have to produce complete stories; instead, they may just produce rough outline of plausible routes to outcomes. Instead of using prior expectations and beliefs to judge a story, the story evokes alternative accounts from the reader.

> Reality is also compared to postcomputed representations, those that are neither consciously nor unconsciously held prior to an event, but which are generated post hoc by the event itself (Kahneman and Miller, 1986)... postcomputed representations focus on counterfactual thoughts of what might have been. The postcomputed or counterfactual representations that are evoked by experience can shape people's reactions every bit as powerfully as the precomputed ones they bring to the experience. (Miller, Turnball, and McFarland, 1990, p. 305)

Counterfactual thinking and the associated simulation heuristic shape the public's judgments about many criminal events and legal decisions such as partitioning responsibility in tort suits (Weiner and Pritchard, 1994), attributing blame to criminal offenders and victims (e.g., Janoff-Bulman *et al.*, 1985), assessing the suspiciousness of actions and reasonable doubt (Miller, Turnball, and McFarland, 1989), compensating victims (Miller and Turnball, 1990), and judging the normality (typicality) of an event (Kahneman and Miller, 1986; Miller, Turnball, and McFarland, 1990). The extent to which people engage in "if only" thinking and the nature of their musing depends on the story features and context. Features that are mutable (could have been otherwise) evoke undoing the story and comparing it to postcomputed alternative scenarios (Kahneman and Miller, 1986; Miller and Turnball, 1990).

Examples of mutable features are near misses of the negative event (e.g., missing a plane by five minutes rather than fifty minutes), out of character actions (e.g., a person with a reputation of honesty stealing money to cover other debts), and apparent alternatives (e.g., a person choosing between several different convenience stores and ending up in the one where a robbery takes place) (Miller, Turnball, and McFarland, 1990). Features are more immutable if they are part of the assumed background of the story rather than the focal point of the story (e.g., whether the story centers around the offender's or the victim's actions), if they are constrained by background variables, and if the harm inflicted is part of the typical harm that occurs during an offense (e.g., a television is stolen during a burglary offense).

How do observers react to crime victims? One possibility is that observers will give victims whose victimization occurred through a mutable action more compensation than victims whose victimization occurred through a less mutable action such as a routine action. Miller and McFarland (1986) proposed that victims who nearly missed their victimization would evoke more sympathy because observers could think of alternative scenarios that have more positive outcomes. They found support for this hypothesis using a story about a victim who was severely injured during a robbery of a convenience store. In the story, they manipulated the mutability of the actions leading to the victimization: (1) in one condition, the robbery took place in the store that the victim most commonly frequented; and (2) in the other condition, the robbery took place in a store the victim did not commonly frequent but had decided to go to "for a change of pace."

They also found that respondents who read about the victimization in the nonroutine store recommended over $100,000 more compensation to the victim than did respondents who read about the victimization in the commonly frequented store. This finding cannot be accounted for by the perceived probability of being robbed across the two stores. The finding suggests that the out of the ordinary action led to more sympathy because respondents thought that the victim almost avoided the victimization; "In line with the counterfactual fallacy, his misfortune—because it need not have been—seemed as though it ought not to have been" (Miller and Turnball, 1990, p. 6).

Other research has found that counterfactual thinking leads to blaming the victim (e.g., Janoff-Bulman *et al.*, 1985; Johnson, 1986). Two theories may explain when observers will blame victims rather than compensate them. When observers are not given an opportunity to compensate victims they will blame them (Miller and McFarland, 1990). Another possibility is that observers will blame victims more when the victims have some control over the course of the crime than when the victimization occurs because of situational reasons such as being in a place at the wrong time.

When a crime is committed, how will people assign blame to a defendant? Consider the following story:

> Neil and his wife went through a nasty divorce and custody battle. Neil's wife was awarded custody of their daughter, but she got to stay with Neil every third weekend of the month. One Friday afternoon, Neil drove to his daughter's elementary school. She was playing with her friends in the schoolyard. Neil waved to her and she got in the car with him. Neil took her to his apartment briefly, and then the two went to a basketball game. It was only the second weekend of the month, and Neil's wife did not know that Neil had picked up the child from school. The girl's friends said only that she had gotten in the car with some man. Neil's wife reported the incident to the police. (Smith, 1993, p. 522)

Is Neil guilty of kidnapping? People may respond based on their knowledge about the definition of kidnapping or beliefs about the characteristics of kidnapping. As an active processor of information, people cannot just read this story and take the information at face value without interpreting it and inferring additional evidence from it. There is a natural tendency to engage in counterfactual thought. For example, they may ask why Neil picked up his daughter on the second week without telling his ex-wife. It clearly must be an unusual practice if the daughter's friends did not recognize him. He should have told his ex-wife unless he planned on upsetting and getting even with the mother; perhaps Neil plans on running away with his daughter and took her to a ballgame in a different city.

One salient, mutable feature in this story is the fact that Neil picked up his daughter on the second week without informing her mother and in direct violation of a custody order. It is a feature that stimulates people to think that he could have acted otherwise. Because Neil's wife was unaware of Neil's plans it is difficult to undo her actions and attribute fault to her for the negative event (i.e., the missing child). The alternative story that Neil's wife maliciously called the police even though she had agreed prior to Neil picking up the child that Neil could take her away for a weekend, is not easily brought to mind and when it is brought to mind it seems less plausible given the facts of the case.

The undoing of this story illustrates a proposition about the assignment of blame: The person whose actions are more mutable (and hence more easily imagined otherwise) will be blamed most for the misfortune (Miller and Turnball, 1990). Counterfactual thinking does not seem completely inconsistent with legal dictate (Miller, Turnball, and McFarland, 1989). As Miller *et al.* (1989) note:

> Exhortations to juries not to convict someone unless they are sure beyond a reasonable doubt invites them to consider the likelihood that a set of occurrences could have come about without the accused being guilty of the offense with which he or she is charged. (p. 584)

In addition to, or instead of their prior knowledge about the definitions of crimes, people may attribute guilt to defendants described in short stories about crime based on the inability to construct alternative accounts other than the one that points to a defendant's guilt. In the story about Neil, a script about child custody battles makes the plot of seeking retribution seem quite plausible, even if it requires going outside the law. The more people can mentally replicate an outcome, the less doubt that they have about its occurrence.

The extent to which a story evokes alternative accounts also determines its perceived normality or typicality. Kahneman and Miller (1986) proposed and demonstrated that perceptions of normality are not solely determined by existing knowledge in memory, but also are shaped by the images and scenarios that a story stimulates through imagination of what might have been. This research has direct implications for how researchers can assess whether prior knowledge shapes judgments. Smith's (1991, 1993) research that shows people are more likely to find a defendant guilty if the scenario has more features in common with their prior knowledge is susceptible to the alternative explanation that atypical stories have more mutable features which evoke alternative accounts.

Stalans' (1993) data speak most directly to the representativeness of the stereotypic knowledge people use in making punishment judgments about abstract cases. In this situation, respondents are given a category label and are asked general questions such as the following: "Are judges too lenient, about right, or too severe in sentencing burglary offenders." This judgement task differs from the task that jurors must make in trials about guilt and innocence. In the sentencing task, the offender has already been labeled a member of a category and the public is asked to judge the blameworthiness of the convicted offender whereas the verdict decision requires jurors to select the category which best fits the evidence against the defendant. For example, in making decisions about the verdict, jurors must decide whether the evidence supports the conclusion that the offender is guilty of murder, guilty of voluntary manslaughter, guilty of involuntary manslaughter, or not guilty.

Jurors in their verdict decisions may misjudge the category membership because in memory a legal label may represent a superordinate category that includes several distinct offenses in the legal code. For example, people may use the word "robbery" more broadly than the legal code. They may exclaim "I have been robbed" when their home was burglarized while they were away (Smith, 1991). The lexicon of the legal system is frequently incompatible with everyday language about crime. Both Smith (1991) and Stalans (1993) found that people write a story about a robbery when they are asked to write a story about the typical burglary, and write a story about a burglary when they are asked to write a story about a typical robbery. Likewise, people use the term, "mugging," to refer to what the legal system defines as a robbery, though they may use it more narrowly than the legal system's definition (Stalans, 1993). Thus, people often have misperceptions about the defining features of specific offenses because the framework of stories about different offenders and offenses is organized differently in memory than the organization of crimes in the legal code. Knowledge about attendant circumstances such as the amount of harm done, the number of offenders, the place, the time, and whether weapons are used, however, may depend on their exposure to crimes.

Conclusions

A great deal of research on information processing has begun to focus on how the structure of prior knowledge shapes information processing. This research shows that a closer examination of the structure of attitudes and prior knowledge illuminates when and why people easily change in the face of subtle or obvious contextual pressures and use prior knowledge to guide decision making. Whether people have simple, consistent prior beliefs or well developed complex beliefs, they use cognitive heuristics such as simulation, availability, and representativeness. The research on involved decisionmakers and on value-connected attitudes illustrates that the reliance on cognitive heuristics is less about low motivation or laziness, and more about efficiency and pragmatism. Indeed, criminal justice professionals also use these heuristics in their decisions about how to sentence actual cases (see Lurigio, Carroll, and Stalans, 1994). Theorists who advocate the "cognitive miser" viewpoint should realize that criminal justice professionals also seek "good enough" decisions rather than optimal decisions.

Much research suggests that even when people use stereotypes and cognitive shortcuts they make decisions that have "good enough" accuracy (Fiske, 1992). In order to determine whether decisions are "good enough," researchers must know the beliefs, images, and values on which people based their decisions. The availability heuristic does not automatically produce biased decisions; it depends on whether the beliefs and images underlying the decisions are unrepresentative or inaccurate and on whether the values considered are irrelevant to the task. Some research has begun to assess people's prior knowledge about crimes and criminals, and has highlighted some of the misconceptions that people may bring to the decision tasks (e.g., Smith, 1993; Stalans and Diamond, 1990; Stalans and Lurigio, 1990; Roberts and Doob, 1990; Roberts and White, 1986).

Future research measuring prior knowledge about crime can begin to assess more carefully and systematically the underlying beliefs, images, and values associated with a category. As our review has highlighted, the availability heuristic also underlies measurement of prior knowledge about crime and criminals, and may produce unrepresentative samples of people's knowledge when they are given abstract open-ended questions under time pressure. Although it is time-consuming, Lord *et al.*'s (1994) concept mapping technique yields information about what beliefs are most accessible, the connection among beliefs, and the array of beliefs available in memory. This technique, moreover, can assess the principled nature of opinions, and whether people hold conflicting values about a category. Closed-ended questions that measure both the variability and average in people's categorical knowledge also may yield more informative data than either abstract open-ended questions or questions asking about the "typical" criminal or crime (see Park and Hastie, 1987; Linville, Fischer, and Salovey, 1989). In addition to a systematic approach to people's prior knowledge about crimes and criminals, the sources of these beliefs and the determinants of the accessibility of these beliefs deserve further examination.

People with conflicting values deserve much closer attention in public opinion research on crime and justice because criminal justice policies and constitutional issues often are implemented by making a choice between conflicting values. Especially for constitutional issues such as unreasonable searches or seizures, privacy, and cruel and unusual punishment, people with conflicting values may provide an indication of the evolving community sentiment in these areas. People with well-formed beliefs and consistent values about a topic may be too closed-minded (irrespective of their politic stance) to give careful consideration to all of the information; indeed our review of the discounting effect and assimilation supports this conclusion.

The literature has also demonstrated that prior knowledge shapes interpretations and responses to both detailed stories and abstract questions. Distortions can occur in both situations. Context and prior knowledge shape how the public assigns meaning to abstract questions and detailed stories. In both situations, public opinion is quite limited without data that tap people's prior knowledge about the situation and that assess the way people form opinions. Durham (1993) suggests that researchers should first use a filter question such as "have you given much thought to the kinds of punishment robbers ought to receive" before respondents provide sentences to detailed stories about robbers. Our review of contextual effects suggest that such filter questions should be placed after questions about punishment preferences about detailed stories to avoid activation of extreme exemplars or unrepresentative abstract knowledge about robbers. In addition, survey researchers should ask questions about the importance of the issue, whether respondents have conflicted beliefs about the topic, and questions to assess whether they have consistent or conflicting values about the topic.

Notes

1. We use beliefs broadly to capture personal experiences, images, emotions, behaviors, and values as Tourangeau and Rasinski (1988) do.

2. Centrality or importance of the attitude was measured with the question, "Would you say your attitude about this issue is very important, important, not very important, or not at all important to you?" Conflict was measured with the question "Would you say you are mostly on one side or the other on this issue or would you say your feelings and beliefs are mixed?"

3. Tourageau *et al.* (1989a) also noted this finding cannot be explained as a demand characteristic in the survey because uninvolved people should be most susceptible to demand characteristics. A demand characteristic is something in the study that makes respondents respond in the way that the researcher wants them to respond or predicts that they will respond.

6

Origins of Crime and
Crime Prevention

In this chapter, we review research on public theories about crime and criminals. At the conclusion of the chapter, we discuss public reaction to crime prevention initiatives. These two literatures are clearly related. Laypersons' views of the causes of crime will determine, in large part, public support for different crime control strategies. For example, there will be little support for crime prevention through social development among people who view offending as an individual aberration rather than a consequence of adverse social conditions.

The large body of literature on public theories of crime is organized in two ways. First, we discuss a question at the heart of public theories about crimes: Why do offenders commit crimes? Are perceptions of criminal offenses grounded more in objective features such as the harm inflicted and moral wrongfulness or subjective elements of intent and motive? Do members of the public hold distorted views about the nature of criminal offenses, criminal offenders, and victims? These questions are addressed as we describe the content of beliefs about specific categories of crimes and criminals. We first provide an overview of the public's general views about crime. Afterwards we turn to the extent to which schemata about specific crimes such as rape, kidnaping, homicide, and burglary contain misconceptions. We also review public stereotypes of offenders, and some of the consequences of these stereotypes.

Beliefs About Why Crimes Are Committed

Why do people commit crimes? For well over a century, criminologists have been conducting empirical research to answer this basic question. Common folk wisdom about the sources of criminal activity also addresses this issue. The public's views of the causes of criminal activity can be synthesized and categorized in several ways. One prominent dimension is whether the cause is located in the offender (e.g., genetic defects, biological problems, poor socialization, mental instability) or in the environment (e.g., was precipitated by the victim or was a result of the offender's lack of employment). This distinction relates to a difference between classical and positivist explanations of crime found in the empirical research (Cullen, Clark, Cullen, and Mathers, 1985).

Classical theorists advocate harsh punishment to deter other people from committing crimes because they see everyone as primarily self-interested and motivated to enhance their own well-being. According to classical theorists, self-interested individuals will break the law when the benefits outweigh the costs (e.g., when easy opportunities co-exist with a low likelihood of official detection, or which result in lenient responses from the court). Positivist sociological theories, unlike classical theorists, locate the source of crime in the environment (e.g., poor socialization, unemployment, poverty, socialization with gang members) whereas positivist psychological theories locate the source of crime in the individual offender as biological deficiencies, mental instability, or deficiencies in moral development.

Criminologists assume that uncovering the causes of crime can lead to ways to prevent crimes in the future as well as to respond to existing criminals. Folk wisdom also assumes that the causes of crime and the responses to crime go hand in hand (Cullen, Clark, Cullen, and Mathers, 1985). Research supports this connection. Individuals who attribute the causes to the environment were less supportive of punishment and more supportive of rehabilitation as the primary objective of sentencing than were individuals who attributed crimes to individual causes (Cullen *et al.*, 1985; Carroll, Perkowitz, Lurigio, and Weaver, 1987). Cullen *et al.* (1985) found similar connections between explanations and sentencing goals for judges, lawyers, and legislators. Carroll *et al.*, (1987) interviewed law students and undergraduate criminology students and found three principal categories of attributions: social (e.g., family problems, criminal associates, and drugs); economic (poverty and inequality); and individual (greedy, lazy, uncaring).

Individuals who supported rehabilitation attributed the causes of crime to social and economic conditions, were older, and supported welfare. On the other hand, advocates of punishment attributed the causes of crime to the individual, believed that the world was a just place, were younger, and did not support welfare. Similar relationships emerged with a sample of probation officers. Thus, for both legal professionals and the public, beliefs about crime and solutions to the crime problem are connected. Beliefs about the causes of crime also may be related to how jurors interpret evidence in court (Pennington and Hastie, 1988).

Several publications provide reviews of the findings from survey data addressing public views about the causes of crimes (Campbell and Muncer, 1990; Erskine, 1974; Flanagan, 1987; Kidder and Cohn, 1979; Furhman, 1988; Roberts, 1992). Here we provide a brief summary of the major points. Before 1960, most of the polls focused on juvenile delinquency (Flanagan, 1987). The most frequent response of the cause of juvenile delinquency in the 1946, 1954, and 1963 Gallup polls of United States residents was lack of parental supervision and parental neglect. Erskine (1974) reviewed the results of Gallup polls in the United States from 1936 and 1978 and concluded: "Six out of ten Americans blame society and its pressures for its own crime rates. Only a third would hold the individual wholly responsible for his unlawful acts" (p. 288).

These findings are quite consistent with the results in other countries. Furnham and Henderson (1983) asked English adults to rate the importance of thirty explanations for delinquency. These researchers found that an absence of parental guidance and neighborhood problems were seen as the most important, and mental instability and genetic defects as the least important causes of crime (see also Jones and Levi, 1987). People tend to explain increasing crime rates primarily in terms of economic conditions creating a need for survival. Explanations for adult criminality also center around environmental causes, but other environmental causes such as socialization, court leniency, and drugs are also mentioned (Flanagan, 1987; in England, Banks, Maloney, and Willcocks, 1974). Roberts (1992) suggests that the different explanations for increasing crime rates compared to an individual's decision to commit crime may be due to respondents using different images of crime to answer these two questions.

The nature of the offense affects the kinds of causal explanations favored by the public. Hollin and Howells (1987) demonstrated that laypersons explained robbery and burglary in terms of poor socialization by parents, but explained rape as a product of mental instability. Surveys suggest that the public generally perceives that alcoholics and heroin addicts have an illness and are morally weak (Haberman and Sheinberg, 1969; Linsky, 1970; Mulford and Miller, 1964; Orcutt, 1976; Pattison, Bishop, and Linsky, 1968). Orcutt (1976) interviewed a sample of undergraduates. Half were interviewed about heroin addicts and the other half about alcoholics. Explanations did not differ for alcoholics and heroin addicts. Respondents differed in their explanations with 55 percent attributing it to both moral weakness and illness, and 34 percent attributing it to illness alone. Few respondents attributed it to only moral weaknesses (5 percent) or to behavioral control (5 percent). Individuals who attributed it to moral weaknesses or behavioral control were more likely to hold the offender responsible.

Explanations about crime also vary across demographic and attitudinal characteristics of respondents. Flanagan (1987) in a review of the Gallup Polls found racial, gender, educational, and age differences. Caucasian respondents focused more on the offender's environment and parental laxity whereas African-American respondents focused more on alcohol abuse and individual dispositions. Women were less likely to attribute increases in the crime rate to court leniency or inadequate law enforcement. As well, women focused more on inadequate socialization and parental authority as explanations for delinquency than did men (Furnham and Henderson, 1983). Younger respondents emphasized unemployment both for delinquency and adult criminality whereas older people focused on mental instability, easy opportunities, and alcohol and drug problems (Flanagan, 1987; Furham and Henderson, 1983). More educated and liberal respondents placed more importance on lack of employment and social inequities than did less educated and conservative respondents (Carroll *et al.*, 1987; Flangan, 1987; Furham and Henderson, 1983). These differences, however, accounted for only a small amount of variability in responses, and did not change the greater importance placed on environmental factors.

Schemata of Criminal Events

Theories about why and how crimes occur are stored in long-term memory and exist at all levels of abstraction. We have theories about why criminals in general commit crimes, and theories about subcategories of crimes such as property crimes, violent crimes, and public disorder crimes (see Forgas, 1980; Sherman and Dowdle, 1974). We also have schemata about specific crimes such as rape, robbery, kidnaping, and burglary, and knowledge about the characteristics and motives of victims and offenders of these crimes.

The criminal law defines each crime with a list of features that must be proved in order to establish that the crime was committed. These features then are both necessary and sufficient to prove a defendant committed the crime. Intuitive theories about crimes, however, may be organized differently (Smith, 1991). People may have categories of crime with substantially overlapping features. For example, research shows that people use the terms "burglary and robbery," and the terms "assault and battery" interchangeably even though the law defines these crimes using different necessary and sufficient conditions (Smith, 1991; Smith, 1993; Stalans, 1993). Public stereotypes about crimes then are fuzzy categories, and may not be consistent with statutory definitions (Smith, 1991).

Along what dimensions do people categorize criminal events? Studies that asked respondents to rate the similarity of different pairs of crimes provide direct evidence that intentionality is one of the dimensions along which people naturally distinguish between crimes and the natural subcategories of crimes. Sherman and Dowdle (1974) discovered that four dimensions were used to classify crimes: whether the victim was an individual or an institution, whether the crime was committed openly or the degree of publicly reported harm; the willingness of the victim; and the degree of premeditation of the offender. Although ratings of seriousness were closely related to the classification of crimes, seriousness was not related to these dimensions.

Stereotypes of Offenders

It is important to understand and address public stereotypes of offenders because as one criminologist observes: "[F]actually incorrect and rigid views of criminals, if held by many, can lead us seriously astray in our attempts both to understand crime and to control it" (Gabor, 1994). If people had a more accurate idea of the range of criminal behavior and the extent to which the public are involved (see Gabor, 1994), they might have more balanced views of certain crime control strategies.

The public perceive crime to consist of a relatively restricted spectrum of behaviors, committed by a small number of individuals (labeled "Offenders"). The reality is that crime is a very diverse phenomenon, encompassing all kinds of anti-social behavior, and has been part of society since Cain slew Abel. A significant proportion of the general public have committed a crime at some time or other. A classic 1947 study of 1700 members of the general public, none of whom had a criminal record, found that fully 99 percent admitted to involvement in at least one of a list of 49 offenses (Wallerstein and Wyle, 1947; see also Gabor, 1994). Since then a wealth of evidence has demonstrated that most people will commit a crime sometime in their lives. Marvin Wolfgang's longitudinal study in the U.S., for example, found that almost half a cohort of adolescents born in 1945 had been arrested by 1975 (Wolfgang and Tracy, 19tk; Tracy, Wolfgang and Figlio, 1990). Similar results have been found for adolescents in Canada (and elsewhere). A study of 2,000 teenagers found that 97 percent admitted to having committed at least one crime (Leblanc and Frechette, 1989). Criminologists are well aware that crime involves a broader range of behaviors, and a greater diversity of individuals than members of the public realize.[1]

A significant body of research in Canada as well as the United States demonstrates that the public have a specific stereotype in mind when they think of the concept "criminal" (see Gabor, 1994, for a review of the research on stereotypes of offenders). Physically unattractive individuals are part of this stereotype. Saladin, Saper and Breen (1988) asked subjects to rate a collection of facial photographs as to the likelihood that the individuals portrayed had committed a serious crime involving violence. Unattractive faces were more likely than attractive faces to be identified as a violent offender. This result has been replicated in several other studies (Gabor, 1994). Although the experimental task was rather artificial, this study demonstrates the finding that the public have a well-defined stereotype of an offender, and this may well have consequences for their attitudes towards, and support for, criminal justice policies (see Gabor and Rattner, 1990).[2]

Stereotypes consist of both visual images and verbal propositions. Many researchers have asked respondents to select pictures of men that resemble criminals in general and specific types of criminals such as robbers, murderers, and rapists (Bull and Green, 1980; Goldin, 1979; Goldstein, Chance, and Gilbert, 1984; Shoemaker, South, and Lowe, 1973; Yarmey, 1993). This research has demonstrated that people may literally hold "pictures in their heads" (Lippman, 1922) or visual images of criminals. Respondents agreed about the facial characteristics of criminals compared to non-criminals (Bull and Green, 1980; Shoemaker *et al.*, 1973; Goldin, 1979; Goldstein *et al.*, 1984). These studies also have confirmed that people hold facial images for sub-types of criminals such as robbers and murderers that are unique consensual matches for these sub-types rather than a simple distinction between "good guys" and "bad guys." Members of the public also distinguish "good guys" from criminals by the characteristics of their voice, though less accurately than face recognition. People believe good guys have deep, relaxed, clear, and variable pitch whereas criminals have soft, unclear, monotone, and tight voices (Yarmey, 1993).

The perception of the offender as different extends to physical stereotypes. Lampe (1982) found that when asked to describe various types of offenders, subjects were most likely to use physical descriptors, such as male, young, unattractive. Psychological characteristics were less frequently employed. These descriptors varied from offense to offense. For example, physical descriptors were used two-thirds of the time to describe murderers, but only in 25 percent of the terms ascribed to shoplifters. There were few sex differences in the attribution of descriptive terms.

In addition to these visual images of criminal faces, people's schemata of crimes can contain objective features about how the crime happened and the amount of harm committed. Objective features can be seen or felt and thus are anchored in an empirically driven reality. For example, the majority of unarmed robberies generally result in few or no injuries requiring medical attention. The severity of physical injuries is an objective feature. Other objective features include the typical place, time of day, number of offenders, whether weapons are used, alcohol or drug involvement, relationship between offender and victim, and the characteristics of the offender and victim. For all of these objective features, researchers can compare people's beliefs about what happens, to what actually does occur for the crimes that are detected and processed in the system.

Many public attitudes towards crime and the criminal justice system's response to crime reflect the view that the typical offender is a "dangerous, relentless predator who is either sick, mad or bad. Many criminals, the public believes, are suffering from mental abnormality or deficiency" (Fattah, 1982, p. 377). Offenders are seen as uneducated, unemployed, young men who are either loners or gang members (Reed and Reed, 1972; Simmons, 1966). In fact a central component of the stereotypical offender relates to social class. Gabor summarizes the research in this area by noting that "Irrespective of the discipline from which this type of research derives, the message is unmistakable: criminals are a distinct group; they are not just different in degree from the rest of us, but fall into a distinct category" (Gabor, 1994, p. 43).

Race and Crime

If the public regard offenders as "outsiders" from mainstream society, it is not surprising that associations are made in the public mind between criminality and race or ethnicity. Research has shown that stereotypes about criminals clearly have a racial element. A 1993 Gallup poll in the United States found that 37 percent of both whites *and* blacks see blacks as 'more likely' than other groups to commit crimes (Gallup Poll Monthly, 1993, p. 37). This attribution of criminality to racial minorities perception transcends national boundaries. Surveys of Canadians in 1994 found that almost half the samples thought that ethnic groups were more likely to be involved in criminal activity. When this subset of respondents was asked to identify the specific group that they had in mind, two-thirds identified "Blacks" (Roberts and Doob, 1996). These surveys did not specify the nature of the crimes, but in all probability, the association between race and crime in the public mind focuses on crimes of violence, street crimes and drug offenses. The racialization of crime is likely to intensify following a ruling by the U.S. Supreme Court in 1996, in which the Chief Justice concluded that certain crimes were in fact associated with certain racial minorities.

Other research in America has found that attributions of criminality are quite race-specific. That is, in addition to attributing more crime to African-Americans than Caucasians, people identify specific crimes with particular racial groups. Respondents in research by Sunnafrank and Fontes (1983) attributed assaults, thefts and muggings to African-Americans, while fraud, embezzlement and counterfeiting were more likely associated with Caucasian-Americans. The perception that some races are more likely to be involved in certain crimes has important consequences. A substantial percentage of African-Americans (42 percent) and Caucasian Americans (56 percent) supported a taxi driver's right not to pick up African-American passengers because of fear for his safety due to having to travel in unsafe neighborhoods. Moreover, 44 percent of Caucasian Americans and 26 percent of African-Americans believed store owners should be able to refuse young African-American men the right to enter their stores at night (The Gallup Poll Monthly, 1993). More importantly, stereotypes about race and crime may result in bias against African-American defendants in criminal trials, a topic we shall explore in a later chapter.

Behavioral Consequences of Stereotypes

These findings explain why a survey found that only 28 percent of respondents said that they would feel "at ease" in the presence of an ex-inmate; only a drug addict elicited a more negative response (Bibby, 1981). Similar results emerge from earlier research: Significant proportions of the public admitted that they would feel uneasy working with an offender on parole. The percentage expressing uneasiness varied from offense to offense, with the highest levels of prejudice associated with offenders convicted of crimes of violence. Thus three-quarters admitted that they would feel uneasy working with a parolee who had committed an armed robbery. Even a parolee who had committed the crime of embezzlement generated uneasiness among 31 percent of respondents (Joint Commission on Correctional Manpower and Training, 1968).

Not surprisingly, this stereotype results in prejudice in the workplace. Other data from the same survey also help to explain some of the difficulties that ex-offenders have in finding employment upon their return to society. Fully 43 percent of the respondents stated that they would hesitate to hire an "ex-convict" as a janitor. More than half would hesitate to hire an ex-offender as a salesman. Since it is socially unacceptable to admit to feeling uneasy in the presence of an ex-offender, (or to hesitate to hire such an individual), it is likely that the percentage of respondents who shared these perceptions of ex-offenders is even higher.[3]

There appear to be differences between Canadians and Americans in terms of reactions to ex-offenders. Research in Canada (Brillon, Louis-Guerin, and Lamarche, 1984) asked a series of similar questions and found more positive reactions on the part of the public. For example, three-quarters stated that they would be in favor of working with someone who had spent time in prison. Two-thirds were favorable to the idea of allowing an ex-inmate to organize recreational activities for children, usually a taboo area in terms of offenders. Finally, fully half the sample were favorable toward allowing an ex-inmate to become a police officer.[4]

The public hold misconceptions about the nature of crime. Beliefs about why crimes occur, offenders' motives, the extent to which offenders typically intend to commit the crime, and the extent to which victims provoke or facilitate the criminal activity also are stored. These beliefs are subjective and address the "mens rea" component of crimes; because these features relate to the minds of criminals, it is much more difficult to address whether people have misconceptions about these features.

The public's theories about crime can be very detailed and organized such that all of the characteristics are organized in a story or event schemata about when, how, where, and why the crime happens, and who is involved. A schema of mugging contains more than a list of typical attributes; it contains dimensions which have a specified range of values. For example, physical harm in a mugging is a dimension which can take on a limited number of values such as broken arm, stab wound, broken hip; if an actual description does not contain information about a dimension then people complete the missing information by inserting the typical value (Stalans and Lurigio, 1990). Schemata are much more flexible than what researchers generally call stereotypes which consist of a label and a list of typical features.

Schemata and stereotypes may shape several legal and personal decisions. Theories about crime may be used to complete the sparse descriptions used in crime seriousness studies, which may distort the findings (Blum-West, 1985; Parton *et al.*, 1991). Theories about specific crimes may contribute to eyewitness accounts of crimes (Yarmey, 1982), to jurors' interpretation of evidence and verdicts (e.g., Kalven and Zeisel, 1966; Pennington and Hastie, 1988), and to the public's desire for harsher punishment (Doob and Roberts, 1984; Roberts and Edwards, 1989). The court also uses public views about crimes and victims to determine whether expert testimony can be introduced on a topic because expert testimony must contribute more than just commonsense. Public theories also may guide reactions to victims and criminals—that is, whether the public provides support to victims or blames them, and whether they give second chances to offenders and are comfortable around them. Theories about crime may also affect people's perceptions of their own personal likelihood of being a victim of certain crimes, and whether they take measures to reduce the risk of victimization.

Individual differences in the content of stereotypes about crime are quite apparent. A significant minority of respondents believe that there are no shades of wrongfulness (Warr, 1989) and some define seriousness as immoral and sex-related acts (Hansel, 1987; for additional findings of individual differences see Forgas, 1980; Howe, 1988; Sherman and Dowdle, 1974;). Individuals who have more exposure to crime through direct experience and personal conversations have more accurate perceptions of the kinds of crime and criminals that come in contact with the legal system than do individuals who rely mainly on media stories (Stalans and Lurigio, 1990; Stalans, 1993). In the following sections, we review the research on public theories regarding specific crimes, or categories of crimes.

Stereotypes of Violent Crimes and Criminals. Most people's image of a violent criminal is one of a single male who quit high school and either is unemployed or is working in an unskilled occupation (O'Connor, 1984; Simmons, 1966). Individuals also have images of what features define murder and manslaughter. Canadian students read homicide summaries where the offender was described as clearly guilty. Respondents without instructions on the law were asked to categorize the homicides as either first degree murder, second degree murder, or manslaughter. Respondents accurately classified 73 percent of the first degree cases, 66 percent of the manslaughter cases, but classified significantly fewer second-degree cases (53 percent) accurately (Higginsbottom and Zamble, 1988).

Smith (1991) found that many people spontaneously mentioned that murder is a planned killing by an armed perpetrator, but she did not assess beliefs about manslaughter. Because media stories often present manslaughter cases as "heat of passion" cases, individuals may often perceive them to occur in the heat of passion. Smith (1991) also assessed prior knowledge indirectly through people's judgments of guilt rather than category assignments. She found that individuals do not use how typical the case is to their prior knowledge for judgments of murder cases, but also do not use intent or violence as sufficient features for finding a guilty verdict (Smith, 1991). Many individuals, moreover, hold misconceptions about robbery, assault, and kidnaping, as supported both in their spontaneous recall of attributes and in their judgments of guilt (Smith, 1991; Smith, 1993).

Definitions and Theories of Rape. In America, rape is legally defined as intercourse with a nonconsenting person or a person who is legally incapable of giving consent (e.g., statutory rape is an adult having intercourse with a consenting minor). Public definitions of rape, however, often extend beyond this definition in ways that fail to classify some incidents as rape even though they meet the legal requirements. Feminist writers have stressed intimidation and domination as the real motives of rape and have shown how the media and socialization fostered misconceptions about rape. According to Brownmiller, "Rape is nothing more or less than a conscious process of intimidation by which all men keep all women in a state of fear" (Brownmiller, 1975, p. 5). Consistent with media images, individuals from different backgrounds agreed that the most credible rape involves a stranger accosting a woman on the street with a weapon and inflicting injuries on the woman during the rape (Williams and Holmes, 1981). The least credible rapes were situations where the husband raped the wife, and where the rape involved no weapons and occurred after the victim either willingly left a bar with the assailant or willingly accepted a ride from an assailant who was an acquaintance (Williams and Holmes, 1981).

These findings accord with other research which shows that the use of force and the resistance of the victim are the two most important predictors of whether respondents define a situation as rape (e.g., Burt, 1980; Bourque, 1989; Krulewitz and Nash, 1979; Krulewitz and Payne, 1978; Lafree, Reskin, and Fisher, 1985; Shotland and Goodstein, 1983). Thus, respondents were more convinced that a rape had occurred if a woman was unwilling and physically struggled than if she was unwilling, but did not physically resist the attack. Respondents attributed more responsibility to the defendant as force and resistance increased (Krulewitz and Nash, 1979; Shotland and Goodstein, 1983). Individuals who support women's equality, however, consider that a rape has occurred based on lack of consent regardless of the level of force (Krulewitz and Payne, 1978). Women with traditional attitudes about sex roles blamed rape victims more when they resisted the attack than when they did not. Conversely, women with more progressive attitudes about women's equality blamed rape victims who resisted the attack more than rape victims who did not resist (Ryckman, Kaczor, and Thornton, 1992).

Kalven's and Zeisel's (1966) study of agreement between judges and juries on verdict illustrates the consequences of the public's stereotypes about rape in juries' decisions about guilt. Juries did not convict defendants of rape when judges would have convicted them in only 12 percent of cases involving strangers or injuries, but failed to convict in 60 percent of the cases in which none of these aggravating factors were present. Moreover, when juries did convict for these "simple" rapes, they convicted the defendant of a lesser charge when the judge would have convicted the defendant of rape. Kalven and Zeisel (1966) suggested that these disagreements derived from the juries' consideration of whether the victim contributed to the act.

Studies involving simulated jurors also find that respondents consider the contributory negligence of the victim as well as the character of the victim (e.g., Borgida and White, 1978; Borgida, 1980; Johnson and Jackson, 1988; Lefley, Scott, Liabre, and Hicks, 1993). Johnson and Jackson (1988) found that college students attributed less responsibility to the defendant and more to the victim when the woman engaged in kissing but said no to intercourse than when a woman did not engage in kissing and said no.

TABLE 6.1   Categories of Myths About Rape and Examples of Attitudinal Statements[a]

Category	Items
Cannot Happen/Victim is Responsible for Prevention	• It is impossible for a woman to rape a man • Even a big strong man can be raped by another man. • A woman can be raped against her will. • 'Nice' women do not get raped. • A raped woman is a responsible victim not an innocent one.
Blaming the Victim	• Most men who are raped by a woman are somewhat to blame for not being more careful. • In forcible rape, the victim never caused the rape. • Women provoke rape by their appearance.
Women Fantasize about Rape	• Many women really want to be raped. • Most women secretly desire to be raped.
Rape is About Power	• All rape is a male exercise in power over women. • Women are trained by society to be rape victims.
Rape is About Sex	• Most rapes occur because the rapist desires sex. • Most rapists are oversexed. • Rape is a sex crime.
Delay in Reporting	• A charge of rape two days after the act has occurred is probably not rape. • Victims who wait several days to report the crime probably are seeking revenge or attention.
Resistance is a Woman's Role	• During a rape, a woman should do everything in her power to resist.
Trauma of Being Raped	• Victims are not upset about being raped.
Normality of Rapists	• All rapists are mentally sick. • Rapists are 'normal' men.

[a]Items are selected from published research. Many additional items have been used to represent these categories

Several studies have measured the public's misconceptions about rape using more global statements and asking respondents the extent to which they agree with each statement. Rape myths are beliefs which are not supported by empirical data on the subject. Table 6.1 provides examples of the categories of myths and statements which support them. A significant minority (20 to 40 percent) of the public support each of these beliefs. The statement that rape is usually an unplanned, impulsive act was endorsed by 37 percent of one sample (Giacopassi and Dull, 1986). About one-quarter of respondents across studies believed women fantasized about being raped (Bourque, 1989; Giacopassi and Dull, 1986; Williams and Holmes, 1981). Many studies found that substantial proportions of respondents attributed some blame to the victim. Past victimization, however, was not associated with less acceptance of rape myths by male or female victims (Burt, 1980; Jenkins and Dambrot, 1987; Struckman-Johnson and Struckman-Johnson, 1992). This finding suggests that lack of empathy with the victim's role is not the source of acceptance in rape myths.

Across studies and ethnicities, women are less accepting of rape myths than are men (Bourque, 1989; Burt, 1980; Calhoun, Selby, and Warring, 1976; Costin and Schwarz, 1987; Field, 1978; Fischer, 1987; Selby, Calhoun, and Brock, 1977; Struckman-Johnson and Struckman-Johnson, 1992). Women also subscribed to fewer myths about rape occurring to men (Struckman-Johnson and Struckman-Johnson, 1992). For both men and women, attitudes supportive of restrictive rights and roles for women are associated with beliefs in rape myths such as sex is the motivation for rape and victims are responsible (Burt, 1980; Field, 1978; Costin and Schwarz, 1987). This finding also emerged in samples of students from England, Israel, and West Germany (Costin and Schwarz, 1987).

In all this research, men were more likely to have attitudes supportive of restricted sex-roles than were women. Beliefs about women's role in society, however, do not completely account for gender differences in the acceptance of rape myths (Field, 1978). African-Americans and Hispanic-Americans are more accepting of rape myths about victim blaming and desire for rape than are Caucasian-Americans. The majority of African-American men (73 percent) and Hispanic-American women (70 percent) believed that rapes could be avoided if women did not provoke them whereas only one-third of Hispanic-American men and one-fourth of Caucasian and African-American women held this belief (Williams and Holmes, 1981). This gender difference between African-American men and women, however, has not been found in other research. This suggests that both African-American men and women are more likely to blame the victim and believe that rape is committed by normal men (Bourque, 1989; Giacopassi and Dull, 1986). Whereas few Caucasian women cited the woman's behavior and character as a cause of rape, 29 percent of African-American women attributed rape to this source.

African-American women are more likely to believe rapes are planned than are Caucasian men and women or African-American men who believe it is an impulsive act. African-American women compared to Caucasian women are more likely to believe that women dream about being raped and cannot be forced to have sex against their will, but African-American men are the most accepting of these myths (Giacopassi and Dull, 1986). In one study, the majority of African-American men (80 percent) believed that women were afraid but curious and excited about rape (Williams and Holmes, 1981).

Some gender and race differences also have been found in the criteria respondents use to evaluate the credibility of a rape victim's story. Bourque (1989) found that African-American men placed more importance on the victim's resistance than did African-American women and Caucasian men and women. Caucasian women focused on information about force and were most likely to judge intercourse between nonconsenting partners as rape compared to Caucasian men or African-American men and women. African-American compared to Caucasian-American women placed more importance on whether the victim resisted the attack.

Lefley *et al.*, (1993) asked rape victims and non-victims to read hypothetical stories of nonconsenusal intercourse and indicate whether a rape occurred, to evaluate the degree of fault of the victim, and to decide whether the man should be arrested. Victims and non-victims responded in the same way. Hispanic men and women placed more fault on the woman than did Caucasian or African-American men and women. Compared to Hispanics, Caucasians believed that forcible date rape was more acceptable when the rape victim was drunk, had gotten the rapist sexually excited, had let the rapist touch her breast, or when they had been dating for a long time (Fischer, 1987). Hispanic men also were more approving of date rape when the rape victim had intercourse with other men or when the rapist had spent a lot of money on her than were Hispanic women or Caucasians.

Several explanations have been suggested to account for these ethnic differences. Field (1978) suggested that sex-role attitudes may be the source, since African-American women are more supportive of restrictive roles for women than are Caucasian women. Another explanation which fits the pattern of ethnic differences is defensive attribution (Giacopassi and Dull, 1986). People attempt to distance themselves from victims by attributing responsibility to them for the crime. Moreover, when they have characteristics in common with offenders, they are less likely to attribute responsibility to offenders and are more likely to attribute it to victims. Giacopassi and Dull (1986) found support for the defensive attribution explanation. Compared to other groups, African-American males were most accepting of five myths: (1) victims are in part responsible for the rape; (2) rape can't happen unless victims want it to; (3) rape is an unplanned impulsive act; (4) false accusations of rape are frequent; and (5) women fantasize about rape. Caucasian men were most accepting of two myths. First, that normal men do not commit rape, and second that rape frequently involves an African-American male offender and a female Caucasian victim.

Do rape myths also exist about who can be a victim of rape? One study found that college students were more accepting of rape myths when a man was a victim than when a woman was a victim, particularly when women raped men (Struckman-Johnson and Struckman-Johnson, 1992). This study found that 22 percent of men and 5 percent of women attributed blame to a man raped by a man whereas 40 percent of men and 12 percent of women attributed blame to a man raped by a woman. Fewer respondents believed a man should be able to escape when the rapist was a man (22 percent of men; 8 percent of women) than a woman (49 percent of men; 27 percent of women). Respondents also believed that a man would be more upset if raped by another man than by a woman. Both men and women (20 percent) believed that a man cannot be raped. A substantially greater number of respondents believed that a married woman cannot be raped by her husband. Differences across ethnicity and gender emerged. Over three-quarters of African-American men and slightly less than half of Hispanic-American men and women held this belief whereas significantly fewer Caucasian men (25 percent) and women (29 percent) and African-American women (34 percent) held this belief (Williams and Holmes, 1981).

Stereotypes of Property Crimes and Criminals. One study has examined the different beliefs held about swindlers and violent criminals. Whereas violent criminals are described as dangerous, uneducated, immature, young males of low intelligence, swindlers are described more positively as male professionals in their thirties who are intelligent, well-mannered, mature, but inconsiderate (O'Connor, 1984). Other studies have examined people's images of burglars and burglary. Over 80 percent of laypersons and probation officers in one study indicated that the typical burglar is single, unemployed, and a high school drop-out, statistics which accord with probation data (Stalans and Lurigio, 1990). Though people differ in their image of burglary, many believe that something of value is taken after the offender has broken into a home or apartment (Smith, 1991). Depending upon their exposure to mass media stories, many individuals believe the typical burglar carries a weapon and ransacks the place (Maguire, 1984; Stalans and Diamond, 1990). This stereotype often leads individuals to acquit offenders who have committed an atypical burglary such as forced entry into a building with intent to commit another felony therein (Smith, 1991). Individuals who spontaneously label these crimes as "breaking and entering," however, are more accurate in their assignments of guilt (Smith, 1993).

Stereotypes of Domestic Violence and Battered Women. Public views about battered women and domestic violence may be used to determine whether expert testimony on battered women can be introduced into trials when battered women kill their abusive husbands (Ewing and Aubrey, 1987; Greene, Raitz, and Lindblad, 1989), and may shape their opinions about how the criminal justice system should handle domestic violence. A few recent studies have examined public theories about domestic violence and battered women. Over half of the respondents believed 70 percent of cases involved men who injured intentionally and with no justification and believed 50 percent of cases involved women who acted in self-defense (Stalans, 1996). Only a small minority of cases (13 percent) were thought to consist of women who intentionally and without justification inflicted injuries on their partner. In this study, women were seen as the recipient of injuries in the majority of cases (70 percent) whereas men were seen as receiving injuries in 15 percent of cases by half of the sample.

Individual differences by gender and race were evident. African-American men compared to other groups believed that a greater percentage of cases involved men who acted in self-defense. Compared to other groups, caucasian women believed that a greater percentage of cases involved men who inflicted injuries without justification whereas Caucasian men were more likely to believe a greater percentage of women use physical violence without justification. Individuals' attitudes toward women's roles and rights, however, explained these race and gender differences. Stereotypes about domestic violence also appear to have social class overtones. Blum-west (1985) interviewed fifty respondents and found that the "impulse killing of a spouse was described as taking place between a young, lower class, married couple in their home during an argument in which the husband, usually described as intoxicated, kills his wife by shooting her with a hand gun" (p. 86). Novice and experienced police officers also believe that lower class couples are more habitually violent and that alcohol use frequently coincides with domestic violence (Stalans and Finn, 1995).

The public has a mixture of accurate and inaccurate knowledge about battered women. Greene *et al.* (1989) found that most jurors were well-informed both about the possibility of violence recurring once it has been used as well as the suffering of the victim. Jurors had fair knowledge about the subjective features of victims' feelings of anxiety, depression, and helpless at changing the situation, and about the victim's beliefs that her husband will kill her, and that leaving will result in further harm. Jurors were not well-informed and disagreed with research supporting these conclusions that battered women: feel dependent and are persuaded to stay by promises to refrain from violence by her husband, can predict when violence will occur, blame themselves for the situation, and deliberately provoke the violence to remove anticipation. Women were better informed than men about the victim's suffering, fear of being killed, fear of further harm on leaving, feelings of dependency, and blaming herself. In another study (Ewing and Aubrey, 1987), fewer women than men attributed some responsibility to the battered woman and believed that the battering was an isolated event. Over half of the respondents over fifty years of age attributed some responsibility to women victims and believed women who stay are masochistic whereas less than one-third of younger respondents held these beliefs.[5]

In addition, stereotypes of battered women contain pictures of their faces. Yarmey and Kruschenske (1995) found that people held two subtypes of battered women: those likely to kill their abuser and those not likely to kill their abusers. Individuals selected in a nonrandom fashion pictures of women who were likely to be battered women who kill and those who do not kill. The faces of battered women who were unlikely to kill were rated as more physically attractive and likeable and as having lower self-respect, having lower-income, less education, and being more neurotic than women not likely to be battered and battered women likely to kill. Women judged likely to be battered and to kill their abuser were perceived as being similar to women judged not likely to be battered on all items.

Crime Prevention

Crime prevention appears to be a priority for members of the public in many countries. For example, preventing (rather than punishing) crime was rated as social priority number two, behind controlling inflation, but ahead of unemployment (Moore, 1985). As well, specific crime prevention initiatives enjoy substantial public support. This finding emerges from polls in Canada and the U.S. which have explored public perceptions regarding the best way to control crime.

An interesting question was put to Americans in 1994. Respondents to a national poll were given a choice of four ways to reduce crime: (1) crime prevention (such as community education and youth programs); (2) law enforcement (more police officers); punishment (defined as better courts and bigger jails) and rehabilitation (e.g., education and work programs for former criminals. They were asked to choose the one area in which the government should spend its money. Given this choice of alternatives, 41 percent chose prevention initiatives, compared to only 19 percent for enforcement and 25 percent for punishment (Maguire and Pastore, 1995). Support for prevention was particularly high among the more educated respondents. Thus over half the sample with post graduate education supported crime prevention, compared to approximately one third with only high school education (Maguire and Pastore, 1995). Clearly then, the American public sees as much if not more merit in crime prevention than punishment.

Similar results emerge from polls conducted in Canada. This is clear from several polls that approached the question in different ways. First, when directly asked to identify the best way to control crime, the most popular option was to reduce the level of unemployment (41 percent). A further 10 percent favored increasing the number of social programs. The criminal justice option of making sentences harsher attracted the support of only one-quarter of the sample (Canadian Sentencing Commission, 1987). Second, when asked who is mainly responsible for preventing crime, more people identified "society in general" than the criminal justice system. Finally, when asked whether the average person or law enforcement agencies should do more to prevent crime, significantly more people (59 percent versus 33 percent) stated that the average person should do more (Environics Research, 1989). Similarly, the British Crime Survey found that the majority of respondents had favorable attitudes towards Neighborhood Watch and other crime prevention programs (Hough and Mayhew, 1985).

Awareness of and Participation in Crime Prevention Programs

There appears to be widespread awareness of at least the major crime prevention programs. In Canada, almost three-quarters of the public were aware of Block Parents. Almost as many knew about Operation Identification and Neighborhood Watch (Solicitor General Canada, 1984). Unfortunately, this awareness does not always translate into active participation. A general finding in several countries is that awareness exceeds participation by a wide margin. For example, in England, although over half the public were aware of Neighborhood Watch, fewer than 1 percent were actively involved in the program (Hough and Mayhew, 1985). Similar results are reported in the United States (Garafalo and McLeod, 1989) and Europe (van Dijk and Steinmetz, 1982).

Why do so few people actively participate, when so many have a favorable attitude? This finding—a positive attitude failing to generate consistent behavior—is a paradox familiar to social scientists for over fifty years now (see LaPierre, 1934)[6]. Contrary to expectation, people in the United States do not become actively involved in crime prevention initiatives on account of a heightened perception of vulnerability to crime (see Lavrakas and Herz, 1982; Washnis, 1976).

Conclusions

Several themes emerged from this literature. First, individuals have many views about crime and criminals which are offense-specific. The content of beliefs about the causes of crime, and schemata all depend upon the specific offense under consideration. Second, research at this stage has not overwhelmingly demonstrated consensus among the public in their views about categories of crimes and criminals. Individuals differ in their perceptions and beliefs based on their exposure to mass media stories and their background characteristics. Misconceptions found in crime stereotypes also show systematic individual differences. Public views about crime and criminals can have several effects on legal and personal judgments. Finally, in terms of crime prevention, it is clear that the public endorse the principle of crime prevention, although in practice this support does not translate into high rates of participation in crime prevention initiatives.

Notes

1. Of course, most of these crimes are relatively minor; only a minority of the public will be processed by the criminal justice system. However, this minority is larger than most people realize, and in many countries is also linked to race (see Tonry, 1995). In England and Wales, by the time they are forty, almost half the male population will have a criminal record (Barclay, 1994).

2. A final component of perceptions of offenders concerns mental instability. Pasewark, Seidenzahl and Pantle (1981) found that community residents overestimated by a significant margin arrest rates among former mental patients. The latter are viewed as a potentially dangerous and unpredictable population.

3. This survey was conducted in 1967. It is likely that attitudes towards ex-offenders have improved since then, although in the absence of a comparable, recent survey it is hard to know.

4. Since this survey was conducted almost twenty years after the American study, it is hard to know whether the discrepancies reflect changes over time, or differences between Americans and Canadians (or, possibly, the influence of both factors).

5. The sample consisted of predominately white, married, well-educated middle class persons. As well, the response rate was very low (16 percent). The characteristics of the sample and the response rate suggest that these results cannot be generalized to the wider population.

6. In a now famous study which spawned a great deal of research, LaPierre found a significant discrepancy between attitudes and behavior in the area of race relations.

7

Evaluating the Police
and the Courts

The basic virtues of the judeo-christian tradition such as honesty and respect for life lie at the core of criminal laws in western nations. The police and the courts exist to protect these societal values through the investigation, prosecution and punishment of violations of the criminal law. Media reports, however, can leave the impression that some police officers violate the very values that they are paid to uphold and enforce. For example, in 1991, the media nationwide broadcast a videotape of White Los Angeles police officers inflicting severe and unnecessary injuries on an African-American man named Rodney King. Most Americans have now seen this videotape. The Greylord scandal in Chicago painted a picture of a court system riddled with corruption—several judges were found guilty of taking bribes to rig verdicts and sentences. In Canada, a great deal of media attention was devoted to the plight of a Montreal cab driver who was left with severe brain damage (and who subsequently died) as a result of injuries sustained while in police custody.

Do the misdeeds of a few tarnish the public's image of the criminal justice system as a whole and undermine societal support for the police and the courts? Who holds the most negative images of the police and courts' honesty, fairness, and respect for citizens' rights? Which neighborhoods have more experience with dishonesty, prejudice, and disrespect? How do respondents' demographic characteristics modify the effects of direct contact on diffuse support for the police and the courts? Are people who support the police also strong supporters of the courts? These questions address the extent to which the public will continue to uphold these institutions even though they know that some officials perform their duties in a dishonest and disrespectful manner.

Diffuse support refers to the amount of good will and respect toward the institution (Easton, 1965). Diffuse support generally has been measured as a set of attitudinal statements about how much respondents would support the existence of an institution if people threaten to abolish it or if the institution made unfavorable decisions. Perceptions about the fairness of an institution (honesty, fair decisionmaking, politeness) also have been used as indirect measures of diffuse support (Gibson, 1991; Tyler, 1990). In this chapter, we follow the tradition of previous research (e.g., Easton, 1965; Gibson and Caldeira, 1992; Tyler, 1990; Tyler and Rasinski, 1991), by distinguishing diffuse support from evaluations of the effectiveness and quality of performance.

Support for, and confidence in the police and courts are necessary for the fair and effective administration of justice. Research shows that individuals who show less support for these institutions are more likely to steal, speed and drive under the influence (Tyler, 1990), and to commit more serious criminal offenses (Hirschi, 1969). As Gibson and Calderia (1992) note: "Diffuse support constitutes a reservoir of institutional goodwill, and is especially useful for the maintenance of an institution when decisionmakers produce public policies with which many of the populace disagree" (p. 1121). When individuals perceive unfair decisionmaking or undignified treatment, they may be less willing to participate in the system as jurors or to seek assistance from the police and courts in resolving their own disputes or responding to victimization. It should be recalled that most crimes come to the attention of the police through the report of a victim or a witness. If victims and witnesses have no confidence in the police, they will not report crimes. This may result in two negative consequences. First, justice will not be done. Second, some victims may seek individual solutions to criminal victimization. There have already been cases of such vigilantes in America and Canada.

Confidence Across Institutions and
Clarification of Diffuse Support

Many opinion polls conducted nationwide in the United States have asked the public: "How much confidence do you have in (institution name)... a great deal, a lot, average, very little, or none?" Confidence is clearly a multidimensional concept that is broader than diffuse support (Flanagan, 1988). For example, confidence may include effectiveness at reducing crime (Flanagan, 1988), favorability of outcomes, solving of crimes, and many other performance characteristics that are based on financial, material, and personal well-being. In contrast, diffuse support focuses on a willingness to defend the institution despite unfavorable outcomes to oneself. Confidence then, may place emotions in the background and perceptions about how authorities do their job in the foreground. Despite the ambiguity surrounding the question's meaning, it has been asked for over two decades.

We use data on public confidence in various criminal justice institutions to highlight some of the central issues that will be addressed in this chapter. Table 7.1 compares public confidence in the police, Supreme Court, and the criminal justice system as a whole, using data from the Gallup Poll conducted nationwide in the United States in 1994. (Data on local courts unfortunately are not available). Two ethnic differences are noteworthy. First, Caucasian-Americans have more confidence in the police than do African-Americans. Only 10 percent of Caucasian-Americans compared to 30 percent of African-Americans have little or no confidence in the police. We will see later that this difference is also found for perceptions of procedural fairness and is slightly less dramatic for direct measures of diffuse support for the police. The second phenomenon that can be seen in Table 7.1 is that a higher percentage of Caucasians have more confidence in the police than in the Supreme Court whereas a similar number of African-Americans have confidence in police and the Supreme Court.

TABLE 7.1   Confidence in Supreme Court, Police and Criminal Justice System Within Ethnicity (1994 Nationwide USA Gallup Poll)

Institution	Caucasian-Americans		African-Americans	
	High[a]	Low	High	Low
Police in General	57%	10%	34%	30%
Police Protection From Personal Violence	47%	9%	38%	11%
Supreme Court	44%	17%	38%	22%
Criminal Justice System in General	14%	50%	26%	50%

[a]The response categories for high were "great deal" and "a lot," and the response categories for low were "very little" or "none." Average was the middle response category that does not appear in this table. This table was compiled from several tables in Maguire, Pastore and Flanagan (1993).

The data on confidence also suggest that Caucasians and African-Americans have similar views on two issues. First, Caucasians and African-

Americans have less disagreement about confidence in the police protecting them from personal violence, with slightly fewer African-Americans having high confidence, but similar numbers of Caucasian-Americans (9 percent) and African-Americans (11 percent) having little or no confidence in the police protecting them from personal violence. Other surveys suggest that fear of victimization or failure to prevent crime does not influence how much the public supports the police. Support primarily depends on whether the public perceives violations of due process rights and ethical standards. The second similarity is that both African-Americans and Caucasians have less confidence in the criminal justice system as a whole than in the specific institutions of the criminal justice system. Half of the Caucasians and of the African-Americans have little or no confidence in the criminal justice system as a whole. The whole seems to be *less* than the sum of its parts.

There are several possible explanations for why people have less confidence in the system as a whole. First, the system may be blamed for doing little to prevent future crimes. Second, the system may be seen as failing to correct authorities who violate ethical standards, and third the system may be seen as unwilling to correct unfair outcomes that result from dishonesty or prejudice. Is this phenomenon unique to the question of confidence or does it generalize to perceptions of the fairness and effectiveness of the system? This question remains unanswered. Research has compared how satisfied people are with an institution such as the courts to how satisfied they are with direct encounters with court officials, but has not compared the system as a whole to its individual institutions.

This chapter focuses on public support for the police and courts. We also explore the public's perception of whether authorities adhere to constitutionally-protected procedural rights in the administration of justice and whether authorities uphold professional standards of honesty, equity and respect. The next chapter provides a comprehensive discussion of public views of the effectiveness of the police at reducing crime and solving crimes as well as their views of the accuracy, adequacy, and fairness of specific arrest decisions. The distinction between procedural justice and distributive justice distinguishes the content of Chapter 7 and Chapter 8. Procedural justice refers to how police officers and courts gather information about a case and whether they recognize citizens' rights and treat citizens with respect; this is the focus of Chapter 7. Distributive justice refers to the fairness of outcomes, and Chapter 8 and 9 focus on the fairness of decisions made from arrest, charging, to jury verdicts. Chapter 9 focuses on the accuracy and fairness of jury verdicts and describes the relationship between outcome fairness and outcome accuracy.

In this chapter, we first examine the public's perceptions of the procedural fairness and ethicality of the police. The next section compares the public's perception of the police with their perception of the courts. We then try to gain an understanding of how people evaluate their own personal encounters with the police and courts, and how these encounters subsequently affect their attitudes. Finally, we show that ethical standards and procedural fairness are the linchpin of citizens' diffuse support for the police and the courts. We also highlight personal and situational characteristics that determine the extent to which specific experiences will change diffuse support. We conclude with a summary of the important conclusions drawn from the literature and questions to be addressed in future research.

Evaluations of the Ethicality and Procedural Fairness of Police

Earlier reviews of the literature conducted in the 1970s (e.g., Decker, 1981; Sarat, 1977; White and Menke, 1978) concluded that the majority of the public holds the police in high esteem and has positive impressions of their ethical standards. This is true in Canada and the United Kingdom as well as America. For example, when members of the public in Canada were asked to rate the ethical standards associated with a list of professions, police officers were second only to physicians (Roberts 1994). In fact, an international comparison involving members of the public in over twenty nations found that attitudes towards the police were most positive in Canada and the United States (Mayhew, 1994).[1] Over 80 percent of respondents in both countries perceived that the police were doing a good job controlling crime. Survey data since then reinforce this conclusion, though the public agrees more about some characteristics than about others. Table 7.2 lists several key characteristics that comprise part of procedural fairness and ethical standards. Table 7.2 also provides a comparison of the views of Caucasian-American, Hispanic-American, and African-Americans about the police based on a nationwide survey of American adults conducted in 1992.

On most of the dimensions, at least half of the respondents in each ethnic group provide very favorable ratings of the police. Two exceptions are noteworthy. First, fewer than one-third of Hispanic-Americans and African-Americans (compared to almost half of the Caucasian-Americans) believed that the police are very honest and maintain ethical standards. Second, 38 percent of the African-Americans compared to half of the Hispanic-Americans and two-thirds of the Caucasian-Americans believed that the police treat people fairly. The most disagreement among the various ethnic groups occurs on normative dimensions, whereas the least disagreement occurs on the purest dimension of self-interest—crime prevention. Ethnic groups have similar views of police efforts to prevent crime, with just over half in all groups providing positive ratings.

TABLE 7.2   Public Perceptions of Fairness and Ethical Standards of Police
Officers

Dimension	Caucasian-American	Hispanic-American	African-American
Honesty and ethical standards (1991)[a]	45%	30%	30%
1992 Gallup poll	43%	NA	29%
1993 Gallup poll	53%	NA	28%
Harris Poll (1992)[b]			
Great deal of respect	68%	51%	51%
Treating people fairly[c]	68%	54%	38%
Helpful and friendly[c]	78%	71%	58%
Solving crimes[d]	61%	57%	43%
Responding quickly to calls for assistance[d]	73%	60%	50%
Preventing crimes[d]	59%	56%	55%

[a]Data are based on the 1991,1992, and 1993 Gallup Polls nationwide surveys of United States residents. The percentages are those who indicated either "very high" or "high." Data were compiled from the 1990, 1992, and 1993 Sourcebooks of criminal justice statistics.

[b]For all dimensions below, data were obtained from tables in the 1992 Sourcebook of criminal justice statistics and are based on the 1992 Harris Poll nationwide survey of United States residents.

[c]The percentages are those who indicated either "excellent" or "very good."

[d]The percentages are those who indicated either "excellent" or "pretty good."

The Use of Excessive Force and Deadly Force

Another interpersonal issue is the use of excessive force by police officers. A poll conducted in 1991 found that a greater number of Americans believed that police brutality occurs more frequently then than three decades earlier. In 1965, 9 percent of respondents believed that police brutality was a problem in their area whereas 35 percent responded this way in 1991 (Gallup Poll Monthly, 1991). When asked the question, "How frequently do you think incidents like this happen [the Rodney King beating] in police departments across the country?", 68 percent indicated that police brutality occurred frequently whereas only 20 percent indicated that police brutality occurred frequently in their local police departments.

Race is the most important divider of opinion with fewer Caucasian-Americans compared to African-Americans and Hispanic-Americans believing that the police often use excessive force (For a detailed review of surveys on excessive force see Flanagan and Vaughn, 1995). In addition, respondents who are younger than fifty years of age, are moderate in their political ideology, claim no religious affiliation, or have some college education are more likely to believe that police brutality exists in their area (Flanagan and Vaughn, 1995). Residents of large cities and those living in the western region of the United States also are more likely to believe that police brutality exists in their area (Flanagan and Vaughn, 1995).

The constitutionality of the police use of deadly force centers on the fourth amendment right to be free from unlawful seizures. Supreme Court Justices must interpret whether a police officer acted justifiably in shooting at a suspect to stop him/her from escaping custody. Public views determine in part whether a shooting was justifiable. Fortunately, the deadly use of police force is relatively rare. Cullen, Cao *et al.*, (1996, p. 449) estimate that approximately 1,000 fatalities occur across the country as a result of police shootings. Professionals have justified the use of deadly force as being necessary to protect society from dangerous criminals. Public opinion is an important consideration in determining the appropriateness of its use. Moreover, public opinion about the police use of deadly force shows marked disagreements between Caucasians and African-Americans.

Should officers have the legal right to shoot suspects who are attempting to escape custody? Public reaction to this question may depend in part on how much they trust the police not to abuse their power, and how much they value individual rights over societal protection through the control of crime. The answer also may depend upon the type of crime the person is suspected of committing. In the case of *Tennessee v. Garner* (1985), the Supreme Court had to decide whether a Tennessee statute which allowed police officers to use deadly force against fleeing property offenders was constitutional. Garner was a fifteen-year-old African-American burglary suspect. When police tried to apprehend Garner, he attempted to escape custody. Garner was unarmed and was attempting to climb a high fence when a Memphis police officer shot and fatally wounded him. Was it reasonable to use deadly force in this way? The Supreme Court concluded that it was excessive in the case of property offenders, but that police officers could use deadly force to stop a fleeing person who was suspected of a violent crime or who threatens the officer with a weapon. While people may support the use of deadly force to prevent the escape of a murder suspect, not even the most extreme crime control advocate would endorse a policy of shooting to prevent the escape of an auto thief or a shoplifter.

A recent study examined public views about the police use of deadly force using a sample of Ohio residents (Cullen *et al.*, 1996). Public opinion concurs with the Court's decision. The vast majority of both Caucasians and African-Americans (over 80 percent) supported the use of deadly force when persons suspected of rape or robbery are attempting to escape police custody. African-Americans and Caucasians, however, held different views about the use of deadly force for escaping persons suspected of burglary or selling drugs. Fifty-two percent of Caucasians but only 39 percent of African-Americans endorsed the use of deadly force to stop persons suspected of burglary. At least for this sample, Caucasians' views diverge from the Supreme Court's opinion. There is far less support for the use of deadly force to stop persons suspected of drug selling: 45 percent of Caucasians and 35 percent of African-Americans supported this action. The researchers found that more general beliefs about government and crime accounted for the difference of opinion between African-Americans and Caucasian-Americans.

Socialization Effects and Ethnic Differences

The dissatisfaction of African-Americans focuses on unethical and unfair treatment rather than the effectiveness of the police to protect them. From 1991 to 1993, almost one-third of African-Americans and Hispanic-Americans adults rated the honesty and ethical standards of the police as low or very low. Similar results are found among younger populations. From 1978 to 1989, nationwide surveys of high school seniors' perceptions of the dishonesty and immorality in the law enforcement and court systems revealed that these perceptions have been rather stable. Slightly fewer Caucasian-Americans than African-American high school students perceived dishonesty in law enforcement to be a considerable or a great problem (Maguire and Flanagan, 1991).[2] The unfavorable evaluation of African-American adults is shared by younger Blacks as well.

Bouma (1973) interviewed 10,000 junior high school students and found that whereas almost all students (91 percent) believed that people would not be better off without the police, Caucasian-Americans and African-Americans disagreed on their perceptions of procedural fairness. The majority of Caucasian-Americans (but only a minority of African-Americans) perceived procedural fairness. Fewer African-American students believed that the police will give them a chance to explain (30 percent compared to 50 percent), and that they try not to arrest innocent people (41 percent compared to 75 percent). Similar results conducted almost twenty years later in England using fourth and fifth graders clarify further the ethnic differences among young students (Waddington and Braddock, 1991). Black teenagers predominately perceived the police as bullies who showed little respect toward youth. In contrast, groups of Caucasian and Asian youths display more variability in their views with some Caucasians and Asians believing the police to be guardians of laws who do not abuse their authority and other Caucasians and Asians believing the police are bullies.

Another important finding emerging from Table 7.2 concerns the issue of solving crimes. Hispanic-Americans and Caucasian-Americans share similar views, and these views are more positive than those of African-Americans. Surveys from 1978 to 1992 also found that African-Americans believed police officers were less courteous to them (Bishop, 1992). A Los Angeles Times Poll in 1990 also found that Hispanics were in the middle between Caucasians and African-Americans on a question about pushing people around: 20 percent of Caucasian-Americans, 36 percent of Hispanic-Americans, and 54 percent of African-Americans held an unfavorable impression of the police. Thus, Hispanic-Americans' discontent seems to focus more on ethical standards and fair treatment, whereas African-Americans' dissatisfaction with the police seems to incorporate other issues such as the inability to solve crimes, police officers' friendliness, and response time. Caucasian-Americans also provided the most favorable ratings of police response time followed by Hispanic Americans and then African-Americans. Response time and solving crimes have an interpersonal component—longer response time and lack of information about police efforts to solve crimes against them may indicate a lack of respect and concern for the citizen.

Many of these dimensions (courtesy, friendliness, fairness, honesty, concern for citizens' rights) comprise evaluations of the demeanor of police officers toward citizens. Demeanor is the most central component of Hispanic-Americans, Caucasian-Americans, and African-Americans adults' and teenagers' attitudes toward the police (Sullivan, Durham, and Alpert, 1987). Demeanor is also the most important influence on people's evaluations of the fairness of procedures accorded to them during personal contact with police officers (Tyler, 1988).[3] Caucasians evaluated the demeanor of police officers more positively than did African-Americans (Hadar and Snortum, 1975).

Alternative Explanations for Ethnic Differences. So far we have highlighted ethnic differences and similarities on several dimensions of police performance without addressing alternative explanations for these differences. Several studies (e.g., Dunham and Alpert, 1988; Smith and Hawkins, 1973; Thomas and Hyman, 1977)[4] find that ethnicity was the variable which bore the strongest relationship to attitudes toward the police. This emerges after controlling for the effects of demographic variables such as age, education, occupation, total family income, area of residence, and perceptual variables such as fear of victimization or perceptions of crime rates. Moreover, direct contact with the police seems unable to account for all differences in perceptions among ethnic groups (Furstenberg and Wellford, 1973; Jacob, 1971; Scaglion and Condon, 1980). Scaglion and Condon (1980), for example, found that an evaluation of the services obtained directly from police was the strongest predictor of attitudes toward the police, but after controlling for this predictor and other demographic variables, ethnicity still accounted for 6 percent of the variability in attitudes toward the police.

The focus on differences and similarities across ethnic groups leaves the impression that because of their ethnic identity or unique socialization, members of a minority group share the same view about the police. Shared views do not arise from identity with the group, but from shared environment. Shared views about the police arise more from a common neighborhood context (Albrecht and Green, 1977; Jacob, 1971; Murty, Roebuck, and Smith, 1990; Schuman and Gruenberg, 1972; Sullivan, Dunham, and Alpert, 1987) and early childhood socialization (see Bouma, 1972; Sarat, 1977; Waddington and Braddock, 1991) than from an individual's membership in an ethnic group.

For example, a study comparing five neighborhoods with homogenous ethnic membership in Florida (Dunham and Alpert, 1988), found that neighborhood context shapes perceptions about police officers. The majority of members in *all* ethnic groups rated police demeanor favorably. Middle-class Caucasian-Americans and Cuban immigrants who had immigrated in 1960, however, rated officers' demeanor more positively than did Cuban immigrants who immigrated in 1980, low-income African-Americans living in a subsidized housing project, and African-American professionals living in a upper-middle class neighborhood. The views of these latter three groups did not differ. Moreover, neighbors in each of these neighborhoods agreed more on their ratings of demeanor than any other attitudinal measure and agreed more with each other than with residents of other neighborhoods. It would appear that consensus about the police results from the influence of a shared environment and experiences rather than from identification with one's ethnic group.

Why African-Americans Differ in Their Perceptions of the Police. We now shift the focus to variation *within* the African-American community to highlight differences among members of the same group. The perception of unethical police standards appears to be especially widespread among urban residents living in ghettos (Albrecht and Green, 1977; Hahn, 1971; Jacob, 1971; Murty *et al.*, 1990). Fully 89 percent of a sample of African-American residents living in a Detroit ghetto after the 1967 riot (Hahn,

1971), believed that most Detroit police officers displayed some dishonesty in performing their duties. Boggs and Galliher (1975) explored the relationship between social class and support for police. They compared a sample of African-American men who lived on the street, in transient housing, or who temporarily slept at different homes over a short period of time to a sample of employed African-Americans living in permanent households. The itinerant, street respondents were more likely to rate police service as poor compared to household respondents. Those who lived in a stable home but had less than a high school education gave more favorable ratings to the police than did those with a high school education. This difference, however, may be due to more requests for assistance among those who are high school educated.

Differences in education do not appear when the effects of contact and other indicators of social class are removed. For example, Murty, Roebuck, and Smith (1990) conducted personal interviews with African-Americans residing in low-crime or high-crime areas. They found that two-thirds had a generally positive attitude toward the police while one-third had a negative attitude.[5] African-Americans in different social classes (as indicated by their place of residence and their occupation) held dissimilar attitudes toward the police. Residence was the strongest predictor of attitudes: Those residing in high crime areas held more negative images than those residing in low-crime tracts.

Differences Across Age Groups

After ethnicity, the second strongest demographic predictor of attitudes toward the police is age. Teenagers and younger adults have less favorable attitudes toward police than do older adults. This finding also generalizes across Caucasian-Americans and African-Americans (Garofalo, 1977; Murty *et al.*, 1990), is found in Canada (Thornton, 1975) and the U.S. (Dunham and Alpert, 1988; Garofalo, 1977; Hadar and Snortum, 1975; Murty *et al.*, 1990; Smith and Hawkins, 1973), and remains after the effects of victimization, education, social class, conservatism, and contact have been removed. Younger people perceived more unfairness on the part of the police (Hadar and Snortum, 1975; Maguire and Flanagan, 1991, Harris Survey; Tyler, 1990), had less respect for the police (Maguire and Flanagan, 1991; Tyler, 1990), rated them as less friendly and helpful (Hadar and Snortum, 1975; Maguire, Pastore, and Flanagan, 1993; Murty *et al.*, 1990) and had less confidence in the police ability to control crime (Flanagan, 1988).

Younger and older respondents in the 1992 and 1993 nationwide Gallup survey of United States residents, however, held similar views of the honesty and ethical standards of police officers (Maguire and Flanagan,

1991). Both younger and older respondents may hold similar views of ethical standards because they rely on the same source for these views: Earlier socialization instructs them that most officials can be trusted and are honest. Younger respondents may develop more negative views of procedural fairness than older respondents because they are more likely to have confrontational encounters with police officers.

Relationship to Political Attitudes

The extent to which political beliefs and other attitudes shape evaluations of the police's demeanor has received very little attention in the literature. This issue is one which may produce some theoretical insights into the differences across ethnic groups. Some research suggests that support for civil liberties is related to perceptions of the respectfulness of police. Almost 80 percent of Caucasian-Americans who did not support any civil liberties gave the police high ratings for respectfulness whereas Caucasian-Americans who supported one or two civil liberties rated police respectfulness as very good (69 percent and 53 percent, respectively) (Block, 1971). This relationship, however, was not found among African-Americans (Block, 1971) or among Hispanic-Americans living in a barrio (Mirande, 1980).

Support for the police has tended to go along with a conservative political orientation. Thus Tyler (1990) found that conservatism was related to support for the police and courts after controlling for gender, race, age education, and income. Zamble and Annesley (1987) found the same result in Canada. Ethnicity may modify the relationship between conservatism and support for the police. Caucasians' support for the police and their evaluations of the procedural fairness of police performance may be based in part on their support for crime control versus due process rights whereas African-Americans may develop support and evaluations based more on their earlier acquired beliefs about whether the police discriminate against African-Americans. This possible variation between ethnic groups may explain the moderately strong correlations found in a primarily Caucasian Canadian sample (Zamble and Annesley, 1987) and Caucasian United States sample (Block, 1971) compared to the significant, but weak correlations found in Tyler's (1990) study which did not examine ethnic differences.

The role of political beliefs has interesting theoretical implications. Although ethnic groups may all agree that the police should be honest, fair, and respectful, Caucasian-Americans who support crime control may hold more lenient standards of which officers' actions constitute excessive force, disrespectful treatment, and unfair decision-making than may ethnic minorities who support due process. Hispanic-Americans and African-Americans may base their support more on earlier socialization about whether police accord equal treatment to all citizens and less on whether police actions are fulfilling the political mission of crime control or due process. Hence, Caucasians may use their political beliefs as filters to assess the fairness and demeanor of police officers and may judge the same action quite differently than African-Americans and Hispanic-Americans who may use absolute standards of decency unaltered by their political views.

Relationship with Fear of Crime and Actual Victimization

Victimization history, fear of crime, and perceptions of crime trends have weak or non-existent relationships to attitudes toward police when the effects of other variables are eliminated. This conclusion generalizes across many samples and different measures. For example, using data collected during 1966 in the midst of urban unrest in the United States, Block (1971) found no significant relationship between the perceived likelihood of being attacked and support for increasing police powers for either Caucasians or African-Americans.[6] Mirande (1980) used identical measures to test whether residents living in a Chicano barrio in a southern California community based support for police power on their fear of victimization. A re-analysis of these data revealed a significant but weak relationship, with those who believed that they were very likely to be attacked more willing to support increased police powers. Thus, even when the environment makes fear of crime a salient concern, it is still only weakly related to support for increasing the powers of the police.

Garofalo (1977) reports one of the most comprehensive tests of the hypothesis that non-victims and those with less fear of victimization will have more positive attitudes toward police than will victims and those with more fear of victimization. Garofalo (1977) tested this hypothesis using data from the National Crime Survey which sampled 22,000 individuals in each of eight cities. Only weak relationships emerged between evaluations of police performance and fear of personal safety or perceptions of crime rates.[7] Perceived threat of victimization or perceptions of crime rates did not shape perceptions of police fairness for residents in Seattle (Smith and Hawkins, 1973), Virginia (Thomas and Hyman, 1977), or Canada (Zamble and Annesley, 1987).

The differences between victims and non-victims are equally small. Garofalo (1977) reports that slightly greater numbers of victims of assaultive violence and robbery without injuries (22 percent Caucasians, 35 percent African-Americans) rated police performance as poor than did non-victims (6 percent Caucasians; 19 percent African-Americans). Other studies, based on samples of U.S. (Smith and Hawkins, 1973) and Canadian residents (Koenig, 1980), indicate that victims who reported their victimization and those who did not report their victimization to the police had similar attitudes toward the police.[8] Maxfield (1988) found that differences between victims and non-victims in England occurred only for those stopped as suspects. Of those stopped as suspects, victims were more likely than non-victims to perceive a lack of politeness on the part of police.

Garofalo concluded that

> the generally low level of associations between ratings of police performance and attitude items which reflect beliefs about crime trends, the fear of crime, and the effects of crime on behavior indicate that the public does not "blame" the police for the problem of crime. (1977, p. 30)

Fear of crime and victimization experiences then may have weak relationships to attitudes toward the police because the public does not attribute to the police the responsibility to control crime. A recent study supports this hypothesis. Dunham and Alpert (1988) found that the majority of Caucasian-Americans and African-Americans disagreed with the statement that only the police can control crime in their neighborhood. Cuban immigrants, however, believed that the police were solely responsible for controlling crime; this misperception may occur because of less familiarity with law enforcement in this country. Likewise, when Canadians were asked who was responsible for preventing crime, fewer than 10 percent identified the police (Canadian Sentencing Commission, 1987).[9]

Evaluations of the Procedural Fairness of Courts

Since 1980, little research has been conducted on the public's perceptions of the fairness of decisionmaking in local courts (for a review of research prior to 1975 see Sarat, 1977). Most public opinion polls on perceptions of the court have focused on the adequacy of sentencing decisions, a topic that will be discussed in Chapter 10. The majority of respondents in a nationwide survey of United States residents believed that local courts and the Supreme Court make decisions in a fair way (63 percent for local; 70 percent for Supreme Court), make decisions only after reviewing all the relevant information (62 percent for local; 73 percent for Supreme Court), give interested citizens an opportunity to express their views (58 percent for local; 50 percent for Supreme Court) and consider all sides before making a decision (74 percent for local; 74 percent for Supreme Court) (Gibson 1989). A nationwide survey conducted in 1995 found that most respondents did not believe that disregarding defendants' rights was a problem in the courts. Ethnicity was related to this opinion: The majority of African-Americans, but only 29 percent of Whites held the view that disregarding a defendant's rights was a problem (Myers, 1996). In the following sections, we compare attitudes toward police and courts, and then consider the personal correlates of attitudes toward the fairness of court procedures.

Comparison of Support for Police and Courts

Although people react more favorably to the police than the courts (Fagan, 1981; Flanagan *et al.*, 1985; Tyler, 1990), research finds that generally those who have supportive attitudes of the police are more likely to have supportive attitudes of the court (Albrecht and Green, 1977; Tyler, 1990). Furthermore, laypersons use their evaluations of the fairness of the police to evaluate the fairness of the judicial process in traffic court (Tyler, 1984) and felony cases (Casper, Tyler, and Fisher, 1988). Based on survey data from 1978 to 1989, a greater number of high school seniors perceived dishonesty to be a problem among police officers (30 percent) than among all courts (24 percent) or the Supreme Court (Maguire and Flanagan, 1991). Whereas Caucasian-American seniors perceived similar levels of dishonesty in law enforcement and courts, a greater number of African-American seniors (13 percentage point difference) perceived dishonesty and immorality as a considerable problem in the law enforcement system than in the court system. Similar numbers of adults in Chicago agreed that police (58 percent) and judges (57 percent) were honest (Tyler, 1990).[10] The police and court system, however, have similar levels of diffuse support and perceived ethicality and fairness.

Most people believe that judges and officers ought to behave and do behave quite similarly (Jacob, 1971). Moreover, these standards for police officers and judges are distinct from the standards set for welfare workers, teachers, and delivery persons. Police officers and judges alike should be honest, fair, hardworking, very strong, and kind. African-Americans and working class Caucasian-Americans have the same standards for both officers and judges, but middle class Caucasian-Americans believe that judges should adhere to impartial justice whereas officers should provide personal service (Jacob, 1971). These differential norms for officers and judges are also found in interviews with victims of violence in England (Shapland, Willmore, and Duff, 1985). These researchers noted that:

> The police are seen as in some way providing a service to victims. ... Victims expect to remain in contact with the case throughout the whole process of prosecution and for that contact to be facilitated by the police. They see the police as independent agents, but agents processing their case who should, therefore, account to victims (and, occasionally, consult them). ... The courts

are given a different role. Judges and magistrates are not thought of as having any obligation to victims. Any especially thorough consideration of the case or kind remarks about the victims' part in the offence or welfare in court are seen not as due, but as a pleasant surprise. ... So the police are judged on their failure to provide a service—an individualized, personal service. (p. 95-96)

Research in the United States also supports the conclusion that people apply different standards to the police and courts. Research in the 1970's (Jacob, 1971; Shapland *et al.*, 1985) showed that Caucasians believed courts should operate as disinterested decisionmakers, and research in the 1980s showed that people having direct experience with courts were more concerned with impartiality, accuracy, and correctability in their evaluations of how fairly they were treated than were individuals that had direct encounters with the police (Tyler, 1990).

Comparison Among Ethnic and Age Groups

The two most consistent and strongest predictors of attitudes toward the police—ethnicity and age—are less consistently related to attitudes toward local courts and the Supreme Court. For example, over time, African-Americans and Caucasian-Americans have demonstrated different levels of diffuse support and perceptions of procedural fairness of the Supreme Court. African-Americans (compared to Caucasian-Americans) were more likely to support the Court during the 1960s, but differences between these ethnic groups had disappeared by the end of the 1970's (For a review of this research see Gibson and Caldeira, 1992). In the late 1980s, African-Americans were less willing than Caucasian-Americans to defend the Supreme Court against threats to abolish it and against reducing its powers (Gibson and Caldeira, 1992).

In contrast to mixed findings for race at the Supreme Court level, race has not been related to views about fair procedures or honesty at the local level. Similar numbers of Caucasian seniors and African-American seniors in 1989 believed that dishonesty and immorality are a considerable or great problem in all the courts and the justice system in general (Maguire and Flanagan, 1991). Ethnicity is also unrelated to beliefs about whether local courts use fair procedures (Tyler, 1990). Race, however, is related to views about less favorable treatment toward African-Americans with fewer Caucasians compared to African-Americans and Hispanic-Americans endorsing this belief (Yankelovich, Skelly, and White, 1978). Age is also unrelated to beliefs about whether local courts (Tyler, 1990) or the Supreme Court (Handberg and Maddox, 1982) use fair decisionmaking procedures.

Effects of Knowledge of the Court

As noted in Chapter 3, the public has little knowledge of the court system either at the local level or the Supreme Court level (see also Sarat, 1977). Paradoxically, several studies in the 1960s and early 1970s suggested that the more knowledgeable citizens were about how the court actually functioned, the less satisfied they were with court performance (for a review, see Sarat, 1977). A nationwide survey of United States residents in 1978 (Yankelovich, Skelly, and White, 1978) clarifies which aspects of the court system people possessing extensive knowledge rated less favorably than did individuals possessing limited knowledge. Yankelovich, Skelly and White (1978) concluded that: "[A] very sobering fact is that those having knowledge and experience with courts voice greatest dissatisfaction and criticism" (p. 1).

Our examination of the tables from which this conclusion is drawn suggests a brighter picture of the relationship between knowledge and attitudes toward local courts. It is true that those with more extensive knowledge of the court (17 percent) were less likely to be confident in state courts than were individuals with average knowledge (23 percent) or limited knowledge (29 percent), but it is unclear what confidence means. Moreover, confidence may vary depending on the institutions that are being compared in the question. The relationship between knowledge and more specific measures can provide more detailed information about the extent to which accurate knowledge lowers support for and perceived fairness of the court.

The greatest difference between those with limited accurate knowledge and those with accurate knowledge occurred for specific performance items related to court administration. Those with limited knowledge believed that these problems occurred less often: delays of at least six months from arrest to trial (limited 26 percent versus extensive 43 percent), too much expense (35 percent versus 42 percent), and not enough judges to handle work (23 percent to 42 percent). Similar numbers of individuals with limited knowledge and those with extensive knowledge perceived that the following procedural problems directly related to fairness occurred often: political considerations influencing court decisions (27 percent versus 26 percent), treating poor worse than rich (24 percent versus 29 percent), treating blacks worse than whites (23 percent versus 21 percent), biased and unfair judges (14 percent versus 10 percent), and disregarding defendants' rights (13 percent versus 4 percent).

The largest gap (only 9 percentage points difference) is in the opposite direction: A greater percentage of those with limited knowledge believed that the court often disregards the rights of defendants. The amount of accurate knowledge was also unrelated to views that judges often failed to put in less than a full day, showed little interest in people's problems, insisted on the letter of the law, and had inadequate training or education. The findings we have reviewed suggest that the *amount* of experience with the court bears little relationship to perceptions of the courts' procedural fairness, ethicality, and impartiality.

Research in the 1960s and early 1970s generally examined only simple two-way relationships between knowledge and views of the court without taking into account other demographic or personal characteristics that could account for the simple relationship. Some research—such as that of Sarat (1975)—carefully distinguished between diffuse support and specific support in the interpretation and analysis. His research clearly indicated that extensive accurate knowledge about the legal system was associated with low levels of satisfaction with how laws are currently created and administered, but did not relate to obligation to obey the law. Similarly, the Yankelovich, Skelly and White (1978) study finds that extensive knowledge produces more discontent about administration of the court than either its procedural fairness or its competence. These earlier studies sometimes have been miscited and overgeneralized in recent publications to paint a much gloomier picture about the impact of knowledge of the court system on support for the courts.

Evaluations of Procedural Fairness:
The Role of Direct Experience

How does direct experience shape the public's satisfaction with the police and the court system? What impact does this have on perceptions of the fairness of police and courts? We begin by examining the role of familiarity with officers as friends, relatives, or acquaintances and the effect of police-initiated contact such as in traffic stops or in the investigation of cases. We then turn to victims' views about how the system treats them and whether their views are grounded in the actual behavior of officials or derive from respondents' prior beliefs and subjective feelings. We conclude this section by reviewing the procedural justice research that has examined the meaning of procedural fairness, and how that meaning changes over personal and situational characteristics.

Familiarity and Police Initiated Contact

Mere familiarity with a police officer as measured by knowing his or her first name, or having a friend or relative who is an officer is not related to evaluations of police performance in Canada (Koenig, 1980) or in the United

States (Scaglion and Condon, 1980; Smith and Hawkins, 1973). Smith and Hawkins noted that establishing programs to foster citizens' familiarity with friendly officers appears to be futile and may reinforce "the minority group conception of enforcement agents, e.g., cops must be authoritarian; they have to work to be friendly" (p. 146). On the other hand, how police handle investigatory stops and requests for assistance from citizens shapes evaluations of police performance and perceptions of the fairness of police in general (Brandl, Frank, Worden, and Bynum, 1994; Boggs and Galliher, 1975; Jacob, 1971; Maxfield, 1988). Brandl and colleagues (1994), using a sample of predominantly African-Americans with low to moderate income, found that satisfaction varied slightly by the type of encounter with the police. Over half were satisfied with the way they were treated during investigatory stops (55 percent) and during requests for assistance (64 percent) whereas a little under half (49 percent) were satisfied with how the police treated them during an encounter reporting their victimization.

Experience with the System's Handling of Personal Victimization

Several studies have examined how victims evaluate the treatment they receive and how these evaluations affect their satisfaction with the system. Studies in the United States have explored the effect of victims' expectations on their satisfaction with police encounters. Such studies have used surveys asked only once (Smith and Hawkins, 1973; Furstenberg and Wellford, 1973) and surveys conducted with the same respondents on two separate occasions (Brandl, Frank, Worden, and Bynum, 1994). Studies which ask questions on two separate occasions can determine whether prior views shape impressions of specific encounters and whether specific encounters shape global beliefs. English research which combines interview data with observations of police conduct or interviews with officers (Maguire and Bennett, 1982; Shapland, Wilmore, and Duff, 1985) provides the best data to address whether police actions actually affect victims' satisfaction or whether satisfaction is more subjective; the English research provides an additional indicator of what actually happened during the encounter.

One of the most comprehensive studies is a longitudinal study of changes in reactions to treatment by the police and the courts. Samples of assault and sexual assault victims were interviewed as their cases were processed through the system in England (Shapland, Willmore, and Duff, 1985). At the first contact, 83 percent of the victims were satisfied or very satisfied with police performance, but fewer victims were satisfied after the interview where they had to commit to prosecution (55 percent of the victims were satisfied). The police were seen to be less efficient, less overworked, more oppressive, less fair, less bureaucratic, more crooked, and less helpful after the committal interview than just after the first contact with an officer. Interviews conducted one to two years after the case was finally resolved suggest that the decline in positive attitudes toward the police was long-lasting. Although victims were less satisfied when they did not want the offense reported or when they wanted to prosecute and the police were unwilling to prosecute, satisfaction had less to do with the outcome of the case than with how the police treated the victim.

As Shapland *et al.* (1985) note "this (dissatisfaction) was almost entirely due to lack of knowledge of what was happening to the case and, for a few, the consequent feeling that the police did not care and were not doing anything—that the police were ignoring both the offence and the victim" (p. 85). This dissatisfaction arose because the police had failed to meet victims' expectations: Almost half of the victims held erroneous beliefs about the police system with 44 percent incorrectly believing that victims had the final decision about prosecution and 55 percent incorrectly believing that victims were required to give testimony after a guilty plea. Dissatisfaction with police handling of victimization also shapes Americans' attitudes towards the fairness of the police (Furstenberg and Wellford, 1973; Smith and Hawkins, 1973).

In contrast to decreasing satisfaction with the police as the case progressed, victims' satisfaction with judges actually improved over the course of the judicial process. This was in part because they were surprised with the friendliness and care displayed by judges. Victims' satisfaction with judges at the final interview, however, was still below the level of satisfaction they had held for the police at the first interview. Because victims expected formality and objectivity from judges, they did not require the judge either to be kind or to keep them informed. This task was delegated to police officers who were expected to provide personalized service. Here we see evidence that pleasant experiences do increase victims' level of satisfaction with the system. Given that satisfaction with the court's handling of the case is moderately related to perceptions of procedural fairness and with respect for judges (see Tyler, 1990), positive experiences may raise support for the court when people expect courts to be formal and to give them little personalized attention.

If satisfaction is grounded entirely in prior beliefs rather than actual behavior, improvements in police behavior will have no effect on victims' satisfaction. That is, impressions of police behavior may be more in the "eyes of the beholder" than in the reality of how police actually treated the victims. Satisfaction, however, does appear to have some grounding in police actions. The police officers in England "tried consciously to be more helpful to sexual assault victims, to keep in touch with them and to keep them informed of exactly what was happening in the case, especially if there was any likelihood of them having to give evidence" (Shapland *et al.*,

1985 p. 88). These actions led to positive results: Sexual assault victims were more satisfied with the police handling of their case than were physical assault victims, even after removing the effects of victims' gender, victims' familiarity with the offender, and agreement or disagreement between police and victim about how to proceed (Shapland *et al.*, 1985). The police made an effort to send the message that they were concerned about and valued sexual assault victims, but exerted less effort to send this message to victims of physical assault.

Other research also shows that satisfaction is grounded in experience. For example, Maguire and Bennett (1982) found that fewer working class burglary victims (32 percent) than middle class burglary victims (49 percent) in England were satisfied with the way the police had handled their case. This discontent among working class victims relates directly to the inferior treatment they received compared to the treatment middle class victims received: fingerprints were taken less often (56 percent versus 77 percent), fewer visits were made by the police (8 percent versus 22 percent had three or more), received advice about security less often (11 percent versus 22 percent) and fewer received notification of the police progress.

Burrows (1986) found that thoroughness of an investigation and whether police provided information about the progress of the case had the strongest influences on victims' satisfaction with the police. Arrest and response time had small (but significant) effects, and interpersonal treatment or providing advice about crime prevention had no significant influence. In both of these studies of burglary victims in England (Burrows, 1986; Maguire and Bennett, 1982), victims seldom felt that police investigation should necessarily result in arrest, and arrest was less important than the police showing concern about the victim's case.

As Maguire and Bennett (1982) noted

> victims were much less concerned with seeing an offender arrested than with receiving what they regarded as the appropriate response to the incident. ... The very routine of investigation—for example, taking fingerprints, recording details, examining the point of entry, questioning neighbors if coupled with a sympathetic attitude and a willingness to listen to the victims' fear was mentioned as having a beneficial effect in helping people to come to terms with what had happened. (p. 137)

These studies reinforce the idea emphasized in United States research on procedural justice (Lind and Tyler, 1988; Tyler, 1988) that people place more importance on the way that they are treated than on nature of the outcome (i.e., whether an offender is convicted).

The Meaning of Procedural Fairness

As we noted earlier, demeanor (politeness and concern for citizens' rights) contributes the most to evaluations of procedural fairness and has been found to be an important factor across a range of legal arenas (for a review see Lind and Tyler, 1988; Stalans, 1994a). Furthermore, the fairness of the procedure matters as much or more than the fairness of outcomes and the favorability of outcomes across many legal arenas including police traffic stops of citizens (Tyler and Folger, 1980; Tyler, 1990), misdemeanor court (Tyler, 1984), family court (McEwen and Maiman, 1984), felony sentencing hearings (Casper, Tyler, and Fisher, 1988), and arbitration hearings and civil trials (Lind *et al.*, 1990).

Tyler (1988, 1990), using panel data from interviews with Chicago residents, has provided the most thorough investigation of the characteristics of an encounter that contribute to evaluations of procedural fairness. He found that the meaning of procedural fairness varied more across situations than across persons. Across all situations, politeness and concern for rights are central to evaluations of the fairness of procedures used by the police and courts. Persons who asked the police or courts for help compared to those involved in police or court initiated encounters were more concerned with the accuracy, impartiality and correctability of decisions.

Demographic variables did not substantially alter the meaning of a fair procedure (Tyler, 1988). Two other personal characteristics, however, did influence the importance placed on different features of the encounter in evaluations of procedural fairness: expectations about fairness and values about procedural fairness. Fairness expectations shaped interpretations of the various features of the encounter and had direct influence on evaluations of procedural fairness. Those who expected fair treatment were more likely to "see" fair treatment than those who expected unfair treatment.[11] Similar findings emerged from interviews with convicted felons involved in felony sentencing hearings (Tyler, Casper, and Fisher, 1989). For both of these studies, prior views do not completely engulf the actual nature of the experience (Tyler, 1990). For example, defendants charged with felonies perceived more procedural fairness if their lawyer had visited them in jail (and thereby provided an opportunity for them to have voice in their case—see Casper *et al.*, 1988).

Expectations also influenced the importance placed on the opportunity to explain. When individuals had little influence over an authority's decision, those who expected fair treatment placed substantial importance on having an opportunity to present their side in forming an evaluation of procedural fairness (the perceived amount of opportunity accounted for 41 percent of the unique variance in procedural fairness evaluations) whereas those who expected unfair treatment placed substantially less importance on opportunity, though it still was a significant consideration (it accounted for 10 percent of the unique variance) (Tyler, 1990).

In addition to holding different expectations about the fairness of the process, people may place a different value on having a fair process. For those who expected to receive fair treatment, having the opportunity to present their case was an important determinant of their evaluation of fairness. Not surprisingly, perhaps, those who expected to receive unfair treatment were far less interested in being able to present their views (Tyler, 1990). These findings suggest that people who value civil liberties more than controlling crime also may define procedural fairness quite differently. This implication assumes that the importance placed on due process should be related to the importance placed on being treated fairly, a hypothesis that needs to be tested in future research.

Relation Between Encounters with Authorities and Diffuse Support

What aspects of encounters with authorities produce changes in diffuse support? Research (Brochner, Tyler, and Schiender-Cooper, 1992; Gibson, 1989; Gibson and Caldeira, 1992; Tyler, 1990) has examined this issue. Tyler (1990) found that the fairness of procedures in specific experiences had more influence on diffuse support than did the fairness of outcomes or the favorability of the outcomes. Evaluations of procedural fairness on diffuse support varied by the nature of the encounters. Respondents placed more importance on procedural fairness when their experience involved the courts, was a dispute, was voluntary, or had an unfavorable outcome than when their experience involved the police, was not a dispute, was involuntary, or had a favorable outcome. Among a sample of high school students, those who valued procedural fairness and perceived fairness were more supportive of the courts than those who valued procedural fairness and perceived unfairness and those who did not value procedural fairness (Enstrom and Giles, 1972). Tyler (1990) also showed that those who valued procedural fairness placed more importance on procedures in determining their support at a given time than do those who do not value procedural fairness.

Do Positive Experiences Raise Support and Negative Experiences Undermine Support?

Brockner, Tyler, and Schiender-Cooper (1992), found that experiences involving procedural unfairness lowered support for the police and court, but experiences involving positive experiences did not raise it. They postulated that this negativity bias occurred because people want to be treated fairly, and are disappointed when they do not receive fair treatment. Their analysis falls short of providing convincing evidence in favor of this view. They ignored the fact that expectations may serve as filters that distort interpretations to confirm what people expected to receive, and did not consider that the value placed on the procedure determines how much influence procedural fairness of a specific experience has on changing diffuse support. Prior analyses of these data, however, demonstrate support for both of these points (see Tyler, 1990).

The idea that people want fair treatment as an explanation for why only negative experiences change diffuse support also falls short of explaining why positive experiences sometimes raise support. It is clear that negative experiences have more influence than positive experiences, but it is not clear that positive experiences have no influence. Prior research shows that positive experiences raised diffuse support for tax audits (Stalans, 1994b) and modestly raised satisfaction with the courts (Shapland *et al.*, 1985) and the police (Brandl *et al.*, 1994). Brandl and colleagues (1994) collected data at three different points in time from a predominantly African-American sample with low to moderate incomes. In keeping with previous research (Tyler, 1990), they found that prior global views of police had a stronger influence on evaluations of specific encounters compared to the influence that specific encounters had on changing prior global views.

In contrast to prior research (Brockner *et al.*, 1992), they found that both positive and negative experiences shaped global views. After controlling for prior global satisfaction, respondents who requested assistance and viewed their contact with police positively were more satisfied with the police in general compared to respondents who did not have any contact in which they requested assistance. In addition, respondents who requested assistance or reported a victimization and viewed their contact negatively were less satisfied with the police in general after controlling for prior views.

Why did one study find only that negative experiences shape support for the police whereas others have found some support for positive experiences? At least three explanations should be tested in future research. First, Brochner and colleagues (1992) used measures that clearly represent diffuse support (e.g., respect for authorities, trust in authorities, acceptance of decisions) whereas research which finds that positive experiences raise support (Brandl *et al.*, 1994; Shapland *et al.*, 1985) have relied on measures of satisfaction. Satisfaction may change more easily than support for the police. However, even if this is the case, satisfaction is related to support for the police, which suggests that positive experiences would raise diffuse support indirectly through raising satisfaction with the police. Second, as we have already stated, the study which claimed that only negative experiences shape diffuse support did not consider how expectations distort interpretations and how differences in values for procedural fairness shape the influence of direct experiences. Third, the studies differ in the nature of their respondents. Brochner and colleagues (1994) analyzed data from a predominantly Caucasian sample with moderate income whereas Brandl and colleagues analyzed data from a predominantly African-American sample with low to moderate income. This last possibility deserves further exploration.

Any explanation of how positive and negative experiences change diffuse support cannot ignore the possibility that different ethnic groups may base diffuse support on different criteria. Some research on public views of the Supreme Court highlights this point. Gibson and Caldeira (1992) explored the ways in which African-Americans and Caucasian-Americans maintain and change their diffuse support for the Supreme Court when faced with decisions unfavorable to themselves or their political views. Data from a nationwide survey in 1987 speak to this issue. In this sample, fewer African-Americans than Caucasian-Americans believed that people should protect the Supreme Court from being abolished as an institution (56 percent versus 71 percent), cared whether the Supreme Court's powers were reduced (55 percent versus 74 percent), and did not want to limit the Supreme Court's power to declare acts of Congress unconstitutional (58 percent versus 71 percent).

Among African-Americans, cohort effects were found: Fewer individuals coming to age during the Warren Era (34 percent) lowered their support for the Supreme Court when faced with the unfavorable outcomes of the recent conservative Supreme Court compared to those born pre-1933 (59 percent) and those born post-1953 (48 percent) who lowered their support. Neither attentiveness to the Supreme Court nor educational level of the respondents can account for this difference. The cohort effects, moreover, do not generalize to Caucasian-Americans because Caucasian-Americans placed more importance on policy outputs in determining their support than did African-Americans. As Gibson and Caldeira noted

> the racial differences are stark: Among whites, there is some tendency for dissatisfaction with the Court's policy outputs to translate into diminished levels of support. But among the blacks, precisely the opposite occurs. Those who are more dissatisfied with recent judicial policies are more supportive of the Court as an institution. This is strong evidence of the resilience of past attitudes toward the institution. (1992, p. 1138)

Ethnic groups, as we have noted earlier, are not homogenous entities, with views common to all members. The Gibson and Caldeira (1992) study suggests that individuals of ethnic groups who have developed support for courts do not readily reduce their support when faced with unfavorable decisions. Do these individuals identify less with their own ethnic group, and maintain their support for courts because they do not care about what happens to other people of their own ethnicity? Lack of identification with one's ethnic group is not the primary reason for maintaining support. Some research (Huo, Smith, Tyler, and Lind, 1995) indicates that identifying with one's ethnic group does not hinder maintaining support for authorities. Huo and colleagues compared three groups of individuals: (1) assimilators—people who identify more with society than with their own ethnic group; (2) biculturalists—people who identify equally with society and their own ethnic group; and (3) separatists i.e., people who identify more with their own ethnic group than with society.

Assimilators as well as biculturalists placed more importance on being treated in a neutral, benevolent, and respectful manner than receiving an outcome that was favorable to them. By contrast, separatists placed more importance on receiving favorable outcomes than on receiving respectful treatment from authorities because they did not identify with the authorities or the group that the authorities represented. This research dealt with procedural fairness and the acceptability of decisions in a public sector work organization. The similarities between the Gibson and Caldeira (1992) research on Supreme court and Huo's and colleagues' research suggest that identification with larger society should foster ethnic minorities' support for the police and courts even when they identify strongly with their ethnic group and perceive inequitable treatment. The implications for society are promising. Authorities do not have to be concerned if people from different cultures do not assimilate completely into the mainstream, but they do need to be concerned if they do not identify with the mainstream in addition to their identification with their own ethnic group (Huo *et al.*, 1995).

Conclusions

Several conclusions can be drawn from the literature reviewed in this chapter. First, substantial evidence has demonstrated that fear of victimization, actual victimization, and perceptions of crime rates have little influence upon support for the police and perceptions of their ethical standards and fairness. Second, even though support for the police and support for the courts are moderately related, different demographic and situational characteristics predict support for these two institutions. For example, race and age are consistently related to attitudes toward the police, but are less consistently related to attitudes toward the courts. Third, ethnic groups, moreover, may develop support for the police in the same way, but some research (Gibson and Caldeira, 1992) suggests that they maintain and change support for the Supreme Court (and perhaps for the local courts) based on different criteria. Fourth, positive and negative contacts may have different influences on support for the police as compared to support for the courts. For example, previous research suggests that the negativity bias may be stronger in encounters with police officers than with court officials because people hold difference expectations for police and courts. Caucasian-Americans believe that the police should provide particularistic service whereas the courts are not obligated to do so (Jacob, 1971; Shapland *et al.*, 1985). These differences in the correlates of support for the police and courts suggest that studies that combine data across police and courts may be masking important differences in the maintenance and change in support for these institutions.

Along similar lines, polls that compare Caucasians to others (lumping African-Americans, Hispanic-Americans and other minorities together) distort the important distinctions that may be made by these different minority groups in their perceptions of police and courts. For example, ethnic comparisons demonstrate that Hispanics and Caucasians have similar perceptions of the police on some dimensions such as friendliness, solving crime, and discriminatory treatment toward African-Americans.

Future research should focus on the interrelationship between political views, specific experiences, and support for an institution within ethnic groups. Whether the importance people assign to crime control compared to due process shapes their perceptions of procedural fairness and support has received little attention, but appears to be a fruitful area of inquiry based on the few studies addressing this issue. Do Caucasian-Americans assign more importance to their political views when evaluating the police and the local courts? Are Hispanic-Americans more similar to Caucasian-Americans than African-Americans in the criteria they use to determine their level of support for the police and the court system? These are some of the questions that future research should address.

Notes

1. By comparison, only 12 percent of residents of Czechoslovakia and 27 percent of Poles shared this positive perception of the police.

2. Data are based a nationwide sample of 12,121 high school seniors in 1989. Similar conclusions can be drawn from nationwide sample taken from 1978 to 1988, though for the classes of 1981, 1983, 1984, and 1987 there exists an 8 to 10 percentage point difference between Caucasian-Americans' and African-Americans' views of considerable or great dishonesty in the courts with fewer Anglo-Americans holding this view.

3. These same items of politeness and concern for the citizens' rights have been labeled as the "dignity of the encounter" (Lind *et al.*, 1990) or the ethicality of the encounter (Tyler, 1990). The label "dignity" shifts the focus toward how police actions may lower self-esteem and self-respect of the citizen whereas the label "demeanor" keeps the focus on how police are perceived to act toward individuals.

4. Smith and Hawkins (1973) categorized race as Caucasian and Asian-Americans compared to African-Americans, Native-Americans, and Hispanic Americans. Studies generally have not studied Asian-Americans' views of the police, but Smith and Hawkins find that they are similar to Caucasian-Americans' views.

5. Respondents rated police on several likert items assessing normative dimensions (honesty, friendly, fairness, kindness) and competence issues (hardworking, harsh, dumb).

6. A significant relationship does exist for the African-American sample using Univariate Optimal Discriminant Analysis with those who perceive that a personal attack is very likely more willing to increase the power of the police, Monte Carlo p < .0027. Though significant the effect strength is .14, which indicates that the relationship is extremely weak.

7. Gamma is a measure of the strength of a relationship between two variables, and ranges from zero to one, with one being perfect and strong relationship and zero being no relationship. The Gammas for the relationship between evaluations of police and fear of personal safety and between evaluations of police and prior victimization range between -.10 and -.18, which are very weak.

8. Gamma is a measure of the strength of a relationship between two variables, and ranges from zero to one, with one being perfect and strong relationship and zero being no relationship. The relationship between victimization and attitudes toward the police was small for both the Seattle sample (Gamma = .12), and the Canadian sample (Gamma = -.17).

9. The most popular response (47 percent) was "society in general," followed by the courts (24 percent).

10. The issue of whether both Caucasian-Americans and African-Americans held similar views of the police and court system was not addressed by Tyler (1990).

11. As Tyler (1990) notes, these connections may also be due to behavioral confirmation. Individuals who expected fair treatment may have acted more responsively toward officers and judges than individuals who expected unfair treatment.

8

Legislative Definitions
of Crimes and Law
Enforcement Priorities

When most people think of criminal justice, they tend to think of criminal *in*justice. This can take many forms. The most serious miscarriages of justice involve judicial errors at the time of trial: Innocent people can be convicted, and the guilty can be acquitted. Sometimes offenders are convicted of the wrong crimes, for example, when a defendant charged with (and guilty of) first degree murder pleads guilty to a less serious offense of manslaughter. This means that he or she receives a much more lenient sentence than is deserved, in light of the seriousness of the crime committed. As well, this perception of injustice includes situations in which the criminal justice system has priorities that do not agree with the public's view. For instance, many people feel that the justice system places too much emphasis on the rights of the offender at the expense of the rights of the victim. Examples of these kinds of problems readily come to mind.

Many of us have thought or told our friends after observing officers giving parking or speeding tickets: "Don't they have anything better to do than write parking or speeding tickets. They should be out there detecting and preventing *real* crime." Such thoughts suggest that there may be important divergences between the public and the police in terms of criminal justice priorities. These perceptions of inaccurate and unfair decisions, however, are based on a biased sample of examples which are easily recalled. This matter raises the two models of criminal justice referred to in Chapter 1. The consensual model of justice assumes that legislative statutes of crimes and criminal defenses and police priorities are consistent with public desires. In contrast, the conflict model suggests that priorities reflect the dominant interests in society. This chapter reviews the research in this area, and tests the assumptions underlying the consensus model of justice.

Chapter 8 provides an understanding of the public's views of the accuracy and fairness of legislative definitions of crimes, of standards for legal defenses which excuse criminal conduct, and of decisions by law enforcement personnel. We start by focusing on whether public views are consistent with legislative statutes defining crimes of attempt, the insanity defense, and the defense of self-defense. Legislative statutes guide police officers' decisions to arrest, prosecutors' decisions about whether to charge people with crimes and prosecutors' decisions about whether to make deals to elicit guilty pleas from offenders (i.e., whether to offer a plea bargain). The next section starts with public views of police competence, and moves to research which compares public views of what priorities the police should have to officers' views of what their priorities should be. In this section, we also examine the differences between ethnic groups in their views about whether the police and courts give favorable treatment to certain segments of society.

Public Definitions of Crimes
and Defenses to Crimes

Criminal laws specify the actions that are criminal and which will be punished. Generally speaking, crimes are defined by the actor's intention and the consequences of the act. For example, first degree murder is defined as the premeditated and unlawful killing of a person. In order to be convicted of murder, the prosecutor must prove beyond a reasonable doubt both that the defendant planned to kill the victim, and that he actually did kill the victim. As well, the intent and the guilty act must also be connected in time. For example, Tom may plan to kill George on Saturday, but on Friday Tom and George are having a very heated argument and in a moment of passion Tom kills George. Because the premeditated intent and the act were not joined, but instead the killing occurred in the heat of passion, Tom is guilty of voluntary manslaughter and not first degree murder.

Over the centuries, philosophers and legal professionals have debated how much importance the law should assign to an offender's mental state such as his or her intent to commit the act. White and Roberts provide a synopsis of this debate. They note that

> Those favoring inclusion of intent in the definition of criminal behavior have suggested that society's moral precepts oppose penalizing people for behavior which they did not intend. It was further argued that people

would be less inclined to conform to the law if they did not think that they could avoid violating it. If this were the case, the law would be seen as unjust, and the public's respect for the law would be diminished. Those favoring strict liability believe that enforcement would be hindered if the prosecution had to prove intent in every case. (1985, p. 456)

Although for most crimes the prosecutor must prove intent as well as the guilty act, people can be held criminally liable even though an injury or death occurred through negligence or recklessness rather than an intent to commit the act. Involuntary manslaughter, for example, is the taking of another person's life through reckless or negligent behavior. Intent is also less important for some behaviors that states have begun to label as criminal. For example, in the past three years, several states have introduced legislation that would hold parents criminally liable for crimes committed by their children using the parents' guns. The justification for this is that the parents acted negligently by allowing their children access to the guns.[1]

In most western nations, a person is held criminally responsible for harmful actions only if the criminal law prohibited the commission of the act and specified a punishment before the person committed the act. Legal definitions of crimes must be specific and describe all the elements of the crime that the prosecution must prove so that people can conform their behavior to the law and will not be subjected to arbitrary persecution by the government. Legislators must decide how much importance to place on the harmful act as opposed to the intentions of the defendant to commit the act. This issue is important in deciding which elements the prosecution must prove, how attempts at crimes will be defined, definitions of insanity, and what will constitute justified self-defense.

Because the public may lose respect for laws which are not consistent with their conceptions of justice, it is important to know how the public balances objective features of the crime (such as the consequences) with subjective features of the crime (such as the defendant's mental state). White and Roberts (1985) examined how much importance a sample of adults placed on the defendant's intention in their decisions about a defendant's guilt. Most of the respondents (80 percent) believed that intent should be a consideration in the verdict decision. However, the majority of subjects (70 percent) believed that a defendant should be found guilty but given a lighter sentence if he/she testified in court that he/she committed the act but did not *intend* to commit the act.

In another study, White and Roberts (1985) asked people to render a verdict and sentence a defendant accused of a theft. In the vignette, the defendant was charged with stealing a watch. He admitted taking the watch, but denied that he had intended to steal. The researchers varied the description of the defendant's defense that he did not intend to commit the crime. In the absent-minded condition, the accused stated that he had put the watch into his pocket intending to pay for it when he left. After examining other merchandise, he had forgotten about the watch by the time he left the store. In the similarity-intent condition, the defendant did not deny taking the watch from a change room, but testified that he had mistaken it for his own watch which was very similar to the stolen watch. The defendant introduced his own watch into testimony as evidence of the similarity between the two watches.

In the witness story, four witnesses gave conflicting testimony concerning the accused's alleged participation in the crime. Two witnesses claimed that the accused was guilty; the other two said someone else was responsible. One witness for each side later admitted that he was preoccupied at the time of the incident and was thus not absolutely sure who was guilty. In the witness story, the defendant did not admit to taking the watch and therefore did not use the intent defense. Thus, the witness story can serve as a comparison for the other conditions which did use the intent defense. For all these conditions, respondents were told that if the prosecution has not proven criminal intent beyond a reasonable doubt then they must find the defendant not guilty.

The findings of this second study clarify the findings from the general survey. Subjects gave a significantly greater number of not guilty verdicts only when the defendant presented objective evidence that substantiated her claim of lack of intent. Respondents were skeptical about the veracity of the defendant's claim that she did not intend to commit the theft when no objective facts supported the claim. The authors note that respondents assume intent from the commission of the act, and require defendants to prove that they did not intend to commit the act, which of course is contrary to the burden of proof required by law. However, many courts

> frequently demand evidence from the accused concerning possession of goods in theft and related cases. According to the 'doctrine of recent possession', the prosecution has to prove that the accused was in possession of goods, and they had been recently stolen. It is then the defendant's responsibility to account for his possession of the goods in a way that will demonstrate his innocence. (White and Roberts, 1985, p. 464)

Interestingly, though skeptical of the defendant's honesty, respondents still favored a more lenient sentence if he claimed it was due to absent-mindedness. Similar to the survey findings, respondents are willing to treat unsubstantiated claims of lack of intent as a mitigating factor in sentencing, but are unwilling to give much importance to such evidence in their verdict decisions.

Punishing an Attempt to Commit a Crime

Legislators are faced with the difficult task of determining at what point in the steps of committing a crime a person should be held accountable even though the actual crime was not completed (Robinson and Darley, 1995). Should people be punished if they merely express an intent to kill someone or to steal something? Individuals may make these statements in moments of anger, when the intent is fleeting (Robinson and Darley, 1995). Perhaps some people mean what they say, but later decide that they cannot carry out the plan because it is morally and legally wrong. Should society base criminal liability on *subjective* grounds of mental state and intentions or on *objective* grounds of behaviors leading up to the commission of an actor's intent to complete a crime?

The legal systems of many countries have adopted either the subjective standard or an objective harmful consequence standard (Darley, Sanderson, and LaMantia, 1996). The Model Penal Code, which has been adopted by thirty-six American states, is an example of a subjective standard to define attempt crimes. "The Model Penal Code [uses the substantial test and] criminalizes attempt at the point when a settled intention to commit the crime has been formed, and a substantial step has been taken towards completing this intention" (Darley, Sanderson, and LaMantia, 1996, p. 409). For example, a person who intends to rob a store takes a substantial step when he/she enters the store to check the location of a safe (Darley, Sanderson and LaMantia, 1996).

The Model Penal Code also requires that attempts be punished as severely as completed crimes (with the exception of attempted murder—see Darley, Sanderson, and LaMantia, 1996). By contrast, the older common law's dangerous proximity test relies on an objective standard which requires the actor's conduct to be in close proximity of completing the crime before liability for attempting the crime is imposed. The common law relies more on the potential for harmful consequences. The actor who intends to rob the store would be held liable for attempted robbery if he or she is caught breaking open the safe. Currently, there is a shift in the United States towards using subjective rather than objective standards when defining crimes of attempt. Is this tendency consistent with community views regarding criminal liability?

Darley, Sanderson and LaMantia (1996) addressed this question using subjects who read scenarios in which defendants were at different stages of attempting a crime (i.e., had merely thought about it, had taken a substantial step toward committing the offense, were about to commit the offense, or had actually completed the act). The respondents then decided upon a verdict and a sentence for the convicted offenders. Their findings indicate little support for the Model Penal Code definitions of attempted robbery or attempted murder. Respondents assigned only a small amount of liability for acts involving only thought or a substantial step. Instead, respondents assigned much more criminal liability and began to view the case as a serious criminal action at the point of dangerous proximity. Thus public views are consistent with the common law notion of attempt crimes.

Moreover, in contrast to the Model Penal Code, the public were less punitive towards offenders guilty of an attempted crime (compared to offenders who succeeded in completing the crime). The authors conclude that:

> If one were to design a legal code that was consistent with our subjects' moral judgments, the crime of attempt would be dealt with in two stages. First, for all steps toward the commission of any crime that fall short of dangerous proximity, regardless of the crime, the code would hold the person liable at a low, perhaps misdemeanor level of offense. ... Second, once dangerous proximity to the offense is reached, without renunciation, then the person has committed an attempted crime, and the offense would therefore be graded in a way that reflected the liability assigned to the actual crime in question, with the sentence proportionately and considerably reduced since the actual crime was not carried out. (Darley, Sanderson and LaMantia, 1996, p. 15)

Impossible Acts

Related to crimes of attempt are impossible act cases. A typical attempted murder case is where a defendant shoots and the bullets miss the intended victim. An impossible act case contains some type of mistake which makes the current situation unable to produce the intended harmful consequence. Consider these impossible act cases.

> A woman attempts to kill her neighbor by shooting him as he lay sleeping; however, unbeknownst to her, the victim had died earlier in his sleep of a heart attack. Setting aside the possible crime of desecrating a dead body, can she be found guilty of attempted murder of an already dead person? A man, trying to kill his wife, drives to a secluded spot, pulls out his gun, puts it to her head, and fires; only then does he realize he forgot to load the gun, and he has brought no bullets with him. Putting aside what must have been an interesting car ride home, can he be found guilty of attempted murder for firing an empty pistol?. (Finkel, Maloney, Valbuena, and Groscup, 1995, p. 596)

Impossible act cases require legislators to attempt to balance subjective factors such as intent with objective factors such as actual harm done or potential harm done.[2]

Finkel and colleagues (1995) asked a sample of undergraduate students to read and decide whether the defendant should be found guilty of attempted murder in one of five cases. Two cases concerned mistakes occurring as a result of the defendant's ineptness: One case concerned a husband who drove to a secluded spot with the intent to kill his wife, but realized he had forgotten the bullets after he fired the gun. The other case concerned a wife who attempted to kill her husband by putting arsenic-laced sugar cubes in his tea, only to later discover that she had put uncontaminated sugar in his cup instead. Another case concerned a mistake occurring through fortuity; this case concerned a person who shot a neighbor who had already been dead for some time. Another case concerned a mistake of perception: "Defendant A aimed and fired his rifle at what he thought to be a person, only to discover that it wasn't a person, but a tree stump" (Finkel *et al.*, 1995, p. 598).

The last case concerned a mistake of belief: "Defendant E attempted to kill a co-worker by buying an effigy doll and sticking pins into the doll's heart repeatedly" (Finkel *et al.*, 1995, p. 599). All respondents found defendants guilty if the mistake occurred through their ineptness (i.e., the cases of no bullets and wrong sugar cubes). Ninety-one percent of the respondents found the defendant guilty of attempted murder when she shot an already dead person. The findings for these three cases are quite consistent with Darley's research which shows that respondents hold defendants liable for attempted crimes when they reach the level of dangerous proximity of completing the act.

In the case where the defendant shot at a tree stump, half of the respondents favored a guilty verdict. This is a substantial drop from the other three cases and the difference appears to lie in how close the defendant came to actually harming someone (Finkel *et al.*, 1995). In the case where the defendant attempted to kill a co-worker with an effigy doll, only 17 percent of the respondents found the defendant guilty. This study shows that respondents make fine distinctions between types of mistakes in their attempt to balance subjective and objective criteria. It also shows that the public can make sophisticated judgments about the complex issues surrounding criminal intent, and offender liability.

The Self-Defense Defense

The defense of self-defense also involves trade-offs between objective criteria of real immediate danger and subjective criteria of the defendant's perception of danger. Defendants who plead not guilty on the grounds of self-defense claim that they harmed or killed someone in order to protect themselves. The "reasonable person standard" is used to determine whether a person acted in self-defense. That is, would a so-called "reasonable person" have acted in a similar fashion when faced with a threat of comparable seriousness? In order for the self-defense claim to be successful under the reasonable person standard, the defendant must show that she was in fear of her life or limb, could not flee, and used only the force necessary to protect herself from the danger threatened by the eventual victim. The reasonable person's perspective views "the situation from outside and makes objective assessments of whether the harm was (1) serious, (2) escapable, and (3) imminent" (Finkel, Meister, and Lightfoot, 1991, p. 586).

The public's view of self-defense, however, lowers liability in certain cases to a greater degree than the law would allow. Robinson and Darley (1995) conducted an experiment to examine the conditions under which people acquitted or gave shorter prison sentences to defendants who acted in self-defense. Respondents were presented with a scenario of a crime and then asked to make liability judgments. For example, did the defendant in the following scenario act in self-defense?

> Paul works in the city and legally carries a gun for his own protection. One night while he is walking down a deserted city street on his way back home, a man jumps out of an alley attacking Paul with a knife. Paul notices that the man is limping and he realizes that he can easily run the half block to his house and be completely safe from his attacker, but instead he pulls his gun and kills the man. (Robinson and Darley, p. 240)

The criminal law would hold Paul responsible for murder because he could easily have avoided the danger. The public, however, has a rather different view that is more sympathetic to the defendant. Though the majority of the public (60 percent) endorse the "retreat" rule, they do not support the punishment called for by the law. The law would require Paul to be sentenced for murder (approximately thirty years in prison) whereas the public assigns an average sentence of 9.6 months in prison. In fact, almost half of the public either assigns no liability or no punishment (Robinson and Darley, 1995). Furthermore, the public would not hold Paul liable for murder if he made a reasonable mistake that he could not safely retreat or if the attack occurred inside his home and he did not retreat. For these two situations, the law also exonerates the defendant (Robinson and Darley, 1995).

The public also agrees with the law that a defendant should be held liable for killing an unarmed attacker. Overall, Robinson's and Darley's study demonstrates that the public agrees with the law's premise that people can defend themselves from attack only with force proportional to that of the attackers. However, the public agrees less with the retreat rule or with the punishment assigned to person's who were faced with provocation from the victim and reacted beyond the legally-defined limits.

Imagine that a teenage boy, named Smith, approaches a man, named Jones, on the subway and demands five dollars. Jones thinks that his life is in danger so he pulls out a gun and kills the boy. After the incident, it is discovered that Jones' fear for his life was not grounded in the objective facts of the situation. He may have perceived a threat to his life, but this perception was unrealistic or unreasonable from an objective perspective. For what types of mistakes will the public accept the subjective factor of the defendant's fear for his or her life? The reasonableness of a mistake becomes less reasonable as objective facts of the context do not support the likelihood of imminent death. Using the story about Smith and Jones, researchers explored public acceptance of the self-defense claim by varying the reasonableness of Jones's belief that he was going to be killed (Finkel *et al.*, 1995).

In the reasonable mistake case, respondents are told that police discovered that Smith had a toy gun. In the dubious mistake case, respondents are told that

> while the teenage still demands five dollars, he does not have a gun in his hand, although he seems to be reaching into his pocket; Mr. Jones fires and kills, and tells the police he thought the kid was going for a gun. Hindsight reveals that the teenager had no weapon, only some note cards saying, 'Thank you for giving to a homeless person.' (Finkel *et al.*, 1995, p. 603)

In the unreasonable mistake version, Smith does not have a gun, does not reach for his pocket, nor make any sudden movements; thus, Jones' perception that his life is threatened is not supported by the circumstances of the case. In the delusional mistake version, Smith is sitting across from Jones on a subway occasionally looking at him and stabbing a pencil into a newspaper. Jones draws a gun and kills him. He tells police that the looks and pencils stabs were warnings that the boy was going to kill him.

Finkel and colleagues (1995) examined the extent to which people would accept the defendant's self-defense claim and acquit him of the voluntary manslaughter charge. They found that over three-quarters of the respondents acquitted the defendant when the mistake was reasonable, only one-quarter acquitted him when the mistake was dubious. Only 4 percent acquitted him when the mistake was unreasonable, and nobody acquitted him when the mistake was delusional. Whether the mistake is objectively grounded determines the success of the self-defense claim, which is consistent with the reasonable person standard.

Battered Women and the Law

The issue of wife assault provides an interesting application of the self-defense defense. Expert testimony on the battered woman syndrome attempts to widen the narrow standard of objective reasonableness to include past history (over many years, in some cases) and the subjective perception of threat from the defendant's point of view. It connects the woman's past history of abuse to the perception of an enhanced threat to what an objective reasonable person, who lacks the history of abuse that the victim has suffer, may see as non-threatening or may see as threats given ample time to leave. For example, an abusive husband may state, "I am going to kill you when I wake up from my nap." Many people may wonder why the battered woman would not simply leave the house instead of resorting to the extreme step of killing her husband. Perhaps they fail to realize that the battered woman has attempted to flee several times only to be tracked down by her abuser and be severely beaten. Accordingly she sees real and imminent danger.

The objective "reasonable" person standard looks at the immediate situation outside the context of the prior abuse, while the subjective standard requires that we also consider the defendant's perspective. Should we use the reasonable person's perspective (an objective test) or view the threat of danger from the defendant's perspective and background (a subjective test)? The objective standard is used in most states, but some states have adopted the subjective perspective. Do community members support such defendants' right to claim self-defense, and what criteria do they use in making decisions about whether a specific defendant acted in self-defense?

Finkel, Meister and Lightfoot (1991) addressed these issues in an experiment which asked students to make judgments about the guilt of three accused persons: a woman who had killed her abusive husband, a woman who had killed the man who raped her, and a woman who had killed teenage boys on a subway when they attempted to rob her. Students were supportive of the self-defense claim with acquittals based on self-defense ranging from 23 percent for the rape case, 27 percent for the subway case, and 63 percent for the battered woman case. Jurors clearly paid attention to context, and especially to the past history of abuse in the battered woman case. In this case, subjective criteria such as the use of past history to see self-defense through the battered woman's eyes, played an important role; the high acquittal rate may also reflect the public's ambivalence about the requirement to retreat. In the rape and subway cases, where past history was absent, jurors made verdict distinctions based in part on objective indicators of harm, namely whether the person had a weapon or threatened force, and whether the killing occurred during the encounter, three hours later, or one month later.

Though expert testimony did not have a direct effect on verdicts, it did change jurors' perceptions of the victim—victims were seen as having

> less capacity for responsible choices and as being more distorted in their thinking and less culpable for her actions... Advocates of the self-defense defense (cites omitted) may indeed have a legitimate concern about the direction expert testimony is taking in battered women who kill cases. (Finkel *et al.*, 1991, p. 598)

Expert testimony appears to shift jurors' concern to the victim's mental state leading to a portrait of a "mentally unstable" individual, but does not lead jurors to believe that the self-defense mitigates her actions.

The examples discussed so far have dealt with the use of force in response to a threat of physical violence. What about threats to a person's property? How do the law and public opinion relate in terms of using force to protect property? Here too, the public favor restrictions on a person's actions. Robinson and Darley (1995) used a series of scenarios in which a man uses force to prevent the theft of his motorcycle. The public were willing to countenance the use of force even when that force was not necessary to prevent the theft. However, they were not willing to acquit a man who killed in order to protect his property from theft. Still, even in this situation, the public assigned punishments that were considerably more lenient than the maximum sentence allowed by the law. Finally, it is important to note that this was an American study. Americans may be more tolerant of this kind of behavior in light of their libertarian traditions and their constitutional right to bear arms.

Not Guilty But Insane

In Chapter 3, we reviewed the discrepancy between public knowledge of the insanity defense, and the way the defense actually functions. Despite the public's misperception about the abuse of the insanity defense, most individuals believe that the insanity defense is justified in some cases (Silver, Cirincione, and Steadman, 1994). When the insanity defense is employed, the fact that the defendant committed the crime is not challenged, but the defendant's mental state at the time of the crime is challenged. The defendant must prove beyond a reasonable doubt that he or she was insane at the time of the crime.

Jurisdictions differ on how they define insanity. Two major distinctions capture the important differences between insanity definitions: (1) whether the defendant was completely impaired or had substantial impairment; and

(2) whether the impairment was one of conduct or one of cognition (Bailis, Darley, Waxman, and Robinson, 1994). For example, the *Model Penal Code* of the American Law Institute, which is used in over half the states, requires that a defendant be sufficiently impaired either to be unable to conform his or her conduct to the law or to understand the criminality of his/her actions. The Model Penal Code requires substantial impairment of conduct or cognitive awareness, but not both. Other definitions such as the Irresistible Impulse Test (which focuses only on impairment of conduct) and the M'Naghten Rule (which focuses only on impairment of cognition) require complete impairment, and thus are more stringent requirements than the Model Penal Code (Bailis, Darley *et al.*, 1994). Research demonstrates that members of the public can and do make the distinction between a cognitive impairment and a conduct impairment (Robinson and Darley, 1995).

What type of legal definition of insanity does the public favor? Bailis, Darley and colleagues (1994) examined this question using a convenience sample of undergraduates and case scenarios that varied only legally relevant information. Respondents were more willing to impose civil commitment and less willing to assign criminal liability when defendants could not conform their behavior to the law than when they did not understand that what they were doing was wrong. Conduct impairment, then was somewhat more important than cognitive impairment, though both were considered in the decisions.

These researchers conducted a second study to extend their findings to cases which contain irrelevant information and expert testimony about the medical diagnosis of the defendant (e.g., paranoid schizophrenia). In this study, respondents also focused on both conduct and cognitive impairment in their decisions, but here also, respondents assigned more importance to conduct impairment than to cognitive impairment in their decisions. Like the Model Penal Code, respondents used both dimensions. Whereas the Model Penal Code requires defendants to prove that they were either cognitively impaired or behaviorally impaired, respondents assigned less criminal responsibility when defendants had *both* conduct and cognitive impairment. Thus, respondents were more conservative than the requirements of the Model Penal Code's definition.

This research then suggests that public views are *not* drastically different from the most prevalent definition of insanity or from the distinctions (cognitive and conduct impairment) made in insanity definitions. The gap between the views of the public and the criminal justice system would appear to involve the administration rather than the nature of the definition of insanity. The public do not oppose the concept, they just believe that it is frequently invoked. And in this perception, as we noted in Chapter 3, they are mistaken.

Defining insanity is one thing. Ensuring that the legal definition is consistently applied is quite another. Over the years, legislators have changed the definition of insanity to ensure that certain kinds of defendants are (or are not) able to use the defense (Finkel, 1991). Since it is a jury that decides whether a particular case meets the criteria for a successful plea of insanity, an important area of research has examined simulated jurors' reactions to different definitions of insanity. If juries are working properly, different definitions of insanity will generate different verdicts. A particular set of facts will give rise to a successful plea under some definitions, but not others. However, research has demonstrated that the verdicts of jurors do *not* vary when different definitions are provided (e.g., Finkel and Handel, 1988; Finkel, Shaw, Bercaw and Koch, 1985; Simon, 1967). Research has shown that jurors understand the differences, but tend to ignore them when arriving at a verdict. Other variables seem to be more important to members of the public. For example, the public are more likely to acquit a defendant by reason of insanity in cases of minor crimes like shoplifting than the most serious crime of murder. (Bailis, Darley *et al.*, 1994). This may have to do with intuitive notions about the amount of premeditation involved. The planned and deliberate taking of life may seem too rational to be carried out by anyone other than a calculating, sane person. On the other hand, a less serious, impulsive act may fall more easily into the realm of mental illness.

Evaluations of Police Competence

In overall ratings of the quality of police performance, African-Americans have more negative views than other ethnic groups (Haung and Vaughn, 1996; Magarita and Parisi, 1979; Newsday Crime Survey, 1989; Skogan, 1978). African-Americans' discontent is not about how well the police prevent crime because just over half in all ethnic groups believe that the police are doing a good or excellent job in this respect. Research also finds that middle class African-Americans and Caucasians have similar views about the quality of police protection (Apple and O'Brien, 1983). African-Americans, however, are less satisfied with police efforts at solving crimes than are Hispanic-Americans and Caucasians-Americans.

Surveys conducted in thirteen cities show that the public's evaluations of police performance vary widely from city to city in the United States (Skogan, 1978). Moreover, differences between African-Americans and Caucasians in their evaluations of police performance also vary from city to city. As Skogan (1978) notes, "To be black and live in Cleveland means to share with whites perceptions of low levels of service. In Chicago, Los Angeles and Philadelphia, on the other hand, blacks perceive relatively low levels of service while whites are quite satisfied with what they receive" (p. 477).

In addition to the overall evaluation of police performance, a limited number of studies have examined public evaluations of police performance for specific tasks. Data from the British Crime Survey are instructive in this regard. The 1992 British Crime Survey asked respondents about an array of police functions. The majority of respondents thought the police were doing a good job at dealing with crowds at public events, handling serious motoring offenses, and responding to accidents and medical emergencies. Respondents indicated that the British police were doing an average job at keeping traffic moving, handling drunken behavior, and detecting and arresting people involved in violent crime. Police were perceived as doing a poor job at routine patrolling and controlling burglary offenses (Skogan, 1996).

The 1995 National Opinion Survey on Crime and Justice asked a series of seven questions about the police (Huang and Vaughn, 1996). Generally speaking, evaluations of the police were positive. Attitudes toward the police were most positive when the question dealt with their friendliness (84 percent held favorable attitudes), and most negative (53 percent held favorable attitudes) when the question dealt with the use of force. Three quarters of the national sample held favorable attitudes to the police when asked to rate the ability of the police to solve crimes or protect the public from crime (Huang and Vaughn, 1996).

Survey data from Ohio provide additional information about public perceptions of police performance in different roles (Bishop, 1992). Over 60 percent of the respondents believed that the police were doing an "excellent" or "good" job at responding quickly to calls, and working with the school on drug education. Half of the respondents thought the police were doing an "excellent" or "good" job at working with neighborhoods to respond to their needs and preventing gang violence in Cincinnati, and only a small percentage of respondents (less than 14 percent) thought police were doing a "poor" job in these areas. In two areas, the majority of respondents indicated that police performance could be better. Over 60 percent of respondents indicated that the police were doing a "fair" or "poor" job in fighting the drug problem, and in investigating citizen complaints against police officers. One-fourth of the respondents indicated that the police were doing a "poor" job at investigating citizens' complaints against the police, with younger African-American adults living in low income households more likely to indicate fair or poor. Younger adults, African-Americans, and those living in low income households also were more dissatisfied with police performance in all areas.

In the following sections, we examine citizens' views about the competence of female police officers, the priorities that police officers should have, and their perceptions of police use of force. We conclude our discussion of police decisions with a discussion of public perceptions about the prevalence of inequitable outcomes by the police and courts.

Evaluations of Women Police Officers

On 12 September 1910, Alice Stebbins Wells of the Los Angeles Police Department became the first woman police officer. The humiliations began on her appointment. Showing her badge to obtain a free ride on a streetcar, she was accused of misusing her husband's. Despite her uniform, the public was reluctant to accept that she had any powers: the idea of police women had been a joke in comic weeklies since the 1850's. (Linda Grant, Independent on Sunday, 9/9/90, p. 23; as cited in Walklate, 1992)

Do stereotypes about gender roles still hamper the public acceptance of women police officers? Research in the 1970s and 80s suggests that the majority of the public accepts women police officers and perceives them as being as competent as men in performing most (but not all) police duties. A 1975 survey of residents in a midwest city clarifies further whether the public perceives women to be as competent as men in performing duties of a police officer (Kerber, Andes, and Mittler, 1977). Over half of the sample had no preference in terms of whether men and women officers handled most situations. However, a significant minority (38 percent) preferred male officers. When the public perceives a difference in competence between men and women officers, this reflects stereotypes about gender roles: Men are perceived as stronger and more aggressive and therefore better able to handle fights, whereas women are seen as more nurturing and therefore better at responding to young children and rape victims.

In addition, men were more likely to judge women officers as more competent in these traditional female roles than were women. The influence of gender stereotypes extends to how references for job candidates describe their candidates' characteristics. An analysis of the content of reference letters revealed that "level-headed" was used to describe male candidates more often than female candidates. Intelligence and a sense of humor were qualities attributed only to male candidates whereas good moral values, dedicated, and reliable were qualities attributed only to female candidates (Walklate, 1992). These different images of men and women in reference letters suggest that gender stereotypes affect both the public image of women officers and the departments' image of officers.

Gender stereotypes may also contribute to the ambivalence in public perceptions of the competence of police women to patrol in a squad car and to answer calls for assistance. These areas generated the most disagreement among respondents in a survey conducted in the 1970s (Kerber, Andes, and

Mittler, 1977). For patrolling in a squad car, 55 percent believed that men were more competent while 42 percent believed that men and women were equally competent. For answering calls for personal assistance, 45 percent believed men were more competent than women whereas 49 percent believed men and women were equally competent. In summary, the public clearly was skeptical of women's ability to handle violent situations, and was divided on the ability of female police officers to handle routine police work such as patrolling and answering calls for assistance.

Senior citizens were overwhelmingly skeptical of women's ability to answer calls for assistance or patrolling, with only 17 percent indicating that women and men were equally competent to handle calls or patrol neighborhoods. As with other stereotypes in criminal justice, education also was strongly related to public perceptions. About half of high school educated or college educated respondents indicated that men and women are equally competent at patrolling or answering calls whereas only 23 percent of respondents without a high school education perceived equal competence. Since these data were gathered over twenty years ago, it is not clear whether stereotypes of female police officers persist to this day.

Public and Police Views Regarding Police Priorities

In an earlier chapter, we reviewed the research on public versus police perceptions of crime seriousness. A related question concerns perceptions of what constitutes a priority for the criminal justice system. If the police priorities do not coincide with the priorities of the public, then the latter are going to be dissatisfied with police service.

Domestic violence has recently received much societal attention and the public has begun to recognize it as a social problem. How does the public want police officers to handle domestic violence cases? A survey in 1987 provides some preliminary findings (Breci and Murphy, 1992). Over half of the respondents thought that the police acting as a service provider was more important than the police role of enforcing the law. Although they wanted police to place service first, half of the respondents said that the police see their role as an authority figure who is there to enforce the law. Men and women agreed about the role of the police, but victims of domestic violence more strongly endorsed law enforcement over service than did respondents who had not been victimized. A survey of police officers found that the officers believed the public wanted them to enforce the law (Breci, 1987).

Although the officers' perceptions are inconsistent with the desires of respondents who have not been victimized, they are quite consistent with the views of actual victims. Stalans (1996) asked people to read a detailed story about a domestic violence situation involving moderately severe injuries and to indicate how they believed the police and courts should handle the situation. She found that the majority of respondents wanted the police to refer the couple to marriage counseling and preferred a guilty verdict coupled with counseling from the court system. Respondents' preferences for these services are based primarily on beliefs about the efficacy of different procedures at reducing conflict and protecting the victim's safety, and are concerned less with retributive justice or the blameworthiness of the offender. This research also found that victims of domestic violence place more importance on the efficiency of the strategy at reducing further violence than on the fairness of the strategy. Certainly, victims have more experience with domestic violence and are more affected by it, thus their views should matter more than the perceptions of the general public whose opinion is not based on direct experience.

Skogan (1996) reviewed the national and regional surveys which asked Britons about their perceptions of police performance and the priorities that the police should have. His review provides important data on public perceptions in this area, which we will now summarize. In several surveys, respondents were provided with a list of police activities and asked to choose five that should be priorities for the police. Skogan noted that the public in England places a very high priority on foot patrol, but a very low priority on officers patrolling areas in their cars, and only an intermediate level of priority on giving crime prevention advice or helping victims. In every jurisdiction, foot patrol "was ranked above responding quickly to calls, and, except nationally above investigating crime and detecting and arresting offenders" (p. 430). Respondents also assigned a high priority to "getting to know local people." Respondents may place priority on foot patrol because they believe it allows officers to be acquainted with the local people, to respond quickly to calls, and to detect and arrest offenders. This perception of the latter two functions, however, is erroneous. Skogan (1996) notes that foot patrol is expensive, competes for funding with other staffing priorities (such as responding quickly to emergency calls), and does not help officers make arrests or clear up crimes.

High-Speed Pursuit Policies

The police occasionally conduct high-speed pursuits in busy urban centers. There is consequently a risk to members of the public, the police as well as the suspect. High speed pursuits have both benefits and costs. One clear benefit is that the suspect may not get away, and additional criminal activity may be prevented. A high cost, however, is the probability that the police, suspect or a bystander could be killed or badly injured in the event that a driver loses control of a car. Consider the following situation:

> There is light traffic on a four lane (not divided) highway. A police officer notices that a car's tailpipe is hanging and may drop off. The car is going at a normal rate of speed. The officer decides to warn the driver that he'd better do something about the tailpipe before he loses it. The officer pulls up behind him and when the driver seems to notice him the officer points to the shoulder. The driver seems to glance at the rear view mirror a few times, looks around from side to side, but continues on. The officer puts the police flashers on and gives him a brief blast of the siren. The driver starts to slow down, but then makes an abrupt turn onto a side road and begins to speed away. (Homant and Kennedy, 1994, p. 431)

Should police officers engage in a high speed pursuit in this situation? This question was posed to a sample of Detroit residents as well as to the police officers employed in their area.[3] A comparison of public and police preferences indicates that "police are more inclined to pursue than the citizens think they are…, and certainly more inclined to pursue than citizens think they should be" (Homant and Kennedy, 1994, p. 431). The majority of the public favored pursuit in this situation, but the police officers were even more in favor of pursuit.

Respondents also were given five policy options on police pursuits that the police department could adopt. The policy options ranged from the least restrictive to most restrictive in terms of the officers' judgment. The least restrictive option was "pure judgment" where officers are given wide discretion and are only cautioned against creating unreasonable danger to the public. The most restrictive option was "pursuit discouraged." According to this policy, officers are told that pursuits are to be avoided except as a last resort to prevent the escape of a dangerous felon. The "limited judgment" policy is where officers are given a detailed list of things to consider before engaging in pursuit and are made aware that they may have to justify their decisions. The policy, however, supports pursuits as long as the risks do not outweigh the benefits. Overall, citizens perceived the existing policy as too permissive and were in favor of tightening restrictions whereas the police perceived the existing policy as too restrictive and were in favor of loosening restrictions. This difference between the public and the police may arise because officers place more importance on fighting crime whereas citizens place more importance on public safety. Or it may reflect differences in perceptions of the actual risks posed to the public by high speed chases.

When Should Police Officers Use Force?

When should the police use physical force against suspects? According to the public, only a limited number of circumstances can justify the use of force by the police. For example, in a national survey conducted in 1980, three-quarters of the sample approved of an officer striking a person if the person was attempting to escape from custody. If the person was attacking the officer with his fists, almost all respondents approved (Williams, Thomas, and Singh, 1983). By contrast, very few (only 8 percent) approved of an officer striking a person if the person was being questioned as a suspect (even in a murder case) or if the person had simply said obscene things to officers (13 percent approved).

The General Social Science Survey has asked about these same situations throughout the 1973 to 1993 period. Opinions have varied more between situations than over time (Flanagan and Vaughn, 1995). For situations involving self-defense, the overwhelming majority of persons support the use of police force. For the less serious situations, people with different demographic characteristics disagreed (Flanagan and Vaughn, 1995). Overall, race divides public opinion, with African-Americans less likely than Caucasians to support the use of force (Williams, Thomas, and Singh, 1983). For escape from custody, support for the use of force varies by demographic characteristics. For example, in 1991, 73 percent of Caucasian-Americans approved of police officers striking a person who was attempting to escape custody whereas only 50 percent of African-American approved of physical force. Persons with lower incomes, those with only a grade school education, and Democrats were less likely to approve of police use of force to stop a fleeing suspect.

Public Perceives Discriminatory Decisions

For several decades, the public's dissatisfaction with the police and the courts has centered around perceptions that police and courts give more favorable decisions to the wealthy and to Caucasian Americans. In a review of research conducted in the 1960s and 70s, Sarat (1977) notes that the perception of unequal justice is one of the most pervasive in the United States. Similar results emerge from national surveys in Canada, Great Britain, France, and Germany (see Roberts, 1992). For example, Brillon, Louis-Guerin, and Lamarche (1984) found that most Canadians agreed with the statement that: "Justice favors the rich over the poor." A 1995 nation-wide survey of Americans found that 57 percent believed that the differential treatment of the poor by the courts was a problem, and African-Americans and Hispanics were more likely to hold this view (Myers, 1996).

Perceptions of favorable treatment of the wealthy, moreover, may shape attitudes toward the police. For example, Albrecht and Green (1977) found that those who hold the least favorable attitudes toward the police also believe that the legal system favors the wealthy. As they noted "negativism toward the police appears clearly connected with cynicism concerning equal justice for all citizens" (p. 77).

People also tend to believe that criminal justice officials discriminate against ethnic minorities. For example, a nationwide sample of Americans in 1993 were asked, "Do you think the American justice system is biased against black people?" Not surprisingly, two-thirds of African-Americans (but only one-third of Caucasian-Americans responded "yes." A nationwide survey in Anerica found similar results: 72 percent of African-Americans, 67 percent of Hispanics but only 35 percent of Caucasians believed that differential treatment of minorities was a problem in the courts (Myers, 1996). Table 8.1 summarizes several recent polls in the 1990s that have addressed police treatment of ethnic minorities. In all these polls, a substantial majority of the African-Americans (65 to 78 percent) believed that the police were tougher on African-Americans whereas between 24 to 58 percent of the Caucasian-Americans and Hispanic-Americans held this belief.[4]

There is more geographical variation in the perceptions of Caucasians and Hispanics. Whereas wide disagreement exists between African-Americans and Hispanics about unequal treatment to African-Americans, only slight differences exist between Hispanics and Caucasians across the surveys. The majority of African-Americans in the L. A. Times Polls (65 percent) perceived the police to be tougher on Hispanics than on Whites, whereas less than half of the Hispanics (47 percent) and one-third of the Caucasians held this belief. Moreover, 66 percent of African-Americans believe that the American criminal justice system is biased against black people whereas 59 percent of Caucasians believe that it is not biased (Saad and McAneny, 1995).

These beliefs are shared by respondents in other countries as well. For example, a survey conducted in Toronto, Canada found that over half the black residents expressed the view that judicial system did not treat black and white persons in the same way. In fact, this view was also shared by over one-third of white respondents as well (Commission on Systemic Racism in the Ontario Criminal Justice System, 1995).

The belief that the criminal justice system is unfair can also influence perceptions of the credibility of witnesses. In the O.J. Simpson case,

TABLE 8.1 Perceptions of Police Treatment of African-Americans and Caucasian-Americans[a]

Sample	Caucasian American[b]	Hispanic American	African American
Nationwide Gallup Poll 1993	35%	NA	74%
Nationwide Newsweek Poll 1992	46%	NA	75%
Los Angeles residents 1990	24%	33%	65%
New York City residents 1987	42%	58%	78%
New York City residents 1985	38%	49%	77%

[a]Respondents were asked the following question: "Compared with whites charged with crimes, are black people charged with crimes treated more harshly or more leniently, or are blacks and whites treated about the same in this country's justice system?"

[b]Percentages are those who indicated "tougher on blacks" to the question: "Are police tougher on whites, treat black and whites equal, or tougher on blacks?"

individuals from different racial backgrounds disagreed about the honesty of L.A.P.D. officer, Mark Fuhrman. A poll in March of 1995 asked respondents whether they believed Mark Fuhrman had actually found the incriminating glove on Simpson's property or whether the detective had planted it there himself. Fifty-eight percent of African-Americans (but only 18 percent of Caucasian-Americans) believed Furhman had planted it. Respondents were also asked, "Do you think the police and prosecutors would have worked as hard on the case as they have if the murder victims have been black rather than white, or would they not have worked as hard?" Race of the respondent was again related to their perception: Two-thirds of African-Americans said 'would not have' whereas only one-third of Caucasian Americans gave this response.

Conclusions

According to the consensual model of how the system administers justice, the decisions of legislators, police officers, and judges should reflect public desires. The Consensual model receives support in some areas of self-defense law, the insanity defense, and the seriousness of violent crimes. The public supports the reasonable person standard of self-defense in cases where defendants mistakenly perceive a threat on their life. Consistent with the law, the public acquits defendants who make reasonable mistakes, but holds defendants responsible when they make dubious, unreasonable, or delusional mistakes about threats on their lives. The public also agrees with the law that people may legally use deadly force within their home to protect themselves from intruders. Both the law and the public believe that a defendant should be held liable for killing an unarmed attacker. The public and the law also support holding people liable for the use of deadly force in the protection of their property rather than their person. The public also makes the distinctions of cognitive and conduct impairment made in statutory definitions of insanity, but are slightly more conservative than the Model Penal Code.

Contrary to the Consensual model, the public expresses different preferences from the current administration of justice for certain types of cases. The public requires defendants to prove that they did not intend to steal. Different countries and states have assigned different importance to the defendant's subjective state of mind—many require that the prosecution prove beyond a reasonable doubt that the defendant committed the crime whereas some allow the court to assume that the defendant intended to commit a theft if stolen goods are in his/her possession. The public thus often places the burden on the defendant to prove that he or she did not intend to steal whereas the law often places the burden of proving the defendant's intent on the prosecution. The public believes white collar crime and drunk driving are more serious than the police do, but for many other crimes the public is more lenient than the law.

The law assigns responsibility to persons attempting murder or robbery much sooner than the public desires. In their assignments of responsibility for both attempt crimes and impossible acts the public place more importance on the potential for objective harm whereas the Model Penal Code definition of attempt crimes places more importance on the intent of the defendant. The public also is less harsh than the law in self-defense cases. The public wants a less severe sentence than that prescribed by the law. People are less supportive of high speed pursuits than are police officers because the public emphasizes public safety whereas police officers emphasize the importance of apprehending a suspect.

The Consensual model assumes that people from different gender, social class, and ethnic backgrounds agree on what is important and receive similar treatment from the criminal justice system. Clearly, research shows that people from different backgrounds perceive the administration of justice differently. The majority of the public believes that the rich receive more favorable decisions than the poor. The majority of African-Americans also believe that the police and courts discriminate against African-Americans whereas less than one-third of Caucasians perceive that African-Americans receive harsher treatments. The majority of Caucasians and Hispanics believe that the police are doing a good to excellent job, but many African-Americans disagree. Whether people from different racial backgrounds agree about police competence, however, varies from city to city. People with different educational backgrounds and from different generations disagree about the competence of women police officers to perform patrol duties and to handle violent situations. Research shows that both men and women from different racial backgrounds want the police to refer couples to counseling for domestic violence; however, people who have actually experienced domestic violence want the police and court to choose strategies which will protect them from further harm.

In much of the research comparing public standards to the law, researchers have not examined whether people from different backgrounds hold similar views. Darley, Sanderson, and LaMantia (1996) have found that respondents who emphasize crime control give more weight to the defendant's intent in their definition of an attempt crime than do respondents who emphasize due process. Future research on the demographic, attitudinal, and situational determinants of the relative weight assigned to objective and subjective factors of crime can begin to provide legislators with needed information about the amount of consensus concerning the priority of these values. The research reviewed in this chapter shows wide disagreement between groups in society about the administration of justice, but has largely not addressed whether the public places the same importance on subjective and objective features of acts in their definitions of crimes and in their judgments of self-defense and the insanity defense.

Notes

1. In Canada, legislation proposed in the province of Manitoba in 1996 would go even further, holding parents financially responsible for property crimes committed by their children (see Roberts, 1996).

2. "Potential harm done" can be considered either a subjective or objective factor. It is a subjective factor because decisionmakers must engage in projecting the outcome under a series of "what if" things worked out differently (Finkel *et al.*, 1995). For example, in the case where the person forgot the bullets, the

decisionmakers must ask what would have happened if the person had remembered the bullets. The answer, of course, is that the victim would be dead. Potential harm, however, is also an objective factor because it is so closely related to the actual results of the crime. We classify "potential harm" as an objective factor because it focuses on the guilty act and the potential result.

3. The response rate for the sample of citizens was 40 percent, which is very low and raises questions about the generalizability of the findings to the larger population. These findings clearly cannot generalize to the opinions of ethnic minority members because the sample contains only four ethnic minorities. The findings, however, do provide interesting trends that can be pursued in future research.

4. Political beliefs may explain part of the reluctance of Hispanic Americans to endorse the view that African-Americans receive tougher treatment in Los Angeles. For this question, only 18 percent of the Republicans compared to 38 percent of the Democrats indicated that the police were tougher on African-Americans; this suggestion is tentative because other alternative explanations could not be examined.

9

The Adversarial System and the Institution of the Jury

Once a defendant is accused of a crime, how should the criminal justice system gather evidence to make a decision about the guilt of the defendant? How does the public want the court to handle the investigation and determination of guilt or innocence? Do they favor a system in which all participants cooperate to find out what happened or do they prefer an adversarial system where actors compete and through this competition the truth about what actually happened emerges? And who should be the decisionmaker—lay people or professionally trained judges? If judges, should they be appointed by the state or elected by the people? The answers to these questions, from a perspective of a consensual model of the administration of justice, require attention to public opinion research.

In this chapter, we review the research on public opinion about their preferences for handling criminal cases. We also review public opinion research on the performance of the jury and the necessity for jury trials. The concept of trial by jury has a long history in European countries and the United States. Jury trials allow lay people to have a direct influence over the outcome of a criminal case. Despite this long tradition, some scholars and professionals criticize the institution of the jury and the role that it plays in our justice system. Critics argue that juries (composed of laypersons) are less likely than professionally-trained judges to arrive at accurate and fair verdicts. Does the public support the jury system or do they side with these critics who call for the limitation of the jury's role in the criminal justice system? This chapter addresses these questions.

Desired Procedures to Resolve
Disputes and Their Accuracy

Many different forums exist to handle disputes, including those constituting crimes. For example, a crime can be handled through plea bargaining, through adjudication at a jury trial, through a mediation session, or by means of informal reprimands or warnings. How do people prefer to handle their disputes, and which forums produce more accurate findings about what actually happened? This section examines public perceptions about different procedural forums for handling disputes, and compares it to research on the amount of bias in different forums.

Preferences for Adversarial and Inquisitorial Procedures

We begin by summarizing the results of research on procedural justice. Thibaut and Walker (1975, 1978) initiated an important line of research on the nature of different dispute resolution procedures. This research includes public perceptions regarding which procedures were fairer than others for resolving certain disputes. Two alternate methods of inquiry are predominately used to handle criminal cases, the inquisitorial system, and the adversarial system. In an inquisitorial system, like the one used in European countries such as France, there is one attorney who is court appointed and assists the judge in investigating the case and presenting the evidence for both sides. Attorneys in the inquisitorial system are neutral and are not advocates for either side. In contrast to this, the adversarial system employs two attorneys representing each side of the dispute. The prosecutor serves as an advocate for the state's position and the defense attorney represents the defendant. The adversarial system is based on the premise that competition will motivate both attorneys to conduct a thorough investigation, which will result in a more thorough and unbiased presentation of the evidence.

Advocates of the adversarial system assert that the lack of competition in the inquisitorial system may produce a less thorough investigation of the case than that which occurs in the adversarial system. Research has tested this assertion. Lind, Thibaut and Walker (1973) assigned law students to either the role of adversarial attorney or the role of inquisitorial attorney. To motivate the students to take their task seriously, the law students were told that undergraduate students were involved in the case as disputants and decisionmakers and that the outcome had real consequences. The law students also had a personal incentive to take the task seriously: They were informed that the magnitude of their payment would depend on how well they performed the task. In addition, the researchers varied the strength of the case against the client: Either 25, 50, or 75 percent of the evidence supported their client.

To test whether the adversarial system produced a more thorough investigation than the inquisitorial system, researchers required the "attorneys" to buy facts about the case (the cost of which would be subtracted from their eventual payment) and examined whether the number of facts bought varied by the role of the attorney. Adversarial and inquisitorial attorneys did not differ in the number of facts they gathered when the evidence was ambiguous (50 percent in favor of one disputant; 50 percent in favor of the other disputant) or favored the adversarial attorney's client. However, when the evidence was more overwhelming against the adversarial client's position, the adversarial attorney bought a greater number of facts than did the inquisitorial attorney.

The researchers also examined the extent of overall bias in the presentation of facts to the court—whether the facts presented in court reflected the universe of facts which the attorneys had received. Inquisitorial attorneys presented an unbiased presentation of facts for all cases as their role required. The adversarial system, however, produced a distorted presentation of the evidence if the case was more clear (75 percent of the evidence favored one disputant's position), but produced an unbiased presentation of the evidence if the case was ambiguous (50 percent favored one disputant's position and 50 percent favored the other disputant's position). For the cases where evidence overwhelmingly favored one disputant, the adversarial system overrepresented the amount of evidence that favored the disputant who had more actual facts against her, but the inquisitorial system provided an unbiased presentation of the facts.

What do these findings say about the accuracy of the adversarial and inquisitorial systems? First, the inquisitorial system appears to provide as thorough an investigation and as an accurate presentation of the evidence for ambiguous cases. When the evidence is overwhelming against one disputant, the adversarial system provides a more thorough investigation, but a presentation which distorts the overall array of evidence against the disputant. This finding can be judged both positively and negatively.

The diligent investigation, but distorted presentation could have a positive benefit: "[I]t would assure that a full investigation would be conducted even if the initial evidence seemed, erroneously, to indicate an 'open-and-shut case'" (Lind and Tyler, 1988, p. 25-26). Inquisitorial attorneys, however, did not prematurely stop investigations. Moreover, other researchers have found additional biasing effects of adversarial systems. Witnesses interviewed by adversarial attorneys present the evidence in a biased way that favors the side for which they are testifying. These biases are much less pronounced when witnesses are interviewed by inquisitorial attorneys (see Sheppard and Vidmar, 1980; Vidmar and Laird, 1983).

Despite the potentially inaccurate outcomes which may result from adversarial systems in certain cases, a consensus exists in terms of public opinion. People from the United States, France, Great Britain, and Germany all prefer adversarial procedures more than inquisitorial procedures for handling their disputes (Thibaut, Walker, LaTour, and Houlden, 1974; for a review see Lind and Tyler, 1988; Lind, 1994). Thus, even in countries like France where trials follow an inquisitorial procedures, citizens prefer pure adversarial procedures over the inquisitorial system (Lind and Tyler, 1988). Regardless of whether respondents imagined they were the disadvantaged party or the disputant who had the advantage, they preferred adversarial procedures. The most important perception shaping their preference was the perceived fairness of the process. Even when respondents were unaware of whether they had the advantage or not, respondents assigned most importance to the fairness of the process as compared to their perceptions about the likelihood of receiving a favorable outcome or their perceptions about the amount of control they would have over the decisionmaking (see Thibaut *et al.*, 1974).

This research indicates that public preferences may be out of line with the actual accuracy of adversarial procedures. The public prefers adversarial procedures over inquisitorial procedures because they are seen as more likely to generate a fair process which in turn will lead to a fair outcome. What is less clear is *why* the public believe adversarial justice is more likely to generate a fair outcome. Confidence in the adversarial mode could spring from some innate distrust of state-controlled adjudication. More recent cross-cultural research with United States, Hong Kong, and Germany citizens further validates the importance accorded to procedural fairness in forming preferences, and reveals that people place importance on procedural fairness because they value relationship issues (Lind, 1994). More recent research, however, has expanded the procedural options available to respondents and has found that people prefer initially to handle their disputes through negotiation or persuasion (see Lind, Huo, and Tyler, 1994).

Jury Structure and Public Views of Accuracy and Fairness

The United States Supreme Court has ruled that a six-member jury is constitutional for criminal cases because it meets the requirements of a fair and impartial jury that is representative of the community (*Williams v. Florida*, 1970). However, research which compares six to twelve-member juries suggests that smaller juries are less thorough in their deliberations, are less likely to foster participation from all members, are more likely to pressure minority members to change their vote without changing their opinion about the truth, and are less likely to represent members of minority ethnic groups (for a review see Hans and Vidmar, 1986).

It also is important to know whether a practice is perceived as fair and accurate because these perceptions shape the public's views about the legitimacy of an institution (MacCoun and Tyler, 1988). MacCoun and Tyler (1988) examined public attitudes towards four types of jury structures: (1) a six-member jury which must reach a unanimous verdict; (2) a six-member jury which can acquit or find the defendant guilty if the majority agrees; (3) a twelve-member jury which must reach a unanimous verdict; and (4) a twelve-member jury which can acquit or find the defendant guilty if the majority agrees. Thus there were two variables, the size of the jury (six or twelve members) and the requirement for a decision (majority or unanimity). Public opinion about these four types of juries was assessed for both a trivial offense (i.e., shoplifting) and a very serious offense (i.e., murder).

Overall, respondents indicated the twelve-person unanimous jury was the most expensive, but that the twelve-person unanimous jury was most accurate, thorough, and fair than were the other jury structures. Moreover, the twelve member unanimous jury was seen as most likely to represent minorities, most likely to listen to holdouts, and most likely to minimize bias. Six-member juries with a majority vote were the least likely to be perceived as fair, thorough, or accurate. This concurs with empirical research showing that jurors attempting to argue a minority position participate less and took a less active role in jury deliberations when the jury operated using a majority rule than a unanimous rule. (For a review of empirical research on jury performance under majority rules see Hans and Vidmar, 1986). Given both the perception of less fairness and less thoroughness of jury deliberations under six-member majority rule, it is fortunate that the Supreme Court ruled that six-member juries must reach a unanimous decision (*Burch v. Louisiana*, 1979). Canadians were split on their opinion about whether unanimous verdicts should be required for twelve person juries; however, they were more likely to favor unanimous verdicts after their jury service was completed (Doob, 1979).

The desirability of these jury structures, however, varied by the seriousness of the crime. MacCoun and Tyler (1988) found that only a little over half of the public favored a trial by a judge alone for the crime of shoplifting whereas most respondents favored a jury trial for the crime of murder. If a jury trial was held, 65 percent of the respondents preferred six-member juries for shoplifting with 43 percent favoring a majority rule and 23 percent favoring unanimity. Six-member juries for shoplifting cases were preferred based solely on the perceived thoroughness of deliberation. Most people probably thought shoplifting cases are clear-cut, and the less expensive six-member jury could do as good a job as the twelve-member jury. By contrast, few individuals preferred a six-member jury for a murder case, and the majority preferred the twelve-person unanimous jury. People desired a twelve-person unanimous jury for murder cases based on their procedural fairness, ability to reduce bias, thoroughness of deliberation, the accuracy of the verdict, and the likelihood that jurors would listen to holdouts.

Individuals made these judgments in the abstract without knowing the details of a case and without placing themselves in the role of defendant or victim. Do people form preferences in a similar way when they are the defendants in a specific case? Consider the following case.

> Imagine that you drive your car home from work one day, and a half an hour later your doorbell rings. When you open your door, two police officers inform you that you are under arrest. They handcuff you, read you your rights, and take you to the police station. The police inform you that a hit-and-run accident has taken place, in which a speeding automobile veered across the sidewalk and struck a pedestrian, resulting in a serious spinal injury that could result in permanent paralysis. ... The victim of this accident gave the police a description of the car and the first four digits of its license plate, and the police matched the identification to your car and noted that the location of the accident is near your home. Eventually, the case comes to trial. Although you are certain of your innocence, the prosecutor insists that his evidence identifies you as the culprit. (MacCoun and Tyler, 1986, p. 342)

Which features of the process will determine your preference—the fairness of the process, the thoroughness of deliberation, the accuracy of the verdict, the reduction of bias, the representation of community members and minorities, or the degree that jurors would listen to jurors whose view was in the minority? What kind of jury structure would you want?

In making this decision, people are faced with a trade-off: They know that larger juries are more expensive, but they also believe that larger juries are fairer in that they are more likely to put aside personal biases and to represent the community and minority members. On the other hand, they may believe that a smaller jury will be more likely to listen to a member who has a different view because there are fewer people against the lone holdout. It is a difficult decision, and they cannot see any difference between six-member juries and twelve-member juries on whether they will arrive at a more accurate verdict. In this hit and run case, students in MacCoun's and Tyler's study recognized that larger juries may be fairer, but they also believed that the size of the jury did not affect the accuracy of the verdict. Because they did not see any difference in accuracy, they did not have an overwhelming preference for a specific jury size.

This study demonstrates that both in the abstract and when faced with concrete cases, people try to balance the trade-offs between the cost of the procedure and the extent to which it is accurate and fair. Because this case involved a serious outcome (i.e., someone was physically injured), people generally placed little importance on the cost of the procedure and instead wanted the deliberations to be as thorough as possible to minimize bias. When people imagine being accused of causing less serious damage (i.e., a hit and run accident in which only a rosebush and bicycle were damaged), they placed more importance on the cost of the procedure, and wanted a procedure that would provide an adequate deliberation but at minimal cost.

MacCoun and Tyler (1988), however, found that procedural fairness shaped preferences regardless of the seriousness of the outcome. Both in the abstract and in response to a concrete case, procedural fairness emerged as an important influence on preferences for six versus twelve-member juries. The accuracy of the verdict (i.e., whether guilty persons will be convicted) had an indirect influence on preferences through two perceptions about the process. First, people who perceived that the deliberations would be thorough also perceived a higher likelihood that guilty persons would be convicted. This relationship between accuracy and thoroughness of the process supports a basic premise of procedural justice research: People assume that fair procedures lead to accurate outcomes (Lind and Tyler, 1988; MacCoun and Tyler, 1988).

Related to this point is the second relationship between accuracy and a process feature. Respondents who believed that jury structure was fairer also believed that guilty persons had a higher likelihood of being convicted. In the study asking about preferences regarding jury structures for shoplifting and murder cases, accuracy of verdict was the procedural aspect most strongly related to perceptions of fairness. In the study using detailed stories about hit and run accidents, verdict accuracy significantly predicted perceptions of procedural fairness after controlling for all other procedural features. Thus, to some extent, what is procedurally fair is what will lead to accurate verdicts. Of course, procedural fairness and verdict accuracy are not synonymous; instead they are distinct concepts which are moderately related to one another. These findings, however, clearly indicate that people do care about the accuracy of verdicts and believe that the likelihood of achieving an accurate verdict is related to the thoroughness and fairness of the process.

When people say a twelve-person jury is fairer than a six-member jury for a specific case, what do they mean by "fair?" Similarly, what is the meaning of fairness when people claim a six-member jury is fairer than a twelve-member jury in a less serious case? The research by MacCoun and Tyler (1988) provides only a partial answer to these questions. In the study using hit and run accidents, they found that verdict accuracy, representation of community members, and representation of minority members significantly explained some of the variability in perceptions of procedural fairness. Beyond these three features, aspects of the deliberation quality (i.e., thoroughness, whether they listen to holdouts, and the ability to minimize bias) and the cost of the procedure did not predict procedural fairness. Much of the meaning of procedural fairness was left unexplained by this study. What are some additional features of six versus twelve-member juries that may contribute to perceptions of fairness? Fairness may be related to perceptions of whether the juries will be consistent across similar cases. Individuals may believe that twelve-member juries are more likely to treat like cases alike because members are more likely to have experience with similar types of cases. Procedural fairness also may be related to perceptions of proportional justice—more serious cases deserve more attention and time than do less serious cases.

Fairness and Accuracy of Jury Verdicts

Trial by jury is a cornerstone of criminal justice systems in the United States, Canada, the United Kingdom, and many other countries. Article Three of the U.S. Constitution provides that "the Trial of all crimes, except in cases of Impeachment, shall be by jury." The sixth amendment of the U.S. Constitution guarantees criminal defendants a jury trial. This guarantee is extended to defendants prosecuted in state criminal justice systems through the due process clause of the fourteenth amendment. Based on the Supreme Court's interpretation of the sixth amendment clause, defendants have a right to a jury trial in all cases excepting petty offenses. Though jury trials have a long tradition in the United States, legal professionals and some academic scholars are skeptical of jurors' ability to make fair and accurate decisions (for reviews of these criticisms see Kalven and Zeisel, 1966; Hans and Vidmar, 1986). Some professionals claim that lay people do not have sufficient knowledge of the law to decide a case, and will often make inaccurate and unfair decisions.

Some vivid case examples where juries may have come to the wrong decision support the criticisms aimed at the jury. The 1992 California state trial of four officers accused of using excessive force against Rodney King provides a vivid and shocking example of an acquittal that many Americans thought was an injustice. The officers were videotaped beating Rodney King as he laid on the ground and attempted to protect his head. Before the case went to trial, the eighty-second videotape was broadcast nationwide. Defense attorneys for the police officers were granted a change of venue to Simi valley, a suburb which is primarily white and where many retired police officers live. A jury of ten Caucasians, one Hispanic, and one Asian eventually found the four officers not guilty. The public's reaction to these acquittals was swift and destructive. An hour after the verdicts were announced, Southeast Los Angeles had become a riot zone—stores were burned and looted, rioters threw stones at passing cars, and innocent bystanders were shot and beaten. Unlike the 1960 riots, this riot was not a pure race riot, but a class riot (Duffy, 1992). Poor people from diverse ethnic backgrounds participated, but the riot had racial overtones and perceptions that the verdict represented racial bias fueled the anger (Duffy, 1992).

The riot itself provided graphic evidence that many people believed that the verdict was unjust. Several nationwide polls conducted after the verdict was announced confirmed that most Americans believed that an injustice had occurred. In a nationwide poll conducted in April 1992, the vast majority of both Caucasian and African-Americans (79 percent) indicated that they had expected the officers would be found guilty, and 62 percent of Caucasians and 92 percent of African-Americans said they would have voted to convict (Church, 1992).

These nationwide polls also asked respondents the following question: "Which describes the reason for the jury's not guilty verdict—poor prosecution, good defense, inadequate evidence, loyalty to police or racism?" Clear differences between Caucasian-Americans and African-Americans emerged. Half of the Caucasians chose reasons relating to the trial (i.e., good defense, poor prosecution, inadequate evidence) whereas only 24 percent of African-Americans cited these reasons. Many African-Americans (45 percent) but few Caucasians (12 percent) identified racism as a factor underlying the verdict. Further highlighting the perception of a racial bias, over 80 percent of African-Americans stated that the verdict would have been different if there had been any African-Americans on the jury, if the police and the man they had beaten had all been Caucasian, or if the police had been African-American and the man they had beaten had been Caucasian. Only half of the Caucasians believed it would have been different if the officers and victim had been a different race, and 64 percent of Caucasians believed the verdict would have been different if any African-Americans had been on the jury (Lacayo, 1992).

Perceptions of the verdict in the O.J. Simpson trial for the murder of Nicole Brown Simpson and Ronald Goldman also are divided by race of respondent. Simpson was acquitted of both murders by a mostly African-American jury. Seventy-eight percent of African-Americans compared to 42 percent of the Caucasian-Americans believed that the jury had made the right decision. Caucasians indicated that they were more pessimistic about the criminal justice system after learning about the verdict:

[F]orty-three percent have less confidence in ethics and professionalism of police; 48 percent have less confidence that jurors won't let racial attitudes affect their judgment; and 51 percent have less confidence that defense attorneys won't resort to unethical tactics. (Urschel, 1995, p. 6)

African-Americans' attitudes towards the system were less affected by the verdict.

Do vivid examples such as the verdicts in the Rodney King case and the verdict in the O.J. Simpson case adequately represent the actual competence and accuracy of the jury as a fact finding institution? The research evidence suggests that juries are in fact as competent and fair as judges in their decision-making. In a landmark study, Kalven and Zeisel (1966) compared the verdicts given by juries in actual criminal cases to what judges said they would have given in 3,576 criminal trials across the United States. These researchers found that the jury can understand the evidence and will use the evidence in decisions about guilt. Kalven and Zeisel noted that "contrary to an often voiced suspicion, the jury does by and large understand the facts and get the case straight, [and]… that the jury's decision by and large moves with the weight and direction of the evidence" (p. 149). Judges and juries agreed on the verdict 78 percent of the time, and disagreed 22 percent of the time. When judges and juries disagreed about the verdict, for most of the time judges wanted to convict and juries acquitted the defendant.

What can explain this leniency bias—juries acquit when the judge said they should convict? Incompetence or lack of understanding of the law is not the answer. In fact, whether the evidence was difficult to comprehend was not related to whether they agreed with the judge on the verdict. Jury sympathy for the defendant or prejudice against the victim also has only a small relationship with judge and jury disagreement (accounting for about 3 percent of the cases). Other research both in the United States and Britain finds similar results, which provides additional confidence in the jury's ability (for a review of this research see Hans and Vidmar, 1986; Horowitz and Willging, 1991).

The fact that juries used a more rigorous interpretation of the concept of "beyond a reasonable doubt" than did judges accounted for some of the disagreements. The most important factor, however, was that juries decided to acquit when a verdict of guilt would result in an accurate decision, but an unfair and unjust one according to commonsense notions of justice. When juries do not base decisions on a strict interpretation of the law, but on their sense of justice, these decisions are called jury nullifications. The jury's "departures from the law were limited, and not due to incompetence but rather the jurors' perceptions of what was fair and just" (Hans and Vidmar, 1986, p. 120).

A final explanation for the leniency bias is differences between judges and juries in terms of the burden of proof or the harm of judicial error. If juries have higher thresholds of proof than judges, this would explain why they would acquit more often. The leniency bias does not seem to be explained by the latter explanation. The judicial system can make two kinds of errors: The innocent can be convicted and the guilty can be acquitted.

Traditionally, the legal system has viewed the former mistake as much more serious than the latter. Some jurists write that it is better that ten guilty parties be acquitted than that one innocent defendant be wrongfully convicted. The public are less asymmetric in their views. When asked which of these two judicial errors was worse, respondents were almost equally split (Dowds, 1994). Although we do not have similar data from judges, it is likely that they would regard a false conviction as far more serious in terms of the administration of justice than a false acquittal. However, since this likelihood runs counter to the results of jury-judge comparisons, it cannot explain the leniency bias on the part of jurors.

The jury is perceived by the public as being no less fair than trial by a judge alone. In a survey of randomly selected adults in a midwestern city (MacCoun and Tyler, 1988), almost all respondents (93 percent) preferred a jury trial over a bench trial for murder cases. For shoplifting cases, however, respondents' views were divided: 56 percent preferred a bench trial and 44 percent a jury trial. Most respondents preferred a jury trial if they were a victim of a crime (68 percent) or were accused of a crime (76 percent). The majority of respondents indicated that compared to trial by judge, trial by jury was more accurate, more thorough, more likely to minimize bias, more likely to represent minorities, and also tended to be more expensive. Ninety percent believed that the jury system was fair. These positive procedural features allowed respondents to support the jury system even though they realized it sometimes made mistakes. On average, respondents estimated that 81 percent of the truly guilty offenders are convicted, and 65 percent of the truly innocent accused persons are acquitted.

Surveys of the general public and jurors reveal the deep public attachment to the concept of trial by jury. When the general public were asked about juries, almost nine out of ten respondents supported the continued presence of juries in the criminal justice system (Angus Reid, 1984). A study which measured attitudes of 644 Canadian jurors before and after their jury service found widespread support for the jury system. The majority of Canadians (over 70 percent) believed that the jury was equally or more likely (than a judge) to arrive at a just and fair verdict (Doob, 1979). Most Canadian judges also held a very favorable view of the jury system, and those with the most favorable views also believed that juries were better able to understand and evaluate the evidence, understand the judges' instructions, and were not likely to wrongfully convict a defendant (Doob, 1979). These results are representative of other western nations as well.

Media Publicity and Jury Verdicts

Most criminal cases receive little public or media attention and are settled following a straight guilty plea or a negotiated plea. A small percentage of cases, however, receive a lot of media publicity—so much publicity that few individuals remain unaware of the case. The O.J. Simpson case is of course the best example of such celebrated cases. Most people in the United States were aware of the fact that O.J. Simpson was on trial for the first degree murders of Nicole Brown Simpson and Ronald Goldman. The media released stories about the evidence such as the bloody glove, the weapon, and Simpson's flight in his white truck down the highway before O.J. was charged and before a jury was selected.

A month after the murders but before the trial had begun, a Gallup poll conducted in July 1994 found that 68 percent of Caucasians said Simpson was guilty while an equal percentage of African-Americans believed that he was innocent. A poll conducted in March 1995 found that the distribution of opinions had not substantially changed; African-Americans and Caucasian Americans were still on opposite sides (Saad and McAneny, 1995). These opinions were founded on a biased sample of evidence available before trial, and from these media stories Caucasians and African-Americans managed to draw different conclusions about the innocence of O.J. Simpson. Respondents in a March 1995 Gallup Poll were also asked: "If you were on a jury in a trial, would you be more willing to believe the testimony of a police officer than another witness who is not a police officer?" (Saad and McAneny, 1995, p. 33). Caucasians were more likely to believe the testimony of a police officers (37 percent said yes) than were African-Americans (18 percent said yes). Thus, the jurors who heard O.J.'s case were not "blank slates." Instead they probably had preconceived notions about the credibility of certain witnesses and about the likelihood that Simpson was guilty as charged.

All of these jurors, of course, said that they could set aside their preconceived notions, but is it possible? Can jurors set aside their previous opinions (formed from media stories) and come to a fair and impartial decision based upon the evidence introduced in court? The public themselves are skeptical about this issue. A Gallup Poll conducted in 1994 found that 46 percent of the respondents believed that the jurors cannot be impartial (McAneny and Saad, 1994). While many people are skeptical of *other* people's ability to set aside their previous opinions, the majority of respondents (66 percent) said that *they* personally could set aside their opinions and reach an impartial and fair decision based on the evidence presented. Most people, however, are too optimistic about their ability to set aside opinions formed from pretrial publicity about cases. Both research which examined people's reactions to real cases and experimental research which manipulated the nature of pretrial publicity indicate cause for concern. Jurors and juries who are exposed to incriminating information before the case are more likely to decide the defendant is guilty than are juries and jurors who have not been exposed to incriminating information (Constantini and King, 1980; Moran and Cutler, 1991; Padawer-Singer and Barton, 1975).

The biasing effects of pretrial publicity, moreover, are not reduced by extensive voir dire, jury deliberations, or explicit instructions from the judge to disregard pretrial publicity (Carroll *et al.*, 1986; Kassin and Wrightsman, 1988; Kramer, Kerr and Carroll, 1990). Pretrial publicity is especially biasing when jurors are exposed to gruesome aspects of the crime rather than information linking the defendant to the crime (Kramer *et al.*, 1990). Thus, the public's skepticism about other people's ability to set aside their opinions should be extended to skepticism about their own reactions, especially when the prejudicial information is emotionally arousing.

Jurors' Prejudices and the Efficacy of Judicial Instructions

In an earlier chapter we reviewed research which showed that jurors' expectations about criminal offenses may interfere with their understanding and adherence to judicial instructions (Smith, 1991, 1993). At this point we turn to research which links these expectations to decisions taken as jurors. As we shall see, jurors have difficulty disregarding information when instructed to do so (for a review see Tanford, 1990) and sometimes make unwarranted inferences.

Public Opinion and the Defendant's Dilemma. Do jurors make unwarranted inferences about a defendant's guilt based on her prior criminal history when it is revealed at trial? The impetus for this research comes from research on actual jury decision-making. Kalven and Zeisel (1966) in their classic work found that the conviction rates for accused with a criminal record were 25 percent higher than for first offenders. This alone does not prove that juries' prejudice against defendants with records was responsible. It is possible that the prosecution's case was stronger for the offenders with records, or that the record group contained a higher percentage of individuals who were actually guilty. For this reason, researchers have adopted an experimental approach to the question, in which simulated jurors are randomly assigned to different conditions, thereby eliminating all other possible explanations.

The question of the effects of criminal record returns us to the subject of public perceptions of offenders. As we noted earlier, many members of the public subscribe to an "us and them" view of offenders and non-offenders. As well, they appear to adhere to a principle of "once an offender always an offender." This has been demonstrated in research showing that the public over-estimate recidivism rates (see Chapter 2). More significantly, the public believe (erroneously, as we have seen) that offenders specialize in their criminal activity in the sense that violent offenders will re-commit violent crimes, drug offenders drug crimes and so on. The dangers for defendants with a criminal record should be clear: If previous convictions are entered as evidence (because the defendant takes the stand in his or her own defense), members of the jury are likely to believe that the person is guilty of the current offense.

This prejudice will be particularly strong if the defendant is currently charged with an offense similar to those prior convictions. This may explain why most defendants choose not to testify in court.[1] This approach too, carries a risk for the defendant. Members of the jury may assume that defendants have a long criminal record simply because they have decided not to testify. Thus Kassin (1995) summarizes the research on inferences made about defendants who do not testify in their own defense: "[P]eople are biased against criminal defendants who remain silent, even when they are specifically admonished not to draw negative inferences" (p. 137). In many respects, it is the classic defendant's dilemma.

Of course, if a defendant with a record does take the stand, and his previous convictions come to the attention of the jury, the trial judge will issue a limiting instruction. The jury will be told that the presence of previous convictions does not mean that the defendant is automatically guilty of the crime for which he is now on trial. The jury may only use the defendant's record to evaluate whether he is telling the truth. The state must still prove all the elements of the current crime beyond a reasonable doubt, and the presence of a criminal record should not be used by the jury to form a direct inference of guilt. The research question, then, is two-fold: Are members of the public unduly influenced by the existence of prior convictions, and if so, can the prejudice created by a record be overcome by limiting instructions from the bench? A number of studies have addressed both parts of the question, and the results are far from encouraging for defendants with criminal records.

The research design used in this research involves comparing the conviction rates of different groups of simulated jurors. Members of one group read a description of a case in which a defendant has a prior conviction, while the other group receives the same description of the case, but without any mention of a prior record. The results are quite consistent across a number of studies conducted in both the U.S. and Canada: The presence of previous convictions raises the probability of a guilty verdict. For example, in a study by Hans and Doob (1976), 40 percent of the juries that heard of an accused's criminal record arrived at guilty verdicts, whereas none of the other juries convicted the defendant. It is important to point out that the strength of the evidence was exactly the same in both conditions. The only difference between the scenarios was the presence of a previous conviction.

As noted, the law allows jurors to consider a defendant's previous convictions in order to establish whether he is a reliable witness. In other words, the record may be used to evaluate the defendant's credibility but not to form a direct inference of guilt. Analysis of the juries' deliberations in this research indicated that the jurors made a direct inference of guilt, reasoning that if he had been convicted in the past, he was probably guilty now. Ratings of the defendant's credibility were unaffected, but conviction rates were higher when the defendant had a prior record, and particularly when the priors were similar to the current charge. This finding has emerged in several other studies in Canada (Doob and Kirshenbaum, 1972; Roberts, 1984), England (Cornish and Sealy, 1973) and the United States (Wissler and Saks, 1985).

These results would not be disturbing if it were the case that such prejudices on the part of jurors could be overcome by appropriate judicial instruction. However, one of the most robust findings in the socio-legal research literature is that judicial instructions are ineffective in a number of contexts, including the misuse of information about prior convictions (see Sue, Smith and Caldwell, 1973; Sue, Smith, and Gilbert, 1974; Tanford and Penrod, 1984; Wissler and Saks, 1985). A recent review of this literature concluded:

> A sizeable literature calls into question the effectiveness of limiting or cautionary instructions from the bench as a means of eliminating the effect of legally inadmissable or prejudicial material. For example, instructions to disregard such factors as inadmissable evidence or a prior criminal record seem to do little to reduce bias. In fact in a few studies, instructions designed to remove a bias actually strengthened the bias. (Kramer, Kerr and Carroll, 1990, p. 412)

With such a consensus in terms of findings across different studies in different countries, the lesson for the law is clear. As noted by Wissler and Saks: "A change of the rules to exclude evidence of prior convictions for defendants would protect defendants while not disabling the prosecutor" (1985, p. 47).

Effects of Prior Acquittals. If prior record information has a biasing effect, what about information relating to prior acquittals? The Supreme Court has recently handed down a decision relating to this question. Consider the following case. Robert Dowling was on trial charged with armed bank robbery. In this trial, Vena Henry testified that two weeks after the robbery, Dowling had burglarized her home. She knew this because she had pulled off his ski mask and recognized him. Dowling had been acquitted of the burglary charge and other charges related to the incident involving Henry. This fact was brought out at his trial for bank robbery. After being convicted of armed robbery, Dowling appealed to the Supreme Court on the grounds that Henry's testimony at trial violated the fundamental fairness of the due process clause and violated the double jeopardy clause of the fifth amendment (for a complete description see Greene and Dodge, 1995).

The Supreme Court rejected these claims and held that the prosecution can introduce information about prior acquittals to establish the identity of the offender because this information does not unfairly prejudice the jury against the defendant (*Dowling v. U.S.*, 1990). Critics of this decision contend that jurors will use this evidence to infer that the defendant has a bad character or to infer that he must be found guilty of the current charge so that he will at least be punished for his past bad deeds. However, many defendants have previous acquittals, and these sometimes come to the attention of the jury. Is this information likely to unfairly prejudice members of the jury against the defendant?

The most recent, and careful exploration of this issue was carried out by Greene and Dodge (1995) who asked adults to read a short trial transcript of the Dowling case. In the transcript, Greene and Dodge varied the defendant's history: A witness either testified that Dowling had no prior record, had a prior acquittal for breaking and entering, or had a prior conviction for breaking and entering. Each respondent read and assigned a verdict under one of these three conditions. In addition, half of the sample received limiting instructions as well as instructions on reasonable doubt whereas the other half received instructions only on reasonable doubt. The limiting instructions told jurors how they could use the information about prior record:

> You are to use the evidence of prior conviction (or acquittal) only to the extent it helps in determining the identity of the person who committed the bank robbery in question. If the testimony does not fall into the aforementioned category, it may be disregarded. (Greene and Dodge, 1995, p. 71)

Greene and Dodge found, consistent with a great deal of other research, that the limiting instruction was ineffective in removing the prejudice (for other issues see Kassin and Wrightsman, 1988; Kassin and Saunders, 1990).

Jurors did not leap to unwarranted inferences about acquittals. For defendants with no prior record and those with a prior acquittal, jurors did not differ in their verdicts or in their perceptions of the dangerousness and credibility of the defendant. Consistent with the research described earlier in this chapter, information about prior convictions, however, did create more negative perceptions of the defendant. Greene and Dodge (1995) found that jurors were more likely to convict and perceived the defendant as more dangerous and less credible when they learned of a prior conviction than when they learned of a prior acquittal or no prior record. Overall, the Supreme Court ruling which allows acquittal information to be presented appears to produce no harm to the defendant, but information about prior convictions (which have different evidentiary rules) does create prejudicial perceptions.

Effects of Prior Jury Experience. Some legal professionals have proposed that jurors with prior jury experience should be disqualified from subsequent jury duty. They base this proposal on the assumption that jurors with prior experience are more conviction prone and have attitudes that are more supportive of crime control than the due process rights of individuals. Several studies have investigated the veracity of this assumption. From a review of the literature, Kerr (1981) concluded that the relationship between juror experience and verdict is small but real. Some earlier research, however, did not find a relationship between juror experience and jury verdict (see Dillehay and Neitzel, 1985). Archival studies, conducted after this review, also support the notion that experienced jurors are more prone to convict. Dillehay and Neitzel (1985) found that with larger numbers of experienced jurors on a jury, the jury is more likely to convict. Himelein, Nietzel, and Dillehay (1991) found that more experienced juries gave significantly more severe sentences than did less experienced juries. Thus, prior experience as a juror may also bias effect the decisionmaking of the jury.

Conclusions

People care about the accuracy and fairness of outcomes from adversarial proceedings. Which matters more, the accuracy or the fairness of outcomes? In some situations, an accurate decision will result in an unfair outcome. For example, juries sometimes acquit a technically guilty defendant because to convict would offend jurors' sense of fairness. When a defendant is on trial for murder because she assisted her terminally ill husband in his wish to die, juries often will acquit when judges would follow the letter of the law and convict the defendant. Thus, when accuracy and fairness conflict, people often place fairness above accuracy. Juries, fortunately, do not abuse their power to deliver fair, but unwarranted acquittals (Horowitz, 1991).

People also choose procedures to handle their disputes based more on fairness than the favorability or accuracy of the outcome. The public recognizes the possibility of wrongful acquittals and convictions from twelve-person juries, but still prefer this institution over a bench trial when defendants are charged with serious crimes. Similarly, as we showed in Chapter 8, the public's discontent with the court centers around perceptions of unfair decisionmaking—that the court provides more favorable decisions to wealthy Caucasians. Fairness in decisionmaking matters a great deal.

Clearly, if community sentiment is followed, the jury will remain a central feature of the criminal justice system in America (and elsewhere) for many years to come. The public holds the jury system in high regard, believing it to be a more fair and accurate institution than decision-making by a judge alone. Here public perceptions are consistent with research on the actual performance of juries: Juries and judges generally agree on the verdicts and juries can comprehend the evidence. When juries deviate from the law, it is out of concern for jurors' conceptions of fairness. The susceptibility of juries to media publicity and inability to disregard evidence already presented are basic human problems, which are not easily overcome through professional training. Nor would it appear that they can be corrected by limiting instructions from a judge. As we noted in Chapter 5, judges too, are susceptible to cognitive shortcuts which can bias their decisionmaking. Thus, in many respects, the jury appears to be as competent as the alternative decisionmaker, the judge.

Notes

1. For example, fully three-quarters of accused fail to testify (Federal-Provincial Task Force on Uniform Rules of Evidence, 1982).

10

Sentencing and Parole

In this chapter we turn to the criminal justice issues of greatest interest to members of the public: sentencing and parole. Since these have also generated the largest number of research studies and polls, we know more about the views of the public in this domain than any other. We also deal with this topic at some length because more than any other issue, sentencing has the greatest impact on offenders' lives. When offenders are sentenced to prison, they are frequently deprived of their liberty for long periods of time. And of course, in the United States, convicted offenders are sometimes deprived of their lives. In the next chapter we explore attitudes towards capital punishment in greater depth.

Throughout this book, we have discussed the relationship between the views of the public and the functioning of the criminal justice system. The influence of the public on policy in the area of sentencing and parole should not be under-estimated. Many sentencing commissions and judges are to some degree affected by public pressure to make sentences harsher. The Chairman of the U.S. Federal Sentencing Guidelines Commission has stated that: "Public input has played a pivotal role in the formulation of the sentencing guidelines" (cited in U.S. Department of Justice, 1987). As well, it is in the area of sentencing policy that politicians are most likely to cite support for their policies. A survey of the American public found that four out of five voters stated that they would be more likely to vote for a political candidate who advocates tougher sentencing policies (Hindelang, 1974). There is reason then, to want to pay particular attention to the results of systematic research into public views of sentencing.

Research upon the punishment preferences of the public is far from new. The first empirical study into public attitudes towards punishment was conducted in the U.S. over eighty years ago (Sharp and Otto, 1909). The authors described the state of the knowledge in the following way:

at present we have nothing better at our disposal than abstract and contradictory statements, the outcome of apparently mere impressions. (p. 341)

If the authors were writing today there would be ample reason to revise this evaluation of our knowledge of public attitudes in this area, as we demonstrate throughout the remainder of this chapter.

Public Interest in Sentencing

Why are the public so interested in sentencing and parole? There are several explanations for the keen public attention to these topics. Some of these reasons have to do with the news media. Unlike other areas of criminal justice, sentencing is highly visible. We seldom read about the activities of the police or the prosecutor in a particular case, but the sentence eventually imposed is frequently publicized. The sentencing decision is at the apex of the criminal process, and there is a great deal of media focus on the "result" that emerges. In many ways, sentencing is the bottom line of criminal justice. Whenever we read or hear about a conviction, the principal question of interest to many people is "What did he get?" The sentence frequently attracts as much public interest as the verdict.

When the public think about crime, their thoughts frequently turn to punishment. Indeed, for many people, the criminal justice process can be reduced to an equation in which criminal behavior is matched by judicial punishment. Or, more precisely, *crime* is matched by *time*, for most people consider punishment to consist exclusively of sentences of imprisonment. As noted in an earlier chapter (3) of this book, most people are unaware of sentencing options aside from incarceration. This fact has important consequences for research into public sentencing preferences. The visibility of the sentencing process also means that people become aware of poor decision-making in a way that is not true for earlier stages of the criminal justice system. If a police officer fails to make an arrest when one is warranted, or if a prosecutor accepts an inappropriate plea bargain, we are unlikely to hear about it. Yet if a judge imposes a suspended sentence for a rape conviction, this is far more likely to come to the attention of the public.

Another reason for the public's interest is that sentencing decisions seem very straightforward, and this makes us all expert judges. Although we know little of the mechanics of policing or the kinds of issues that confront a prosecutor, most people feel that intuitively they know what kinds of sentences are appropriate for what kinds of cases. In fact, research has demonstrated that when people react to reports of sentencing decisions, they are usually very confident of their opinions. This was demonstrated in a study conducted a few years ago in Canada.

Members of the public from Canada and the United States[1] were given a number of sentencing stories from the newspapers to read. The stories were not selected in advance. They were just the stories that happened to appear in the newspapers at that time. Afterwards people were asked two simple questions: "Is the sentence reported in the story too harsh, too lenient or about right?" and "How confident are you of your opinion?" As one might expect (in keeping with survey data), the vast majority of people felt that the sentences reported in this selection of stories were too lenient. More interestingly, though, the second question revealed very high levels of confidence. Even though they were evaluating sentences on the basis of minimal amounts of information (the newspaper stories were very brief, typically only a short paragraph), for well over half the stories people indicated that they were very confident of their evaluations of the sentences imposed (Doob and Roberts, 1983).[2] When a judge imposes a sentence, it is often a complex decision which may take into account several sentencing purposes and a number of mitigating and aggravating factors. Little of this information makes its way into the brief newspaper paragraph that eventually reaches the public. And yet people are willing to make fast, confident judgments about the sentence imposed.

The Purposes of Sentencing and Imprisonment

Let us begin our review of research in this area by addressing the most basic question: Why punish? What exactly do the public expect from the sentencing system? Laypersons' sentencing preferences cannot be understood without knowing something about the purposes of sentencing endorsed by the public, and in fact many opinion surveys have explored the purposes of sentencing. There are several sentencing purposes. These include general and specific deterrence, incapacitation, rehabilitation, punishment and doing justice.

One reason for the research interest in this question is that divergences between the courts and the public in terms of punitiveness could be explained by differences between the judiciary and the public in terms of the purposes sentencing is supposed to serve. After all, sentencing purposes determine in large part the nature and quantum of punishment imposed (e.g., Hogarth, 1971; McFatter, 1978; Palys and Divorksi, 1986). As is the case elsewhere in the criminal justice system, theory determines practice: If a judge adopts a rehabilitation-oriented sentencing theory, the sentences that he or she imposes will differ from those imposed by a deterrence-oriented sentencer.

The findings of surveys in this area cannot be easily summarized; there is little consistency across polls or over time. It is not possible, therefore, to say that the public favors one sentencing purpose over *all* the others. Some of this inconsistency can be attributed to the diversity of approach in terms of methodology. Pollsters have frequently elected a "menu-style" approach, in which respondents are allowed to choose a single purpose from a list provided by the interviewer. In other surveys, respondents have been asked to rank-order sentencing purposes or to assign a numerical score reflecting the importance of each purpose. And some polls ask respondents to consider the purposes of sentencing generally, while in others they are asked about the relevance of specific purposes for specific offenses.

When given a choice, members of the public appear to endorse many purposes (as do judges). An American poll (Jamieson and Flanagan, 1989) found the greatest support for special deterrence (79 percent rated it "very important") but rehabilitation received almost as much support (rated "very important" by 72 percent of the respondents). Clearly, the public view punishment as serving multiple purposes: In fact, five sentencing purposes were rated as being very important by at least two-thirds of the sample.

There are obvious deficiencies to the menu-style approach to this question. The results may be a function of respondents' relative familiarity with different purposes. Deterrence, for example, may attract support from the public simply because it is more familiar to people than a sentencing goal such as incapacitation. General deterrence has a great deal of intuitive appeal; most people see the principle of deterrence at work in everyday life, and extrapolate to criminal behavior. They may well reason that if parking fines can discourage double-parking (and for most drivers this is the case), the threat of sentences of imprisonment should be able to deter people from committing bank robbery. The underlying principle is the same; the stakes are just higher. Most people expect deterrence to function in the area of criminal behavior, and for this reason general deterrence attracts a fair degree of support in surveys of the public.

The Contrast Between What People Do and What They Say They Do

Another reason for regarding these surveys with some skepticism is the underlying assumption that responses reflect the actual purposes behind sentencing decisions favored by the public. Research in the field of social psychology (e.g., Nisbett and Wilson 1977) has shown that self-reports are often discrepant with reality. That is, when people are asked to state what factors influenced their decisions, they are sometimes quite inaccurate. There have been many demonstrations of tasks in which people are asked to make decisions based upon a number of factors. Afterwards, subjects state which factors influenced them the most. When these self-reports are compared with objective analyses of the actual influence of these factors, discrepancies emerge. Subjects fail to report factors that did influence their decisions, and sometimes report that particular factors had influenced their behavior when experimental evidence suggested the absence of any such influence (see Nisbett and Ross, 1980, for a summary of this literature).

It is possible that people believe they are sentencing according to one principle (e.g., deterrence) and yet in fact are guided by another. This certainly seems to be the case for some judges. McFatter (1982) found little concordance between the purposes that judges rated as being important and the purposes that actually governed their sentencing decisions. For example, individuals who rated doing justice as the most important sentencing purpose were not the ones who followed this purpose when actually assigning penalties. Similarly Levin (1966) found that judges imposed sentences on the basis of a few purposes but were unaware of this fact. As Konecni and Ebbesen (1982, p. 235) note: "The fact that judges talk about numerous factors may have nothing to do with the causal factors that control their decisions." In short, direct questions may not be the optimal method of ascertaining public preferences regarding sentencing purposes.

An alternative research strategy consists of gathering sentencing decisions from members of the public and inferring from statistical analyses of these data, the kind of model that underlies public views of sentencing. A couple of studies have explored the issue of sentencing purpose from this perspective. An example will illustrate the point. Suppose a group of people were given scenarios to read, and asked a number of questions about the offender and the offense, including the kind of sentence that should be imposed. Thus they might be asked to estimate the likelihood that the offender will re-offend. If the statistical analysis showed a powerful negative association between ratings of likely recidivism, and severity of sentence, we would conclude that preventing crime is an important sentencing purpose endorsed by the public.

On the other hand, if the only significant correlation was between subjects' ratings of crime seriousness and severity of sentence, then we would conclude that just deserts is the most important sentencing purpose from the public's perspective. Warr, Meier and Erickson (1983) and Roberts and Gebotys (1989) conducted research of this kind, and found that the most powerful predictor of sentence severity was in fact the seriousness of the offense. This suggests that the just deserts sentencing philosophy is the most important purpose underlying public sentencing preferences. However, when asked to rate the importance of different sentencing purposes, general deterrence received the highest ratings. To put it another way, the subjects *pursued* a just deserts sentencing model, yet *rated* general deterrence as being the most important sentencing purpose. These results imply that public opinion regarding sentencing is more influenced by retributivism (just deserts) than utilitarianism (general deterrence, for example).

This conclusion is supported by the results of the most recent national poll in America to have addressed the issue of sentencing purpose. Unlike other polls, this one found a clear consensus among members of the public. The National Crime and Justice Survey found much stronger support for retribution (51 percent) than for rehabilitation (21 percent), incapacitation or deterrence (both 13 percent—see Gerber and Engelhardt-Greer, 1996). It is interesting to note that while the percentage of respondents endorsing retribution varied across demographic categories, it still received more support than any of the other sentencing purposes. As we shall see in a later chapter, preferences for sentencing purposes changed when the question shifted to the reasons for sentencing juvenile rather than adult offenders.

Offense-Specific Sentencing Purposes

While differing in emphasis from the responses of actual judges, public reactions are nevertheless just as complex. For example, support for different purposes varies from offense to offense. In a national survey conducted in the U.S. (Jacoby and Dunn, 1987), rehabilitation was the purpose endorsed by most respondents (85 percent) for arson, and yet the fewest respondents (50 percent) for a crime such as forcible rape. Likewise in Canada, if the crime was relatively minor, the sentencing purpose endorsed by the greatest number of respondents was individual deterrence, but when asked to consider instead serious crimes such as sexual assault or robbery, the percentage of respondents supporting individual deterrence fell while support for incapacitation grew (Canadian Sentencing Commission, 1987). David Indermaur (1990) reports similar findings using a sample of Australian respondents. It is hard therefore to make statements about sentencing purposes favored by the public, since they endorse several aims simultaneously with support for any particular aim depending upon the nature of the crime under consideration (and perhaps also the kind of offender being sentenced).

Purpose of Prisons and Criminal Record

Offender characteristics also affect public preferences for different sentencing purposes. This was demonstrated in some research conducted in Ohio. Respondents were asked to identify the purpose of prison for first time offenders and for repeat offenders. When asked about first offenders, only 9 percent stated that prisons should serve as a punishment. The vast majority (75 percent) of Ohio residents said that changing behavior was the principal purpose of prisons for offenders without a criminal history. For repeat offenders, however, punishing or isolating from society were the purposes endorsed by three-quarters of the sample. Changing the behavior of recidivists was seen as the purpose of prison by fewer than 20 percent of respondents (Governor's Office of Criminal Justice Services, 1984).

A final caveat about the literature on sentencing purposes is that these findings must be seen in the context of public knowledge, which was reviewed in Chapter 3. How much public support would be found for the utilitarian sentencing purposes of deterrence and incapacitation if people were aware of the limitations upon their efficacy? Many people are in favor of "Three Strikes" sentencing legislation, but do they know how much crime will be prevented by these policies, or how much they will cost? While we cannot review the empirical research on the effectiveness of sentencing in this book, it does seem clear that the public have more faith in deterrence and incapacitation than is warranted, in light of the findings from systematic research.

Public Views and Views of Criminal Justice Professionals

One issue that has not been fully explored concerns the relationship between public and professional sentencing philosophies. If the public are eclectic in their sentencing preferences, wishing to retain multiple purposes, what about criminal justice professionals? The best data on the question come from polls conducted in several American states, the results of which revealed significant concordance between the public and criminal justice professionals. For example, in Colorado, rankings of sentencing purposes derived from the public were remarkably similar to rankings of the same purposes derived from criminal justice officials (see Mande and English, 1989, Table 7). Here also the purpose of sentencing varies as a function of the nature of the offense. Diamond and Stalans (1989) found that judges assigned more importance to general deterrence and as a result imposed harsher sentences (than did laypersons) on a first offender convicted of selling eleven grams of cocaine. Similar differences in the importance assigned general deterrence in cases of burglary emerged for lay and professional magistrates (Diamond, 1990). It would seem then that the views of the public are not that discrepant with the views of criminal justice elites, including members of the judiciary.

To summarize, it should come as no surprise that the public are eclectic in their support for sentencing purposes. After all, judges also support different sentencing purposes on different occasions. While some judges may lean towards one purpose rather than another, no judge sentences purely for deterrence (for example) in all cases. In this respect, the public are no different then, from the judiciary.

Proportionality in Public Views of Sentencing

A central question addressed by researchers concerns the relationship between crime seriousness and punishment severity. According to the just deserts sentencing philosophy, there should be a strong relationship between the severity of punishments, and the seriousness of the crimes for which they are imposed. This is referred to as the proportionality principle in sentencing. It means that the more serious crimes are punished more severely than the less serious offenses. How do the public react to the question of proportionality in sentencing? There can be little doubt that a strong association between public assessments of seriousness and severity permeates our culture. For example, politicians in many countries make allusion to the notion of proportionality in sentencing.[3]

What can empirical research tell us about this issue? Hamilton and Rytina (1980) conducted face-to-face interviews with Boston residents, who were asked to evaluate the seriousness of a list of crimes as well as the relative severity of a list of punishments. On average, the degree of association between the seriousness of a particular crime and the severity of the assigned penalty was very high. The principle of proportionality was therefore strongly supported by respondents in the research. Blumstein and Cohen (1980) explored similar ground using a mail survey. Once again impressive correlations emerged to support the just deserts principle of proportionality (see also White, 1975; Gebotys and Roberts, 1987).

The crime seriousness-sentence severity relationship is however more complex than this research would suggest. Innovative research by Peter Rossi and his colleagues (1985), employing the factorial survey approach, found that the relationship between crime seriousness and punishment severity was far from perfect. As Rossi, Simpson and Miller (1985) note: "[T]here is no one-to-one direct relationship between the seriousness measures of crimes and desired sanctions" (p. 89). Subjects in the research were affected (once again, like judges) by characteristics of the offenders, the victims, and the consequences of the crime. This means that public sentencing preferences are influenced by factors other than the seriousness of the offense. One obvious example of such factors is the extent of the offender's criminal record, to which we now turn.

Criminal Record and the Sentencing Process

After the seriousness of the crime (or even before, in some American states—see Roberts, 1996), the most important variable determining sentence severity is the nature and extent of the offender's criminal history. Accordingly, it is worth exploring this issue from the perspective of the public. A sentencing model based strictly on proportionality leaves little room for an offender's previous convictions: A sentence imposed upon an offender with six robbery convictions would be no more severe than the sentence imposed for a robbery committed by an offender with only two priors. The reason for this is that the seriousness of the robbery (the harm inflicted or threatened) is unaffected by the extent of the offender's record.[4] However, public sentencing preferences are to a degree influenced by criminal history information: Penalties assigned to recidivists increase as a direct function of the number of priors. After the level of harm inflicted, the nature of the defendant's criminal history is the most important determinant of sentence severity (e.g., Applegate *et al.*, 1996). In this sense, there is a similarity between public sentencing preferences and sentences prescribed by the state and federal sentencing guidelines commissions (Roberts, 1996).

However there is a limit to public support for the use of harsher penalties for recidivists. This has been demonstrated in recent American research. One of the most controversial sentencing changes in recent years is the so-called "Three Strikes" law contained in the 1994 Federal Crime Bill. The "Three Strikes" provision echoes similar pieces of legislation at the state level which prescribe very severe penalties for repeat offenders. In some states this means that an offender can receive a very severe sentence for a felony which itself may not that serious, so long as the two prior felonies were serious (see Greenwood *et al.*, 1996). America is not alone in having such legislation. Similar proposals have been advanced by the British Home Secretary, and there have been calls for comparable reforms in Canada. Many sentencing theorists would regard this as a violation of the principle of proportionality (see above) since the penalty can be disproportionately harsh, relative to the seriousness of the crime of which the offender has just been convicted. The offender's criminal record becomes a more important determinant of the current sentence than the seriousness of his latest conviction.

On the face of things, it would seem that the public strongly support such policies. When a representative sample of Americans were asked if they were in favor of a law requiring the imposition of life imprisonment upon anyone convicted of a violent felony for the third time, almost 90 percent responded affirmatively (cited in Lacayo, 1994). A similar result emerged from another poll, which also showed that race was the only demographic variable to have an influence on responses: 68 percent of blacks supported the law, compared to 88 percent of whites (Maguire and Pastore, 1995). However, once again, the poll result must be qualified by the findings from more detailed and sophisticated methods of gauging popular opinion.

There are in fact important limits upon public support for these "Three Strikes" sentencing laws. Finkel, Maloney, Valbuena and Groscup (1996) found that while the public supported the use of criminal record in the sentencing process, this support did not extend to those laws that demand very harsh laws for crimes committed by recidivists. Similar results were found by Rossi, Berk and Cambell (1996), who used a large representative sample of the American public. These researchers concluded that "there did not seem to be widespread support for habitual offenders sentencing such as is usually found in "three-strikes-and-you're out" legislation" (p. 9).

This conclusion contradicts to a degree, the poll result just cited. The solution would appear to be that the recidivist statutes that impose severe penalties upon recidivists *regardless* of the seriousness of the third felony, are out of step with public opinion. The public, it would seem, favor harsh, mandatory penalties for violent recidivists, but only if the third (i.e., the triggering) offense is also of a very serious nature. This is why there was so much public outcry and media attention paid, in 1995, to cases in which offenders were sentenced to life imprisonment for offenses that were not that serious.[5] (For further information on public opinion and the role of criminal record, see Roberts, 1996).

Truth in Sentencing

An important issue in the area of sentencing is the relationship between the sentence of imprisonment imposed in court, and the sentence as served by the offender. The intervention of parole and other early release mechanisms means that few offenders serve the complete term of imprisonment in an institution. This absence of "truth in sentencing" attracts the attention of sentencing theorists, and the public too, are clearly concerned about the issue. This conclusion is based upon several surveys which have found that the public wish to see a closer fit between the sentence imposed and the sentence served. To a limited degree, the public perception reflects a view that the problem is worse than it really is. This conclusion can be drawn from research in which members of the public are asked to estimate the proportion of a sentence that is actually served in prison rather than on parole in the community. These surveys find that the public under-estimate the percentage of time that is served in prison before the inmate obtains release on parole.

A great deal of the public concern about the absence of truth in sentencing focuses on life prisoners, who, in most jurisdictions, return to the community after a decade inside (although they usually remain on parole, and can in theory be returned to the institution at any point up to their death). A survey from England illustrates the tenor of public opinion. Dowds (1994) reports that almost nine out of ten respondents supported the position that a life sentence should mean that an offender spends the remainder of his or her natural life in prison. There is more consensus on this issue than any other in the area of sentencing, even the general issue of sentencing or attitudes towards capital punishment. Similar results emerge in Canada and elsewhere.[6]

Attitudes Toward Sentencing Severity

Are the courts more lenient than the public? This critical question has been addressed repeatedly over the past thirty years, and more than any other it exposes the limitations of public opinion surveys as an adequate measure of the views of the public. Members of the public are generally believed to be harsher than judges. More public criticism is directed at the sentencing decisions of judges than any other issue in criminal justice. Ray (1982), for example, concluded: "There is very clearly a stark gap between actual sentencing practice and what the public see as appropriate sentencing practice.. the gap between the judiciary and the public is so gross that nothing can disguise it" (p.442). This perception is shared by many policymakers, criminal justice professionals and politicians. But is this a correct reading of public opinion? Discussion of this issue has tended to focus on the results of polls in which respondents are asked the following question: "In your view, are sentences too harsh, about right, or not harsh enough?"

The question has never failed to generate the result that the vast majority of the public in all countries covered in this survey expressed their desire for harsher penalties. In fact, the question concerning sentencing severity generates a more consensual response than any other issue in criminal justice, including capital punishment. For example, polls published in 1994 revealed that 81 percent of respondents in the U.S. (Maguire and Pastore, 1994) and exactly the same percentage in Canada (Roberts, 1994) feel sentences are not harsh enough. Twenty years earlier, the percentage expressing this view was 79 percent in the United States (Sourcebook of Criminal Justice Statistics, 1987) and 75 percent in Canada (Fattah, 1982). A slightly different question asked on the 1995 National Crime and Justice Survey found a similar result: 61 percent of the public responded that the harshness of the courts was a problem, and of these almost all meant that sentences were insufficiently harsh (Myers, 1996). This perception is widespread throughout the western world. In Australia, 76 percent favored harsher sentences when responding to this question (Indermaur, 1987). In England, 79 percent of respondents agreed with the statement that "Too many convicted criminals are let off lightly by the courts" (Dowds, 1994; see also Hough and Moxon, 1988). Finally, the emphasis on leniency also emerges from qualitative analyses of public opinion, such as Focus groups (see Hough, 1996; Doble, 1987, p. 23).[7]

On the face of things, then, the public appear to want more punitive sentencing. For criminal justice researchers, the data summarized here represent the point of departure. For many politicians, these data also represent the point of arrival. The poll findings have also been interpreted to mean that sentencing cannot become more lenient, for fear of further alienating an already disenchanted public. But are the public really as punitive as these results suggest? Careful research refutes the conventional wisdom which portrays the public in this way. First, we should deal with some methodological problems associated with research on this issue. Before this material however, we point out an important qualification regarding the poll results just cited.

Several researchers have asked a second question after the one dealing with sentence severity. Specifically, people have been asked what type of offender they had in mind when answering this question. In one of these studies, almost half of the respondents who stated that sentences were too lenient also stated that they had been thinking of violent, recidivist offenders (Doob and Roberts, 1983; Brillon, Louis-Guerin, and Lamarche, 1984). Violent recidivists account for a very small percentage of all offenders processed by the courts. The clearest way of establishing what kind of offender is in the public's mind when they answer the question about sentence severity is to pose two separate questions, one about violent recidivists and the other about offenders in general. When this was done with a sample of Canadians, the results were clear. Four-fifths of the sample believed sentences were too lenient when asked about violent offenders. However, when asked about non-violent offenders, less than half the sample believed sentences were too lenient (Angus Reid, 1984). An important qualification then, of the general poll finding is that sentences are not harsh enough for a small group of offenders, namely those convicted of crimes of violence.

When the public think of sentencing and parole, they tend to think of the worst case scenarios. This is particularly true for the more serious crimes. When most people think about murder, they bring to mind the most heinous homicides. In America this means people like the multiple murderers Wayne Gacy or Geoffrey Dahmer. For Britons it means offenders like Myra Hindley and Geoffrey West. For Canadians, the name of Clifford Olsen, a mass murderer now serving a life sentence, is frequently heard.

The range of criminal behavior—in terms of crime seriousness and offender culpability—escapes the attention of the general public (as well as politicians).

Relative Punitiveness of the Public and the Courts

Difficulties in Comparing Public Opinion and Sentencing Patterns

It is far from easy to make appropriate comparisons between the views (or sentencing patterns) of judges and public opinion. One obvious methodological difficulty concerns the question of whether the public are responding with an accurate perception of the system. For example, do the public have a realistic idea of the extent to which early release on parole affects time served in prison? As noted in Chapter 3, the public hold inaccurate perceptions of what happens to offenders, and these mis-perceptions are biased in the direction that would lead the public to see the system as lenient. If the public under-estimate the proportion of a sentence served in prison, this will have an impact on their response to questions regarding the appropriate sentence length for various crimes.

Role of Plea Bargaining

Before turning to the results of research comparing sentences derived from the courts with sentences favored by the public, one other issue warrants discussion. An important factor contributing to public disenchant-ment with sentencing patterns is the role of plea bargaining. Deals made prior to sentencing have an important impact on the severity of the sentence eventually imposed, and the public have a very negative view of these negotiations between the prosecutor and the defendant or her legal representatives. This topic has infrequently been explored by researchers, but the few polls that exist demonstrate widespread opposition.

In theory, both sides of the dispute gain by a plea bargain. The prosecu-tor saves the time and expense of a trial, in which a conviction may not be possible. Victims and witnesses save the inconvenience and sometimes the indignity of having to testify. Defendants receive a more lenient sentence than if they had pled guilty but been convicted following a trial. In reality, the issue is complex, and it is not clear who benefits, and the practice of accepting a guilty plea has been widely criticized. The public are very critical of plea negotiations. This is clear from research in America and Canada. Fagan (1981) found that a substantial majority of the American public disapproved of plea negotiations with defendants, a result that was replicated in 1988 (Shriver, 1989).

Cohen and Doob (1988) conducted a representative survey of the Canadian public and found that four out of five respondents disapproved of plea bargaining. There was little demographic variation in attitudes. Moreover, the link between attitudes towards plea bargaining and views of sentencing were clear. People who regarded plea bargaining as unacceptable also thought that sentences were not harsh enough.[8] Respondents regarded plea bargaining as nothing more than a means by which offenders could evade receiving their just deserts. Finally, the presence of information about a plea bargain in scenarios had the impact of changing public evaluations of criminal justice professionals. For example, if subjects read about a case in which a plea bargain had taken place, they had more negative views of the prosecutor.[9]

Are the Courts Really More Lenient than Public Opinion?

Two principal strategies have been adopted by researchers to compare public attitudes to judicial practices. In many studies, "sentences" derived from surveys of the general public have been compared to actual sentencing patterns (e.g., Gibbons, 1969; Boydell and Grindstaff, 1972; Grindstaff, 1974; Warr, Meier and Erickson, 1983; Hough and Mayhew, 1985; Hough and Moxon, 1985; Zimmerman, Alstyne and Dunn, 1988; Diamond and Stalans, 1989; Mande and English, 1989; Roberts and Doob, 1989; Diamond, 1990; Zamble and Kalm, 1990) or sentences prescribed by penal codes (e.g., Samuel and Moulds, 1986). Comparisons have been made between public responses to attitudinal data derived from judicial officers such as judges and probation officers (e.g., Gottfredson and Taylor, 1984; Fichter and Veneziano, 1988; Ouimet; 1990; Tremblay, 1990). Other studies have compared the public and the courts using a single case history (e.g., Doob and Roberts, 1984) or a series of high-profile cases (e.g., Ray, 1982).

Contrary, perhaps, to expectation, the preponderance of evidence from all these studies—using different approaches—supports the view that the public are not harsher than the courts, or at least are not as consistently harsh as the poll findings would suggest. There are exceptions, but this is true for almost all research questions in the social sciences. In what follows, we have tried to convey a sense of the general findings. Because the issue of sentence severity cuts across international boundaries, we draw on research from representative surveys from the four countries surveyed in this book.

United States. Diamond and Stalans (1989) compared sentences derived from laypersons and judges in Illinois. The penalties favored by the public were no more severe, or in some cases even less severe, than those imposed by the judges. Fichter and Veneziano (1988) compared the sentencing preferences of citizens to those derived from a sample of judges. In comparisons involving nineteen offenses, the public were harsher for one offense (manslaughter) but the judges were harsher than the public in the remaining eighteen cases. This finding—of a public that is not necessarily harsher than the courts—is to be found in other U.S. studies as well, some going back over forty years (e.g., Rose and Prell, 1955; Parker, 1970; Williams, Gibbs and Erickson, 1980; Warr, Meier and Erickson, 1983; Gottfredson and Taylor, 1984; Samuel and Moulds, 1986; Thomson and Ragona, 1987; Diamond and Stalans, 1989; Mande and English, 1989; English, Crouch and Pullen, 1989). Two exceptions to this pattern are studies by Blumstein and Cohen (1980), in which public sentences were one-half to two times longer than time actually served, and a study by Zimmerman, Van Alstyne and Dunn (1988).

In addition to studies that find few differences between sentences favored by the public and the criminal justice system, there are others in which dramatic differences are found, with the public being markedly less punitive. Mande and Crouch (1984) compared public and professional reactions to a case of aggravated robbery in which the offender had a substantial criminal record. Over 85 percent of the criminal justice professionals, but only 67 percent of the public favored imprisonment. Differences in terms of the sentence lengths favored by judges and the public were even more striking. On average, the criminal justice professionals favored sentence lengths of sixty months, while the average sentence length from the public was only thirty-six months. In a related study (Mande and English, 1989) comparisons of average sentence lengths showed that the sentences recommended by criminal justice professionals were more severe than those favored by the public in ten out of fourteen cases. Finally, Secret and Johnson (1989) provide the most thorough examination of racial differences in American attitudes towards punishment. He notes some convergence between the attitudes of Blacks and Whites since 1980. Overall, he concludes that "Existing differences are small and generally disappear when socio-economic, sociological, political and demographic factors are controlled" (p. 370).

Canada. Roberts and Doob (1989) compared incarceration rates derived from a survey of the Canadian public with the actual incarceration rates for ten common offenses. For some crimes, public sentencing preferences were harsher than the courts, for others the courts were harsher. Overall, however, the results showed considerable similarity between public opinion and judicial practice. Another way of looking at these data is to convert them to numbers of offenders incarcerated. If the sentencing decisions of the public had actually been applied to the offenses in question, the result would have been 81,863 admissions to custody. In fact, 92,415 offenders were actually sent to prison over the period.[10] Similar results have been found in other Canadian studies (see Doob and Roberts, 1984; Zamble, 1990; Zamble and Kalm, 1990). The counter-example to this trend in Canada is the study by Tremblay, Cordeau and Ouimet (1990).

Great Britain. Analysis of data from the British Crime Survey (Hough and Moxon, 1985) shows that for a series of crimes, the opinions of the public in terms of dealing with offenders coincided with the actual treatment of offenders by the courts. For example, 85 percent of the British Crime Survey respondents favored incarceration as the sentence for robbers and 92 percent of sentences in cases of robbery were in fact terms of imprisonment. Mike Hough and David Moxon (1985) concluded: "These findings suggest that policy-makers and courts can treat with a degree of scepticism the claims often made by the media that public opinion demands a tougher line with offenders. The BCS offers no evidence to suggest widespread punitive attitudes among the public" (p. 171).

Australia. Walker, Collins and Wilson (1988) asked a representative sample of Australians to assign the most appropriate sentence for a series of offenses. The authors note: "The average response shows broad agreement with typical court decisions" (p. 150). For some offenses, the public responses were more punitive than the courts, although not to the extent that one might expect on the basis of the poll results showing that the vast majority of the public feel sentences are too lenient. Thus for armed robbery, 88 percent of the public favored incarceration, while 80 percent of the convictions had in fact resulted in imprisonment.

Public Attitudes Toward Sentencing Alternatives

Finally, further light is shed on the alleged punitiveness of the public by research exploring popular views regarding alternatives to incarceration. If the public are as punitive as suggested by polls, they are unlikely to support alternative sanctions such as restitution. However, several studies have found widespread public acceptance of this disposition. In a typical study, respondents are presented with a case study and are asked if restitution should be considered as a punishment for the offender.

Research in several countries (e.g., Galaway, 1984; Boers and Sessar, 1989; Bae, 1991) has demonstrated that the public endorse the use of restitution in a fairly wide range of cases, and that they are at least as accepting of restitution as are criminal justice professionals such as judges and prosecutors. For example, in a U.S. study (Bae, 1991), the researchers found that criminal justice officials in Minnesota were less supportive (than the public) of restitution as an alternative punishment to imprisonment for property offenders (see Bae, 1991 for a review of this literature). Mande and English (1989) also report convincing data that support a reversal of the accepted view of the public. In a series of cases, members of the public were more supportive of community corrections than were judges. If the public really are that much harsher than the courts, this result would seem unlikely.

It is often said that the public will support community-based sanctions but only for minor crimes. The data from this Colorado study are worth examining more closely, for they offer impressive refutation of this interpretation. Using aggravated robbery as the offense of comparison, these researchers found that only 14 percent of offenders convicted of this offense had in fact received a community-based sentence; 76 percent had been imprisoned. However, only 30 percent of the public endorsed incarceration for this kind of offense; almost half of the public sample favored a community-based alternative to incarceration.

These results will come as a surprise to many criminal justice professionals and politicians. Surveys of these groups have shown that they have an exaggerated view of the punitiveness of the public, particularly as it relates to sentencing alternatives. There are many examples of this in the literature. In 1985, a survey found that fewer than one-quarter of criminal justice decision makers believed that the public would support the use of alternatives to incarceration. In fact, surveys of the public in that state (Michigan) found that fully two-thirds of the public approved of the use of such alternatives (see Immarigeon, 1986).

Importance of Restitution

The public are very supportive of the use of restitution, although they do not always think of alternatives such as this when responding to surveys. If, however, alternatives such as restitution are made salient to respondents, then an important result emerges: There is a significant decline in support for imprisonment. This too has been demonstrated in a number of studies. In one, people were asked to choose the most appropriate penalty for a first offender convicted of burglary. They were given a choice of imposing one of four sentences: prison, a fine, a period of probation, or fine plus a probation. Under these conditions, about one third chose prison. Respondents were then asked the following: "How, instead of [answer chosen in preceding question] would you be in favor of having the offender be ordered by the court to do a certain number of hours of work beneficial to the community or the victim?" In response to this question, almost half of the subjects who had chosen prison as the appropriate sentence stated that they would be in favor of the restitution based sanction in "all or most cases" (Doob and Roberts, 1988). We would draw two conclusions from studies generating such findings. First, when answering questions about sentencing options, people tend to think of prison above all other sanctions. Second, the initial response (favoring imprisonment) is not necessarily that strongly held.

Electronic Monitoring and House Arrest

Few studies have examined public support for intermediate, community sanctions. This is surprising, in light of their increasing importance to the sentencing process in North America and Europe (see Morris and Tonry, 1990). Elrod and Brown (1996) conducted a survey of New York residents to explore support for house arrest as a sanction. As with other sanctions, support varied as a function of the seriousness of the offense. Seventy-one percent supported house arrest for minor crimes such as theft, while only 15 percent endorsed it for more serious offenses such as crimes of violence or drug crimes. Interestingly, support for the use of Electronic House Arrest was based upon the perception that incarceration for this profile of offender was self-defeating.

Sentencing Decisions by Lay Versus Professional Judges

The studies reviewed so far all involved comparisons between responses from groups of judges (or actual sentences) and responses from samples of the public. Another way of comparing public views with judicial practice consists of comparing the sentencing decisions taken by lay and professional magistrates. This is possible in jurisdictions such as England and Wales, where sentencing is carried out by laypersons as well as judges trained in the conventional legal manner. Diamond (1990) examined the sentencing preferences of these two groups and found the lay magistrates to be as lenient as their professional counterparts on both simulated cases and actual decisions.

Taken together, the research reviewed here does do not sustain the conclusion that the public is overwhelmingly more punitive than the courts. (See Makela, 1966) for similar findings in countries other than the four included in this volume). It has long been argued that criminal justice reforms that involve non-carceral options are likely to encounter resistance from the public. Ryan (1983) notes:

> The construction of public opinion should be of more than passing interest to civil servants and politicians... It is, after all, they who are constantly

> arguing that reforms, say shorter sentences or more alternatives to prison, are impractical because public opinion would not tolerate more 'soft options.' (p. 120)

As we have seen, when the public are given information about alternative dispositions, support for incarceration declines significantly (Doble and Klein, 1989). In other words, support for non-carceral sanctions has in part been lacking due to public ignorance of such sentencing options. The findings reviewed here suggest that the movement for increased use of such options will not generate the degree of public opposition that some suggest.

We believe that the research summarized here qualifies, to a significant degree, the perception that the public are much more punitive than the courts. But it would also be a mistake also to think that judicial practice is consistently more severe than public opinion. In all likelihood, while the views of the public and the decisions of the courts are fairly close, generalizations are risky. It seems probable that the public are harsher than the courts for some offenses while for other types of crimes the courts are harsher. Overall, however, the differences between the two have been overstated. The public are likely to "under-punish" offenses such as perjury and other crimes against the administration of justice because they fail to appreciate the true seriousness of these crimes. On the other hand, the public may "over-punish" crimes such as assault a police officer believing these to involve a very serious degree of harm.[11]

Public Sentencing Preferences and Sentencing Guidelines

A practical question lies behind this research on public attitudes to sentencing. As noted earlier, an important consideration for sentencing commissions in America is public attitudes. It would be interesting to know then, whether the sentencing guidelines in use across the country conform to the views of the general public. A recent study by Rossi, Berk and Campbell (1995) enables us to draw some conclusions about this issue. A representative sample of Americans was asked to sentence offenders, and then their responses were compared to the sentences prescribed by the federal sentencing guidelines. Overall, the results indicated that the guideline ranges were quite similar to the sentences favored by the public. Across the entire range of offenses, the median guideline sentence was 2.5 years, while the median sentence derived from the public was only slightly higher at three years. These researchers concluded that their findings indicated that the federal guidelines "map rather well onto the central tendencies of public wishes" (Rossi *et al.*, 1995, p. 20). The only major area of discrepancy involved drug offenses. The federal guidelines favor very harsh penalties for people convicted dealing in illegal drugs such as crack cocaine. The public however, were not supportive of such harsh penalties for this kind of offender.

How Does the Perception of Leniency in Sentencing Arise?

When most people think about sentencing, their "top-of-head" reaction is to believe that sentencing is very lenient. We saw in Chapter 3 that public *knowledge* of the sentencing process is poor, and biased towards a negative view of the system. Where does this misperception of a lenient system come from? A nation-wide poll in Canada in 1987 found that 96 percent of the public cited the news media as their primary source of information about sentencing (Canadian Sentencing Commission, 1987). There is no reason to believe that this result is exclusive to Canadians. As noted in Chapter 3, when a sentence is reported in the news media, little information is given which might explain an otherwise lenient sentence. Writers have long observed this. Over 100 years ago, the jurist Stephen noted that "Newspaper reports are necessarily much condensed, and they generally omit many points which weigh with the judge in determining what sentence to pass" (Stephen, 1883, p. 90). This substantiates the observation made by one sentencing expert who noted that "judges who deal with robbers, rapists and other serious offenders by means of suspended sentences, fines or probation provoke storms of protest from newspapers and readers who [...] were not told of the reasons for such leniency" (Walker, 1981, p. 114).

The power of the news media to determine public views in the area of sentencing was clearly demonstrated in a study conducted a few years ago by Anthony Doob and one of the authors of this book (Doob and Roberts, 1988). Members of the public from Canada and the U.S. were recruited to participate in a criminal justice experiment. Half of the subjects were asked to read the newspaper account of a sentencing decision, while half were asked to read a summary of the court documents pertaining to the case. Afterwards, subjects in both groups were asked the same set of questions. Since participants were randomly assigned to experimental condition (i.e., media version or court documents version), we can be sure that any differences between groups in terms of their reaction to the case are due to the version that they read, and not other factors.

The critical question posed was whether the sentence imposed in the case was too harsh too lenient or about right. Subjects who had read the news media account had a very different view of the sentence. Almost two-thirds of the media condition participants expressed the view that the sentence was too lenient, while over half of the people who had read the court documents thought that the sentence was too harsh. In other words, although the sentence was the same in both conditions, the interpretation of that sentence was very different. As well, subjects had very different views of the judge, the offender and the offense, depending upon which version of reality they had just read. This effect has subsequently been replicated using other cases, and other samples of subjects (see Roberts and Doob, 1990, p. 462). Members of the public, it would appear, are often getting information about sentences of the court that leads them to believe that these sentences are too lenient.[12]

Attitudes Toward Parole

Attitudes towards early release from prison have not been studied as often as attitudes toward sentencing. This is rather surprising, in light of the widespread public criticism which focuses upon parole when the news media report a serious crime was committed by a parolee. In reviewing this material, it should be recalled that the public in Canada at least hold several misconceptions of parole. For example, they over-estimate the release rates and the recidivism rates of parolees (see Chapter 2 and 3). The same may well be true in America.

In general, the U.S. public supports the concept of parole. For example, a poll conducted in 1984 (Jamieson and Flanagan, 1986, Table 2.12) found that 82 percent endorsed the view that "parole supervision is useful in deterring crime and in helping the individual to adjust to the community." As well, the percentage of respondents who favor the abolition of parole is small. A poll conducted in Canada in 1986 found that less than one quarter of respondents favored parole abolition (Roberts, 1988a).

Nevertheless, accompanying this positive reaction towards parole, is the widespread perception that parole has become too easy to obtain, and should be granted at a later point in the sentence, to fewer inmates. Two-thirds of the Canadian public see their parole boards as being too lenient (Roberts, 1988a) approximately the same percentage as those who regard sentences as being too lenient (Sacco and Johnson, 1990). Fully 70 percent of respondents to a 1987 poll in Canada supported the view that "parole boards release too many offenders on parole" (Canadian Criminal Justice Association, 1987). In the U.S., over 80 percent of the public who were surveyed in 1993 supported a proposal to make parole more difficult (Maguire and Pastore, 1993). This was higher than the percentage of respondents who favored the imposition of harsher sentences. Unlike the perception of leniency in sentencing, attitudes towards parole have not always been so negative. Thirty years ago, a Harris poll found that half the population agreed with the view that the parole grant rate was "about right now." Only 14 percent of respondents in 1967 believed that parole should be used less often (Joint Commission on Correctional Manpower and Training, 1968).

As with the questions dealing with sentencing, the public have a concrete image of an offender in mind when responding to the issue of parole. When asked "When answering this question (about the release of offenders on parole) what kinds of offenders were you thinking of?", over half the sample were thinking exclusively of violent offenders (Canadian Criminal Justice Association, 1987). There is significant correlation between the two attitudes, suggesting that people who perceive sentencing as being lenient also perceive parole as being lenient (Roberts, 1988a). Most members of the public would favor restricting parole release to certain offenders. The same survey revealed that two-thirds favored restricting parole to inmates serving time for non-violent crimes.

Following the views of the public on the issue of parole would seem to result in longer periods of imprisonment, with a greater percentage of sentences served in prison. However, it should be recalled that the public opposition to parole is largely founded upon inaccurate perceptions of parole release rates. That is, most people over-estimate the percentage of inmates granted parole, as well as the percentage of offenders on parole who fail to complete the term of their sentences in the community without re-offending. This suggests that correcting misperceptions about parole would result in greater support for community-based corrections, although this specific hypothesis remains to be tested empirically.

General Versus Specific Measures of Public Opinion

In Chapter 1 we argued that public opinion can only be fully understood by using a number of different research methodologies. On its own, the large-scale representative survey is simply not sufficient. Nowhere is this more true than with respect to sentencing and parole. We would argue that the surveys of public attitudes that have been conducted are at best an over-simplification, and at worst misleading about the tenor of public views. The central deficiency of a public survey is that it usually poses a simple question which encourages (and indeed compels) people to respond in a simple way. Are sentences too harsh or too lenient? Is parole too easy or too restrictive? Like Russian dolls, these kinds of questions contain many others: sentences for what kinds of crimes? What kinds of offenders? Recidivists? First Offenders?

As for parole, the same questions can be asked, in addition to others concerning the offender's institutional conduct, life plans after release and so on. A single poll lacks specificity, as well as information. In this sense, criminal justice polls suffer from a deficiency not associated with political surveys. No further elaboration is needed in a political survey: Either you are going to vote Democrat or Republican, Conservative or Labour, Liberal or New Democrat, there is no in-between response.

A solution to this problem involves studying public opinion in a context in which respondents have a great deal more information at their disposal. This might be termed the *case history* approach, and has been followed by several researchers. The general strategy is to give people a specific case description to read, thus allowing them sufficient time to consider the many aspects of the case. When this kind of approach is followed, researchers have uncovered some interesting results. The typical finding has been that when confronted with a specific case, the public are less punitive than when answering a general question. We shall summarize some research findings from several studies, and discuss some actual jury decision-making data from Canada that illustrate the point. Before getting to the research, however, let's consider a sentencing decision handed down in Canada which illustrates the point.

Probation for Homicide

The accused was convicted of manslaughter, the unintentional taking of human life. The maximum penalty for manslaughter in Canada is life imprisonment, although the average sentence actually imposed is around six years in prison (Roberts, 1995). Jean-Francois Rubio was convicted of shooting his father and received a sentence of three years probation. Knowing just these bare facts, ask yourself the usual question: "Was this sentence too severe, too harsh or too lenient?" Most people would agree that on these facts at least, the sentence sounds disproportionately lenient, in light of the gravity of the crime. However, when people learn more about the circumstances leading to the commission of the offense, their views tend to change.

Rubio, a young man, had lived in a climate of continual harassment in which his father had beaten him and driven his mother to take refuge in a hostel for battered women. On the day of the killing, the father had abused the son continually, with the result that the accused felt driven to kill his father. After the shooting, Rubio immediately turned himself in to the police. He co-operated fully with the investigation, and expressed a great deal of remorse. He had no criminal history, and by the time the court heard his case, had spent a year in pre-trial detention.

In short, there were powerful grounds of mitigation to reduce the severity of the sentence. Learning these details, many people regard the sentence as being appropriate. Of course, some people will still think that Rubio should have served a significant period of custody, on account of the fact that he had killed someone. The point we simply make is that a term of probation for manslaughter generates an immediate, punitive response, in part because our natural tendency is to think of the crime alone and not of any possible grounds for mitigation.

As well, when most people think about manslaughter or sexual assault, what comes to mind are images of the most serious instances of such crimes. For example, with regard to manslaughter, people may think of cases that are closer to murder, but which resulted in a manslaughter conviction. The same can be said for public images of offenders: Ask most people to describe the average offender, and they will give you a description of a recidivist violent offender, when such individuals are far from typical of offenders in general. Stalans and Diamond (1990) directly tested this hypothesis that the public have a distorted view of the typical offender. Using survey and experimental data, these researchers found that respondents' images of typical cases of burglary were inconsistent with the cases that were actually sentenced. Dissatisfaction with sentencing trends was in part a reflection of an inaccurate perception of the seriousness of the average case of burglary.

Sentencing

Several studies have tested what we term the "specificity" hypothesis. In one, subjects were assigned (at random, so that the groups would be equivalent before the study began) to read one of two accounts of a real case of manslaughter. One account was relatively brief, providing few details beyond the name of the offense and the sentence imposed on the offender. In the longer version of the same case, a summary of actual court documents was provided to subjects. Participants in both conditions were then simply asked the now-familiar question about the severity-leniency of the sentence. It was clear that perceptions of the sentence differed greatly depending upon the experimental condition to which subjects had been assigned. Thus 80 percent of subjects who read the "short" version evaluated the sentence as being too lenient, whereas only 14 percent of the subjects in the other condition shared this view (Doob and Roberts, 1983). This finding—that global measures of punitiveness do not tell the whole story—has subsequently been replicated in other research (e.g., Zamble and Kalm, 1990).

Parole

Comparable results emerge in the area of parole. Subjects in a study by Cumberland and Zamble (1992) were given scenarios to read. Each scenario described an inmate who was applying for early release on full parole. There were two types of crimes: aggravated assault including robbery, and burglary. The experiment began with a global measure of attitudes towards parole. Consistent with nation-wide surveys of the public at the time, (Roberts, 1992), approximately four out of five subjects in the study were dissatisfied with the parole system. However, the results indicated substantial support for the granting of early release in particular cases. A substantial majority of subjects endorsed release on parole even for a violent recidivist. The researchers concluded: "As in the case of sentencing, the specific case method indicates that people are more liberal and flexible than is suggested by responses to global questions" (Cumberland and Zamble, 1992, pp. 452-453).

We have argued that when people are given more information (such as a case history or scenario), they are less punitive than general surveys would suggest. To this point however, we have drawn on simulation studies, in which members of the public have clearly been aware that they are in a research study. This awareness may have influenced their responses. For example, it may have made them more liberal in their reactions, when in reality they remained implacably opposed to releasing a violent inmate on parole. As research in social psychology has long demonstrated, subjects' behavior is sometimes different when they are in a research study. However, there is evidence from actual jury decision-making which sustains the same hypothesis.

A Case History: Early Parole for Inmates Serving Life Terms in Canada

As noted earlier in this chapter, most Canadians are opposed to parole for inmates convicted of crimes of violence. Not surprisingly then, fully 80 percent of Canadians responded to an opinion poll by stating their opposition to granting parole to inmates serving life sentences for murder (Roberts, 1988; 1994). According to the *Criminal Code* of Canada, people convicted of first degree murder are sentenced to life imprisonment. In practice, this means that they must remain in prison for at least twenty-five years without the possibility of parole. However, there is also a provision in the Canadian *Code* which allows such life term inmates to apply, at the fifteen-year mark, for a review of their parole eligibility dates.

This review consists of a judicial hearing at which a jury will decide whether the inmate can apply for parole earlier than the twenty-five-year mark. The jury considers evidence brought forward relating to the inmate's progress in prison, his plans for the future as well as any other information introduced by the defense or the prosecutor. After hearing all this testimony, the jury can refuse the applicant's request for early parole or it can pick a year between fifteen (when the inmate became eligible for a review) and twenty-five. The provision was introduced in 1978, with the result that by 1996, almost eighty life-term inmates had had their cases reviewed by juries across the country. The results of these reviews shed some interesting light on the nature of public attitudes to parole.

If the survey results told the whole story about public attitudes towards parole, the outcomes of these parole eligibility reviews would be easy to predict. After all, if over 80 percent of the public oppose parole in general, then it is unlikely that murderers applying for early parole would receive a positive response from jurors. This is particularly true in light of the widespread public support for "truth in sentencing." However, over three-quarters of the applicants under this provision have received a reduction in their parole ineligibility, with the majority being allowed to apply for full parole immediately (Roberts, 1994). These results suggest that the survey is picking up on general dissatisfaction with parole, and a degree of diffuse punitiveness. However, when confronted with an actual case, and when they are asked to make a decision which will affect the life of a specific individual, people are more inclined to respond with leniency.

Conclusions

What conclusions should policy-makers draw from the findings that we have reviewed in this chapter? One is that a complex and emotional topic such as sentencing cannot be adequately researched in the way that market researchers explore preferences for soft drinks. Before concluding that the public endorse harsher sentencing or that they oppose parole for inmates serving life terms, legislators and criminal justice officials should take a careful look at the research that has accumulated over the past forty years in several countries. Another lesson is that politicians should refrain from promising the public more in terms of crime control benefits than can be delivered by the sentencing process. Part of the disillusionment with sentencing in America and elsewhere can be attributed to false expectations. Members of the public are encouraged to believe that significant reductions in crime rates can be achieved by harsher sentencing, including mandatory penalties. Primed to expect sentencing to function as a crime control mechanism, the public are likely to continue to be disappointed with the sentencing process, and this disappointment will manifest itself in opinion polls.

The public favor a mixed model in terms of sentencing purposes. They strongly endorse the notion of proportionality, and just deserts sentencing, but the public also feel that crime prevention and rehabilitation of offenders is important too. Although there is considerable support for the use of criminal record in the sentencing process, as noted earlier, there are clear limits to public support for very harsh recidivist laws such as the "Three Strikes" sentencing policies that now exist in several states and at the federal level. Most polls find the public favor harsher sentencing policies. However, when more sophisticated research is conducted, it appears that sentences imposed by courts and sentences favored by the public are much closer. In addition, those members of the public who favor harsher sentencing have a specific category of offender in mind: violent recidivists. As well, there is a tendency for people to be very punitive when confronted with a general question, but to be far less punitive when deciding what sentence is appropriate after having been given details about a specific case. This phenomenon also appears to hold for the issue of parole.

A theme which emerges from the research on public attitudes towards punishment is that there is clear support for a bifurcated response to sentencing offenders. Offenders convicted of the most serious crimes, particularly those involving violence or the threat of violence, provoke a strong punitive response, although not always a response that is harsher than sentencing patterns in contemporary America. On the other hand, for other kinds of offenders such as those convicted of economic crimes, property crimes and the like, the public are willing to support non-punitive sentencing strategies. There is one qualification to this conclusion: When property offenders have long criminal histories, the public shift to a more punitive response.

Pollsters will doubtless continue to conduct, and the news media will continue to report, polls in which the public are simply asked whether sentences are too harsh or too lenient. And in all probability the public will continue to state that the courts are too lenient. In light of this, it is important that the results of more refined research be made available to policy-makers. For sentencing commissions interested in knowing how well their guidelines fit community views, it is clearly important to have more research such as that carried out by Peter Rossi and his colleagues.

Notes

1. This study found no significant differences between the responses of Canadians and Americans.

2. There was also evidence suggesting that the general view of sentencing affected the specific evaluation of a particular disposition: Those respondents who thought that sentences in general were too lenient were more likely to rate any

specific sentence as too lenient (Doob and Roberts, 1983).

3. For example, Margaret Thatcher, the former British Prime Minister, once spoke of "the very real anxiety of ordinary people that too many sentences do not fit the crime," a clear reference to the absence of proportionality in sentencing (Economist, 1985).

4. According to a desert-based sentencing theory, there should be a discount for first offenders, who are seen as being less culpable: They can claim that the offence was "out of character." With repetition however, this appeal for mitigation becomes less plausible (see von Hirsch, 1982; Roberts, 1996).

5. For example, in 1995, an offender was sentenced to twenty-five years to life in California for stealing a pizza. Although only a felony petty theft, it was his third felony conviction. The story received widespread national and international attention. It was the topic front-page stories in other countries as well (see Globe and Mail, October 28, 1995).

6. Part of the public dissatisfaction with the intervention of parole is founded upon an inaccurate perception. People over-estimate the number of inmates who obtain parole, and they under-estimate the proportion of the sentence that is served in custody—see Chapter 3.

7. The perception of leniency plays into other perceptions about crime and justice. One of the most well-documented public associations is between the perception of leniency and a rise in crime rates. When Canadians were asked to identify the factors responsible for any rise in the crime rate, the most frequently chosen response was "A justice system that is too lenient" (Macleans, 1995).

8. Of those who approved of plea bargaining, 55 percent thought that sentences were not harsh enough. Of those who disapproved of plea bargaining, 83 percent felt sentences were not severe enough. This is a statistically significant difference.

9. The perception that plea bargaining permits defendants to evade justice, or obtain very lenient punishments is itself a misperception. Whatever the advantages and disadvantages of plea bargaining, systematic research suggests the practice is of greater benefit to the prosecutor than the defendant. Indeed, researchers have found that it is no "bargain" at all for the defendant.

10. The offenses included in this study were high-profile crimes of the kind with which the public are most familiar (e.g., break and enter). These offenses are also the ones for which the public are most likely to demand harsh penalties. If the researchers had selected other crimes (such as offenses against the administration of justice), discrepancies between the public and the courts might well have been even greater. In short the offenses chosen for this study were ones on which most agreement would be found, thus making it a conservative test of the public punitiveness hypothesis.

11. While some officers are undoubtedly the victims of very serious assaults, many cases of this category of offence are not that serious, amounting to little more than resisting arrest, or challenging the authority of the arresting officer.

12. It is interesting to note that the public appear aware that they are not getting all the facts from the news media. A majority of Canadians were of the view that the media do not provide them with adequate information in the area of sentencing (Doob and Roberts, 1988).

11

The Death Penalty

This chapter is devoted to public attitudes towards the ultimate punishment: the death penalty. As we are all aware, capital punishment raises complex moral, ethical and constitutional issues. In this chapter, the focus is almost exclusively on criminal justice in America, as it is alone in the western world in executing offenders. As of April 30, 1995, 3,009 prisoners were under sentence of death in the U.S. (Maguire and Pastore, 1995). There are several reasons for devoting an entire chapter to the issue of capital punishment. First, as noted in the first chapter, public attitudes towards the death penalty have received more attention from researchers and pollsters than any other single issue in the area of criminal justice.

Second, research on public opinion has been instrumental in determining whether (and how) the death penalty is used in America. And finally, it is worth exploring this issue because it represents the most extreme form of government intrusion into the lives of its citizens. This may explain why the debate over the utility and the morality of executing offenders has been around for generations, and will probably continue to be part of public discourse in America for some time. Even in nations that have abandoned execution as a legal punishment for decades, groups and individuals continue to call for re-instatement of capital punishment for offenders convicted of murder. One of the principal arguments made for re-instatement is that the vast majority of the public support the death penalty, and that it is undemocratic to ignore such a broad degree of consensus.

Power of the Death Penalty as Cruel
and Unusual Punishment

In America, there is a dual interest in public opinion regarding the death penalty. First, because we want to know what the people think about such an extreme criminal justice policy, and second because there are constitutional implications. The Eighth Amendment of the U.S. Constitution prohibits the government from imposing "cruel and unusual punishment." According to the Supreme Court, the phrase "cruel and unusual punishment" derives its meaning from "the evolving standards of decency that mark the progress of a maturing society" (*Trop v. Dulles*, 1958, p. 101). In *Furman v. Georgia* (1972), the Court ruled that death penalty statutes were unconstitutional because they permitted arbitrary and capricious decision-making. In the Furman decision, the Court did not declare the death penalty unconstitutional *per se*, but it did clearly indicate that community sentiment was central in determining this issue. In *Gregg v. Georgia* (1976), the Court ruled that the death penalty for murder was constitutional *per se*, and cited the fact that thirty-five states had passed death penalty statutes since the 1972 Furman case, and one state-wide referendum had been held in which the majority of the public voted in favor of the death penalty.[1]

For several decades social scientists have recognized the need to provide the Court with empirical evidence regarding the nature of public attitudes towards the death penalty. Unfortunately, the Supreme Court has not yet recognized the need to adhere to an adequate social science analysis of these data. This is regrettable, for researchers have demonstrated the weaknesses of relying on responses to broad questions about whether the public generally supports the use of capital punishment. We now know much more about who supports the death penalty, and for which crimes and which categories of offenders. In the following sections, we examine the empirical literature relating to public support for the death penalty. In addition to the nature of death penalty attitudes, we examine the sources which contribute to these attitudes and the circumstances under which the public opposes the death penalty. As well, we explore the extent to which people's attitudes change when confronted with rational, instrumental arguments.

The Stability and Nature of Death Penalty Attitudes

As we have noted, public opinion plays a central role in the judicial determination of whether the death penalty constitutes cruel and unusual punishment. An examination of death penalty attitudes over time shows that since 1982, support for capital punishment has been relatively stable: between 70 and 75 percent of the public (Ellsworth and Gross, 1994). In fact, with the exception of a brief period at the end of the 1960s,[2] support for the death penalty has been over 60 percent since 1936 (see Zeisel and Gallup, 1989).[3] In 1936, 62 percent of the American public were in favor of the death penalty, 33 percent were opposed and 5 percent expressed no opinion (cited in Erskine, 1974). Most recently, a Gallup poll in 1994 found that 80 percent of Americans support the death penalty for a person convicted of murder (Moore, 1994). This pattern is consistent with surveys conducted in other western nations. A representative poll in Canada found that 70 percent of the public favored the return of capital punishment (Angus Reid, 1995). This figure has changed little in Canada since the death penalty was abolished in the 1976. However, as we noted in Chapter 1, these surveys have several limitations.

Though the polls are measuring relatively stable opinions, the phrasing of questions and the context of questions may influence the outcome. In national polls, wording changes do not make a great difference in support for the death penalty (Ellsworth and Gross, 1994), but the salience of media attention to a specific issue does shape public support for the death penalty for specific crimes (e.g., rape; see Bohm, 1987; Bohm, 1991; Ellsworth and Gross, 1994). As well, support for capital punishment declines significantly when the alternative of life imprisonment without parole is mentioned. This can be demonstrated by examining poll data from 1994. When Americans were asked whether they favor or oppose the death penalty for murder, three-quarters responded in favor, one-quarter were opposed (Maguire and Pastore, 1994).

However, when asked "What should the penalty be for murder—the death penalty or life imprisonment with no possibility of parole?", only 50 percent chose the death penalty, while 32 percent chose life imprisonment, with 11 percent chose the response "it depends"[4] (Maguire and Pastore, 1995). The death penalty polls that are most often cited ask the latter question, and hence overstate the level of public support for capital punishment. Another important problem is that these broad questions fail to accurately gauge the limits of support: For whom and for which crimes is the death penalty an acceptable, even preferred punishment? Later sections of this chapter will address these questions. We begin with an examination of the reasons underlying public support for, or opposition to, the death penalty.

Justifications for Death Penalty Opinions

Across studies, most demographic characteristics show inconsistent relationships with support for the death penalty. Education shows mixed results across fifty years of Gallup Poll data (Bohm, 1991), a significant, but small effect in other studies (Barkan and Cohn, 1994; Kelley and Braithwaite, 1990; Stinchcombe et al., 1980; Young, 1991, 1992), and no effect in other studies (e.g., Keil and Vito, 1991). Old and young people generally hold similar attitudes toward the death penalty (Barkan and Cohn, 1994; Keil and Vito, 1991; Kelley and Braithwaite, 1990). Surprisingly, perhaps, conservatism, (when measured as political affiliation), also shows inconsistent effects across studies (Bohm, 1987; Kelley and Braithwaite, 1990). The inconsistent findings for conservatism may occur because it has several distinct, but related, dimensions (Kelley and Braithwaite, 1990). Kelley and Braithwaite (1990) found that only anti-union sentiment and opposition to social services were related to death penalty support.

Two consistent effects have emerged across studies. First, support for the death penalty is generally higher among men than women (Barkan and Cohn, 1994; Bohm, 1991; Ellsworth and Gross, 1994; Kelley and Braithwaite, 1990; Keil and Vito, 1991). Second, ethnic differences have also emerged across a number of studies. In a review of Gallup poll data over a fifty-year period (1936 to 1986), Bohm (1991) demonstrates an average ethnic difference of about 20 percentage points with African-Americans less likely to support the death penalty than Caucasians. For example, a 1994 Gallup poll shows that 82 percent of Caucasians but only 64 percent of African-Americans support the death penalty (Moore, 1994).

Unfairness in Administration

Several studies suggest that Americans believe that the death penalty is unfairly administered. The vast majority (80 percent) of respondents in random samples from Nebraska and New York as well as 80 percent of jurors who had served on capital cases in South Carolina indicated that the death penalty is "too arbitrary," with some offenders receiving prison terms while other, equally culpable defendants are sentenced to death (Bowers, 1993). People recognize that African-Americans are more likely to receive the death penalty than are Caucasians convicted of crimes of comparable seriousness. A little over 40 percent of Nebraskans and New Yorkers agreed that the death penalty was imposed in a racially biased manner (Bowers and Vandiver, 1991a,b). Three-quarters of Nebraskans agreed that defendants who can afford a good lawyer almost never get executed (Bowers and Vandiver, 1991a). A nation-wide Gallup poll in 1991 found that 45 percent believed that racial bias existed and 60 percent believed that a social class bias existed in the administration of the death penalty (Gallup and Newport, 1991). Three-quarters of African-Americans but less than half Caucasian Americans agreed that racial bias existed. Similar findings were found in the 1985 Gallup poll. The racial difference in the perception of discrimination against African-Americans may explain in part why members of this ethnic group are less likely to support the death penalty.

Recent studies also find that racial prejudice and negative stereotyping by Caucasians contribute to Caucasians' greater support for the death penalty (Barkan and Cohn, 1994; Kelley and Braithwaite, 1990). Racial prejudice explains death penalty attitudes even after controlling for demographic characteristics, political attitudes, fear of crime, and views of human nature. In Australia, individuals who had more sympathy for aboriginals and non-English speaking immigrants were more opposed to the death penalty. Respondents with the least amount of sympathy for minorities were far more likely to support the death penalty than those with the most amount of sympathy (Kelley and Braithwaite, 1990).

Symbolic and Emotional Nature of Death Penalty Attitudes

Many people acquire attitudes toward the death penalty during childhood, and these attitudes become connected to their ideological self-image (e.g., Tyler and Weber, 1982). Death penalty attitudes generally are based more on emotions and symbolic attitudes than on rational reflection (e.g., Ellsworth and Ross, 1983; Ellsworth and Gross, 1994; Tyler and Weber, 1982). Survey data support this conclusion: Most people agree that they learn to be for or against the death penalty before they learn the reasons why (Bowers and Vandiver, 1991a, b).

The symbolic nature of death penalty support is also found in the reasons people give to justify their support. Retribution is the most common justification cited by the public (Ellsworth and Gross, 1994; Warr and Stafford, 1984; Zeisel and Gallup, 1989). In response to an open-ended question asking the reasons for their positions regarding the death penalty, 50 percent of proponents in a 1986 Gallup poll cited retribution and 40 percent of opponents stated that it is wrong to take a life (Zeisel and Gallup, 1989). Based on national surveys over time, "retribution ('a life for a life') has been a more popular reason than the belief in deterrence" (Ellsworth and Gross, 1994, p. 29; Harris 1986, p. 453). Most proponents say they would support the death penalty even if deterrence was found to be ineffective, and most opponents say they will oppose it even if deterrence is effective (Ellsworth and Ross, 1983). These findings suggest that death penalty attitudes reflect emotional, rather than rational reactions to ways of reducing murder rates.

Finally, evidence of the strength of public support for the death penalty for certain offenders at least, comes from a Gallup poll conducted in 1994. This survey preceded the standard question by raising the possibility that the use of the death penalty would inevitably mean that some innocent individuals would be wrongfully executed. Specifically, respondents were asked the following question: "Some experts estimate that one out of 100 people who have been sentenced to death were actually innocent. If that estimate were right, would you still support the death penalty for a person convicted of murder or not?" Even when the specter of the ultimate injustice was made salient, three-quarters of the American public stated that they still supported capital punishment. The level of support was unchanged from polls in which false convictions were not mentioned. Fully four out of five men held this view (Maguire and Pastore, 1995). This result is further evidence of public support for the crime control versus due process model of criminal justice. The American public appear willing to countenance the judicial murder of innocent people in order to obtain whatever benefits are associated with the execution of guilty offenders.

Support for the Death Penalty Limited to Specific Offenses

Another important qualification on public support for capital punishment is that it is restricted to certain categories of offenses, and certain types of offender. As well, the extent of public support for the death penalty varies according to the specific circumstances surrounding the commission of the offense. This means that people tend to oppose legislation which automatically sentences offenders to death, regardless of the presence of any mitigating factors. After the Furman decision, several states attempted to reduce the arbitrary nature which characterized the administration of the death penalty by passing mandatory capital punishment laws. Under these statutes, all offenders convicted of specified categories of murder would automatically be sentenced to death (see Ellsworth and Gross, 1994, p. 36). When polls give respondents a choice between a discretionary death penalty and a mandatory death penalty which would apply to all convicted murders, the public prefers the discretionary death penalty. Ellsworth and Gross (1994) reviewed the Harris poll data across several years and found that fewer than 30 percent favored a mandatory death penalty. Supreme Court Justices' intuitive notions of community sentiment in this area are correct. Noting public sentiment in this area, they declared that mandatory death penalty laws were unconstitutional (*Woodson v. North Carolina*, 1976; *Roberts v. Louisiana*, 1976).

Which crimes are candidates for the death penalty from the public's perspective? This question has been addressed by several national opinion polls. (For a review of these surveys see Ellsworth and Gross, 1994). Several southern states have prescribed the death penalty for the crime of rape, not just murder. Is this consistent with public opinion, or are the public in favor of capital punishment only for premeditated murder? In 1977, the Supreme Court, citing empirical evidence on community sentiment, declared that the death penalty was cruel and unusual punishment for the crime of rape (*Coker v. Georgia*, 1977).

Justice White, in a concurring opinion, asserted that public attitudes must determine whether the death penalty is a disproportionate punishment to the crime for which it is imposed. He noted that few nations still punish rape by executing the rapist, and that while many states re-enacted death penalty statutes for murder after the Furman decision, the crime of rape was not included in the list of crimes for which offenders could be executed. In support of this position, he cited national opinion poll data showing little support for the death penalty for rape and cited the fact that few juries endorse the death penalty for rape. There may have been a shift in attitudes over time. In 1978, a Gallup poll revealed that only 32 percent supported the death penalty for rape, which further suggests that the Court correctly assessed community sentiment. More recent polls in 1986 and 1988, however, show that half of the respondents favor the death penalty for rape, which is perhaps due to the salience of rape in the media and the feminist movement (Ellsworth and Gross, 1994).

Not surprisingly, then, the public appears to favor the death penalty more for crimes involving a killing than for other crimes (Ellsworth and Gross, 1994). In a 1993 Gallup poll, 44 percent were opposed to extending the death penalty to other crimes (Gallup Poll Monthly, 1993, p. 31). The characteristics of the murder, however, are important. A survey in Kentucky found that 76 percent favored the death penalty if the murder was deliberate and premeditated. Almost as many favored the death penalty if the case involved multiple victims or if the murder was committed while the convicted person was under the influence of drugs (Keil and Vito, 1991). Support for the death penalty then, depends upon the heinousness of the crime, and perceptions of the killer's motivation and intention (Pennington and Hastie, 1986; Keil and Vito, 1991). It does not appear to be the case then that all murders provoke a desire among members of the public for the execution of the offender. Consistent with this conclusion, the next section describes public opposition toward imposing the death penalty for a negligent homicide that occurred during a commission of a felony.

Death Penalty for Felony-Murder

Many countries and thirty-four states in America allow juries to sentence accessories to a murder to death (as well as the principal actor) if a killing occurred during a commission of a felony (Finkel and Duff, 1991). For example, two robbers (Tom and John) plan to rob a convenience store. Tom watches the door while John demands the money from the clerk. In the course of the robbery, John shoots and kills the clerk. Should Tom receive the death penalty even though he did not actively participate in the killing, and did not carry a gun, but knew John was carrying a gun? The felony-murder rule allows the criminal justice system in certain states to execute Tom as well as John because the law concludes from the general intent to commit a felony that the principal (John) intended to kill. This intention to kill is effectively transferred to the accessory, Tom (e.g., Finkel and Duff, 1991; Robinson and Darley, 1995). Both the accessory and the triggerman in a felony-murder are seen as having the same degree of culpability (called the accessorial liability rule) and hence if convicted, both can be sentenced to death (Finkel and Smith, 1993). Many felony-murder state statutes also allow the execution of defendants when a bystander is accidentally shot by another third-party at the scene (e.g., the police, the clerk, or another bystander).

Does the felony-murder rule violate the Eighth amendment's prohibition against cruel and unusual punishment because it provides what the public believes is disproportionate punishment for the crime? In two cases (*Edmund v. Florida*, 1982; *Tison v. Arizona*, 1987), the Supreme Court considered whether the death penalty for accessories in felony-murder was cruel and unusual punishment. Consider the case of *Edmund v. Florida*:

> Earl Edmund was the getaway driver, sitting in a car when his companions, Sampson and Jeanette Armstrong, attempted to rob a farmhouse in Florida. In the ensuing attempt, the Armstrongs shot and killed Thomas and Eunice Kersey. Edmund was charged with felony-murder. In Florida, the felony-murder rule permits an unintended death occurring during the commission of a felony (e.g., robbery) to be treated as first-degree murder. ... Edmund was found guilty of felony-murder and given the death sentence. (Finkel and Smith, 1993, p. 130)

Does the death penalty for Edmund constitute cruel and unusual punishment? The majority of the Supreme Court Justices in Edmund concluded that the death penalty was cruel and unusual punishment for an accessory who neither killed nor intended to kill and played only a minor role in the felony (i.e., getaway driver).

Consider the facts in the case of *Tison v. Arizona*:

> The Tison brothers, Ricky and Raymond, participated in breaking their father, Gary Tison, and his cellmate, Randy Greenawald, out of Arizona State Prison, without a shot being fired. Two days later, while driving a Lincoln, they had a flat tire; with no spare, their father instructed them to flag down a motorist in order to steal a car. The Lyons family stopped and was taken into the desert at gunpoint. John Lyons asked the Tisons to leave his family there with some water, and Gary Tison sent his sons to get some water. As the sons were returning, they heard the shots. All four members of the Lyons family were killed. Ricky and Raymond were found guilty and

sentenced to death as accessory felony-murderers. (Finkel and Smith, 1993, p. 130)

Should the Tison brothers be sentenced to death or are their actions similar to Edmund's actions in the previous case? The majority of the Supreme Court Justices upheld the death penalty as an appropriate punishment for the Tison brothers. The Court asserted that the Tison brothers had substantially participated in the crime and had displayed a reckless indifference to human life, even though they neither killed nor intended to kill. The degree of participation, then, would appear to be critical. Where do the public stand on the issue of the capital punishment for offenders convicted of felony-murder?

Several studies (Finkel, 1990; Finkel and Duff, 1991; Liss, Finkel, and Moran, 1994; Finkel and Smith, 1993; Robinson and Darley, 1995), using experimental manipulations in simulated cases and convenience samples of undergraduates and adults, have examined whether community sentiment supports treating accessories and principals alike, and supports treating principals of a felony-murder with as much severity as people convicted of premeditated murder. Community sentiment is consistent with the dissenting Justices' views in felony-murder cases heard by the Supreme Court (Finkel and Duff, 1991).

For example, Finkel and Duff (1991) found both full and partial nullifications in verdict decisions as well as significantly fewer respondents wanting the death penalty for triggermen in felony-murder cases than for triggermen in premeditated murder cases. Whereas 64 percent of the subjects wanted the death penalty for triggermen in premeditated murder cases, in felony murder cases none wanted it for the driver, only 2 percent wanted it for the lookout, only 6 percent wanted it for the sidekick, and only 17 percent wanted it for the triggerman (Finkel and Duff, 1991). Moreover, whereas all mock jurors found the defendants guilty of robbery charges, only 42 percent of the defendants were found guilty of first degree murder, which suggests that more than half the mock jurors nullified the assumption in the felony-murder rule that intent to commit the robbery transfers to intent to commit first degree murder. Canadians, too, distinguish between offenders convicted of premeditated murder and others who kill during the commission of another offense, without having planned to do so. Ninety-three percent supported the death penalty for cases of premeditated murder, whereas only 60 percent supported execution as a penalty for offenders who committed murder during a burglary (Focus Canada, 1987).

In all of these studies, respondents differentiate between accessories and principals felony-murder: Compared to principals, accessories are less likely to be found guilty and less likely to receive the most severe sentence. Even children in second grade give sentences proportional to the culpability of the actors and reject the felony murder rule that principals and accessories should be treated the same (Liss, Finkel, and Moran, 1994). These findings suggest that the accessorial liability doctrine is inconsistent with community sentiment. The public prefers proportional justice whereas the doctrine requires equal treatment for all participants in a felony-murder.

In both the Tison case and the Edmund case, the Supreme Court Justices conducted what can only be described as a poor social science analysis of legislative statutes and verdict decisions (see Finkel and Duff, 1991, for a detailed description of the Court's opinion in these cases). A more adequate analysis of legislative statutes across jurisdictions shows that only a minority of the jurisdictions would allow for the death penalty when a defendant is similar to Edmund (i.e., does not kill or intend to kill and has minor to less substantial participation in the felony such as a getaway driver, but a killing takes place during the commission of the felony). Likewise, only a minority of the jurisdictions would allow for the death penalty when a defendant is similar to the Tison brothers (i.e., does not kill but has moderate to substantial participation in the felony and shows reckless indifference to human life) (Finkel, 1993). Aggregate jury data, which were not reviewed by the Court, also demonstrated reluctance on the part of both jurors and the prosecution to support the execution of accessories as well as principals in felony murder cases (see Finkel, 1990). Thus, multiple methodologies converge to suggest that accessories should be treated more leniently than triggermen in felony-murder cases, and that community sentiment does not favor the death penalty for accessories to murder.[5]

There is a more general lesson regarding public opinion to be learned from this line of research. The public's position on felony-murder cases shows that people make relatively sophisticated distinctions in terms of the culpability of offenders. They clearly reject a simplistic position that favors imposition of the death penalty on anyone convicted of murder. As well, they are interested in establishing degrees of culpability—between offenders who set out to kill, and others who set out to commit another crime but who end up becoming accessories to murder. Underlying the public's position on this topic may be a sense of fairness in the allocation of punishment. They see the unfairness of treating accessories and principals with the same severity.[6]

Support for the Death Penalty Limited to Specific Criminals

Juvenile Offenders. Should juvenile offenders and mentally deficient offenders be liable for execution if they are convicted of murder? These are among the most contentious questions in the death penalty literature. There are of course strong arguments against executing both categories of offender, on the grounds that they are less responsible for their actions, and hence less culpable of their crimes, than adult offenders without mental deficiencies. Nevertheless, the Supreme Court has held that the death penalty is constitutional for both categories of offender.

In contrast to America, all European countries, Canada, and many other nations prohibit the execution of juvenile offenders. By 1986, 281 juvenile offenders had been executed for crimes committed under the age of 18 in the U.S. (Streib, 1988). It is interesting to note that most juvenile offenders were sentenced to death for a murder committed while in the process of another felony (Ogloff, 1987). There are therefore dual grounds for opposing the death penalty for most murders committed by juveniles: Not only are the offenders young, but they have committed the kind of murder that is considered less serious, namely a felony murder, and which fails to find the support of the public as a crime for which execution is an appropriate punishment.

In 1988, the Supreme Court held that the death penalty is unconstitutional for juveniles who committed the crime at the age of fifteen or younger in states who do not have minimum age limitations (*Thompson v. Oklahoma*, 1988). In 1989 the Supreme Court held that the death penalty was constitutional for offenders who committed the crime at the age of sixteen (*Wilkins v. Missouri*, 1989) and at the age of seventeen (*Stanford v. Kentucky*, 1989). In all these cases, the Court stated its preference for "objective indicia" such as legislative statutes to gauge community sentiment over attitudinal data from opinion polls. The Court appears more confident of measures that are closer to the behavior of carrying out executions such as the passage of legislation allowing the death penalty for juveniles. As the cases of Stanford and Wilkins illustrate, different interpretations of "objective indicia" fuel heated battles between Justices on the Supreme Court. Justice Scalia, for example, does not count the fifteen states without capital punishment in his count of the states that bar executions of juveniles, and concludes that a majority, much less a consensus, is not shown in the data (Finkel, 1993).

Justice Brennan in a dissenting opinion, however, labels Scalia's analysis a "distorted view" because the fifteen non-death penalty states are not included (Finkel, 1993). In the end, both the minority and majority make basic social science errors in analyzing the data, and arrive at widely disparate conclusions:

> [T]he plurality gets answers of 41 percent [of states barring executions of sixteen-year-olds] and 32 percent [barring executions of seventeen-year-olds], clearly less than a majority; the minority gets 91 percent [barring executions of sixteen-year-olds], and 82 percent [barring executions of seventeen-year-olds], clearly a substantial majority. (Finkel, 1993, p. 71)

When Finkel (1993) analyzed the data using appropriate scientific assumptions, over half of the states barred executions for sixteen-year-olds (58 percent) and seventeen-year-olds (52 percent), which was significantly higher than the percentage that barred executions for adults (29 percent). These data provide some evidence that community sentiment (as measured by the existence of legislative statutes) is against the execution of juvenile offenders. As we have mentioned earlier, legislative statutes, however, are a very indirect and error-prone measure of community sentiment. Jury sentencing data were also cited by Justice Brennan to support the view that the evolving standard of decency does not want executions of juveniles; unfortunately, the numbers are uninformative because the Justices either use the wrong denominator or provided no denominator (Finkel, 1993).

The Supreme Court places little value in public opinion polls on account of their weaknesses. These include problems such as the use of a single measure, confusing wording of the questions, lack of detail about the cases, and the absence of real consequences. In national polls conducted in the United States which have these problems, support for the death penalty for juveniles has risen since 1936 when it was first asked (Ellsworth and Gross, 1994). In 1965, 21 percent favored the death penalty for juveniles. This increased to 44 percent in 1988 and 57 percent in 1989 (Ellsworth and Gross, 1994). In September 1994, 60 percent favored the death penalty for a convicted teenager who commits murder (Moore, 1994). McGarrell and Sandys (1996) found that 59 percent of a statewide random Indiana sample supported the juvenile death penalty.

Other research suggests that a majority of the public is opposed to the death penalty for juveniles. Skovron, Scott, and Cullen (1989) found that two-thirds of their sample in 1986 were opposed to the state passing a law to allow the death penalty for juveniles over the age of fourteen. When Georgia residents were given a choice between life imprisonment or the death penalty for persons convicted of murder before they turned eighteen, two-thirds favored life imprisonment (Clearinghouse on Georgia Prison and Jails, 1987).

These survey data, however, do not tell us whether the public believes the age of the juvenile should determine whether the death penalty is appropriate. Two studies, using the experimental method and hypothetical scenarios of children on trial for first degree murder as adults, have tested the hypothesis that people consider age in making death penalty decisions and whether the heinousness of the crime constrains how much importance people give to the youthfulness of the offender in their death penalty decisions (Finkel, Hughes, Smith, and Hurabiell, 1994). Data on the reasons for mock jurors' sentences showed quite clearly that age is the primary factor that persuades individuals not to impose the death penalty. The power of youth to mitigate the severity of punishment declines as the crimes become more heinous.

However, even for the most heinous crimes, the majority of respondents still did not favor imposition of the death penalty on juveniles. As Finkel *et al.*, (1994) concluded:

> In a most heinous case, in which we would expect the age effect to be most muted and in which approximately 60 percent gave the death penalty to a 25-year-old, approximately 25 percent gave it if the defendant was 13, 14, or 15, and approximately 35 percent gave it if the defendant was 16, 17, or 18; thus, for the latter two groups, 75 percent and 65 percent of the DQ [death qualified] community refuse to give the death penalty. (p. 19)

A comparison of these studies with the national opinion poll data suggest that the majority of people do not support the death penalty for juveniles when questions are framed to highlight the behavioral consequence of the preference (e.g., enactment of a state law, a decision of death in a jury) and when they are given alternatives such as life imprisonment. As with the felony-murder rule then, criminal justice practice is at odds with community sentiment. Finally, as noted earlier in this chapter, executing juveniles runs contrary to public opinion in other countries as well. More Canadians were opposed to, rather than in favor of executing juveniles, although there was a strong majority in favor of the death penalty for adult offenders (Brillon *et al.*, 1984).

Mentally Retarded Offenders. In 1986, Jerome Bowden, a mentally handicapped African-American was executed in the state of Georgia. He was not the first, and will not be the last mentally deficient defendant to be executed in America. The Supreme Court ruled in 1989 (*Penry v. Lynaugh*) that the death penalty can legally be imposed on mentally retarded offenders convicted of murder principally because it believes that the public condones the execution of this category of offender. The Court is clearly wrong in this interpretation of public opinion research. Two Gallup Polls in 1988 and 1989 showed that only a minority (22 percent and 27 percent) favored the death penalty for mentally retarded offenders.

Surveys in many states as disparate as Georgia, Texas, Florida, South Carolina, and New York also show little support for the execution of mentally retarded offenders. (For a description of these surveys see Reed, 1993). McGarrell and Sandys (1996) found that only one-quarter of Indiana respondents favored the death penalty for mentally retarded adult offenders. Additional indicators of community sentiment such as the development of habilitative programs for persons with mental retardation, judges' and juries' sentencing decisions, legislative activity, and federal statutory enactments suggest that the Supreme Court has misjudged public sentiment (Reed, 1993).[7]

For example, five states with death penalty legislation (Georgia, Kentucky, Tennessee, New Mexico, and Maryland) have statutes that ban the execution of mentally retarded offenders, and at least fourteen states have habilitative programs for mentally retarded individuals in prisons (Reed, 1993). In addition, twenty-four states have also considered a complete ban on executions for mentally retarded offenders, but for a variety of reasons did not pass the legislation, and seven states have taken no action on this issue (Reed, 1993). Here we have a more fine-grained analysis of legislative statutes—one that includes whether legislative bodies have *considered* the ban and the *reasons* for failure to pass the ban. This helps to provide an answer to the question of whether community sentiment or political lobbying groups played a role in the decision. In this area, multiple indicators of community sentiment converge to indicate that the majority of the public does not support the death penalty for mentally retarded individuals.

Power of Instrumental Arguments to Change Death Penalty Attitudes

The last issue relating to public opinion and the death penalty raises a theme we have explored in a number of different domains in throughout this book: the effects of information upon attitudes. In an earlier chapter, we noted widespread public ignorance of many criminal justice statistics. We argued that an important priority for the criminal justice system in all the countries included in our survey of public opinion is to provide the public with better information. Educating the public so that they become more informed is necessary if criminal justice policy-development is to proceed without irrational opposition from the community. How does this apply to the domain of capital punishment? What happens to public support for the death penalty when people are given information about the administration of capital punishment?

As noted earlier, people are uninformed about the nature of the death penalty in contemporary America. The public know very little about how it is actually administered, believe that it is much cheaper than life imprisonment, and believe that it deters potential murderers (Ellsworth and Ross, 1983). This raises an interesting research hypothesis: Will individuals who support the death penalty change their attitude once they receive accurate information about its costs and benefits? Clearly, the costs and benefits of the death penalty affect some people's support for it. A sizable minority of respondents mention the cost of keeping people in prison or fear of murderers being released from prison as one reason for their support for capital punishment (see Ellsworth and Gross, 1994).[8] Information about the costs and benefits of the death penalty, however, will probably persuade only individuals who are ambivalent toward the death penalty.

Several studies have examined the extent to which people are persuaded by instrumental arguments. In a classic study in the area, Lord, Ross, and Lepper (1979) presented undergraduate students who were opposed the death penalty as well as those who supported the death penalty with research on how much the death penalty deters other people from committing murder. Each student read two research reports. One study supported the student's *a priori* view about the death penalty, and the other study contradicted the student's view. In this sense, the information provided to subjects was "balanced," with one study supportive of capital punishment, the other opposed. Along with each study, students received criticisms of each study and rebuttals to these criticisms. After rending all this material, subjects in the study were asked to rate the scientific validity of the two studies, as well as to indicate the strength of their own death penalty opinion at the end of the study.

If the subjects in the study were reasoning rationally, we might expect the attitudes of the two groups to converge. Since the research evidence is mixed, and therefore supports both sides, pro and anti-death penalty individuals should become somewhat less sure of their position. Under these conditions, it would be reasonable to expect opinions to be come less extreme. After all, if the data are mixed, one should not have a strong opinion either way. Paradoxically, this manipulation had a boomerang effect.

After reading about these studies, all participants more strongly endorsed their *original* view: Those who opposed the death penalty were more strongly opposed, and those who supported the death penalty were more strongly in favor of it. Moreover, subjects were selective in their reactions. Both the proponents and the opponents of the death penalty rated the report that supported their view as more convincing and better conducted than the report that did not support their view. This study suggests that people discount and ignore arguments when these arguments are inconsistent with their prior beliefs.

The Lord *et al.* (1979) findings, however, may apply only to people whose attitudes about the death penalty are connected to other political and moral attitudes. Research finds that respondents with more accessible attitudes about capital punishment discounted research reports on the effectiveness of the death penalty to a greater extent than did those who held weaker attitudes (Houston and Fazio, 1989). Sarat and Vidmar (1976) also found that over half of the respondents who were uncertain or did not strongly oppose or favor the death penalty changed their opinions when they read utilitarian and humanitarian arguments, whereas few individuals who strongly held their beliefs changed their opinions.

McGarrell and Sandys (1996) found that the majority of individuals who strongly support the death penalty (59 percent) still endorsed the death penalty when given the option of life imprisonment without parole, but half of those who strongly support the death penalty changed their mind when given the option of life imprisonment plus work and restitution. By contrast, half of the individuals who somewhat favor the death penalty change to life imprisonment without parole when given the option, and the majority of these individuals endorse life imprisonment without parole plus work and restitution. These findings suggest that individuals are more open to change when they are ambivalent about the death penalty. Moreover, this pattern of change suggests that retribution is the underlying motivation for those who strongly support the death penalty.

Before leaving the Lord *et al.* study, it is worth noting a more general lesson to be learned. The results of the research confirm that we do not react to information in a "cool" unbiased way. Our beliefs influence, and in fact may determine what kinds of information we acquire and how we evaluate that information. This means that it is going to be hard to change public perceptions based upon strong beliefs. For example, if people strongly believe that sentencing patterns are very lenient or that many offenders on parole commit further crimes, these opinions are going to guide their reactions to stories that disconfirm their views. It would be unreasonable then, as we point out in an earlier chapter, to expect the public to behave like research scientists, evaluating data and revising theories in a scientific manner.

Several studies support the conclusion that many people are ambivalent about the death penalty. When asked how strongly they feel about their death penalty attitudes, two-thirds of respondents in a national Gallup poll indicated very strongly and one-third indicated not so strongly (Zeisel and Gallup, 1989); this is a measure of attitude involvement. From Zeisel and Gallup's data on strength of death penalty sentiment, one-third of the respondents are open to change and may not discount instrumental arguments. Further supporting the validity of the responses on strength of sentiment, Zeisel and Gallup (1989) found that 28 percent of supporters indicated that they would oppose the death penalty if it had no deterrent effect and life sentence without parole were available, and 4 percent of opponents indicated that they would support it if they were convinced that the death penalty was a deterrent. Other data also suggest that a sizable minority are ambivalent about the death penalty. Over 40 percent of a Nebraska sample and over 55 percent of a New York sample agreed that they have moral doubts about the death penalty, and that they are personally uncomfortable with it (Bowers and Vandiver, 1991a,b).

Bowers (1993) argued that many people are ambivalent about the death penalty, and if alternatives were available that provided a meaningful and harsh sentence, people would endorse these alternatives rather than the death penalty. Bowers (1993) further suggested that policymakers and scholars had been misreading the overwhelming support for the death penalty found in national polls: It merely indicates that in the absence of harsh and just punishment, people will endorse the death penalty.

To test this hypothesis, Bowers posed the following question to respondents: "If convicted murderers in this state could be sentenced to life in prison with absolutely no chance of ever being released on parole or returning to society, would you prefer this as an alternative to the death penalty?" When this alternative is made clear, many people who support the death penalty in the abstract change their minds and endorse life imprisonment without parole. Adding restitution to the victims as a requirement convinces still more people to change their minds.[9] Over three-quarters of a sample of Indiana respondents supported the death penalty in response to standard poll question, but when life imprisonment without parole coupled with restitution to the family was presented as an alternative, only 26 percent supported the death penalty.

Self-described conservatives, however, were less likely to change their mind and endorse the alternative punishment than were moderates or liberals (McGarrell and Sandys, 1996). This finding supports prior research (e.g., Lord *et al.*, 1979; Sarat and Vidmar, 1976): People were less likely to change their attitude in the face of a demand to do so when their political beliefs served as the basis for their attitude about the death penalty.[10] To summarize, between one-third and two-fifths of the public have weak attitudes toward the death penalty and are open to change through rational persuasion.[11]

Effects of Information: Testing the Marshall Hypothesis

A number of studies have tested what has become known as the Marshall hypothesis. The name derives from Justice Thurgood Marshall's opinion in *Furman v. Georgia*. In that judgment, Marshall noted that public opinion must be knowledgeable about the issue. He further concluded that if Americans knew the facts about the death penalty, if they were aware of its limited deterrent effect (relative to life imprisonment) as well as the inequities of application, more of them would oppose capital punishment. This hypothesis is easily testable in an experimental setting: If public support for the death penalty is founded upon ignorance of the facts, educating them about the true state of affairs should dampen public enthusiasm for executing offenders convicted of murder.

Several researchers have tested the Marshall hypothesis (e.g., Sarat and Vidmar, 1976; Vidmar and Dittenhoffer, 1981) and the results have generally supported the hypothesis, although not always to the extent that Justice Marshall might have predicted. A systematic evaluation of the hypothesis was published in 1991. Bohm, Clark and Aveni used a sample of students, some of whom were enrolled in a special class on the death penalty, while the "control" condition consisted of students enrolled in other courses offered at the same time. The death penalty class met for two hours a day, five days a week for four weeks. Unlike some laboratory research, the "manipulation" in this study was quite intensive: Students were exposed to forty hours of discussion about capital punishment. In addition there were extensive readings. At the end of the four weeks, they would have known more about the death penalty than 99 percent of the general public. In short, they can definitely be considered an informed population.[12]

The results of this study showed (1) that subjects were uninformed about the death penalty before taking the course, and (2) that a significant shift in attitudes occurred for certain individuals. Students who became more knowledgeable as a result of taking the death penalty course shifted away from supporting the death penalty. The shift was by no means complete: A majority of study participants still favored capital punishment. African-Americans and women, particularly African-American women, once they became informed about the death penalty were most likely to change opinions and oppose the death penalty.

Another study also compared students who acquired knowledge about the death penalty through a college course to students who did not acquire such knowledge (Bohm and Vogel, 1994). This study also found that information about the death penalty only made a difference for certain kinds of individuals. Crime victims were less likely to support the death penalty after becoming informed. However, death penalty supporters were less likely to agree that there is a danger in executing an innocent person whereas death penalty opponents believed the opposite; this finding suggests that people assimilate certain information in a biased manner to support their initial beliefs. Nevertheless, these careful experiments demonstrate both that the American public is uninformed about the issue, and that some Americans are not as supportive of the death penalty as would be suggested by a poll asking a simple question such as "Are you in favor of, or opposed to, the death penalty?"

Consistent with the notion that death penalty attitudes are open to change, Zimring and Hawkins (1986) suggested that political elites should lead public opinion rather than follow it, and argued that if the death penalty were abolished, public support for capital punishment would decline substantially. Kelley and Braithwaite (1990) tested this hypothesis using a representative nation-wide sample of Australians. They found that respondents who lived in a state that had abolished the death penalty thirty years earlier were less supportive of the death penalty than were respondents who lived in other states. Though this difference is significant, "it is not large: 5 percent over a generation." (Kelley and Braithwaite, 1990, p. 551). This finding suggests that when the death penalty was abolished some people changed how they socialized their children to think about the death penalty. It may also suggest that the Zimring and Hawkins "educative" hypothesis takes time to have an effect, and does not necessarily have an impact on all members of society.

How stable are changes in attitudes about the death penalty which are based on informed knowledge? Bohm, Vogel, and Maisto (1993) examined this issue. Students who completed a month-long college course on capital punishment were significantly more opposed to the death penalty after becoming informed about it. This attitude change, however, did not last. Students completed a questionnaire on their attitudes toward the death penalty two or three years after taking the course. These data showed that after two or three years their attitudes had rebounded to near where their attitude was before taking the death penalty class.

Conclusions

In this chapter, we have explored the nature of community sentiment towards the death penalty, and the role it plays in determining the government's use of capital punishment. Supreme Court Justices often use intuition and anecdotal experiences to assess where community sentiment stands on an issue. Moreover, when the Court considers social science evidence, the Justices often draw faulty conclusions from the data. The Court often misses the mark of contemporary standards of what is cruel and unusual punishment for specific crimes. In judging what was cruel and unusual, the Court has declared that the death penalty for juveniles, mentally retarded offenders, and accessories to felony-murder meet the standards of decency of an evolving society, but social science evidence suggests that the majority of the public does not support the death penalty for these crimes. The Court, however, correctly interpreted community sentiment when it declared that mandatory death penalty statutes and that the death penalty for rape were unconstitutional. The research reviewed in this chapter suggests that many Supreme Court Justices are skeptical of social science evidence, and others misinterpret data.

Research demonstrates that members of different ethnic groups disagree about the appropriateness of these measures. African-Americans are less supportive of the use of the death penalty than are Caucasian-Americans. This finding supports the conflict model's image of justice. Individuals with more power in society will be more likely to endorse measures that protect their property and position in society than will individuals with less power in society (e.g., minorities). Moreover, minorities are less likely to endorse capital punishment, but are more likely to be executed if convicted of a capital crime. Research shows that African-Americans are disproportionately sentenced to death (Bohm, 1989).

Finally, we stress the need to educate the American public about the nature and effects of capital punishment. It is important to educate the public about all aspects of criminal justice, but the stakes are so much higher with capital punishment. At the present time, one of the justifications for the continued use of the death penalty in the U.S. (when other nations have replaced execution with life imprisonment) is the widespread public support for capital punishment. This support has been over-stated, and is founded in part upon a lack of information. Until such time as the public knows more about the issue, we should be skeptical of claims for the legitimacy of the death penalty based upon public opinion.

While central to the issue, public support for the death penalty is not sufficient to guarantee the constitutionality of this punishment. The Supreme Court Justices, especially liberal due process justices, emphasize the value in maintaining the dignity of human life in their assessment of what is cruel and unusual. For example, Bohm (1989) notes that Justices Stewart, Powell, and Stevens in *Gregg v. Georgia* accorded priority to dignity when they stated:

> [P]ublic perceptions of standards of decency with respect to criminal sanctions are not conclusive. A penalty also must accord with *the dignity of man*, which is the *basic concept underlying the Eighth Amendment*... the Eighth Amendment demands more than a challenged punishment be acceptable to contemporary society. The Court also must ask whether it comports with the basic concept of *human dignity* at the core of the Amendment. (emphasis in original; as cited in Bohm, 1989, p. 174-75)

However, in recent cases in the 1980s and 1990s, the Court has indicated that the concept of dignity has been met in its rejection of social science evidence which demonstrates racial biases. The court also ignores social science evidence indicating that the death penalty serves no instrumental function to deter other potential murderers; by ignoring this evidence, the administration of the death penalty does not challenge the image of humankind as a humane society (Bohm, 1989).

Notes

1. Fourteen states (Alaska, Kansas, Hawaii, Iowa, Maine, Massachusetts, Michigan, Minnesota, North Dakota, New York, Rhode Island, Vermont, West Virginia, Wisconsin) do not allow the death penalty for any offenders.

2. Gallup polls in 1965 and 1966 recorded 45 and 42 percent respectively in favor of the death penalty for persons convicted of murder (see Maguire and Pastore, 1995, Table 2.56).

3. Since this issue has been repeatedly explored since the 1930s, occasionally polls show exceptions. For example, Erskine (1970) cites a Gallup survey conducted in 1965 which found the public almost evenly divided between opponents and proponents of capital punishment. This survey would appear to be an exception; the general trend is for proponents to outnumber opponents by a margin of 2:1.

4. A further 7 percent chose neither, other, don't know or refused to respond (see Maguire and Pastore, 1995, Table 2.55).

5. The public does not reject completely the purpose behind the felony murder rule, which is to hold felons responsible for the danger that they create in committing felonies. As Robinson and Darley (1995) noted: "[F]rom our respondents' view, the felony-murder rule is on the right track but simply goes too far. The subjects would support a felony-murder rule that significantly aggravates negligent killings during a robbery but only to the level of manslaughter for principals and to something less than that for accomplices, not to the level of murder as the current doctrine does. In other words, they would support a 'felony-manslaughter rule' with a standard 'accomplice discount'" (p. 178).

6. Another reason for the discrepancy between the public and the court with regard to felony murder may be that the public are unaware of one of the principal justifications for the felony-murder rule, namely to deter potential offenders from carrying firearms when they commit crimes.

7. The data presented for judges' and juries' decisions, however, suffer from the same problem as jury decisionmaking data for juvenile death penalty trials: It is unclear how many cases of mentally retarded persons have been *considered* for the death penalty and in how many cases the prosecutor did not pursue the death penalty.

8. General fear of crime, however, does not have a significant effect (Barkan and Cohn, 1994; Kelley and Braithwaite, 1990) or has only a very small effect (Tyler and Weber, 1982) when the effects of other predictors such as political attitudes are removed.

9. These findings have been replicated in a survey of Indiana residents (McGarrell and Sandys, 1996) and in a national poll.

10. Ellsworth and Gross (1994) note that Bowers' questions are strongly worded and may place demands on the respondent to choose the alternative because the respondent thinks the interviewer wants them to do so.

11. Ellsworth and Gross (1994) use an "undecided" response to determine how many would change their attitudes in the face of persuasive arguments. As Ellsworth and Gross (1994) note, around 8 percent of respondents on national polls say they are undecided about support or opposition for the death penalty. This measure of attitudinal involvement, however, is extremely indirect, and biased by the fact that most people are compelled to provide some answer rather than volunteer that they are undecided.

12. Manipulation checks conducted by the researchers showed that the experimental manipulation (participation in the seminar) did increase students' knowledge about the death penalty.

12

Privacy and Free Speech

Several constitutional issues in the United States depend upon the standards and opinions of the public: Privacy and free speech are two prime examples. A consensus among the majority of a community is essential in determining whether a police officer has conducted an unreasonable search and seizure. In some exceptions to constitutional rights—such as laws prohibiting the distribution of obscene material—community sentiment is central to assessing whether particular materials are obscene or are legitimate expressions of free speech. In other constitutional areas (such as the state's regulation of abortion), some Supreme Court Justices are concerned about the legitimacy of Court decisions that may not have popular support. We have noted that when the public loses confidence in the judicial system, a number of negative consequences ensue. For example, when Court decisions run contrary to popular conceptions of justice, jurors may decide to acquit or convict a defendant of a less serious charge. This is known as jury nullification: Jurors make decisions that defy the evidence and the law.[1] Thus, the Supreme Court Justices believe that public opinion is directly relevant to the reconciliation of some constitutional issues, and in other areas may shape the justice system through concerns about the Court's legitimacy or through jurors' focus on the fairness of a law in specific cases.

In this chapter, we review research on community attitudes towards privacy and obscenity. As with other issues covered in this book, we shall compare the research on community views to the Supreme Court Justices' assertions about community sentiment for a particular issue. As we noted in Chapter 1, there are several methods to assess community sentiment. These include representative public opinion polls, experimental manipulations using hypothetical scripts, analysis of real and mock jury decisions, voting behavior on issues, and legislative statutes. Court[2] Justices often use anecdotal experiences and intuitive notions to determine the nature of public opinion. In addition, the Supreme Court Justices rely on empirical indicators of community sentiment. As we have already seen with regard to the death penalty, members of the Court are not scientists and often fail to follow the rules of good research.

Justices fail to appreciate a basic tenet of science called triangulation. This approach to research consists of employing multiple ways of measuring a single concept such as community sentiment. It provides a more reliable assessment of the concept than single measures or methods. When multiple methods produce the same result, we can have more confidence in the veracity of conclusions drawn (Ellsworth, 1988). All measures have biases, but if different approaches arrive at the same conclusion, then these biases alone cannot explain the result. In contrast to this approach, the Court often looks for a single method that provides the most "valid" measure of community. It prefers what it calls "objective indicia" such as the passage of legislative statutes and real jury decisions in cases to gauge community sentiment (e.g., Finkel, 1993; Finkel and Duff, 1991). The Court then often takes a historical approach to gauging community sentiment, one that can miss the mark on contemporary standards of decency or contemporary expectations of privacy. Moreover, as we will see, Supreme Court Justices sometimes draw inappropriate conclusions from their attempts at analyzing legislative statutes and jury verdict data (Finkel, 1990).

Supreme Court Justices may place more importance on legislative statutes as a measure of public opinion for two reasons. First, they are concerned with how people will react toward federal intrusion on the rights of states and attempt to mitigate negative reaction by acknowledging the right of states to differ in how they regulate their citizens. Second, they may believe that indicators closer to *behavior* are more valid than indicators that measure mere preference, which may be uninformed and uncommitted opinions. Legislative statutes, however, are at best only very indirect measures of community sentiment. They may misrepresent community sentiment in several ways (Finkel, 1990; Stalans and Henry, 1994). Statutes may be historically dated. They also may have been enacted on the basis of misperception of the public desires, or they may represent the influence of powerful lobbying groups. As well, they are constrained by the fact that legislators cannot enact statutes on matters that the Court has declared unconstitutional and often consider the Court's position before enacting a statute. In this sense they may reflect legislators' perceptions of Supreme Court decisions, rather than public opinion *per se*.

Public Versus Judicial View of Privacy

The meaning of privacy is not explicitly defined by the American Constitution. Instead, Supreme Court Justices have constructed the legal meaning of "privacy" through their interpretations of the first, fourth, fifth, ninth, and fourteenth amendments. Privacy encompasses at least three concerns (Melton, 1983). One such concern is the right to make decisions about one's body without government interference, and the protection from governmental interference with one's body or mind as guaranteed in the first, ninth, and fourteenth amendments. Another component is protection from unreasonable searches and seizures of one's home and possessions. This protection is guaranteed by the fourth amendment. The final issue is the right to grant or deny access to information about oneself (e.g., medical or school records) and the right to protection from governmental acquisition of information about oneself through coercion (e.g., the police using physical force to obtain a confession to a crime) or intrusion (e.g., the police obtaining medical, bank, or school records without consent). Public opinion has a bearing on the first two concerns, but less on the right to grant or deny access to information about oneself because this right generally revolves around the balance between informed consent and government's need for the information.

Community Sentiment Regarding Government's Interference with One's Body

The most salient example of freedom from government's interference with a person's autonomy is the abortion issue. In the 1973 case of *Roe v. Wade*, the Supreme Court Justices drew upon medical legal history to determine the public's attitudes toward abortion procedures over the centuries. In the Roe case, the majority of the Court declared unconstitutional a Texas statute that made abortion a criminal offense. This Supreme Court decision gave women the right to choose whether to have an abortion or not. In the 1990s, the Supreme Court Justices have also been aware of public opinion on abortion as they have made decisions in recent cases which have sought to overturn or limit the Roe decision. As Finkel (1995) notes, the plurality in *Planned Parenthood of Southeastern Pennsylvania v. Casey* was concerned that if the Court's decision was not grounded in community sentiment, the Court would lose some of its legitimacy. In this case, the conservative Supreme Court upheld the Roe decision.

Several Gallup polls have asked the public about their reaction to the conservative Court's decisions in recent abortion cases. In 1989, the Supreme Court in its decision in *Webster v. Reproductive Services* turned the abortion issue into a political one when it decided that state statutes could prohibit the use of public facilities and employees to perform or assist in abortions except those undertaken to save the mother's life. In 1989, 44 percent of the American public expressed strong disapproval of the Webster decision and another 10 percent expressed disapproval (Hugick and Hueber, 1991).

In the 1991 *Rust v. Sullivan* decision, the Supreme Court ruled that the federal government could withdraw funds from clinics that informed women that they had the option to abort a pregnancy. The Rust decision dealt with the issue of free speech, and the Supreme Court decisions that government could provide negative reinforcement not to talk about abortion curtailed medical clinic employees' right to free speech. Thus, the Rust decision was dubbed the "gag rule." The majority of individuals who believed abortions should be legal under certain circumstances (63 percent) disapproved of the Rust decision because of their concerns about the limitations placed on free speech (Hugick and Hueber, 1991). Even 40 percent of those who believed abortion should always be illegal disapproved of the Rust decision. Liberals, democrats, college graduates and higher-income individuals were more likely to disapprove of the Rust decision than were conservatives, Republicans, high school graduates and lower-income individuals. Across the nation, 66 percent were in favor of Congress passing a law that would allow federally-funded clinics to provide information about abortions (Hugick and Hueber, 1991).

Public Attitudes Toward Abortion. National Gallup polls since 1975 have asked the following question: "Do you think abortions should be legal under any circumstances, legal only under certain circumstances, or illegal in all circumstances?" About half of the respondents from 1975 to 1993 have favored the legality of abortion only under certain circumstances. The problem is that the circumstances giving rise to the abortion (e.g., rape, threat of death, after twenty-four hour waiting period) are left unspecified. In 1975, similar proportions of the public believed abortion should always be legal or believed abortion should never be legal. Since 1990, fewer people have endorsed the view that 'abortion should never be legal'. The percentage has dropped from 22 to 13 percent and a greater number of people have endorsed the view that 'abortion should always be legal' (it has subsequently increased from 22 to 32 percent). This trend suggests that more people are joining the pro-choice side of the abortion issue. However, other questions suggest that the pro-life position still attracts a substantial minority. The Gallup poll in 1988, 1989, and 1991 asked respondents: "In 1973, the Supreme Court ruled that states cannot place restrictions on a woman's right to an abortion during the first three months of pregnancy. Would you like to see this ruling overturned, or not?" Between 34 and 42 percent responded affirmatively (Hugick and Hueber, 1991). The majority, however, disagreed and felt that Roe should stand, which is consistent with the Court's decision. Individuals on both sides of the abortion debate hold strong opinions, which are connected to political and religious views (Scott, 1991). Who disapproves of abortion? Not surprisingly, perhaps, Republicans, lower-income and high school educated Americans have higher pro-life (i.e., anti-abortion) sentiments based on eighteen years of Gallup poll data (McAneny and Saad, 1993). Individuals who are more religious also are more likely to be pro-life.

Active Euthanasia and Right to Die Cases. Does societal interest in the preservation of life supersede a terminally ill individual's right to ask someone to help them die? This privacy issue about the government's interference with one's body clearly raises similar moral issues as those surrounding the abortion issue. McClosky and Brill (1983), using a 1978-1979 nationwide survey of U.S. residents, compared the general public, community leaders, police officers, and the legal elite on their opinion about whether people should have the right to die free from government interference. A consensus emerged among this diverse group. Over 70 percent of the respondents in each of these categories believed that the victim's family should have the right to stop treatment that sustains life in a permanently comatose accident victim. There was less agreement, however, about whether a person suffering from a painful, terminal illness should have the right to choose when and how they die: 59 percent of the mass public, 66 percent of community leaders, 66 percent of police officers, and 81 percent of the legal elite supported a person's rights in this respect.

Consistent with the majority opinion in these surveys, the Supreme Court in the Cruzan case (*Cruzan v. Director, Missouri Department of Health*, 1990) declared that individuals have a qualified right to die. However, not all acts of euthanasia are protected. Disconnecting a life-support machine is an example of passive euthanasia. Providing a patient with lethal drugs at their request or shooting them are examples of active euthanasia. This form of euthanasia is considered unethical by many people and since 1991 has been a crime in several states. But the difference between active and passive euthanasia is sometimes difficult to make and courts often provide rulings that blur the distinction (Finkel, Hurabiell, and Hughes, 1993).

Community sentiment about euthanasia shapes jurors' decisions about whether the person who killed a terminally ill person is guilty of first degree murder or some less serious crime, such as manslaughter (Finkel, Hurabiell, and Hughes, 1993; Horwitz, 1988). Many jurors consider extra-legal factors, which lead them to acquit a clearly guilty defendant who acted morally and mercifully, or to find the defendant guilty of a lesser charge—these verdict patterns are evidence of nullification of the law. For example, Finkel *et al.*, (1993) examined the question of whether people's sentiment about the right to die would affect their verdicts in cases of active euthanasia. Evidence in the case showed that the husband had planned and intentionally killed his terminally ill wife. Participants in this jury simulation rendered a verdict which was inconsistent with a strict interpretation of the letter of the law. They did so for a variety of different reasons.

Some people viewed the issue as a private one outside the scope of the law, and this often led them to acquit the defendant. Other people acknowledged the "law's place, but not its current position; others reflect a common sense rather than legal view of crime elements (e.g., malice or heat of passion); still others reflect an uncommon view of actor as extension of the patient, rather than as independent agent" (Finkel *et al*, 1993, p. 504-505). These views also often led to acquittals or to guilty verdicts of a lesser charge, or to guilty verdicts of murder with a recommendation for leniency. As with other criminal justice issues that we have examined, there is a general lesson here. This research demonstrates that when legislatures and courts create and uphold laws contrary to public sentiment, community sentiment still shapes the system of justice through jury deliberations and verdicts that nullify the law.

Public Views of Intrusiveness and
Fourth Amendment's Search and Seizure Cases

The Fourth amendment of the U.S. Constitution states:

> The right of the people to be secure in their persons, houses, papers, and effects, against unreasonable searches and seizures, shall not be violated, and no Warrants shall be issued, but upon probable cause, supported by Oath or affirmation, and particularly describing the places to be searched, and the persons or things to be seized.

The amendment regulates where and when police officers can conduct searches without a warrant or without the consent of the person being searched. The types of searches that police generally conduct can be grouped into two broad categories: searches with or without a warrant. The fourth amendment places the judge between the citizen and police as a impartial decisionmaker who must determine whether officers have enough evidence to justify the granting of a search warrant. Most searches, however, are conducted without warrant because individuals simply consent to the search. If individuals deny officers' requests, the fourth amendment prevents police from searching just anywhere or anyone or seizing or temporarily detaining anyone at anytime. In short, the police must act reasonably. Reasonableness is not judged from the perspective of a police officer nor a criminal, but instead is judged from the perspective of an innocent person (Slobogin and Schumacher, 1993a).

The landmark case of *Katz v. U.S.* in 1967 re-defined the meaning of the term "search" as it applies to warrantless searches. Before *Katz*, the Court employed the "trespass doctrine" which defined the reasonableness of a search by whether the police had a legal right to be on the premise. In the *Katz* decision, the Court defined search from the point of view of people who may be searched rather than the places that may be searched. *Katz* created the rule of a "reasonable expectation of privacy that society is prepared to recognize." This rule means that the Court determines whether a warrantless search was unreasonable based upon whether the average innocent person would reasonably expect to keep private the places and items that were searched. Slobogin and Schumacher (1993a) succinctly highlight the scope of a "search" under this definition: "an action by law enforcement officers that does not infringe on 'reasonable expectations of privacy' is not a 'search', and therefore need not be authorized by a warrant, or be based on probable cause, or be in any other way 'reasonable'" (p. 729). Officers who are legally at a residence, for example, may seize any apparently incriminating items that are in plain view. The Court also defines a seizure from the point of view of persons who may be seized. The Court in several cases has determined whether a defendant was seized based on whether "a reasonable person would have believed that he was not free to leave" (For additional details on these cases see Slobogin and Schumacher, 1993a).

Notwithstanding their support for the police and crime control in general, the public cherish their privacy, and are unwilling to allow police officers free reign in order to reduce crime. In a 1978 nationwide survey of U.S. residents, at least 74 percent of the general public, community leaders and legal elite indicated that the protection of their home against searches without a warrant was extremely important (McClosky and Brill, 1983). Three-quarters of respondents also indicated that their right to privacy in their correspondence or phone conversations was extremely important. Another poll found that 92 percent of a U.S. nationwide sample believed that the police should never, without first obtaining a court order, be allowed to open the mail of members of an organization who had not been convicted of a crime. Four out of five respondents believed that bank records should be kept strictly private (McClosky and Brill, 1983).

More recent polls further document the public's reluctance to give up their right to privacy. In 1993, the Gallup Poll asked a national sample of U.S. citizens: "Would you favor or oppose the following activities in high-crime areas in order to help reduce crime?" (Gallup Poll Monthly, 1993, p. 32). The overwhelming majority of both Caucasians and African-Americans opposed allowing police to search a home without a warrant and allowing police to wiretap telephone lines of suspects. Caucasians and African-Americans disagreed about whether police should be allowed to stop and search anybody they suspect of having committed a crime. The majority of Caucasians favored this measure whereas the majority of African-Americans were opposed. The disagreement over police "stops" may occur because Caucasians are less likely to believe a random stop will happen to them. African-Americans are more often subjected to random stops than are Caucasians. Whereas three-fourths of Caucasians believed that police should be allowed to hold someone they suspect of having committed a crime for twenty-four hours without bail, only 54 percent of African-Americans supported this measure.

As with other areas of criminal justice, there is an element of "us" versus "them" to this issue. The public appears quite willing to give up the privacy rights of known criminals who are suspected of planning new crimes. Support for this conclusion derives from 1978-79 nationwide survey of U.S. residents (McClosky and Brill, 1983). Over 70 percent of the general public, community leaders, and legal elite indicated that tapping telephones with a legal warrant can be justified when used against known criminals suspected of planning new crimes. Ninety-four percent of the police supported this action. Of course, this question is limited to situations where the police already have some evidence against the person and have obtained a legal warrant. Even without a warrant, all of the groups cited overwhelmingly supported the use of dogs in airports to help police locate narcotics in suitcases or lockers. The public, however, is in less agreement about whether the police should be able to search a person's car for narcotics or stolen goods: 58 percent of the mass public, 59 percent of community leaders, 31 percent of legal elite, and 67 percent of police officers believe that officers should be able to search under these conditions. For this item, it is clear that legal elite and the mass public hold differing opinions.

In making decisions about the "reasonableness" of searches and seizures, rather than consulting social science surveys, the Court generally uses its own ideas about what society deems reasonable and what society considers intrusive. Should police officers be allowed to trespass onto your open but private fields in search of evidence (e.g., marijuana plants) even though you have "No trespassing" signs posted? Should police officers be allowed to board and delay buses so that they can ask people to consent to a search of their luggage? The Supreme Court says yes, officers should be allowed because society expects that people (including the police) may ignore their no trespassing signs, and society believes that officers' boarding buses to request consent to a search is not very intrusive. Is the Court right in its conclusions about public perceptions of intrusiveness?

Only one contemporary study has addressed the public's views about the intrusiveness of different searches and seizures (Slobogin and Schumacher, 1993a,b). This research used a convenience sample which was comprised of undergraduates, law students, U.S. adults, and Australian adults. The respondents were asked to read fifty brief descriptions of searches and seizures (e.g., boarding a bus and asking to search your luggage), and to rate each description on the level of intrusiveness of each search or seizure. Respondents were randomly assigned to read one of four versions. The versions varied whether the description was personalized (e.g., *your* garbage can) or impersonal (e.g., *a* garbage can), and whether the description did or did not describe the purpose of the search (e.g., looking for evidence of forgery). The descriptions of different searches and seizures were obtained from Supreme Court cases so that the researchers could determine whether the Supreme Court Justices had guessed correctly about where community sentiment stands on specific types of searches and seizures.

As with other issues, the Court's conclusions regarding public opinion were incorrect. The public perceives entering private fields and the use of dogs as searches requiring some reasonable suspicion on the part of the officer. In contrast, the Court believes that entering open fields and dog sniffs do not violate societal expectations of privacy and are not searches. Whereas the public believes that officers who board buses and ask passengers to consent to a search of their luggage is a very intrusive seizure, the Court has ruled that it is reasonable because the detention is short and a reasonable person would believe that they can deny the request. The Court also concludes that innocent people have little expectation of privacy about information revealed or obtained by their secretaries, their chauffeurs, or by bank employees who may be working undercover for police agencies. Moreover, the Court has held that certain employers can obtain blood from their employees using hypodermic needles and can obtain urine samples to check for illegal drug usage. The majority of Supreme Court Justices think that the public sees these actions as reasonable and not very intrusive, but they are wrong; the public clearly viewed these actions as being intrusive.

The court's conclusions in several areas of searches, however, are consistent with the desires of community sentiment. The Court concluded that actions such as helicopter surveillance, safety inspections of homes, searches of suspects' garbage left on the curb are not intrusive and therefore constitute reasonable actions. The public agrees. The public also agrees with the Court that an officer either following you in a police car or stopping you at a nighttime roadblock is not intrusive. However, if the stop lasts ten minutes, it is considered to be intrusive.

According to the Supreme Court, community sentiment about "intrusiveness" and "privacy" should be from a personal perspective and not from the observer's perspective of what may happen to someone else (Slobogin and Schumacher, 1993b). People rated searches and seizures as being more intrusive when they judged them from a personal perspective than from the perspective of an observer (Slobogin and Schumacher, 1993b). People also rated seizures as being more intrusive when they did not know the purpose of the search than when they did know the purpose. In Chapter 5, we noted that judges often use the same heuristics and have similar biases in their decisionmaking as lay people. Supreme Court Justices may underestimate societal expectations in certain areas because they take an impartial observer's perspective and are often faced with clearly guilty defendants (Slobogin and Schumacher, 1993b).

If the fourth amendment protection is to be effective, it has to be properly enforced. An important part of the fourth amendment right to be secure in one's person, places, and effects from unlawful searches and seizures is the enforcement of this right. The U.S. Supreme Court decided in the case of *Mapp v. Ohio* (1961) that an important part of this fourth amendment right was that a defendant has the right to exclude evidence obtained in an illegal search and seizure from a state trial on his or her guilt. The exclusionary rule holds that any evidence police officers obtain during an illegal search and seizure must be excluded from both state and federal criminal trials. A 1979 nationwide survey of U.S. residents asked: "if a person is found guilty of a crime by evidence gathered through illegal methods: (1) he should be set free or granted a new trial; or (2) he should still be convicted if the evidence is really convincing and strong" (McClosky and Brill, 1983, p. 246). Three-quarters of the legal elite indicated that the defendant should be set free or granted a new trial whereas only half of the community leaders and police officers and only 37 percent of the general public held this view. Clearly, the opinion of the mass public depends upon whether they take the perspective that the event could happen to them. This too may reflect the public dichotomy between "law-abiding citizens" and "offenders." When the public focuses on known criminals or defendants, they may conclude that this event could not happen to them, in which case they are less fastidious about evidentiary issues.

Third-Party Consent Searches. According to the Supreme Court, police officers can conduct a warrantless search of a home if they first obtain the consent of the suspect (*Schneckloth v. Bustamonte*, 1973) but also the consent of a third-party such as a spouse or roommate (*United States v. Matlock*, 1974). The legitimacy of third-party consent searches is based on two legal concepts: common authority and the assumption of risk (Kagehiro and Taylor, 1988). Common authority refers to the doctrine that individuals who have possession and control of a premise can validly consent to a search, but if a premise is in the exclusive use of one person, then a third-party cannot consent to a search. When a third-party validly consents to a search of a shared premise, any incriminating evidence can be used against anyone with "common authority" over the premise. The "assumption of risk doctrine" holds that individuals who share a premise with other individuals have no reasonable expectation of privacy that the others will not allow searches and take the risk that a co-resident may unilaterally consent to a search (e.g., *United States v. Hendrix*, 1979). Thus, the Court allows third-parties to consent to a search of a shared premise separately and independently of the co-resident's view of the matter. For example, the third-party can consent to a search when the co-resident is away from the premise. The third party can also provide consent when the co-resident either is present but protesting against the search, or is absent, but has clearly indicated a desire not to allow people to search the premise.

Does the public's perception of personal privacy correspond with the Court's ruling on third-party consent searches? Research has addressed this question using undergraduate students who read scenarios describing a police's request for a search, and then judged the third-party's right to consent to a search and whether the consent was voluntary (Kagehiro, 1990; Kagehiro and Taylor, 1988; Kagehiro, 1988; Kagehiro, Taylor, Laufer, and Harland, 1991). How the police asked for permission to search determined the public's perceptions about the voluntariness of the consent (Kagehiro, 1988). The public also believed that the right of the third-party to consent to a search depends upon the circumstances surrounding the search. Respondents believed that third-parties have the right to consent to a search when a suspect is absent, but do not have this right when the suspect is present and protesting (Kagehiro and Taylor, 1988).

Beliefs about the consent rights of third-parties also depend upon whether the police find incriminating evidence. When evidence is found and the suspect is absent by chance, most respondents agreed that societal expectations permitted the third-party to allow police to search the house. Substantially fewer agreed, however, when the suspect was present and protesting against the search (Kagehiro, Taylor, and Harland, 1991). When the police fail to find any evidence and the suspect is present and protesting, most agreed that the third-party has a right to consent to a search whereas significantly fewer agreed when the suspect is absent and no evidence is found. People may believe that a third-party has more right over a protesting suspect when no evidence is found because they see no harm to the suspect and believe that the third-party has a right to avoid guilt by association in this circumstance. These findings suggest that respondents perceived that a third-party has only a very limited right to consent to a search when the suspect is present and protesting (Kagehiro and Taylor, 1988).

Community Standards and
Judgments of Obscene Materials

The first amendment of the U.S. Constitution allows individuals to express themselves freely through words, body language, and visual art or signs. Free speech allows individuals to keep their autonomy and dignity.

> Contemporary liberal defenses of free speech often take the shape of a rights argument, in which freedom of speech follows from a recognition of the dignity and autonomy of the speaker. Just as dignitarian concerns bar the state from forcing a criminal defendant to speak (the Fifth Amendment), the First Amendment erects a similar defense of individual dignity and autonomy by barring the state from silencing the would-be speaker. ... The right of free speech describes the relationship not simply between the state and the subject, but between individuals dedicated to principles of mutual respect. (Douglas, 1995, p. 177, cites omitted)

Not all expressions, however, are protected. Public officials can regulate expressions that may cause riots or public danger so long as their actions are directed at controlling a reasonable public danger rather than the *content* of speech. The classic example is that it is illegal to yell "fire" without cause in a crowded movie theater. For a long time, a legitimate possibility of harm has been an exception to a protection to speak freely.

Court Ruling on Obscenity

Public officials cannot sanction speech just because they find it distasteful. Obscenity, however, is an exception. The Supreme Court has long held that obscene materials such as hard core sex scenes are not protected by the First Amendment (*Roth v. U.S.*, 1957; *Memoirs v. Massachusetts*, 1966; *Miller v. U.S.*, 1973) because since the colonial days, as the Supreme Court notes (*Roth v. U.S.*, 1957), the government has made illegal lewd speech. Thus, the justices using this historical fact concluded that the meaning of the free speech clause did not include obscene materials. Unlike yelling fire without cause, obscene material may not put people in immediate physical danger, but may undermine the moral standards of the community and may cause harm to specific individuals. Some opinion data suggest that the public do favor the regulation of obscene materials. Though the questions are vague about the meaning of pornography, the General Social Survey has included items to assess opinions about the regulation of pornography. Thus, in 1988, 43 percent favored a complete prohibition, seven percent favored decriminalization, and the remainder favored some degree of regulation of pornographic materials.

Support for regulation is not without limits; it varies by the type of pornography. As well, the public make a clear distinction between private viewing and public displays. A 1986 Gallup Poll found that only 36 percent wanted to ban videos for home viewing, while fully three-quarters favored a ban on the presentation of sexual violence in movie theaters (Wu and McCaghy, 1993). Wu and McCaghy (1993) conducted a telephone survey to assess the correlates of attitudes toward the regulation of pornography. Respondents were asked whether they agreed that it should be legal to sell, rent or show sexually explicit materials to adults. Unfortunately, the undefined term, "sexually explicit" leaves much to the respondents' imaginations. The researchers found that younger persons, males, less religious persons, and single persons were more likely to approve of legalizing pornography. Not surprisingly, as beliefs in the harmfulness of pornography increased, individuals were less likely to favor legalization. Beliefs in support of sexual privacy, on the other hand, increased support for legalization.

The Supreme Court has made it difficult for people to judge whether they are violating obscenity laws because community standards determine what is obscene. In *Miller v. U.S.* (1973), the Supreme Court created a three-prong test of obscenity in which the decisionmaker (judge or jury) must decide: (1) whether the average person, applying contemporary community standards, thinks the work in its entirety, appeals to a shameful, morbid, and unhealthy interest in sex (i.e., a prurient interest); (2) whether the work depicts or describes sex in a way that goes beyond the limits of candor or blatantly offends community standards (i.e., "a patently offensive way"); and (3) whether the work, taken as a whole, lacks serious literary, artistic, political or scientific value. Community standards of decency, thus, are central in determining whether a particular work violates obscenity laws. Prior to the Miller decision, a national community standard was the appropriate reference point. The Miller decision changed the standard to a local one, and gave states the task of defining the meaning of "local." Most states ask jurors to apply the average community standard of their county, but some states such as Tennessee and Texas ask jurors to apply the average community standard of the entire state.

Use of Survey Evidence by the Courts

Given the direct relevance of community standards in obscenity cases, do courts frequently rely on social science evidence such as a survey of a random sample of community members to establish what is the standard in a community? Some courts occasionally do, which suggests that they are beginning to recognize the value of opinion poll data to resolve this question (See Scott, 1991; Linz *et al.*, 1995). Scott (1991, p. 31) quotes the Indiana Court of Appeals in *Saliba v. State* (1985) which held:

> Expert testimony based on a public opinion poll is uniquely suited to a determination of community standards. Perhaps no other form of evidence is more helpful or concise... and its admission may be necessary in the sense that no other evidence would be as good as the survey evidence or perhaps even obtainable as a practical matter.

As we will see, this court is right to be skeptical that jurors can accurately ascertain community standards without social science evidence. These courts are the exceptions in what is generally a rather bleak rejection of empirical data. The U.S. Supreme Court believes that prosecutors do not need to present expert testimony such as opinion surveys to prove that materials go beyond what the community will tolerate because the material can speak for itself (*Paris Adult Theatre v. Slaton*, 1973). This omission makes obscenity cases quite different from other criminal cases because in all other criminal cases prosecutors have the burden of proving each element of a crime (Scott, Eitle, and Skovron, 1990).

The Supreme Court, however, has decided that defendants in a criminal trial are allowed to introduce relevant expert testimony which may include the discussion of a community survey (*Kaplan v. California*, 1973). It is not just any survey, however, that will be accepted by the courts—the survey must pass the test of "circumstantial guarantees of trustworthiness" (Linz *et al.*, 1995). In order to be trustworthy, a survey must meet the standard of social science such as whether acceptable survey techniques were used (e.g., random sampling), correct statistical methods were employed, whether the correct universe was examined, and whether appropriate methods and questions were used. Courts have begun to reject telephone surveys and to insist that surveys be conducted after respondents have viewed the questionably offensive material. Just because a survey is admitted into evidence, however, the jury or judge still does not have to rely on it in making its verdict decision. In both the U.S. (see Scott, Eitle, and Skovron, 1990) and Canada (Coons and McFarland, 1985), decisionmakers have ignored expert testimony and have relied on their own views of community standards in reaching decisions. The most optimistic interpretation of most courts' position is that they accept survey data but only with a high degree of skepticism.

Can Jurors Apply the Miller Test?

In order to make fair decisions that follow the Miller test, a community standard must exist, jurors must accurately know this standard, and jurors must be able to set aside their own personal standards and use the community standard. Much research has begun to question whether jurors can accurately apply the Miller test. First, research findings have been inconclusive about whether a single standard exists in most communities (Brown, Anderson, Burggraf, and Thompson, 1978; Herrman and Bordner, 1983; Massey, 1970; Wallace, 1973). Herrman and Bordner (1983), using a randomly selected sample of southern residents, found consensus on perceptions of community standards for certain types of sex acts. The majority of respondents (66 percent or higher) indicated that the community did not tolerate depictions of rape, homosexuality, or group sex. For adultery and total nudity, the respondents showed no consensus in perceptions of community standards. Thus, whether consensus exists may vary by the nature of the sexual activity depicted. The findings of another study suggest that other factors may also affect the degree of consensus. Wallace (1973) found that respondents rated the offensiveness of pictures portraying the same theme (e.g., coital activity) quite differently, which indicates that if respondents are applying a standard it does not necessarily lead to the same rating of similar pictures. The issue of whether a single community standard exists, thus remains unresolved.

Several studies have found that personal standards are moderately related to perceptions of community standards (Herrman and Bordner, 1983; Scott, 1991; Scott, Eitle, and Skovron, 1990). Scott (1991) found that respondents' own personal standard was the best predictor of their perception of the community's standard in eighteen of twenty samples. Demographic characteristics did not consistently or substantially shape perceptions of what the community tolerated or accepted (Scott, 1991). These findings call into question whether jurors are able to put aside their personal standards and accurately assess and use the community standard in making decisions in obscenity trials.

The cognitive limitations of laypersons reviewed in Chapter 5 also suggest that jurors may not be able to accurately assess community sentiment. The two samples that did not show a relationship between personal standards and perceptions of community standards had heard media stories about a high number of arrests and guilty verdicts for distribution of obscene materials (Scott, 1991). Researchers (Linz, Donnerstein, *et al.*, 1991) suggested that the discrepancy between personal standards and perceptions of community standards may occur because respondents exposed to these media stories may infer from these stories that community members must be intolerant if the police and prosecutors are actively seeking these cases. From this research, misperceptions about community standards may either occur through individuals' willingness to generalize from media stories about prosecutions to what the community tolerates or through individuals' use of their personal standards to guess the community standard. Linz *et al.*, (1995) provide a concise summary of the implications of these findings: "By ignoring this potential bias, the Court may be maintaining a convenient legal fiction—the belief that jurors can accurately gauge community standards in spite of compelling evidence to the contrary" (p. 135).

Are Courts Regulating the Right Obscene Material?

In order to be prosecuted under any obscenity law, the Supreme Court has held that the material must have sexual content. Generally, hard-core sex acts without violence have been prosecuted. What kind of acts do individuals find obscene? Linz *et al.*, (1995) have conducted one of the most methodologically-sound studies to date on this issue. The study itself was used in expert testimony for the defense side in an obscenity trial. The researchers evaluated the level of community tolerance for a hard core pornography film in which a defendant was being prosecuted for its distribution in Western Tennessee. Respondents were randomly selected from the Western Division of the Federal Western District of Tennessee. They answered a survey about their own personal acceptance and the community's tolerance of hard-core sex films before viewing the film, and after viewing the film rated their acceptance of the film and the community's tolerance for the film.

In order to determine whether other acts were tolerated, respondents were asked to indicate their personal acceptance and the community's tolerance if the film had contained rape and bondage or had contained actors under the age of 18. Respondents held similar views of their personal acceptance and the community's tolerance of the "hard core pornographic" film before and after viewing the film: The majority found the film personally acceptable, and perceived it as being tolerated in the community. Most people indicated that films depicting rape and bondage and films depicting children under 18 engaging in sexual acts were personally unacceptable, and would not be tolerated by the community. Community standards thus support the regulation of child pornography and of violent sex films that show rape and bondage.

In addition, some respondents were randomly selected to rate scenes from a violent film that did not contain explicit sexual themes. Less than half found this footage personally acceptable, but the majority still believed that the community tolerated films of this nature. People may derive a perception of community tolerance for violent movies from their wide availability and lack of regulation even though about half of the community finds them personally unacceptable. It is unclear, however, whether people want to prosecute the distributors of such films. Though people in opinion polls express disapproval of the amount of violence on television, at the same time they are against government regulation (See Linz *et al.*, 1995).

Conclusions

In this chapter, we have highlighted the role of community sentiment in determining constitutional issues. We have seen how Supreme Court Justices often use intuition and anecdotal experiences to assess where community sentiment stands on an issue. Given these methods, the Court often misses the mark of contemporary standards of privacy and free speech. In the privacy arena, courts' decisions on drug testing in employment settings, the search of open fields, and the boarding of buses were inconsistent with the available research on this topic. Here, Supreme Court Justices may incorrectly interpret community sentiment because they take a neutral observer perspective and face (for the most part) clearly guilty defendants (Slobogin and Schumacher, 1993a). Moreover, people did not believe that third-parties should have an independent right to consent to a search of a common dwelling when the suspect was present and protesting. The Court, however, correctly surmised community sentiment when it declared that searches of garbage on curbs, and night time roadblocks did not violate public expectations.

In other areas of constitutional law such as obscenity cases, the Supreme Court has delegated the task of determining community standards about what is obscene to jurors in obscenity trials. Here, representative and valid surveys of the community on what is obscene are given a secondary and subordinate position: The prosecution need not prove the community standard because the material can speak for itself, and the defense may be allowed to present experts who testify about community surveys, but the jurors can ignore this testimony and use their own judgment. Much research suggests that jurors may not cognitively be able to perform correctly the Miller test and thus may render unfair outcomes.

Other areas of constitutional law illustrate the indirect ways that community sentiment shapes the criminal justice system. The abortion decisions highlight the importance that the Supreme Court accords to maintaining its legitimacy. The active euthanasia cases demonstrate the ways in which laws which are inconsistent with community sentiment may be nullified through the jury rendering verdicts of acquittal or convictions of less serious charges. To conclude, the research literature reviewed in this chapter demonstrates that many Supreme Court Justices are skeptical of social science evidence, while others misinterpret social science findings.

Notes

1. In Canada, the trials of Henry Morgenthaler provide an example. This physician was repeatedly put on trial for performing illegal abortions. Every time he was tried he was acquitted by jurors who had little sympathy with the law.

2. Throughout this chapter, we use the phrase, "The Court," to refer to the United States Supreme Court. When the words, court or courts, are not capitalized, these words refer to lower trial and appellate courts. In referring to European or Canadian courts, we identify the country.

13

Juvenile Crime and
Juvenile Justice

The criminal law accords differential treatment to special categories of offenders, including people convicted of crimes committed before the have attained the age of majority. Most countries have separate justice systems for youthful offenders. In this chapter we discuss public reaction to juvenile crime, and the treatment of young offenders by juvenile courts.

Juvenile justice has become one of the most hotly-debated criminal justice issues in America, Canada and the United Kingdom. Great public concern exists in all three countries, especially Canada, where a vigorous debate has arisen surrounding legislative amendments to the juvenile justice system. Public attention to youth crime has been growing for years, in part as a result of several incidents that attracted a great deal of public interest. In England, the killing of five-year old Jamie Bulger by two ten-year olds shocked the nation. In Canada, several homicides were committed by young persons, including one murder of two elderly people in Quebec, and the murder of a taxi driver by teenage girls. To many members of the public, such crimes are hard to comprehend. More than that, they seem novel. For many people, teenage murderers are a new phenomenon. Criminality is usually attributed to adults, not children. But even such high profile cases as the Bulger murder are far from new. There are historical precedents for the Bulger murder in England. In America, people who have seen the 1958 film "Compulsion" will recall the murder committed by two college students, Loeb and Leopold. Nothing in the past of these two boys would have predicted that they would commit first degree murder, and the crime was as shocking to residents of Chicago in the 1920s, as the Bulger murder was to Britons in Liverpool today.

The debate over crime by young people then is far from new. Concern about crime by the young goes back to ancient Greece, where several writers complained about the decline in juvenile morality, which manifests itself in criminal behavior. Today, many people read of homicide by young people, and think that society has recently become much worse. Evidence of the public's mood can be seen in successive polls conducted in the United States and Canada. An American survey conducted in 1982 found that 81 percent of the public disagreed with the statement that "The juvenile crime problem is not really as serious as most people are saying." (Opinion Research Corporation, 1982). In Canada, the public were asked on two occasions whether they thought that the behavior of young people had changed over the previous five years. In 1990, 47 percent endorsed the view that young persons had become worse; by 1993 the percentage sharing this view had risen to 64 percent.

In addition, there is concern about the way in which the juvenile justice system responds to teenage crime. Many members of the public hold the perception that the juvenile justice system itself may in part be responsible for juvenile criminality. Once again, case-histories probably have an important impact on the public. In England, public dissatisfaction focused on a case in which a teenager who had committed a long series of robberies was then sent on holiday by the authorities. In Canada, television interviews with some young offenders received a great deal of airtime. These offenders were seen laughing at the severity of penalties imposed under the Young Offenders Act. Incidents such as these have provoked an increase in public support for more punitive treatment of juvenile offenders. For example, in 1994, a poll in Canada found that three-quarters of the public favored facilitating the transfer of young offenders to adult court, and almost as many endorsed the creation of detention centers where young offenders would be required to perform manual labor. Many people feel that the juvenile justice system is too lenient, and this is itself a cause of juvenile criminality. But is the system that lenient? And how much do members of the public really know about the severity of juvenile courts? As Triplett (1996) notes, until very recently, researchers have paid little attention to exploring public opinion regarding youth crime and juvenile justice. With the growth in public concern, however, this is now changing.

Knowledge of Juvenile Justice Trends

The Perception of Leniency

There are parallels between public perceptions of juvenile justice and sentencing at the adult level. Most people believe that the juvenile courts are too lenient, and this perception has been around for some time. For example, a national opinion survey conducted in the U.S. in 1981 found that fully four out of five respondents agreed with the view that juvenile courts were too lenient (Opinion Research Corporation, 1982). The same result can be observed in surveys going back to 1964 (Parker, 1965). As we have seen in an earlier chapter, a similar percentage of Americans hold the view that adult courts are insufficiently harsh towards convicted offenders. The same is true in Canada, where the public perception of youth courts appears to be that young offenders are treated with great leniency. Statistics show otherwise. Leesti (1992) summarizes youth court data showing significant proportions of young offenders being sentenced to custody. As well, many of the young offenders sentenced to custody (secure or open) have been convicted of non-violent crimes. Thus one-quarter of young offenders convicted of property offenses received a custodial disposition (see Leesti, 1992, Table 1).

An early study conducted in Washington state found a result which echoes findings at the adult level. A sample of the general public first indicated that juvenile courts were too lenient. However, when they themselves were asked to sentence juveniles, they chose penalties for youthful offenders that were less strict than those actually handed down by the juvenile courts (see Parker, 1965). Once again, then, when it comes the issue of leniency, the public have the perception that the system is easier than it in fact is. The author of the report describing this research noted that: "Indeed, the actual dispositions handed out by the court are more severe than the preferred levels identified by many citizens" (Parker, 1965, p. 265).

There is not a great deal of information on public knowledge of the juvenile justice system, but what exists shows that this is one of the areas of criminal justice in which the public ignorance is widespread. A typical result is that which emerged from a survey in California in 1988. Although that state had some of the most punitive youth sentencing policies, which resulted in longer juvenile terms, only 17 percent of the general public were aware of this (Steinhart, 1988). Most members of the public simply assumed that the juvenile courts were lenient, in the absence of any data to support this assumption.

Another public misperception seems to be that youth courts have become more lenient in recent years. This does not appear to be the case. Markwart (1992) presents a great deal of information about the use of incarceration in youth courts both before and after passage of the Young Offenders Act in Canada. For example, he notes that the average daily sentenced population in the third year after implementation of the YOA was 148 percent greater than in the last year under the Juvenile Delinquents Act. He writes: "It is difficult to arrive at any other conclusion but that the implementation of the YOA has apparently been associated with a substantially *increased* reliance on incarceration" (1992, p. 247, emphasis added). More recent data show that there has been very little change in the incarceration rate for young offenders. In 1986-87, 24 percent of all youth court dispositions were custodial. This rose slightly to 26 percent for the year 1990-1991 (see Leesti, 1992; Reitsma-Street, 1994). A Toronto study found that more sentences involving custody were being handed down as a result of passage of the Young Offenders Act.

There are parallels with adult crime issues. The public in America, Canada and elsewhere share the perception that youth crime is increasing at an alarming rate, and is becoming increasingly more violent. In the major survey of Americans' attitudes towards juvenile crime, over four-fifths of the sample felt that the amount of serious juvenile crime had increased in their particular state. Data from California provide a good illustration of the phenomenon. In 1988, respondents were asked about the rate of juvenile crime within the past five years. There was a great deal of consensus in responses: Over 80 percent endorsed the view that the juvenile crime rate had gone up. However, analysis of the actual statistics reveals a very different picture. Arrests actually declined by 11 percent of the period, with arrests for violent felonies declining by 21 percent (Steinhart, 1988). The researcher who made these comparisons concluded that "The public's perception of juvenile crime activity bears little relationship to the facts" (Steinhart, 1988, p. 7).

From 1973 through 1988, the juvenile arrest rates for violent offenses remained relatively constant. The trend however has changed since 1988.

> The years between 1988 and 1991 saw a 38 percent increase in the rate of juvenile arrests for violent crimes. The rate of increase then diminished, with the juvenile arrest rate increasing little between 1991 and 1992. This rapid growth moved the juvenile rate for violent crime in 1992 far above any year since the mid-1960s. (Snyder and Sickmund, 1995, p. 6)

Though juvenile crime has increased, "less than one-half of 1 percent of juveniles in the U.S. were arrested for a violent offense in 1992" (Snyder and Sickmund, 1995, p. iv).

As well, juveniles are responsible for only a small minority of crimes: In America, juvenile offenders accounted for 13 percent of crimes recorded by the police in 1992 (Snyder and Sickmund, 1995, p. 3). In Canada, the proportion is even lower: Only 7 percent of violent crimes reported to the police (and resulting in a charge) involved a young offender (Canadian Centre for Justice Statistics, 1995). The public however believes that juveniles are responsible for a substantially higher percentage than this. Thus a Gallup poll in 1994 asked respondents to estimate the percentage of violent crimes committed by juveniles. Only 6 percent gave the correct answer. Most people generated an estimate considerably in excess of the actual statistic. Almost half the sample estimated the figure to be over 40 percent (Moore, 1994).

Knowledge of Youth Crime Legislation

In 1984, significant changes to the treatment of young offenders were introduced in Canada. The Juvenile Delinquents Act was replaced by a completely new Young Offenders Act. The public have a highly negative view of the new Act (see Hruska and Eisenberg, 1991 for a summary of public attitudes towards the YOA), but have little awareness of its provisions and effects. The public do not understand the philosophy and specific provisions of the Act, and probably regard it as yet another manifestation of leniency on the part of the criminal justice system. Shortly after the YOA became law, the public were asked whether they had heard of the Act: Fewer than one quarter were aware of the legislation (Angus Reid, 1984a). That has now changed, in large part as a result of the widespread news media attention to serious crimes committed by young offenders. Nevertheless, widespread public ignorance of the nature of the Young Offenders Act remains. A more recent nation-wide survey (Decima Research, 1993) found that almost half the sample admitted that they were "not at all" or "not very" familiar with the Act.

In 1989, Canadians were asked if they thought that treating juveniles in a different way from adults would lead to an increase or decrease in juvenile crime. Slightly over half the respondents in 1985, and 60 percent in 1989 believed that this provision would lead to an increase in juvenile crime. This seems to corroborate the view that the public regard the YOA as responsible, in part, for increases in juvenile offending. According to systematic research on the impact of the YOA, this public perception is without foundation. Carrington and Moyer, for example,

> found no evidence in UCR data to support the popular myth that the YOA has resulted in more, and more serious, youth crime in Canada. The mean rate of police-reported youth crime in Canada was about the same in 1985-90 as in 1980-84. This was in spite of the addition to the youth population.
> ... of young people who had been classified as adults under the Juvenile Delinquents Act. (1994, p. 22)

As well, the public perception emerging from polls in 1994 and 1995, that youth crime rates are rising fast, would appear to be a misperception. Doob, Marinos and Varma (1995) examined youth crime statistics and concluded that "crime generally and youth crime in particular are probably not increasing, or, if they are increasing, they have not reached a level that should alarm us" (p. 25). Sprott (1995) explored public knowledge of the Young Offenders Act and found that misperceptions were widespread. For example, most members of the public greatly under-estimated the percentage of young persons convicted of assault who were incarcerated. In fact the public subscribed to many misperceptions, and "In most cases, the public incorrectly believes the [Young Offenders] Act to be more lenient than it actually is" (Sprott, 1995, p. 41).[1]

Purpose of Juvenile Courts

If juvenile courts shared the same purpose and punishments as adult courts, there would be no need for a dual system of justice. The emphasis in juvenile justice has always been more upon the rehabilitation and treatment than mere punishment. The argument has been made that young offenders are less culpable than adults convicted of the same kinds of offenses, and accordingly should be punished less harshly. Where do the public stand on this issue? The results of a number of different polls are consistent.

The public clearly support the principle of a separate juvenile justice system. In 1982, fully three-quarters of the public agreed that the main purpose of the juvenile court system should be to treat juvenile offenders rather than to punish them (Opinion Research Corporation, 1982). When respondents to a more recent national survey were asked whether the main purpose of the juvenile court system should be to treat and rehabilitate or to punish young offenders, four-fifths chose treatment compared to only 12 percent who chose punishment. A further 10 percent chose "both equally" (see Schwartz, 1992). Support for rehabilitation at the adult level is not as strong, as we noted in Chapter 10. The question was made quite explicit in a 1988 poll: 71 percent agreed with the statement that "It is more important to emphasize rehabilitation for juveniles than it is for adult criminals" (Steinhart, 1988).

The most recent nationwide poll in America asked members of the public to identify the purpose of sentencing adult and juvenile offenders. In an earlier chapter we noted that the most popular sentencing purpose for adults was retribution. However, when the question related to juveniles, the results were quite different. Exactly half the sample endorsed rehabilitation, more than any other purpose (Gerber and Engelhardt-Greer, 1996).

The public are also influenced by the manner in which the question is posed. A poll conducted for the L.A. Times in the same year asked a more leading question. Respondents were asked: "In your view, should juveniles who commit violent crimes be treated the same as adults, or should they be given more lenient treatment in a juvenile court?" With its emphasis on the violence of the crime, and the leniency of the response in juvenile courts, this formulation generated a different response: 68 percent favored treating juveniles in the same manner as adults (Maquire and Pastore, 1995). However, there is an element of ambivalence in all this. While the vast majority favor rehabilitation over punishment, there is also widespread support for processing some juveniles through the adult system. Fully half the national sample in the juvenile justice survey agreed that "A juvenile charged with a serious property crime should be tried as an adult." When the question dealt with a juvenile charged with a serious violent crime, the percentage agreeing increased from 50 percent to 68 percent (Schwartz, 1992). The percentage supporting transfer was almost as high (62 percent) for a juvenile charged with selling large amounts of illegal drugs. Canadians are divided on the issue of the separate treatment of young offenders. When asked whether young defendants should be tried in adult courts, or whether there should be special provisions and sentences for young offenders, the sample split fifty-fifty (Roberts, 1994).

Transferring Juvenile Accused to Adult Court

The juvenile and adult criminal justice systems are not entirely separate. In most countries, mechanisms exist which permit the transfer of a juvenile offender from the juvenile to the adult level. Usually such transfers are reserved for offenders charged with the most serious crimes, such as murder. Under certain circumstances then, it is possible to transfer juvenile offenders to adult court. A transfer decision is more than a decision about jurisdiction for the ensuing trial. It is primarily a decision about the punishment that can be imposed, in the event of a conviction. For example, in Canada, a young offender convicted of murder at the youth court level is liable to receive a penalty of up to ten years in prison. If transferred and convicted in adult court, the mandatory penalty would be life imprisonment, with the requirement to serve at least twenty-five years in prison prior to becoming eligible for parole. The choice to try juveniles in adult court shifts the goal of sentencing away from rehabilitation and towards a more punishment-oriented system.

Legislators, criminal justice professionals and academicians often cite public demand for harsher punishment as a justification for statutory changes in transfer decisions (e.g., Bureau of Justice Assistance, 1992; Champion and May, 1991; Feld, 1987; Juvenile Justice Reform, 1987). Twelve states provide prosecutors with the choice to bypass judicial hearings and try juveniles as adults. At least twenty-four states have implemented legislation that bypasses a judicial hearing and automatically transfers to adult court juveniles who have committed certain felonies such as murder. These statutes are known as *automatic legislative transfers*. Where do the public stand on the issue? Is it the case that they favor transferring juveniles, as many people claim?

One study (Schwartz, 1992) using a national telephone survey asked respondents if they agreed or disagreed with the statement "A juvenile who is charged with a serious violent crime should be tried as an adult." Over two-thirds of respondents agreed with the statement. The National Opinion Survey on crime and Justice, conducted in 1995, also asked a series of questions about transferring juvenile offenders to adult court. Respondents were asked whether various kinds of offenders should be transferred. Results indicated strong support for transferring defendants charged with a serious violent offense and juveniles charged with selling illegal drugs. Fully 87 percent supported a waiver for the first kind of juvenile defendant, and 69 percent for the latter (see Triplett, 1996).

Similar results emerged in Canada, where 88 percent of the public stated that they approved of legislation allowing young offenders accused of "crimes like murder" to be transferred to adult court (Hruska and Eisenberg, 1991). From these results, we might be tempted to conclude that the public strongly support transferring juveniles to the adult court level. This would be a mistaken conclusion. Neither of these polls specified the details surrounding the felony. It is not clear that people support transfers for *all* felonies or just the most serious ones that they happen to be thinking of when responding to the question.

As we have already seen, research has shown that people are more punitive (in this case this would mean supporting automatic transfers) when they are responding to abstract, nonspecific questions than when they are given concrete cases to consider. This has been demonstrated in terms of sentencing adults, and the death penalty (see Chapters 10 and 11). In order to have an adequate test of the question, subjects would need to have details about the relevant criteria used in legislative transfers. One of the injustices of automatic transfers is that they ignore the possibility that important mitigating factors may be present.

An obvious example of a factor which should mitigate the punishment is the presence of a history of childhood abuse. Evidence of such abuse is sometimes used to support a self-defense argument. Juveniles who kill their abusive parents may have done so because they were in fear for their life. As well, if childhood abuse was an important factor, it may reduce the seriousness of the offense, from first degree murder to voluntary manslaughter. Statutes that do not consider the possibility of childhood abuse and automatically try abused juveniles convicted of murder as adults may be inconsistent with community sentiment.

In order to test this possibility, as well as to provide a more adequate exploration of public views regarding juvenile transfers, Stalans and Henry (1994) provided subjects with a series of scenarios. After reading the cases, subjects were asked whether the young accused should be tried in juvenile or adult court. Several factors were manipulated in the scenarios, and the effects of these variables on the critical question of transfer shed light on the views of the public in this area. Age played a role. If the juvenile accused was sixteen years old, people were more likely to recommend transfer than if he was only fourteen. In this respect, the public are consistent with legislation which also treats older juveniles as more appropriate targets for transfer to adult court.

Criminal record also had an influence on subjects' responses: When the accused was described as having two prior juvenile convictions, the public were more likely to favor transfer to adult court than if he was a first offender. The effect of prior record has also emerged in several nationwide surveys. When the public was asked whether juveniles convicted of their first crime should be treated the same or less harshly as adults, 40 percent said less harshly. However, the vast majority of the public (over four-fifths) said that recidivist young offenders should be treated with the same severity accorded repeat adult offenders (Sourcebook of Criminal Justice Statistics, 1995). This too, is consistent with the role of criminal record at the adult level. As for the critical question of childhood abuse, it had the effect of moderating public support for transferring juveniles to adult court.

The consequences for the criminal justice system are clear. Although many states have created automatic legislative statutes that require adult trials for all juveniles accused of murder and felony one crimes, such legislation runs contrary to community sentiment. Public opinion in this area (as others reviewed in this book) is sensitive to the contextual features of the offense. These findings demonstrate that citizens are relatively sophisticated decision-makers and consider the juvenile's prior record, age, history of childhood abuse as well as the relationship between the victim and the accused in forming their recommendations about trying juveniles as adults. The emerging trend to make more frequent transfers to adult court is therefore inconsistent with community sentiment.

There are also parallels between public perceptions of juvenile delinquency and the insanity defense. It will be recalled that the more serious the crime, the less likely were the public to accept a plea of not guilty by reason of insanity. For juveniles, it would appear that the public feel that the most serious crimes require adult maturity, so that if a sixteen-year old commits murder, the act itself is evidence of adult maturity. There are clear weaknesses to this reasoning. First, many homicides are spontaneous gestures committed without reflection. In this sense, one might expect adults to be less, not more, likely to commit such a crime. Second, in evaluating whether a young person charged with homicide should be treated like an adult, the public are using the charge, not a conviction, and the reasoning becomes circular.

Sentencing Juvenile Offenders

Another feature common to most criminal justice systems is the existence of stepped-down punishments for juveniles. Even for juveniles transferred to adult court, the penalties are less severe. This is consistent with public opinion. There was a consensus on this issue: Almost two-thirds of the respondents disagreed with the assertion that a juvenile convicted of a crime should receive the same sentence as an adult.

A Canadian Gallup poll in 1994 asked respondents the following question: "How do you think society should deal with juveniles (those under age 18) who commit crimes?" Fifty-two percent chose to "give the same punishment as adults," 31 percent chose the option to place "less emphasis on punishment [and] more on rehabilitation" (Moore, 1994).[2] When juveniles had been convicted of their second offense, 83 percent of the public favored treating them like adults. Clearly then, as with other areas of criminal justice, the public are sensitive to the circumstances of the case. As well, we see once again the importance of an offender's criminal history in determining public reaction. The differential treatment of juvenile offenders is reserved for first offenders.

The public are also opposed to the prospect of sending juveniles to serve their sentences in adult prisons. For example, 83 percent disagreed with such a policy for juveniles convicted of a serious property crime. A study conducted in California reached the same conclusion. Californians overwhelmingly rejected a proposal to confine juveniles and adults in the same institution (Steinhart, 1988). Earlier research asked respondents to provide sentences for fourteen-year old and twenty-two-year old looters in a riot. For the juvenile offender, over half supported the use of probation whereas for the adult offender, only 21 percent felt that he should be placed on probation (Louis Harris and associates, 1968).

The preference for more lenient penalties can also be seen in responses to questions dealing with specific sentencing decisions. For example, when asked how they would sentence a juvenile convicted of a serious property crime, only one respondent in ten favored secure custody. Even for a juvenile convicted of a violent crime, more than half the sample favored some kind of community-based sanction, such as intensive probation or community residence.[3]

Schwartz (1993) provides an analysis of the role of demographic variables in public attitudes towards the treatment of juvenile offenders. Specifically, with regard to the issue of punitiveness, the results indicated that males, and respondents who were afraid of becoming a crime victim were most punitive. That is, these groups were more likely to favor trying juveniles in adult courts, giving juvenile offenders adult sentences and so forth. An interesting interaction emerged between parental status and race.

Adults who had children were less likely to support punitive policies. However, while African-Americans were less punitive than Caucasians, compared to other groups, respondents who were African-American and parents favored harsher penalties for juvenile offenders convicted of crimes involving violence. Schwartz speculates that this may reflect the differential probability of such individuals being the victims of crimes.

There are important parallels between public attitudes to sentencing juveniles and adults. We have noted in an earlier chapter that people who respond to polls by choosing the response that sentences are too lenient, are thinking of the worst kinds of offenders. The same phenomenon emerges at the level of juvenile justice. Sprott (1995) replicated this finding with a sample of Canadians. She found that the majority of people who believed that sentences for young offenders are too lenient were thinking about violent, recidivist young offenders. In contrast to this, people who were thinking of all offenders when responding to a question about sentence severity at the juvenile level, were far more likely to believe that sentences are appropriate.

Visiting the Sins of the Children on Their Parents

A number of jurisdictions have introduced legislation that holds parents responsible for crimes committed by their children, even in the absence of any evidence of negligence. For example, legislation proposed in Canada in 1996 would effectively hold parents responsible for any loss or damage arising from crimes committed by their children. As a solution to rising juvenile crime, the argument has been made that such a measure would promote a greater degree of parental interest in, and control over, young persons. It has also been argued that the public are likely to be in favor of such legislation. No American poll of which we are aware has addressed this issue directly. With regard to crimes committed by juveniles who use their parents firearms, Americans favor punishing the parents. Thus when Americans were asked in 1995 whether "Parents should be charged with a crime if their children injure themselves or others with a gun kept in their household," over half the respondents were in agreement (Adams, 1996). Canadians appear to differ from Americans on this issue. A representative survey of Canadians conducted in 1994 found most members of the public to be opposed to a measure which would make parents financially responsible for crimes committed by their children (Roberts, 1996).

Conclusions

Residents of several countries are concerned about what they perceive to be a rise in the volume or seriousness of youth crime. As with some other criminal justice perceptions, the public are misinformed. Youth crime rates have not been rising steadily as many people suppose. By a large margin, members of the public believe that the goal of juvenile courts should be rehabilitation and not punishment. There is widespread support for a separate juvenile court system, although this is qualified by a desire on the part of the public to permit the transfer of the more serious offenders to adult court. It is not the case that the public favor blanket transfers of all juvenile offenders convicted of a serious felony, or even of murder. The public are interested in learning about the details of the case. As with other areas of criminal justice, the public have little concrete knowledge of statistical trends in juvenile justice.

Notes

1.   As with sentencing at the adult level, Sprott (1995) finds that the misperceptions of youth justice can be traced back to inadequate news media coverage. For example, over the period covered by the research, over 5,000 cases were sentenced in youth court. Only twelve cases were reported by the media, and only one newspaper story discussed the justification for a sentence. Sprott concludes: "Thus, it is reasonable to expect that the public has little understanding of these issues" (p. 43).

2. Thirteen percent chose the option "depends on the circumstances," while 3 percent chose some other response.

3.   When the current serious violent crime committed by the juvenile was his second such offense, the percentage favoring the imposition of a term in a secure residence rose considerably. This is consistent with the impact of criminal record on public preferences for sentences at the adult level (see Chapter 10).

14

Gun Control

Regulating the acquisition of lethal weapons is a topic that is never far from the headlines. One of the causes of this constant interest is media coverage of mass murders involving firearms. The killing of fourteen young women in Montreal in 1989, and the murders of sixteen schoolchildren in Dunblane, Scotland in 1996 are examples of two such tragedies.[1] In the aftermath of these terrible crimes, there have been many calls for more restrictive legislation which, it was argued, would have prevented the offenders from acquiring their guns. And the most well-known piece of gun control legislation in America—the Brady Bill—was a direct result of the assassination attempt on President Reagan which left several people seriously wounded. Whether governments should regulate the possession of guns by private citizens is an issue that has generated endless political debates. The debate about gun control is especially heated in the United States for two reasons. First, because the prevalence of firearms is higher in America than any other western nation.[2] Second, because regulating the acquisition of firearms has obvious constitutional implications. The second amendment of the U.S. Constitution states that citizens have the right to bear arms and form state militia.

Proponents and opponents of gun control interpret the second amendment in different ways. Supporters of regulating possession of guns by private citizens see the second amendment as not granting an absolute right to bear arms, and as having an obsolete historical purpose of preventing the federal government from suppressing a state militia. Opponents of gun control perceive the second amendment as guaranteeing them an absolute right to bear arms for individual protection and state militia. In fact, groups in several states have formed militia to reinforce their second amendment right to bear arms such as semi-automatic weapons. The federal government has had several confrontations with these militia over violations of gun law regulations and other criminal laws. Confrontations such as those that occurred at Waco, Texas and Ruby Ridge have led to the deaths of private citizens as well as law enforcement officers. These conflicts have further intensified and divided the public on this issue.

In addition to the constitutional implications, the public also believes that gun control may affect the control of crime and has implications for the protection of one's home and life. Supporters of gun control believe that banning certain weapons and using other regulatory procedures such as pre-purchase waiting periods will reduce the overall rate of violent crimes. In contrast, opponents of gun control pursue a different logic, best encapsulated in their oft-repeated slogan "guns don't kill, people do." Opponents argue that severe punishments for violent crimes is the way to deter potential offenders.

In this chapter, we review the research on public opinion about gun control. Since attitudes towards gun control are so bound up with the ownership of firearms, we first examine the extent of public possession and ownership of guns, and then turn to public views about a variety of proposals to control access to guns.

Possession and Ownership of Guns

The actual number of guns possessed by Americans is difficult to determine because many guns are not registered and there is no reliable method for counting these unregistered guns. Estimates, however, indicate that the number of guns possessed by private citizens has increased significantly over time. The Bureau of Alcohol, Tobacco, and Firearms in the United States "estimates there were 54 million rifles, shotguns, and handguns in the United States in 1950, 104 million in 1970, 165 million in 1980, 201 million in 1990, and 211 million in 1992/1993" (Jacobs, Foster, and Seigel, 1995, p. 6).

> During the 94-year period between 1899 through 1993, an estimated 76.1 million handguns, 80.5 million rifles, and 69.9 million shotguns became available in the United States. ... The number of handguns produced and imported for sale in the United States increased 35 percent over the past 10 years, rifles rose 137 percent while shotguns sales grew only 11 percent. (Jacobs *et al.*, 1995, p. 8)

Several public opinion polls have been conducted over the past few decades to estimate the number of people who have guns in their possession. Approximately 50 percent of respondents to Gallup Polls conducted from 1959 to 1993 indicated that they had a gun in their home. Surveys from 1973 to 1993 at the National Opinion Research Center found that between 40 to 47 percent said they had a gun in their home. Taking into account the margin of error associated with any survey, these results suggest that between about 37 to 54 percent of United State residents have a firearm of some description in their residence. The most recent national poll addressing this issue found that 56 percent of respondents stated that there was a gun in their household (Adams, 1996). This same survey found that 45 percent owned guns primarily for sport, 20 percent primarily for protection, and 27 percent for both sport and protection (Adams, 1996).

There are clear differences between America and other western nations in this respect. In Canada, for example, less than 3 percent of homeowners report possessing a handgun whereas 20 percent of homes in the United States have a handgun (Mauser, 1990). An even smaller percentage of the British public own firearms. Surveys are less accurate at estimating ownership of semi-automatic weapons because many people may be hesitant to admit that they possess one of these weapons. The Bureau of Alcohol, Tobacco, and Firearms (BATF) estimates that United States residents in 1989 owned three million semi-automatic weapons (cited in Jacobs *et al.*, 1995). Legal bans on ownership of certain types of semi-automatic weapons in 1986 and in 1994 have reduced the number of these weapons manufactured or imported into the United States. The BATF estimates that between 700,000 to one million semi-automatic weapons would have been imported into the United States if the legal bans had not been enacted.

Gun owners are not a homogenous group, but a large percentage share certain demographic characteristics. Over the years, Gallup surveys and the National Opinion Research Center Surveys have found consistent demographic differences in ownership. Men, whites, those with only a high school education, Republican, and Southerners were more likely to own firearms (see Jacobs, 1995). One of the largest differences is gender: Only one-third of women own the guns in their homes whereas over 85 percent of men own the guns in their homes (Jacobs *et al.*, 1995). The majority of gun owners report knowing where their gun is located and how to use it, and a little over 40 percent say their gun is stored loaded. As well, almost one-fifth of respondents indicated that they have at some time carried their guns on their person.

Views About Gun Control Laws

In light of the high profile of the gun control issue, it is not surprising that each year for the last twenty years, Gallup has asked Americans the following question: "In general do you feel that the laws covering the sale of firearms should be made more strict, less strict, or kept as they are now?" The majority of the public has always supported stricter laws. Over the twenty years an average of 65 percent supported stricter laws (Moore and

Newport, 1994). The 1995 National Crime and Justice Survey found that 61 percent of the public agreed with the position that the laws covering the sale of firearms should be made stricter (Adams, 1996). Public concern about the availability of guns as a cause of crime can also be seen in responses to a poll conducted in 1994. Respondents were asked to evaluate a number of alternative explanations for the fact that American society is more inclined to violence than other societies. The second most popular explanation in the eyes of the public (endorsed by 70 percent of the sample) was the "easy availability of handguns" (Maguire and Pastore, 1995). Similarly, when asked about the high rate of homicide in America (compared to Canada or Europe), the most cited explanation of this phenomenon was the response "It is easier for people to buy guns here than in other countries" (Maguire and Pastore, 1995).[3]

The public in other countries are even more supportive of gun control legislation. For example, in Canada, 77 percent of respondents supported tighter restrictions on firearms ownership (Decima, 1993). Support varies by the background of the respondents, but the majority of respondents from all backgrounds indicate that laws should be stricter. Whites, men, rural dwellers, and republicans were less likely to support stricter laws (about a 20 percentage point difference) than were African-Americans, women, urban dwellers and democrats. Not surprisingly, gun owners are less supportive of controls on the acquisition of firearms: 55 percent of gun owners wanted stricter laws, 36 percent wanted them kept the same, and 8 percent thought they should be less strict (Jacobs *et al.*, 1995). The NCJS poll in 1995 found even starker differences between gun owners and non-owners with regard to restricting access to firearms: Less than half the gun owners (43 percent) wanted stricter gun control laws compared to three-quarters of non-owners (Adams, 1996).

The Gallup poll in 1993 also asked respondents whether they supported no restrictions on owning guns, some restrictions, or believed all guns should be illegal for everyone except for police and other authorized persons. The majority of adult respondents (73 percent) favored some restrictions, and of those who favored some restrictions half favored major restrictions (such as banning ownership of handguns and certain semi-automatic weapons), while 47 percent favored minor restrictions (such as instituting waiting periods before purchase of a handgun). One in five adults, however, believed it should be illegal to own a gun. Gun owners were less likely to endorse the view that it should be illegal to own a gun (only 6 percent held this belief). However, almost all gun owners (83 percent) favored some restrictions. Of the gun owners who favored some restrictions, the majority (60 percent) favored only minor restrictions such as waiting periods (Moore and Newport, 1994).

The frequency and publicity of these nationwide media polls on the issue of gun control suggest that gun control is a very important public policy issue for the public. As Mauser and Kopel noted

> a person who read only media polls might develop the impression that a substantial tightening of gun laws is a very important public policy objective for a very large majority of the American people. But when pollsters ask the general open-ended question, "What should be done about violent crime?" the percentage of people who answer "gun control" is often smaller than the sampling error. (1992, p. 77)

For example, the Harris Poll in 1994 asked respondents what were the two most important issues for the government to address. Results indicated that less than 5 percent of the public believed that gun control was one of the two most important issues confronting America (see Jacobs *et al.*, 1995, p. 108). Similarly, only 1 percent of the respondents in a 1993 Gallup poll named gun control as the most important non-economic problem.

These polls suggest that gun control is not a top priority for the public. Other polls also indicate that the public does not see additional controls on firearms to be the solution to the crime problem. A 1993 poll asked respondents to list the most important cause of violent crime in the United States. Only 8 percent indicated the availability of guns and only 9 percent thought that gun control was the single most important thing that can be done to help reduce violent crime in the United States (Jacobs *et al.*, 1995). In this same poll, 30 percent indicated that more gun control laws would be the least effective method in reducing violent crime.

When a 1994 Gallup poll asked respondents what they thought contributed to violent crime, "Seventy percent believed that the easy availability of guns contributed a lot to violence in American society, 89 percent indicated lack of adult supervision of children, 61 percent thought television contributed a lot, and 60 percent named movies" (Jacobs *et al.*, 1995, p. 121). Thus, the availability of guns is seen as a contributing factor, but is not as the sole or primary contributor to violent crime. Moreover, gun control appears to rank below other methods of controlling violent crime such as preventive programs, an increase in the effectiveness of prosecution and the imposition of harsher penalties on convicted felons.

Support for Permits and Waiting Periods

The requirement that prospective gun owners obtain a permit before purchasing a gun is considered by most people to constitute a minor restriction on the public's right to bear arms. As such, it is supported by the majority of the public in several nations. Most nation-wide polls conducted between 1959 and 1978 have found that the majority of the public supported the requirement of obtaining a permit before purchasing a gun (for a review see Lester, 1983). Moreover, support for a further requirement that purchasers obtain a permit from the police has been relatively stable across fifteen years of Gallup polls in both the United States and Canada (Mauser, 1990). A 1978 U.S. Gallup poll and a 1977 Canadian Gallup poll asked respondents: "Do you favor or oppose a law which would require a person to obtain a police permit before he or she could buy a firearm?" Over four-fifths of the public in both Canada and the U.S. supported this legal requirement. Police permits, however, have been required by law in Canada since 1978. In contrast, police permits have received more debate and have not been enacted in all states in the United States (Mauser, 1990). Recent polls also show similar support for gun permits. A more recent Canadian poll in British Columbia in 1988 also found that 86 percent supported a law requiring police permits (Mauser, 1990). Similarly, a Roper Center 1993 poll found that 81 percent favored requiring a police permit before the purchase of a gun (Jacobs *et al.*, 1995).

The conditions surrounding the acquisition of firearms, however, have received much debate. After much debate, Congress finally enacted the Brady Handgun Violence Prevention Act in 1993. The so-called Brady Bill established a waiting period throughout the country, the purpose of which is to allow local law enforcement authorities to conduct checks on prospective handgun purchasers. The goal of these checks is to uncover evidence of mental instability or criminal propensity, as well as to serve as a "cooling off period" which might prevent some impulsive crimes committed with a firearm.

The Brady Act applies only to handgun sales by licensed dealers and requires dealers to send the purchaser's sworn statement to the law enforcement officials within one day of purchase.

> With the passage of the Brady Law, all states have a waiting period. They either comply with the federal five-day business waiting period or have alternative requirements. Nine states have instant background checks. Fourteen states require permits or licenses to purchase handguns while seven states require permits for long guns. (Jacobs *et al.*, 1995, p. 26)

Nationwide polls find overwhelming public support for the Brady Law. A 1993 Gallup Poll found that 87 percent of the respondents favored the Brady Bill, both substantial majority of gun owners (82 percent) and non-owners (90 percent) supported the Brady bill (Moore and Newport, 1994).

However, as with other surveys, this poll failed to address one of the central issues debated by Congress: whether a five day waiting period should be enacted now or whether the quality of criminal records should first be improved before background checks were made mandatory

(Mauser and Kopel, 1992). The quality of police records is such that many individuals may be "cleared" for purchase of a gun even though they have a prior arrest or conviction. The Republicans in Congress wanted to make the records more accurate before enacting a law such as the Brady Bill. The public opinion poll data provide only a picture of public opinion with the assumption that background checks yield accurate results (Mauser and Kopel, 1992). Another problem with the media polls on the Brady Bill is that these polls did not address the alternative that was being considered in Congress: whether there should be an instant background check or a five day waiting period (Mauser and Kopel, 1992). A 1991 poll conducted by the Lawrence Research Firm found that 78 percent of the respondents preferred the waiting period over the instant background check (Mauser and Kopel, 1992). This same poll also indicated that only one-third of the public supported two features of the initial proposed Bill: making the check optional and allowing lawsuits against police when it appears that they conducted an insufficiently thorough check of the individual who purchased the firearm (Mauser and Kopel, 1992).

Support for Other Minor Restrictions

The registration of guns is another minor restriction that has received consideration. The majority of citizens in both the U.S. and Canada support a law requiring registration of guns. Most Canadians (83 percent), however, are overwhelmingly in favor of such a law whereas there is less consensus in the United States with only 67 percent supporting the law (Mauser, 1990). More recent surveys in both countries also find that the majority of the public supports registration. A 1988 survey of British Columbia residents found that 82 percent supported registration (Mauser, 1990). A 1994 Gallup Poll found that 81 percent favored the registration of all handguns and 71 percent of all gun owners favored registration of handguns (Moore and Newport, 1994). A 1992 Gallup poll of teenagers found that 70 percent of all teenagers supported firearm registration. Though registration is widely supported by the public, only seven states require registration of handguns. Thus, requiring registration was favored across numerous sectors of society, including gun owners and teenagers.

A 1993 Gallup poll also has addressed other measures of gun control that would impose minor restrictions on public possession of firearms. Two restrictions are supported by over 80 percent of the respondents: mandatory safety classes in order to qualify to own a gun (89 percent support); and limiting the purchase of guns to one firearm a month (72 percent support) (Moore and Newport, 1994). Virginia, which is a major source of illegal guns for neighboring states, enacted a one gun per month law to curb this illegal trafficking, and a recent survey of Virginia residents found overwhelming support for the law (83 percent indicating approval, see Kauder, 1993). Another poll conducted in 1994 explored whether the public favored requiring a license to shoot a gun. Three-quarters of the respondents supported requiring a license to shoot a gun similar to the license required to drive a car (Jacobs *et al.*, 1995). Clearly, the public endorses proposals that may reduce the incidence of accidents and violence committed during the commission of crimes, as long as they do not interfere with the right to own guns. Respondents in the 1993 Gallup poll, however, were split on whether to support a law that would impose a high tax on bullets: 55 percent support and 43 percent oppose such a law (Moore and Newport, 1994).

Concealing Handguns. Some states have recently loosened the requirements for carrying a concealed weapon. A 1995 nationwide survey found that two-thirds of Americans opposed making it easier for citizens to carry concealed weapons legally (Adams, 1996). Gun owners, in contrast, were more likely to favor the loosening of concealed weapon laws.

Banning Handguns. Handguns are often used in the commission of violent crimes. "Handgun Control, Inc., an organization committed to stronger federal handgun legislation, reported that in 1992, handguns killed 36 people in Sweden, 97 in Switzerland, 60 in Japan, 128 in Canada, 33 in Great Britain, 13 in Australia, and 13,220 in the United States" (Jacobs *et al.*, 1995, p. 57). Gallup has asked conducted several surveys on the banning of handguns over the period 1980 to 1993 in the United States. In this time, at least half of the respondents in each survey have opposed a law that would ban the possession of handguns. Only the 1959 Gallup poll revealed a majority of respondents (60 percent) in support of a law that would ban handguns. A 1993 Gallup poll indicates that the majority of the public (60 percent) and gun owners (83 percent) oppose banning the possession of handguns (Moore and Newport, 1994). Seventy-two percent of the respondents, however, supported a law banning cheap handguns. The opposition toward banning handguns is not as strong in Canada. In a 1975 Gallup poll, 81 percent of Canadians favored a law which would forbid the possession of handguns except by the police and other authorized persons (Mauser, 1990). Similarly, 63 percent of Canadians living in British Columbia favored a ban on handguns in a 1988 poll (Mauser, 1990).

Banning Semi-Automatic Weapons. Several Gallup polls have asked respondents to state whether they would favor or oppose a ban on the manufacture, sale, and possession of semi-automatic assault guns, such as the AK-47. In the 1993 poll, 77 percent favored the ban. The problem with these polls is that the question is ambiguous—the AK-47 is a fully automatic weapon which has been banned in the United States since 1986 (Mauser and Kopel, 1992). A 1994 Gallup poll asked respondents: "In your view, should

Congress pass the crime bill in its original form as Clinton supports it, or should Congress change the bill to remove the ban on assault weapons?" Fifty-seven percent of respondents favored retention of the ban whereas 30 percent favored its abolition. Unfortunately, the term "assault weapon" is left undefined, and it is doubtful that many people knew the actual details of the crime bill. "Most states that studied the semi-automatic issue debated proposals for a total ban. Total bans were rejected in over two dozen states and enacted in two (California and New Jersey)" (Mauser and Kopel, p. 75).

It is very important to know the details of the semi-automatic weapons because many hunters use semi-automatic rifles that hold five to ten bullets; the debate surrounding semi-automatic weapons is intensified over a concern that law-abiding citizens will be deprived of the use of semi-automatic weapons for the legitimate purpose of hunting. A 1992 New York Times poll found that 79 percent of the general public and 76 percent of gun owners favored a ban on semi-automatic military-style rifles that hold up to thirty bullets (Jacobs *et al.*, 1995). It is unclear where the public stands on other types of semi-automatic weapons because the questions posed in most of the polls have been flawed. Clearly, however, the public does want some restrictions on the acquisition of semi-automatic weapons. A Virginia poll found that 81 percent favored requiring a permit in order to purchase a semi-automatic weapon (Mauser and Kopel, 1992). Similarly, a Wisconsin poll found that 91 percent were in favor of requiring the owners of semi-automatic rifles to register their weapons with the state (Mauser and Kopel, 1992).

Banning Ownership of Guns for Certain Groups of Citizens. Much concern is expressed about juveniles obtaining and carrying weapons. This practice, however, is all too common. A 1990 nationwide survey of students in ninth to twelfth grade were asked whether they had carried a weapon such as a knife, gun, or club during the previous month. About 5 percent said they had carried a firearm, and it was usually a handgun (Snyder and Sickmund, 1995). A study surveyed 835 male serious offenders incarcerated in six juvenile correctional facilities in four states and 758 male students in ten inner city high school facilities (Jacobs *et al.*, 1995). Nine percent of this sample reported having used a weapon to commit a crime. Eighty-four percent of the juvenile offenders and 45 percent of the students reported that they had been threatened with a gun or shot at on the way to or from school in the previous few years. Most of the juveniles and students thought it would be easy to get a gun, and more than half of the juveniles and 8 percent of the students had stolen a gun. Forty-five percent of the juveniles had bought, sold, or traded a lot of guns. Seventy-two percent of the juveniles and 18 percent of the students had dealt drugs and most had carried weapons while they were dealing drugs.

Does the public want juveniles to be able to own guns legally? A 1993 Gallup poll revealed that the majority of the public (over 87 percent) supported a law that would bar individuals under eighteen years of age from purchasing a gun (Moore and Newport, 1994). Despite this overwhelming support, by the end of 1993, only sixteen states had laws prohibiting the possession of handguns by juveniles (Synder and Sickmund, 1995). Four additional states had enacted statutes prohibiting the possession of firearms by juveniles at the end of 1994, and other states are currently debating the issue (Jacobs et al., 1995). Most state statutes that allow juveniles to possess firearms appear not to reflect public views on this issue.

The majority of the respondents to a 1993 Gallup poll supported a law that would bar persons with prior convictions from purchasing a gun (Moore and Newport, 1994). Public views appear consistent with federal law making it illegal for anyone, "whether licensed or not, to sell or otherwise transfer a gun to any person included in the "high risk" category—convicted felons, drug abusers, and persons with mental defects" (Jacobs et al., 1995, p. 17). People convicted of crimes, however, have access to guns. A nationwide survey of prisoners revealed that almost half the respondents acknowledged that at some point they had owned a firearm (Jacobs et al., 1995). Moreover, about two-thirds of all armed violent offenders carried guns, and over half of these offenders had actually fired their guns during the commission of the offense (Jacobs et al., 1995). Over half of the offenders said they carried a weapon to scare the victim whereas 30 percent carried a weapon for self-protection.

The Reasons for Support or Opposition to Gun Control

There are at least three types of justification that may underlie support for gun control: personal instrumental reasons, sociotropic instrumental reason, or ideological reasons (Tyler and Lavrakas, 1983). The personal instrumental perspective suggests that support or opposition to gun control is related to people's beliefs about their personal welfare. For example, people may want tighter laws restricting access to gun because they fear that they will be a victim of a violent crime or people may want the unrestricted right to bear arms to protect themselves from violent crime. The sociotropic instrumental perspective argues that people support gun control because they are concerned about the overall crime rate and believe gun control laws can effectively curb violent crimes.

The ideological perspective asserts that people's political and philosophical views affect their support or opposition to gun control. Kleck (1996) drew upon the nationwide General Social Surveys to explore the concerns that affect the public's support for police permits before purchasing a gun. He found that prior victimization and personal fear of crime did not affect their opinions on this issue. Moreover, respondents living in high crime areas and respondents living in low crime areas held a similar view on this issue. Support for police permits was determined by an ideological perspective and varied by membership in different social groups. Gun control support was highest among better educated, higher income liberals who did not own guns or hunt. Tyler and Lavrakas (1984) examined the concerns underlying support for banning handguns in two urban midwestern cities. Similar to Kleck, they found little support for the personal instrumental perspective: Fear of crime was only weakly related to support for the ban. They, however, did find that concern about the crime rate and a belief that gun control laws could reduce crime were related to support for the ban, which provides some support for the sociotropic perspective. Clearly, the reasons underlying support may vary by the type of restriction proposed. A 1995 survey found that individuals with less confidence in the police were more likely to support liberal concealed weapon laws and to support less strict gun purchase laws (Adams, 1996).

Fear of personally being a victim of a crime may be unrelated to support for gun control laws because some of those with high fear may want guns to protect themselves. Gallup polls conducted in the U.S. in 1985 and in Canada in 1987 revealed that the majority of the public (at least 68 percent) believe that it is sometimes justified for retail store owners to use firearms to protect themselves and their property (Mauser, 1990). A 1988 British Columbia survey found that 58 percent favored store owners being licensed to have a small handgun to use if necessary in the event of an armed robbery, but 59 percent opposed home owners being licensed to have small handguns to use if necessary in the event of an armed robbery (Mauser, 1990). In 1981, a Gallup poll revealed that 16 percent bought a gun for self-protection, and by 1993, 30 percent said they bought a gun for self-protection (Jacobs et al., 1995). Part of the opposition to banning handguns may be that people believe law-abiding citizens will be deprived of an opportunity to protect themselves. A 1992 New York Times poll found that 56 percent thought that banning handguns would keep guns away from law-abiding citizens (Jacobs et al., 1995). These surveys suggest that some members of the public oppose gun control because they want the opportunity to protect themselves.

Conclusions

Governmental control over citizens' ownership of and access to firearms has received much attention in the media and from politicians. The widely publicized polls on public support for stricter gun control laws, however, may over-simplify the public's views and overstate public support for more restrictive gun control legislation. The survey data on gun control indicates that many people hold complex views about the topic. The type of restriction often affects the extent to which the public endorse greater restrictions. Moreover, the public may consider different concerns in forming judgments about their support for specific restrictions. For relatively minor restrictions such as police permits, the belief in the right to bear arms may not be a primary concern. On the other hand, for major restrictions such as banning handguns the belief in the right to bear arms may be a central consideration. The strength of the public's belief in the right to bear arms may explain why the majority of Americans oppose laws banning handguns, whereas most Canadians and Europeans favor such laws. Similarly, differences in the strength of the belief about the right to bear arms and the assimilation into cultures that value hunting and target shooting may account in part for why women, African-Americans, Democrats, higher income, and more educated respondents are more likely to support stricter gun control legislation.

Differences in attitudes between countries and the importance of background characteristics of respondents suggest some support for the conflict model of justice. The conflict model of justice suggests that the powerful members of society may impose their views on the less powerful. Consistent with the conflict model, legislative statutes on some proposed gun control strategies appear to be out of step with public desires (in America at least). A substantial majority of the public supports laws requiring registration of handguns and semi-automatic weapons, but only a few states require such registration. Similarly, there is public consensus that juveniles should be prohibited from possessing guns, but only twenty states have enacted laws prohibiting those under eighteen from having guns. Such discrepancies may be explained in part by the fact that those opposed to gun control are more likely to act on their beliefs (Schuman and Presser, 1981). Additionally, the National Rifle Association is a powerful lobbying group with over two million members. Some legislative actions, however, are consistent with expressed public opinion. Legislators' reluctance to enact statutes banning handguns appears to have public backing. Similarly, legislative statutes requiring waiting periods or police permits before the purchase of a gun reflect community sentiment on this issue. The issue of gun control and public views on this topic encompass a wide range of strategies which will continue to be debated for many years.

Notes

1. Incidents such as these have occurred in many countries. In 1996, thirty-five people were killed in Port Arthur, Tasmania.

2. The proportion of households with firearms is higher in Switzerland, but this is an anomaly—almost all these weapons are state-owned and are relinquished at the conclusion of the householder's period of active military service.

3. Sixty percent cited easy access to handguns as a major reason, and 22 percent as a minor reason for the higher homicide rate in America. Only 16 percent responded that access to handguns was not a reason.

15

Drawing Conclusions

Throughout the course of this volume we have reviewed public knowledge and attitudes towards a wide range of criminal justice topics. What have we learned? A number of conclusions stand out.

Educating the Public

First, it is clear that whatever the issue, public attitudes to criminal justice are founded upon an imperfect knowledge base. The insanity defense is one example, but there are many others. The greatest gaps between knowledge and opinion arise when the public perception is related to a populist ideology. Thus in the area of sentencing, most Americans (along with Canadians and Europeans) believe that sentences are too lenient. Part of the reason for this belief is that the public adhere to an ideology that the criminal justice system *in general* is to easy on offenders. It would be inconsistent of members of the public to hold the view that the system is tilted towards the defendant or offender, while at the same time believing that sentences are appropriate or too harsh.

There are lessons for researchers here, but more importantly it seems incumbent upon the criminal justice system to strive to educate the public to a greater degree than at present. Improving public knowledge of crime, and the limits of the criminal justice system will go some considerable way towards improving public satisfaction with criminal justice in America. Gaps will remain between the judicial process, or the actions of criminal justice professionals and the views of the public, but at least these will be founded upon a more realistic comprehension of the problem.

At the present time, much public dissatisfaction with criminal justice in America is in part a result of false expectations. Nowhere is this more true than in the area of sentencing. Many members of the public feel that the sentencing process is responsible for containing or even reducing crime rates across the nation, and that if crime is escalating (as it always seems to be), then sentencing should be harsher. As we have noted earlier, this is a misperception. There is a role for the sentencing process in the area of crime prevention, but it is a very limited role. Even sweeping changes to the severity of penalties (in either direction) will have only a very small impact on the overall crime rates.

If the public are not made more aware of the true state of affairs in the area of punishment, the result will be the passage of more repressive legislation. We are not the first to underline the importance of public education in this area. After reviewing recent research on public attitudes to punishment in the United Kingdom, the leading public opinion researcher in Europe concluded that:

> One thing is clear. If sentencers do nothing to stimulate a better public appreciation of their sentencing decisions, the government will take action to respond to public disenchantment with court sentences. And in the current political climate, the most likely government response is not public education, but the imposition of statutory minimum sentences and other devices to curb sentencing discretion and toughen up sentences. (Hough, 1996, p. 212)

Although Hough was writing about England and Wales, the same argument applies to other countries as well.

The Deliberative Poll approach to public opinion described in Chapter 1 may be a useful way of improving public legal knowledge, as well as exploring public opinion. A summary of the British poll on crime conducted in 1994 was televised to a national audience. As such it may well have had the effect of improving public awareness of criminal justice. Certainly the individuals who personally participated in the week-end learned from their experience. Significant improvements in knowledge accompanied the shifts in opinion documented earlier in this book. For example, at the end of the sessions, 80 percent of the participants knew that Britain has a larger prison population than other western European countries (see Fishkin, 1995, Appendix). If similar shifts in knowledge were observed in the television audience that watched the coverage of the weekend, then the technique holds promise for educating the public.

Another public education challenge for politicians concerns the costs of criminal justice. All too frequently the public are simply asked if they support a given crime policy such as "Three Strikes" legislation or manda-tory prison terms for drug dealers. It is an inappropriate question to pose. In many respects it is comparable to a survey which asks people if they support capital punishment for offenders convicted of murder without giving respondents the alternative of life imprisonment. Criminal justice initiatives that cost a lot of money (such as mandatory terms for drug dealing) should be put to the public with a price tag. The choice should not be between supporting or opposing mandatory sentences, but between endorsing the use of these penalties *or* some other criminal justice response to individuals who sell illegal drugs. Mandatory penalties may not be the most effective response, but they are certainly the most expensive.

In addition to information about costs, the public should be given specific alternatives, rather than just being asked whether they support or oppose a particular policy. For example, if the public were asked whether they think that making sentences harsher will reduce crime rates, most people would probably agree. However, if a more balanced question is asked, if the public are required by the poll to choose the most effective way of controlling crime, the results will be quite different. As we saw in an earlier chapter, when the question is posed in the broader manner, only one respondent in four chose making sentences harsher, while more than half the sample chose a non-criminal justice option, such as reducing unemployment or increasing the number of social programs.

This procedure of placing alternative policies before the public is observed in other areas of social policy. In the area of transportation for example choices are offered the public between subsidizing high-speed rail links or constructing and improving highways. Applying a similar logic to criminal justice suggests that the public should not be asked whether they favor increased spending for prisons, but rather to allocate criminal justice expenditures among the police, the courts and the prison system.

Researching Public Opinion

Although we have reviewed studies employing a diversity of approaches, the representative public opinion survey is still the methodology of choice in the field. Perhaps the most important lesson we have learned from this review is that while it is still the most useful tool, there are important limitations, and these must always be considered when evaluating the results of surveys. These restrictions can be overcome by supplementing survey research with more refined and complex experimental work. Attitudes towards the death penalty provide the most compelling example of this, but it is a general point which we believe applies to all the criminal justice issues that we have reviewed. The difficulty is that the news media are accustomed to reporting the results of snap-shot surveys of the public. The findings of more careful research that follow in the wake of the one-question surveys, are unfortunately confined to scholarly publications with comparatively restricted audiences.

We perceive an important distinction between public support for a policy in broad terms, and public support for a policy when applied to specific individuals. Unless support for a policy stands up at the level of an individual, we would not accept the position that the policy meets with the approval of the public. The danger with general questions is that the respondent loses sight of the consequences of a criminal justice policy. Once again the sentencing literature is instructive. Part of the support for harsher penalties springs from the fact that respondents to a sentencing survey have a generic offender in mind, one that is more serious than the average case. Survey researchers need to provide specific case histories in order to establish the limits of public support and also to circumvent the stereotypical image of offenders that most people have in their minds when answering surveys of this nature.

We would argue that the fact that criminal justice policies have important impacts on the lives of individual offenders means that researchers have a duty to ensure that subjects in a study or respondents to a survey have as much information as they need to make an informed choice about criminal justice topics. A higher threshold than that which is associated with other polls is advisable under these conditions.

Thirty years ago, a Presidential Commission concluded that:

> The Commission believes that there is a clear public responsibility to keep citizens fully informed of the facts about crime so that they will have facts to go on when they decide what the risks are and what kinds and amounts of precautionary measures they should take. Furthermore, they cannot judge whether the interference with individual liberties which strong crime control measures may involve is a price worth paying. (President's Commission on Law Enforcement and the Administration of Justice, 1967, pp. 52-53)

We agree with this position, although we would go further and add that the public can only be expected to rationally participate in the debate over criminal justice policy when they have an accurate idea of the extent of the problem, and the relative effectiveness (and costs) of various solutions. To date, efforts to educate the public about the phenomenon of crime, and the functioning of the criminal justice system have largely been ineffective.

Educating Criminal Justice Professionals

It is equally important to educate criminal justice professionals about the true nature of public opinion. There are numerous examples in which professionals have had a distorted view of the views of the public. Usually, we have found, the error is asymmetrical: Politicians and policy-makers assume that members of the public are more hawkish regarding crime policies than is in fact the case. For example, Smith and Lipsey (1976) found that over half the public favored a conjugal visitation program for prison inmates. These researchers concluded that their research "suggests that the appraisal of public concern by legislators, prison administrators, and criminologists is often incorrect... The traditional perception of a public intolerant of innovation in penal practice is not based on present day fact" (Smith and Lipsey, 1976, p. 122). The same statement holds today about a number of other criminal justice issues.

There is a great danger in the misuse of public opinion research findings, whether at the hands of Supreme Court justices, criminal justice administrators or politicians. We are not alone in this apprehension. Flanagan and Caulfield noted over a decade ago that: "the improper use of public opinion data in policy development has been likened to the manner in which a drunk employs a lamp post: for support rather than illumination" (p. 31, 1984).

We would argue that contextual information must always be supplied. The public need some context before being asked to respond to questions about crime and justice. In a similar fashion, the consumers of public opinion research need context in order to interpret the significance of poll results. Pollsters and researchers in the area of public opinion have an obligation to provide this context, and politicians have an obligation to take the contextual information into consideration before rushing to judgment about the nature of community sentiment.

There are two possible reactions to the findings we have summarized in this volume showing the public's lack of knowledge about crime and criminal justice. One extreme would suggest that there are few advantages, and great dangers, associated with consulting the public on criminal justice issues. We would reject this perspective. In a contemporary democracy, public consultation takes place on all important social questions, almost regardless of the level of public awareness of the issues. The public probably knew little about the likely benefits of signing the North American Free Trade Agreement or the advantages of military intervention in the Gulf war, yet few would deny the importance of gauging the nature of community sentiment regarding these and other social issues.

The challenge to researchers is to ensure to the greatest degree possible that research generates results that reflect the opinion of informed members of the public. This means using multiple methods of research, appropriate research designs, replication of findings and other research tools that are now commonplace as research on public opinion becomes more sophisticated. The enterprise of understanding public opinion towards crime and criminal justice cannot advance unless more structure is brought to the field. The haphazard accretion of poll results tells us little about community opinion. What is needed is a more systematic data-base which tracks public attitudes to all important issues in criminal justice. The results of each individual snap-shot survey can then be seen in context of previous findings using a similar methodology, but independent samples of respondents.

There is one important public misperception that has implications for many criminal justice issues. As noted in an earlier chapter, the public tend to see offenders as a separate category of citizen, readily identifiable and relatively unchanging in their anti-social behavior. This is at best an antiquated view of deviance. If the public realized that criminality takes many forms and cuts across all demographic categories, they would be less supportive of crime control policies founded principally upon a desire to isolate and punish, rather than rehabilitate and reform.

Finally, we must not lose sight of the principal reason for conducting research into public views of crime and justice. Crime itself is by its very nature anti-social and destructive. But criminal justice policies too can have deleterious effects on offenders, families of offenders, victims, their families and society in general. A central goal of good government is to ensure that the steps we take as a society to fight crime are not only effective, just and humane, but also consistent with the informed opinion of the very communities that criminal justice policies are created to protect.

References

Abel-Smith, B., M. Zander, & R. Brooke. 1973. *Legal Problems and the Citizen*. London: Heinemann.

Adams, K. 1996. "Guns and Gun Control." In T. J. Flanagan & D. R. Longmire (eds.), *Americans View Crime and Justice: A National Public Opinion Survey*. Thousand Oaks, CA: Sage Publications.

Akman, D. D., A. Normandeau, & S. Turner. 1967. "The Measurement of Delinquency in Canada." *Journal of Criminal Law, Criminology, and Police Science*, 58:330-337.

Albrecht, S., & M. Green. 1977. "Attitudes Toward the Police and the Larger Attitude Complex: Implications for Police-Community Relationships." *Criminology:An Interdisciplinary Journal*, 15:67-86.

Alderman, J. 1984. "Goetz and Bumpurs Cases Divide New York By Race." *Daily News Poll Eyewitness News*, 1-2.

Alemika, E. 1980. "Policing and Perceptions of Police in Nigeria". *Police Studies*, 11: 161-176.

Alpert, G.P., & R.G. Dunham. 1986. "Community-Policing". *Journal of Police Science and Administration*, 14:212-222.

"Americans Say Police Brutality Frequent". March, 1991. *The Gallup Poll Monthly*. 306: 53-56.

Anderson, C. 1983. "Abstract and Concrete Data in the Perseverance of Social Theories: When Weak Data Lead to Unshakeable Beliefs." *Journal of Experimental Social Psychology*, 19:93-108.

Andrews, P. 1985. "Mellow Attitudes Help Police Gain Stature". *Seattle Times*, p. 1.

Angus Reid Associates. 1984a. *Canadians' Attitudes Toward the Justice System*. Toronto: Angus Reid Associates Inc.

————. 1984b. *Canadian Unity Information Office Survey*. Toronto: Angus Reid Associates Inc.

————. 1994. *Public Opinion on Crime*. Toronto: Angus Reid Associates Inc.

Apple, N., & D. J. O'Brien. 1983. "Neighborhood Racial Composition and Residents' Evaluation of Police Performance". *Journal of Police Science and Administration*, 11: 76-84.

Applegate, B., F. Cullen, B. Link, P. Richards & L. Lanza-Kaduce. 1996. "Determinants of Public Punitiveness Toward Drunk Driving: A Factorial Survey Approach". *Justice Quarterly*, 13:57-79.

Ashworth, A. 1992. *Sentencing and Criminal Justice*. London: Weidenfeld and Nicholson.

Austin, W., & T. Williams. 1977. "A Survey of Judges' Responses to Simulated Legal Cases: Research Note on Sentencing Disparity." *Journal of Criminal Law and Criminology*, 68:306-310.

Bae, I. 1991. *A Survey on Public Acceptance of Restitution as an Alternative to Incarceration for Property Offenders in Hennepin County, Minnesota*. Ph.D. dissertation, University of Minnesota.

Bailis, D., J. Darley, J. Waxman, L. Tracy & Robinson, P. 1994. *Community Standards of Criminal Liability and the Insanity Defense*. Paper Presented at the American Law and Society Meetings, Santa Fe, New Mexico.

Bala, N. 1994. "What's Wrong with YOA Bashing? What's Wrong with the YOA? Recognizing the Limits of the Law." *Canadian Journal of Criminology*, 36:247-270.

Banks, C., E. Maloney, and H. D. Willcocks 1975. "Public Attitudes to Crime and the Penal System. *British Journal of Criminology*, 15:228-40.

Bar-Hillel, M. 1982. "Studies of representativeness." In D. Kahneman, P. Slovic, & A. Tversky (eds.), 69-83. *Judgment Under Uncertainty: Heuristics and Biases*. Cambridge University Press: London.

Barclay, G. (ed.), 1994. *Digest 2. Information on the Criminal Justice System in England and Wales*. London: Home Office.

Barkan, S. E., & S. F. Cohn. 1994. "Racial prejudice and support for the death penalty by whites". *Journal of Research in Crime and Delinquency*, 31(2):202-209.

Bell, D. J. 1982. "Police Uniforms, Attitudes, and Citizens". *Journal of Criminal Justice*, 10:45-55.

Bertrand, F. 1982. "Public Opinion About Criminal Justice Issues: Some Caution About Poll Data." *Impact*, 1:11-20.

Bibby, R. 1981. "Crime and Punishment: A National Reading." *Social Indicators Research* 9:1-13.

Bird, R. E. 1984. "The Rule of Law in an Instant Society". *American Psychologist*, 39(2): 158-162.

Birnbaum, M. H., & S. S. Stegner. 1981. "Measuring the Importance of Cues in Judgment for Individuals: Subjective Theories of IQ as a Function of Heredity and Environment". *Journal of Experimental Social Psychology*, 17:159-182.

Bishop, G. F. 1992. *The Greater Cincinnati Survey: Fall 1991*. Cincinnati, OH: Institute for Policy Research University of Cincinnati.

Black, J. B., J.A. Galambos & S. J. Read. 1984. "Comprehending Stories and Social Situations." In R. S. Wyer & T. K. Srull. (eds.), *Handbook of Social Cognition*, 3:45-86.

Block, R. L. 1971. "Fear of Crime and Fear of the Police. *Social Problems* 19:91-101.

Blumstein, A., & J. Cohen. 1980. "Sentencing of Convicted Offenders: An Analysis of the Public's View." *Law and Society Review* 14:223-261.

Blum-west, S. 1985. "The Seriousness of Crime: A Study of Popular Morality." *Deviant Behavior* 6:83-98.

Boers, K. & K. Sessar. 1989. "Do People Really Want Punishment? On the Relationship Between Acceptance of Restitution, Needs for Punishment and Fear of Crime." In *Developments in Crime and Crime Control Research*, K. Sessar & H-J. Kerner. (eds.), New York: Springer-Verlag.

Boggs, S. L., & J. F. Galliher. 1975. "Evaluating the Police: A Comparison of Black Street and Household Respondents." *Social Problems* 22(3):393-406.

Bohm, Robert M. 1987. "American Death Penalty Attitudes: A Critical Examination of Recent Evidence." *Criminal Justice and Behavior* 14(3):380-396.

Bohm, R. M. 1989. "Humanism and the Death Penalty, with Special Emphasis on the Post-Furman Experience." *Justice Quarterly* 6(2):173-218.

―――. 1987b. "Myths About Criminology and Criminal Justice: A Review Essay." *Justice Quarterly* 4:631-642.

Bohm, R. M. 1986. "Crime, Criminal and Crime Control Policy Myths". *Justice Quarterly* 3(2):193-214.

Bohm, R. M., & R.E. Vogel. 1994. "A Comparison of Factors Associated with Uninformed and Informed Death Penalty Opinions." *Journal of Criminal Justice,* 22(2):125-143.

Bohm, R.M., R.E. Vogel & A. A. Maisto. 1993. Knowledge and death penalty opinion: A panel study. *Journal of Criminal Justice* 21(1):29-45.

Bohm, R.M., L. J. Clark & A. F. Aveni. 1991. "Knowledge and Death Penalty Opinion: A test of the Marshall hypothesis." *Journal of Research in Crime and Delinquency,* 28(3):360-387.

Borgida, E. 1981. "Legal Reform of Rape Laws". In L. Bickman (ed.), *Applied Social Psychology Annual.* Beverly Hills: Sage.

Borgida, E., & P. White. 1978. "Social Perception of Rape Victims: The Impact of Legal Reform." *Law and Human Behavior* 2:339-51.

Bottomley, K. & K. Pease. 1986. *Crime and Punishment: Interpreting the Data.* Milton Keynes: Open University Press.

Bouma, D. H. 1972. "Youth Attitudes Toward the Police and Law Enforcement." In JT.Curran, A. Fowler, & R.H. Ward. (eds.), *Police and Law Enforcement* 3:219-238. New York: AMS Press.

Bourque, L.B. 1989. *Defining Rape.* Durham, NC: Duke University Press.

Bowers, W. 1993. "Capital Punishment and Contemporary Values: People's Misgivings and the Court's Misperceptions." *Law & Society Review* 27:157-175.

Bowers, W. & M. Vandiver. 1991a. "New Yorkers Want an Alternative to the Death Penalty." *Executive Summary of a New York State Survey Conducted March 1-4, 1991.*

Bowers, W. & M. Vandiver. 1991b. "Nebraskans Want an Alternative to the Death Penalty." *Executive Summary of a Nebraska State Survey Conducted April 26-28, 1991.*

Boydell, C. and C. Grindstaff. 1972. "Public Opinion and the Criminal Law: An Empirical Test of Public Attitudes Towards Legal Sanctions." In: C. Boydell, C. Grindstaff, and P. Whitehead (eds.), *Deviant Behavior and Societal Reaction.* Toronto: Reinhart and Winston.

Bracki, M.A. & G. Connor. 1975. "Survey of Police Attitudes Toward Rape in Du Page County, Illinois." *Crisis Intervention* 6:28-42.

Brandl, S. G., J. Frank, R. E. Worden, & T.S. Bynum. 1994. "Global and Specific Attitudes Toward the Police: Disentangling the Relationship." *Justice Quarterly* 11(1): 119-134.

Breci, M. G., & J. E. Murphy. 1992. "What Do Citizens Want Police to Do at Domestics: Enforce the Law or Provide Services?" *American Journal of Police* 11(3):53-68.

Breci, M. G. 1987. "Police Officers' Values on Intervention in Family Fights." *Police Studies* 10:192-202.

Bridges, J. S. 1991. "Perceptions of Date and Stranger Rape: A Difference in Sex-Role Expectations and Rape-Supportive Beliefs." *Sex Roles* 24:291-307.

Brillon, Y., C. Louis-Guerin, & M-C. Lamarche. 1984. *Attitudes of the Canadian Public Toward Crime Policies*. Ottawa: Ministry of the Solicitor General Canada.

Brockner, J., T. R. Tyler & R. Cooper-Schneider. 1992. "The Influence of Prior Commitment to an Institution on Reactions to Perceived Unfairness: The Higher They Are, The Harder They Fall." *Administrative Science Quarterly* 37:241-261.

Brown, C., J. Anderson, L. Burggraf & N. Thompson. 1978. "Community Standards, Conservatism, and Judgments of Pornography." *Journal of Sex Research* 14(2):81-95.

Brownmiller, S. 1975. *Against Our Will*. New York: Bantam Books.

Bull, R. H. C., & J. Green. 1980. "The Relationship Between Physical Appearance and Criminality." *Medical Science and Law* 20:79-83.

Burch v. Louisiana 441 U. S. 130 1979.

Bureau of Justice Assistance 1992. *Accountability In Dispositions of Juvenile Drug Offenders*. (NCJ 134224). U.S. Department of Justice: Washington, D.C.

Burrows, J. 1986. "Burglary Investigations: Victims' Views of Police Activity. *Policing* 2: 172-183.

Burt, M.R., 1980. "Cultural Myths and Supports for Rape." *Journal of Personality and Social Psychology* 38:217-230.

Burtch, B. & R. Ericson. 1979. *The Silent System*. Toronto: Centre of Criminology, University of Toronto.

Butow, D. 1992. "Days of Rage." *U.S. News & World Report* 112(18): 20-36.

Calhoun, L., J. Selby & L.Warring. 1976. "Social Perception of the Victim's Causal Role in Rape: An Exploratory Examination of Four Factors." *Human Relations* 29(6):517-526.

California Assembly Committee on Criminal Procedure. 1975. "Public Knowledge of Criminal Penalties." In *Perception in Criminology*. R. L. Henshel & R. A. Silverman. (eds.), Toronto: Methuen.

Callins v. Collins, 114 S.Ct. 1127 1994.

Campbell, G. 1993. *An Examination of Recidivism in Relation to Offence Histories and Offender Profiles*. Ottawa: Statistics Canada, Canadian Centre for Justice Statistics.

Campbell, A. & S. Muncer. 1990. "Causes of Crime: Uncovering a Lay Model." *Criminal Justice and Behavior*, 17:410-19.

Canadian Centre for Justice Statistics. 1994. *Canadian Crime Statistics*. Ottawa: Statistics Canada.

Canadian Criminal Justice Association. 1987. *Attitudes Toward Parole*. Ottawa: Canadian Criminal Justice Association.

Canadian Sentencing Commission. 1987. *Sentencing Reform: A Canadian Approach*. Ottawa: Ministry of Supply and Services Canada.

Cann, A., L. Calhoun & J. W. Selby. 1980. "Attributions for Delinquent Behaviour: Impact of Consensus and Consistency Information." *British Journal of Social and Clinical Psychology* 19:33-40.

Carlson, J. M., & T. Williams. 1993. "Perspectives on the Seriousness of Crimes." *Social Science Research* 22:190-207.

Carlson, H.M. & M.S.Sutton. 1979. "Some Factors in Community Evaluation of Police Street Performance." *American Journal of Community Psychology* 7(6):583-591.

Carrington, P. & S. Moyer. 1994. "Trends in Youth Crime and Police Response, Pre and Post-YOA." *Canadian Journal of Criminology* 36:1-28.

Carroll, J. S. 1978. "Causal Theories of Crime and Their Effect Upon Expert Parole Decisions." *Law and Human Behavior* 2:377-88.

Carroll, J. S., W. T. Perkowitz, A. J. Lurigio & F. M. Weaver. 1987. "Sentencing Goals, Causal Attributions, Ideology, and Personality." *Journal of Personality and Social Psychology* 52(1):107-118.

Carroll, J. S., N. L. Kerr, J. J. Alfini, F. M. Weaver, R. J. MacCoun & V. Feldman. 1986. "Free Press and Fair Trial: The Role of Behavioral Research." *Law and Human Behavior* 10:187-201.

Carter, D. L., 1985. "Hispanic Perceptions of Police Performance: An Empirical Assessment." *Journal of Criminal Justice* 13:487-500.

Carte, G.E. 1973. "Changes in Public Attitudes Toward the Police: A Comparison of 1938 and 1971 Surveys." *Journal of Police Science and Administration* 1(2):182-200.

Casper, J. D., K. Benedict & J. L. Perry. 1989. "Juror Decision Making, Attitudes, and the Hindsight Bias." *Law and Human Behavior* 13:291-310.

Casper, J. D., T. R. Tyler, & B. Fisher. 1988. "Procedural Justice in Felony Cases." *Law & Society Review* 22:483-507.

Chackerian, R. 1974. "Police Professionalism and Citizen Evaluations: A Preliminary Look." *Public Administration Review* 34(2):141-148.

Chaiken, S., & S. M. Yates. 1985. "Attitude Schematicity and Thought-Induced Attitude Polarization." *Journal of Personality and Social Psychology* 49:1470-1481.

Champion, D. J., & L. G. Mays. 1991. *Transferring Juveniles to Criminal Courts: Trends and Implications*. New York: Praeger.

Church, G. L. May, 1992. "The Fire This Time: As Los Angeles Smolders." *Time*. 20-25.

Clearinghouse on Georgia Prisons and Jails, 1987. *Juveniles and the Death Penalty: Poll Documents Voters' Opinion*. Atlanta, GA: Clearinghouse on Georgia Prisons and Jails.

Clifford, F. & D. Ferrell. 1992. "Angelenos Condemn King Verdicts, Rioting, Poll Finds." *The Times Union*, Wednesday, May 6, Section A, page 11.

Cohn, S. F., S. E. Barkan & W.A. Halteman. 1991. "Punitive Attitudes Toward Criminals: Racial Consensus or Racial Conflict?" *Social Problems* 38:287-96.

Cohen, S. A. & A. N. Doob. 1989. "Public Attitudes to Plea Bargaining." *Criminal Law Quarterly* 32:85-109.

Coker v. Georgia, 433 U.S. 584 1977.

Commission on Systemic Racism in the Ontario Criminal Justice System. 1995. *Report of the Commission on Systemic Racism in the Ontario Criminal Justice System*. Toronto: Queen's Printer for Ontario.

Constantini, E., & J. King. 1980. "The Partial Juror: Correlates and Causes of Prejudgment." *Law & Society Review* 15:9-40.

Converse, P. E. 1964. "The Nature of Belief Systems in Mass Publics." In D. E. Apter (ed.), *Ideology and Discontent*, 206-261. London: The Free Press of Glencoe.

Cook, R. L., & T. R. Stewart. 1975. "A Comparison of Seven Methods for Obtaining Subjective Descriptions of Judgmental Policy." *Organizational Behavior and Human Performance* 13:31-45.

Coombs, C. H. 1967. "Thurstone's Measurement of Social Values Revisited Forty Years Later." *Journal of Personality and Social Psychology* 6:85-91.

Coons, W.H., & P. A. McFarland. 1985. "Obscenity and Community Tolerance." *Canadian Psychology* 26(1):30-38.

Corbett, C. & F. Simon. 1991. "Police and Public Perceptions of the Seriousness of Traffic Offenses." *British Journal of Criminology* 31(2):153-164.

Cordner, G. W. 1986. "Fear of Crime and the Police: An Evaluation of a Fear Reduction Strategy." *Journal of Police Science and Administration* 14(3):223-233.

Cornish, W. & A. Sealy. 1973. "Juries and the Rules of Evidence." *Criminal Law Quarterly* 16:208-223.

Correctional Services of Canada. 1993. *Basic Facts About Corrections in Canada. 1993 Edition*. Ottawa: Ministry of Supply and Services Canada.

Correctional Services of Canada. 1994. *Basic Facts About Corrections in Canada. 1994 Edition*. Ottawa: Minister of Supply and Services.

Costin, F., & N. Schwarz. 1987. "Beliefs About Rape and Women's Social Roles: A Four-Nation Study." *Journal of Interpersonal Violence* 2:45-56.

Cox, T. C. & M. F. White. 1988. "Traffic Citations and Student Attitudes Toward the Police: An Examination of Selected Interaction Dynamics." *Journal of Police Science and Administration* 16(2):105-121.

Cruzan v. Director, Missouri Department of Health, 110 S. Ct. 2841 1990.

Cullen, F. T., B. G. Link & C. Polanzi. 1982. "The Seriousness of Crime Revisted: Have Attitudes Toward White Collar Crime Changed?" *Criminology* 2:83-102.

Cullen, F. T., B. G. Link, L. F. Travis. III & J. F. Wozniak. 1985. "Consensus in Crime Seriousness: Empirical Reality or Methodological Artifact?" *Criminology* 23(1): 99-118.

Cullen, F. T., K. E. Gilbert & J. B. Cullen. 1983. "Implementing Determinant Sentencing in Illinois: Conscience and Convenience." *Criminal Justice Review* 8:1-16.

Cullen, F. T., G. A. Clark, J. B. Cullen, & R. A. Mathers. 1985. "Attribution, Salience, and Attitudes Toward Criminal Sanctioning." *Criminal Justice and Behavior* 12:305-331.

Cullen, F. T., S.E. Skovron, J. E. Scott & V. S. Burton. 1990. "Public Support for correctional treatment: The Tenacity of Rehabilitative Ideology." *Criminal Justice and Behavior* 17:6-18.

Cullen, F.T., L. Cao, J. Frank, R.H. Langworthy, S. L. Browning, R. Kopache & T. J. Stevenson. 1996. "Stop or I'll Shoot: Racial Differences in Support for Police Use of Deadly Force." *American Behavioral Scientist* 39(4):449-460.

Cumberland, J. & E. Zamble. 1992. "General and Specific Measures of Attitudes Toward Early Release of Criminal Offenders." *Canadian Journal of Behavioural Science* 24:442-455.

Darley, J. M., C. A. Sanderson & P. S. LaMantia. 1996. "Community Standards for Defining Attempt: Inconsistencies with the Model Penal Code." *American Behavioral Scientist* 39(4):407-422.

Decima Research. 1993. *A Report to the Department of Justice*. Ottawa: Decima Research.

Decker, S. H. 1981. "Citizen Attitudes Toward the Police: A Review of Past Findings and Suggestions for Future Policy." *Journal of Police Science and Administration* 9(1): 80-87.

Decker, S. H. 1985. "The Police and the Public: Perceptions and Policy Recommendations." In R.J. Homant & D.B. Kennedy, (eds.), *Police and Law Enforcement* 3: 89-105. New York: AMS Press.

Department of Justice. 1988. *An Analysis of Public Attitudes Towards Justice-Related Issues 1986-1987*. Ottawa: Research Section, Department of Justice.

Diamond, S. 1990. "Sentencing Decisions by Laypersons and Professional Judges." *Law an Social Inquiry* 15:191-221.

Diamond, S. & L. J. Stalans. 1989. "The Myth of Judicial Leniency in Sentencing." *Behavioral Sciences and the Law* 7:73-89.

Dieter, R. C., 1993. "Sentencing for Life: Americans Embrace Alternatives to the Death Penalty."

Dillehay, R. C., & M. T. Nietzel. 1985. "Juror Experience and Juror Verdicts". *Law & Human Behavior* 9(2):179-191.

Doble, J. 1987. *Crime and Punishment: The Public's View*. New York, NY: Prepared by The Public Agenda Foundation for the Edna McConnell Clark Foundation.

Doble, J., & J. Klein. 1989. *Punishing Criminals: The Public's View. An Alabama Survey*. New York: The Edna McConnell Clark Foundation.

Doleschal, E. 1970. "Public Opinion and Correctional Reform." *Crime and Delinquency* 2: 456-76.

Doleschal, E. 1979. "Crime -- Some Popular Beliefs." *Crime and Delinquency* 25:1-8.

Doob, A. N. 1979. *Studies on the Jury*. Ottawa, Ontario: Canada Law Reform Commission.

Doob, A. N. 1985. "The Many Realities of Crime." In: *Perspectives in Criminal Law*, E. L. Greenspan & A. N. Doob.(eds.), Aurora, Ontario: Canada Law Book.

Doob, A.N. & H. Kirshenbaum. 1972. "Some Empirical Evidence on the Effect of S. 12 of the Canada Evidence Act upon the Accused." *Criminal Law Quarterly*, 15:88-96.

Doob, A. N., V. Marinos & K. Varma. 1995. *Youth Crime and the Youth Justice System in Canada. A Research Perspective*. Toronto: University of Toronto, Centre of Criminology.

Doob, A. and J.V. Roberts. 1982. *Crime and the Official Response to Crime: The Views of the Canadian Public*. Ottawa: Department of Justice Canada.

_____. 1983. *An Analysis of the Public's View of Sentencing*. Ottawa: Department of Justice Canada.

_____. 1984. Social Psychology, Social Attitudes and Attitudes Toward Sentencing. *Canadian Journal of Behavioural Science* 16:269-280

Douglas, L. 1995. "The Force of Words: Fish, Matsuda, Mackinnon, and the Theory of Discursive Violence." *Law & Society Review*, 29(1):169-190.

Douglas, K. & J. Ogloff. 1997. "Public Opinion of Statutory Maximum Sentences in the Canadian Criminal Code: Comparison of Offences Against Property and Offences Against the People." *Canadian Journal of Criminology*, in Press.

Dowds, L. 1994. *The Long-eyed view of Law and Order: A decade of British Social Attitudes Survey Results. (Draft Report)*. London: Home Office.

Dowling v. U.S., 110 S.Ct. 668 1990.

Duffy, B. (May, 1992). "Days of Rage." *U.S. News & World Report* 112(18):20-26.

Dunham, R. G., & G. P. Alpert. 1988. "Neighborhood Differences in Attitudes Toward Policing: Evidence for a Mixed Strategy Model of Policing in a Multi-Ethnic Setting." *The Journal of Criminal Law & Criminology* 79(2):504-523.

Durham, A. M. III. 1988. "Crime Seriousness and Punitive Severity: An Assessment of Social Attitudes." *Justice Quarterly* 5:131-53.

Durham, A. M. III. 1993. "Public Opinion Regarding Sentences for Crime: Does it Exist?" *Journal of Criminal Justice* 21:1-11.

Durkheim, E. 1964. *The Division of Labor in Society*. Translated by George Simpson. New York: Free Press.

Eagly, A. H. & S. Chaiken. 1993. *The Psychology of Attitudes*. New York: Harcourt Brace Jovanovich College Publishers.

Easton, D. 1965. *A Systems Analysis of Political Life*. Chicago: University of Chicago Press.

Economist. 1985. Untitled Article. July 20, p. 51.

Edmund v. Florida, 458 U.S. 586 1982.

Edwards, C. 1987. "Public Opinion on Domestic Violence: A Review of the New Jersey Survey." *Response to the Victimization of Women and Children* 10:6-9.

Ellis, D. May, 1992. "L.A. Lawless." *Time*, 26-29.

Ellsworth, P.C. & L. Ross. 1983. "Public Opinion and Capital Punishment: A Close Examination of the View of Abolitionists and Retentionists." *Crime and Delinquency* 29(1):116-169.

Ellsworth, P. C., & S. R. Gross. 1994. "Hardening of the Attitudes: Americans' Views on the Death Penalty." *Journal of Social Issues* 50(2):19-52.

Ellsworth, P. C. 1988. "Unpleasant Facts: The Supreme Court's Response to Empirical Research on Capital Punishment." In K. C. Haas & J. A. Inciardi (eds.), *Challenging Capital Punishment: Legal and Social Science Approaches*, 177-211. Newbury Park, CA: Sage Publications Inc.

Elrod, P. & M. Brown. 1995. *Predicting Public Support for Electronic House Arrest: Results from a New York County Survey*. Charlotte: University of North Carolina.

English, K., J. Crouch & P. Pullen. 1989. *Attitudes Toward Crime: A Survey of Colorado Citizens and Criminal Justice Officials*. Colorado: Colorado Department of Public Safety, Division of Criminal Justice.

Engstrom, R. L., & M. W. Giles, 1972. "Expectations and Images: A Note on Diffuse Support for Legal Institutions." *Law & Society Review* 6:631-636.

Environics Research Group. 1987. *Survey of Public Attitudes Toward Justice Issues in Canada*. Toronto:Environics Research Group Limited.

————. 1989a. *A Qualitative Investigation of Public Opinion on Sentencing, Corrections and Parole. Final Report*. Toronto: Environics Research Group Limited.

————. 1989b. *The Focus Canada Report: 1989*. Toronto: Environics Research Group Limited.

Erez, E. (1984). "Self-Defined "Desert" and Citizens' Assessment of the Police." *Journal of Criminal Law and Criminology* 75(4):1276-1299.

Erickson, M. J., & J. P. Gibbs. 1979. "On the Perceived Severity of Legal Penalties." *Journal of Criminal Law and Criminology* 70:102-16.

Erksine, H. 1974. "The Polls: Causes of Crime." *Public Opinion Quarterly* 50:288-298.

Evans, S. S., & J. E. Scott. 1984b. "The Seriousness of Crime Cross-Culturally: The Impact of Religiousity." *Criminology* 22(3):39-59.

Ewing, C.P. & M. Aubrey. 1987. "Battered Women and Public Opinion: Some Realities About the Myths." *Journal of Family Violence* 2:257-264.

Fagan, R.W. 1981. "Public Support for the Courts: An Examination of Alternative Explanations." *Journal of Criminal Justice* 9:403-417.

Fagan, R.W. 1987. "Knowledge and Support for the Criminal Justice System." *Criminal Justice Review* 12:27-33.

Farrell, R. A. & M. D. Holmes. 1991. "The Social and Cognitive Structure of Legal Decision-Making. *Sociological Quarterly* 32(4):529-542.

Fattah, E. 1982. "Public Opposition to Prison Alternatives and Community Corrections: A Strategy for Action." *Canadian Journal of Criminology* 24:371-385.

Fazio, R. H., & M. P. Zanna. 1981. "Direct Experience and Attitude-Behavior Consistency." *Advances in Experimental Social Psychology* 14:161-202.

Fazio, R. H., & C. J. Williams. 1986. "Attitude Accessibility as a Moderator of the Attitude-Behavior Relation: An investigation of the 1984 Presidential Election." *Journal of Personality and Social Psychology* 51:505-514.

Fazio, R. H. 1989. "On the Power and Functionality of Attitudes: The Role of Attitude Accessibility." In A. R. Pratkanis, S. J. Beckler, & A. G. Greenwald. (eds.), *Attitude Structure and Function*, 153-179. Hillsdale, NJ: Erlbaum.

Feagin, J. R., & P. R. Sheatsley. 1971. "Ghetto Resident Appraisals of a Riot." *Public Opinion Quarterly* 32:352-362.

Federal-Provincial Task Force on Uniform Rules of Evidence. 1982. *Report of the Federal-Provincial Task Force on Uniform Rules of Evidence.* Toronto: Carswell.

Fedorowycz, O. 1992. "Break and Enter in Canada". *Juristat Service Bulletin* 12(17).

Feld, B. C. 1987. "The Juvenile Court Meets the Principle of the Offense: Legislative Changes in Juvenile Waiver Statutes." *Journal of Criminal Law & Criminology* 78: 471-484.

Fichter, Michael & C. Veneziano. 1988. *Criminal Justice Attitudes - Missouri.* Jefferson City, Missouri. Missouri Department of Corrections.

Field, H.S. 1978. "Attitudes Toward Rape: A Comparative Analysis of Police, Rapists, Crisis Counselors, and Citizens." *Journal of Personality and Social Psychology* 36:156-179.

Figlio, R. M. 1975. "The Seriousness of Offenses: An Evaluation by Offenders and Non-Offenders." *Journal of Criminal Law and Criminology* 66:189-201.

Finkel, N. J., R. Shaw, S. Bercaw & Koch, J. 1985. "Insanity Defenses: From the Jurors' Perspective". *Law and Psychological Review* 9:77-92.

Finkel, N. J., & S. F. Handel. 1988. "Jurors and Insanity: Do Test Instructions Instruct?" *Forensic Reports* 1:65-79.

Finkel, N.J. 1990. "Capital Felony-Murder, Objective Indicia, and Community Sentiment." *Arizona Law Review*, 819.

Finkel, N. J. & K. B. Duff. 1991. " Felony-Murder and Community Sentiment: Testing the Supreme Court's Assertions." *Law and Human Behavior* 15:405-423.

Finkel, N. J. 1991. "The Insanity Defense: A Comparison of Verdict Schemas." *Law and Human Behavior*, 15(5):533-555.

Finkel, N. J., K. H. Meister & D. M. Lightfoot. 1991. "The Self-Defense Defense and Community Sentiment." *Law and Human Behavior* 15(6):585-602.

Finkel, N. J., S. T. Maloney, M. Z.Valbuena & J. L. Groscup. 1996. "Lay Perspectives on Legal Conundrums: Impossible and Mistaken Act Cases." *Law and Human Behavior* 19(6):593-608.

Finkel, N.J. 1993. "Socioscientific Evidence and Supreme Court Numerology: When Justices Attempt Social Science." *Behavioral Science and the Law* 11:67-77.

Finkel, N. J., M. L. Hurabiell & K. C. Hughes. 1993. "Right to Die, Euthanasia, and Community Sentiment: Crossing the Public/Private Boundary." *Law and Human Behavior* 17(5):487-506.

Finkel, N.J. & S.F. Smith. 1993. "Principals and Accessories in Capital Felony-Murder: The Proportionality Principle Reigns Supreme." *Law & Society Review* 27(1):129-156.

Finkel, N.J., K.C. Hughes, S. F. Smith & M. L. Hurabiell. 1994. "Killing Kids: The Juvenile Death Penalty and Community Sentiment." *Behavioral Science and the Law* 12: 5-20.

Finkel, N. J. 1995. *Commonsense Justice*. Boston, MA: Harvard University Press.

Fischer, G.J. 1987. "Hispanic and Majority Student Attitudes Toward Forcible Date Rape as a Function of Differences in Attitudes Toward Women." *Sex Roles* 17(2):93-101.

Fischoff, B. 1975. "Hindsight or Foresight : The Effect of Outcome Knowledge on Judgment Under Uncertainty." *Journal of Experimental Psychology: Human Perception and Performance* 1:288-299.

Fiske, S., & S. Taylor. 1991. *Social Cognition*. Reading, MJA: Addison-Wesley.

Fiske, S. T., & S. L. Neuberg. 1990. "A Continuum of Impression Formation, from Category-Based to Individuating Processes: Influences of Information and Motivation on Attention and Interpretation." In M. P. Zanna (ed.), *Advances in Experimental Social Psychology* 3:1-74. San Diego, CA: Academic Press.

Fiske, S. T. 1992. "Thinking is For Doing: Portraits of Social Cognition from Daguerreotype to Laserphoto." *Journal of Personality and Social Psychology* 63(6): 877-899.

Flanagan, T. 1987. "Change and Influence in Popular Criminology: Public Attributions of Crime Causation." *Journal of Criminal Justice* 15:231-243.

Flanagan, T. J., & K. Maguire. 1990. (eds.), *Sourcebook of Criminal Justice Statistics - 1989*. Washington, D.C.: U.S. Department of Justice (Bureau of Justice Statistics).

Flanagan, T. J., E. F. McGarrell & E. J. Brown. 1985. "Public Perceptions of the Criminal Courts: The Role of Demographics and Related Attitudinal Variables." *Journal of Research in Crime and Delinquency* 22:66-82.

Flanagan, T. J. 1988. *Public Support and Confidence in the Police: A Multidimensional View of Attitudes Toward Local Police.* Paper Presented at the Annual Meeting of the Academy of Criminal Justice Sciences. San Francisco, California.

Flanagan, T. J. 1985. "Public Perceptions of the Criminal Courts: the Role of Demographic and Related Attitudinal Variables." *Journal of Research in Crime and Deliquency* 22 (1):66-82.

Flanagan, T.J. 1985. "Consumer Perspectives on Police Operational Strategy." *Journal of Police Science and Administration* 13(1):10-21.

Flanagan, T.J. & M. S. Vaughn. 1995. "Public Opinion About Police Abuse of Force." In W. A. Geller & H. Toch (eds.), *Police Use of Excessive Force and its Control: Key Issues Facing the Nation*, 113-151. Washington, D.C.: Police Executive Research Forum.

Flanagan, T. J. 1987. "Change and Influence in Popular Criminology: Public Attributions of Crime Causation." *Journal of Criminal Justice* 15:231-43.

Fletcher, J. 1991. "Policing, Police Culture and Race: Police Attitudes in the Canadian Cultural Context." Unpublished Manuscript. Toronto: Centre of Criminology, University of Toronto.

Focus Canada. 1987. *Attitudes Toward Capital Punishment*. Focus Canada Report.

Forgas, J. P. 1980. "Images of Crime: A Multidimensional Analysis of Individual Differences in Crime Perception." *International Journal of Psychology* 15:287-299.

Furnham, A. & M. Henderson. 1983. Lay theories of delinquency. *European Journal of Social Psychology* 13:107-120.

Furnham, A. 1988. *Lay Theories: Everyday Understanding of Problems in the Social Sciences*. New York: Pergaman Press.

Furman v. Georgia 408 U.S. 238 1972.

Furstenberg, F. F. & C. F. Wellford. 1973. "Calling the Police: The Evaluation of Police Service." *Law & Society Review* 7:393-406.

Fyfe, J. J. 1988. "Police Use of Deadly Force: Research and Reform." *Justice Quarterly* 5: 165-205.

Gabor, T. 1994. *Everybody Does it! Crime by the Public*. Toronto: University of Toronto Press.

Gabor, T. & A. Ratner. 1990. *Criminal Stereotypes Revisited: A Review of the Literature*. Ottawa: Department of Criminology, University of Ottawa.

Galaway, B. 1984. "Survey of Public Acceptance of Restitution as an Alternative to Imprisonment for Property Offenders." *Australian and New Zealand Journal of Criminology* 17:108-117.

Galaway, B. & J. Hudson. 1990. *Criminal Justice, Restitution and Reconciliation*. Monsey, N.Y.: Criminal Justice Press.

Gallup. 1989. *The Gallup Report. Number 285*. Princeton, N.J.: The Gallup Poll.

Gallup, A., & F. Newport. 1991. "Death Penalty Support Remains Strong." *The Gallup Poll Monthly*, 40-45.

Gallup Poll Monthly 1991. "Americans Say Police Brutality Frequent," 53-56.

Gallup Poll Monthly. 1993. "Americans Discouraged by Government's Ineffective War on Crime." 28-32.

Gallup Poll Monthly. 1995. "Black Americans See Little Justice For Themselves," 32-35.

Gallup Canada. 1969-1990. *The Gallup Report*. Toronto: Gallup of Canada Ltd.

Gamson, W. A., & J. McEvoy. 1972. "Police Violence and its Public Support." In J.F. Short & M.E. Wolfgang (eds.), *Collective Violence*, 329-342. Chicago: Aldine.

Garofalo, J. 1977. *Public Opinion About Crime: The Attitudes of Victims and Nonvictims in Selected Cities*. Albany, New York: Criminal Justice Research Center.

Garofalo, J. 1981. "Crime and the Mass Media: A Selective Review of Research." *Journal of Research in Crime and Deliquency* 18(2):319-350.

Garrett, K. A. & P. H. Rossi. 1978. "Judging the Seriousness of Child Abuse." *Medical Anthropology* 1:1-47.

Gartner, R. & A. Doob. 1994. "Trends in Criminal Victimization: 1988-1993". *Juristat Service Bulletin* 14(13).

Gebotys, R. J., & J. V. Roberts. 1987. "Public Views of Sentencing: The Role of Offender Characteristics." *Canadian Journal of Behavior Science* 19:479-488.

Gebotys, R. G., J. V. Roberts & B. DasGupta. 1988. "News Media Use and Public Perceptions of Crime Seriousness." *Canadian Journal of Criminology* 30:3-16.

Gebotys, R. J., & B. Dasgupta. 1987. "Attribution of Responsibility and Crime Seriousness. *The Journal of Psychology* 121(6):607-613.

Giacopassi, D.J., & R. T. Dull. 1986. "Gender and Racial Differences in the Acceptance of Rape Myths Within a College Population." *Sex Roles* 17(1-2): 93-101.

Gibbons, D. C. 1963. "Who Knows What About Correction?" *Crime and Delinquency* 9: 137-144.

————. 1969. "Crime And Punishment: A Study In Social Attitudes." *Social Forces* 47: 391-397.

Gibbons, D., J. Jones & P. Garabedian. 1972. "Gauging Public Opinion about the Crime Problem." *Crime and Delinquency* 18:134-146.

Gibson, J. L. 1980. "Environmental Constraints on the Behavior of Judges: A Representational Model of Judicial Decision-Making." *Law & Society Review* 14(2):343-370.

Gibson, J. L. 1989. "Understanding of Justice: Institutional Legitimacy, Procedural Justice, and Political Tolerance.' *Law & Society Review* 23.

Gibson, J. L., & G. A. Caldeira. 1992. "Blacks and the United States Supreme Court: Models of Diffuse Support." *The Journal of Politics* 54(4):1121-1143.

Gibson, J. L. 1991. "Institutional Legitimacy, Procedural Justice, and Compliance with the Supreme Court Decisions: A Question of Causality." *Law & Society Review*, 25(3): 631-635.

Gilbert, D. T., P. W. Perlham & D. W. Krull. 1988. "On Cognitive Business: When Person Perceivers Meet Persons Perceived." *Journal of Personality and Social Psychology* 54(5):733-740.

Glauser, M. J., & W. L. Tullar. 1985. "Communicator Style of Police Officers and Citizen Satisfaction with Officer/Citizen Telephone Conversations." *Journal of Police Science and Administration* 13(1):70-77.

Glauser, M.J. & W. L. Tullar. 1985. "Citizen Satisfaction with Police Officer/Citizen Interaction: Implications for the Changing Role of Police Organizations." *Journal of Applied Psychology* 70(3):514-527.

Glick, H. R., & G. W., Jr. Pruet. 1985. "Crime, Public Opinion and Trial Courts: An Analysis of Sentencing Policy." *Justice Quarterly* 2:319-343.

Globe and Mail. 1995. "Life for Theft of Pizza." October 28, p.1.

Gordon, M. & L. Heath. 1981. "The News Business: Crime and Fear." In *Reactions to Crime*, D.A. Lewis (ed). Beverly Hills: Sage.

Goldin, S.E. 1979. *Facial Stereotypes as Cognitive Categories.* Unpublished Doctoral Dissertation. Carnegie-Mellon University, Pittsburg, PA.

Goldstein, A. G., J. Chance. & B. J. Gilbert. 1984. "Facial Stereotypes of Good Guys and Gad Guys: A Replication and Extension." *Bulletin of the Psychonomic Society*, 22:549-552.

Gordon, M. & L. Heath. 1981. "The News Business: Crime and Fear." In: *Reactions to Crime*, D.A. Lewis (ed.), Beverly Hills, California: Sage.

Gottfredson, S. D., B. D. Warner & R. B. Taylor. 1988. "Conflict and Consensus About Criminal Justice in Maryland." In: N. Walker & M. Hough (eds.), *Public Attitudes to Sentencing: Survey From Five Countries*, 178-202. Brookfield, Vt: Gower.

Gottfredson, S. D., K. L. Young & W. L. Laufer. 1980. "Additivity and Interactions in Offense Seriousness Scales." *Journal of Research in Crime and Delinquency* 16: 26-41.

Gottfredson, S., & R. B. Taylor. 1984. "Public Policy and Prison Populations: Measuring Opinions About Reform." *Judicature* 68:190-201.

Governor's Office of Criminal Justice Services. 1984. *Ohio Citizen Attitudes Concerning Crime and Criminal Justice*. Columbus, Ohio: Governor's Office of Criminal Justice Services.

Graber, D. 1980. "Media and Public Images of Criminals and Victims." In *Crime News and the Public*, Praeger Publishers.

Grabosky, P.N., J. B. Braithwaite & P. R. Wilson. 1987. "The Myth of Community Tolerance Toward White-Collar Crime." *Australian and New Zealand Journal of Criminology* 20:33-44.

Grant, L. 1990. *The Independent on Sunday*, 23.

Greene, E., A. Raitz & H. Linbblad. 1989. "Juror's Knowledge of Battered Women. *Journal of Family Violence* 4:105-125.

Greene, E., & M. Dodge. 1995. "The Influence of Prior Record Evidence on Juror Decision-Making." *Law and Human Behavior* 19(1):67-78.

Gregg v. Georgia, 428 U.S. 153 1976.

Grindstaff, C. F. 1974. "Public Attitudes and Court Dispositions: A Comparative Analysis." *Sociology and Social Research* 58:417-426.

Haberman, P.W., & J. Sheinberg. 1969. "Public Attitudes Toward Alcoholism as an Illness." *American Journal of Public Health* 59:1209-16.

Hadar, I. & J. R. Snortum. 1975. "The Eye of the Beholder: Differential Perceptions of Police by the Police and the Public." *Criminal Justice and Behavior* 2(1):37-54.

Hagan, J. & C. Albonetti. 1982. "Race, Class and the Perception of Criminal Injustice in America." *American Journal of Sociology* 88:329-55.

Hahn, H. 1971. "Ghetto Assessments of Police Protection and Authority." *Law and Society Review* 6:183-194.

Hamilton, V. L., & S. Rytine. 1980. "Social Consensus on Norms of Justice: Should the Punishment Fit the Crime?" *American Journal of Sociology* 85:1117-44.

Hamilton, D. L. & D. M. Mackie. 1990. "Specificity and Generality in the Nature and Use of Stereotypes." In Thomas K. Srull & R. S.Wyer, Jr., (eds.), *Advances in Social Cognition* 3:99-110. Hillsdale, New Jersey: Lawrence Erlbaum Associates, Publishers.

Hanberg, R., & W. S. Maddox. 1982. "Public Support for the Supreme Court in the 1970's." *American Politics Quarterly* 10(3):333-346.

Hans, V. P. & A. N. Doob. 1976 "Section 12 of the Canada Evidence Act and the Deliberations of Simulated Juries." *Criminal Law Quarterly* 18:235-253.

Hans, V. P. & D. Slater. 1983. "John Hinckley Jr. and the Insanity Defense: The Public's Verdict." *Public Opinion Quarterly* 47:202-212.

Hans, V. P., & N. Vidmar. 1986. *Judging the Jury.* New York: Plenum Press.

Hans, V. P. 1986. "An analysis of Public Attitudes Toward the Insanity Defense." *Criminology* 4(2):393-415.

Hann, B. & B. Harman. 1986. *Full Parole Release: An Historical Descriptive Analysis.* Ottawa: Solicitor General Canada.

Hansel, M. 1987. "Citizen Crime Stereotypes -- Normative Consensus Revisted." *Criminology* 25(3):455-485.

Harris, L. & associates. 1968. *The Public Looks at Crime and Corrections.* Washington, DC: Joint Commission on Correctional Manpower and Training.

Hawkins, S. A. & R. Hastie. 1990. "Hindsight: Biased Judgments of Past Events After the Outcomes are Known." *Psychological Bulletin* 107:311-327.

Herrman, M. S. & D. C. Bordner. 1983. "Attitudes Toward Pornography in a Southern Community." *Criminology: An Interdispciplinary Journal* 21(3):349-374.

Hewer, P. & A. Birkenmayer. 1994. "Conditional Release Decision-Making in Canada, 1992-1993." *Juristat Service Bulletin* 14(2).

Higginbottom, S. F. & E. Zamble. 1988. "Categorizations of Homicide Cases: Agreement, Accuracy and Confidence of Public Assignments." *Canadian Journal of Criminology* 30:351-366.

Higgins, E. T., & G. King. 1981. "Accessibility of Social Constructs: Information Processing Consequences of Individual and Contextual Variability." In N. Cantor & J. Kihlstron. (eds.,. *Personality, Cognition, and Social Interaction,* 69-121. Hillsdale, NJ: Erlbaum.

Hilton, N. Z. 1993. "Police Intervention and Public Opinion." In N. Z. Hilton (ed.), *Legal Responses to Wife Assault.* Newbury, CA: Sage.

Hilton, N.Z. 1989. "When is an Assault Not an Assault? The Canadian Public's Attitudes Toward Wife and Stranger Assault." *Journal of Family Violence* 4(4):323-337.

Himelein, M. J., M. T. Nietzel & R. C. Dillehay. 1991. "Effects of Prior Juror Experience on Jury Sentencing." *Behavioral Sciences and the Law* 9:97-106.

Himmelfarb, A. 1990. "Public Opinion and Public Policy". *Forum on Corrections Research* 2:20-22.

Hindelang, M. J. 1974. "Public Opinion Regarding Crime, Criminal Justice, and Related Topics." *Journal of Research in Crime and Delinquency* 11:101-116.

Himmelfarb, A. 1990. "Public Opinion and Public Policy." *Forum on Corrections Research* 2:20-22.

Hirschi, T. 1969. *Causes of Delinquency.* Berkeley: University of California Press.

Hochstedler, E., & C. M. Dunning. 1983. "Communication and Motivation in a Police Department." *Criminal Justice and Behavior* 10(1):47-69.

Hoffman, P. B., & P. L. Hardyman. 1986. "Crime Seriousness Scales: Public Perceptions and Feedback to Criminal Justice Policymakers." *Journal of Criminal Justice* 14:13-31.

Hogarth, J. 1971. *Sentencing as a Human Process.* Toronto: University of Toronto Press.

Hoinville, G. & R. Bowell. 1978. *Survey Research Practice*. London: Heinemann.

Horton, A.L., K. M. Simonidis, L. L. Simonidis. 1987. "Legal Remedies for Spousal Abuse: Victim Characteristics, Expectations, and Satisfaction." *Journal of Family Violence* 2(3):265-279.

Hollin, Clive R. & K. Howells 1987. "Lay Explanations of Delinquency: Global or Offence-Specific?" *British Journal of Social Psychology* 26:203-10.

Homant, R.J., D. B. Kennedy & R. M. Fleming. 1984. "The Effect of Victimization and the Police Response on Citizens' Attitudes Toward Police." *Journal of Police Science and Adminstration* 12(3):323-332.

Homant, R. J., & D. B. Kennedy 1994. "Citizen Preferences and Perceptions Concerning Police Pursuit Policies." *Journal of Criminal Justice* 22(5):425-435.

Horowitz, I. A. & T. E. Willging. 1991. "Changing Views of Jury Power: the Nullification Debate, 1787-1988. *Law and Human Behavior* 15(2):165-182.

Horowitz, I. A. 1988. Jury nullification: "The Impact of Judicial Instructions, Arguments, and Challenges on Jury Decision-Making." *Law and Human Behavior* 12(4):439-453.

Hough, M. & P. Mayhew. 1985. *Taking Account of Crime: Key Findings from the Second British Crime Survey. Home Office Research Study No. 85*. London: Her Majesty's Stationary Office.

Hough, M. & D. Moxon. 1985. "Dealing with Offenders: Popular Opinion and the Views of Victims." *The Howard Journal* 24:160-175.

Houston, D. A., & R. H. Fazio. 1989. "Biased Processing as a Function of Attitude Accessibility: Making Objective Judgments Subjectively." *Social Cognition*, 7(1):51-66.

Howe, E. 1988. "Dimensional Structure of Judgments of Crimes." *Journal of Applied Social Psychology*, 16:1371-1393.

Howells, K., M. McEwan, B. Jones & C. Mathews. 1983. "Social Evaluation of Mental Illness" (Schizophrenia) in Relation to Criminal Behaviour." *British Journal of Social Psychology*, 22:165-166.

Hruska, H. & T. Eisenberg. 1991. *The Young Offenders Act - An Environmental Analysis*. Ottawa: Department of Justice, Communications and Public Affairs.

Hsu, M. 1973. "Cultural and Sexual Differences on the Judgment of Criminal Offenses: A replication Study of the Measurement of Delinquency." *The Journal of Criminal Law and Criminology*, 64:348-353.

Hugick, L. & G. Hueber. 1991. "Two-Thirds Oppose Supreme Court's Latest Abortion Ruling." *The Gallup Poll Monthly*: 36-39.

Huo, Y. J., H. J. Smith, T. R Tyler, T. R., & E. A. Lind. 1995. *Superordinate identification, subgroup identification, and justice concerns: Is separatism the problem; is assimilation the answer?* American Bar Foundation Working Paper Series #9410.

Immarigeon, R. 1986. "Surveys Reveal Broad Support For Alternative Sentencing." *Journal of the National Prison Project*, 9:1-4.

Indermaur, D. 1987. "Public Perception of Sentencing in Perth, Western Australia." *Australian and New Zealand Journal of Criminology* 20:163-183.

Indermaur, D. 1990. *Perceptions of Crime Seriousness and Sentencing: A Comparison of Court Practice and the Perceptions of a Sample of the Public and Judges*. Canberra: Criminology Research Council of Australia.

————. 1990. *Perceptions of Crime Seriousness and Sentencing: A Comparison of Court Practice and the Perceptions of a Sample of the Public and Judges.* Criminology Research Council of Australia.

Insight Canada. 1994. *Perspectives Canada.* Toronto: Insight Canada Research.

Jacob, H. (1971). "Black and White Perceptions of Justice in the City." *Law & Society Review* 6:69-78.

Jacobs, N. R., C. D. Foster & M. A. Seigel. 1995. *Gun Control Restricting Rights or Protecting People. The Information Series on Current Topics.* Wylie, Tx: Information Plus.

Jacoby, J. E. & C. S. Dunn. 1987. *National Survey on Punishment for Criminal Offenses.* Paper presented at the National Conference on Punishment for Criminal Offenses, Ann Arbor, Michigan. November.

Jaffe, P.G., E. Hastings, D. Reitzel & G. W. Austin. 1993. "The Impact of Police Laying Charges." In Z. Hilton (ed.), *Responses to Wife Assault: Current Trends and Evaluations.* Newbury Park: Sage Publications.

Jamieson, K. & T. Flanagan (eds.), 1987. *Sourcebook of Criminal Justice Statistics - 1986.* Washington, D.C.: U.S. Department of Justice, Bureau of Justice Statistics.

————. 1989. *Sourcebook of Criminal Justice Statistics - 1988.* Washington, D.C.: U.S. Department of Justice, Bureau of Justice Statistics.

Janoff-Bulman, R., C. Timko & L. L. Carli. 1985. "Cognitive Biases in Blaming the Victim." *Journal of Experimental Social Psychology* 21:161-77.

Jefferson, T. 1988. "Race, Crime and Policing: Empirical, Theoretical and Methodological Issues." *International Journal of the Sociology of Law* 16(1):521-539.

Jefferson County Survey. 1982. Louisville, KY: University of Louisville, Urban Studies Center.

Jenkins, M.J., & F. H. Dambrot. 1987. "The Attribution of Date Rape: Observer's Attitudes and Sexual Experiences and the Dating Situation. *Journal of Applied Social Psychology* 17:875-895.

Jenkins, P. & B. Davidson. 1990. "Battered Women in the Criminal Justice System: An Analysis of Gender Stereotypes." *Behavioral Science and the Law* 8:161-170.

Johnson, J., & L.A. Jackson. 1988. "Assessing the Effects of Factors that Might Underlie the Differential Perception of Acquaintance Versus Stranger Rape." *Sex Roles* 19:37-45.

Johnson, J. T. 1986. "The Knowledge of What Might Have Been: Affective and Attributional Consequences of Near Outcomes." *Personality and Social Psychology Bulletin* 12:51-62.

Joint Commission on Correctional Manpower and Training. 1967. *The Public Looks at Crime and Corrections.* Washington D.C.: Joint Commission on Correctional Manpower and Training. (Publication available from American Correctional Association, College Park: MD.)

Jonas, A. & E. A. Whitfield. 1986. "Postal Survey of Public Satisfaction with Police Officers in New Zealand." *Police Studies* 9(4):211-221.

Jones, S. & M. Levi. 1987. "Law and Order and the Causes of Crime: Some police and Public Perspectives." Howard *Journal of Criminal Justice* 26:1-14.

Junvenile Justice Reform: A Model for the States. 1987. Ann Arbor, MI: Rose Institute and American Legislative Exchange Council.

Judd, C. M., R. A. Drake, J. W. Downing & J. A. Krusnick. 1991. "Some Dynamic Properties of Attitude Structure: Context-induced Response Facilitation and Polarization." *Journal of Personality and Social Psychology* 43(2):193-202.

Kagehiro, D. K., R. B. Taylor, W. S. Laufer & A. T. Harland. 1991. "Hindsight Bias and Third-Party Consentors to Warrantless Police Searches." *Law and Human Behavior* 15(3):305-314.

Kagehiro, D. K. 1988. "Perceived Voluntariness of Consent to Warrantless Police Searches." *Journal of Applied Social Psychology* 18:38-49.

Kagehiro, D., R. Taylor & A. Harland. 1991. "Reasonable Expectations of Privacy and Third-Party Consent Searches". *Law and Human Behavior* 15:121-138.

Kagehiro, D. K. & R. B. Taylor. 1988. "Third-Party Consent Searches: Legal vs. Social Perceptions of "Common Authority." *Journal of Applied Social Psychology* 18:1274-1287.

Kagehiro, D.K. 1990. "Psycholegal Research on the Fourth Amendment." *Psychological Science* 1(3):187-193.

Kagehiro, D. K., & W. S. Laufer. 1990. "The Assumption of Risk Doctrine and Third-Party Consent Searches. *Criminal Law Bulletin* 26:195-209.

Kagehiro, D. K., R. B. Taylor, W. S. Laufer & A. T. Harland. 1991. "Hindsight Bias and Third-Party Consentors to Warrantless Police Searches." *Law and Human Behavior* 15(3):305-314.

Kahneman, D. & D. T. Miller. 1986. "Norm Theory: Comparing Reality to its Alternatives." *Psychological Review* 93(2):136-153.

Kahneman, D., & A. Tversky. 1982. "The Simulation Heuristic." In D. Kahneman, P. Slovic, & A. Tversky (eds.), *Judgment Under Uncertainty: Heurisitics and Biases*. 201-208, Cambridge University Press: New York.

Kahneman, D., P. Slovic & A.Tversky. 1982. *Judgment Under Uncertainty: Heuristics and Biases* (eds.), Cambridge University Press: New York.

Kalven, H. & H. Zeisel. *The American Jury*. Boston: Little, Brown Company.

Kaplan v. California 413 U.S. 115 1973.

Kappeler, V., M. Blumberg & G. Potter. 1993. *The Mythology of Crime and Criminal Justice*. Prospect Heights, Ill.: Waveland Press.

Kassin, S. M. 1995." The American Jury Handicapped in the Pursuit of Justice." In G. L. Mays & P. R. Gregware (eds.), *Courts and Justice: A Reader*. Prospect Heights, IL: Waveland Press, Inc.

Kassin, W. & Saunders. 1990. "Dirty Tricks of Cross-Examination: The Influence of Conjectural Evidence on the Jury." *Law and Human Behavior* 14:373-

Kassin, S. M. & L. S. Wrightsman. 1988. *The American Jury on Trial: Psychological Perspectives*. New York: Basic Books.

Katz v. United States, 389 U.S. 347 1967. (Harlan, J., concurring)

Kauder, N. B., 1993. "One-Gun-a-Month: Measuring Public Opinion Concerning a Gun Control Initiative." *Behavioral Sciences and the Law* 11:353-360.

Keil, T. J., & G. F. Vito. 1991. "Fear of Crime, and Attitudes Toward Capital Punishment: A Structural Equations Model." *Justice Quarterly* 8(4):447-464.

Kelley, J., & J. Braithwaite. 1990. "Public Opinion and the Death Penalty in Australia." *Justice Quarterly* 7(3):529-563.

Kerber, K. W., S. M. Andes & M. B. Mittler. 1977. "Citizens Attitudes Regarding the Competence of Female Police Officers." *Journal of Police Science and Administration* 5(3):337-347.

Kerr, N. L. 1981. "Effects of Prior Juror Experience on Juror Behavior." *Basic and Applied Social Psychology* 2:175-193.

Kidder, L., & E. Cohn. 1979. "Public Views of Crime and Crime Prevention." In I. Frieze, D. Baral & J. Carroll (eds.), *New Approaches to Social Problems*. San Francisco: Jossey-Bass.

Kleck, G. 1996. "Crime, Culture Conflict and the Sources of Support for Gun Control: A multilevel Application of the General Social Surveys." *American Behavioral Scientist* 39(4):387-404.

Klecka, W. R., & A. J. Tuchfarber. 1978. "Random Digit Dialing: A Comparison of Personal Surveys." *Public Opinion Quarterly* 105-114.

Klein, R. J., I. Newman, D. M. Weis & R. F. Bobner. 1983. "The Continuum of Criminal Offenses Instrument: Further Development and Modification of Sellin and Wolfgang's Original Criminal Index" *Journal of Offender Counseling Services and Rehabilitation* 7:33-53.

Knight, D. W. 1965. "Punishment Selection as a Function of Biographical Information." *Journal of Criminal Law, Criminology and Police Science* 56:325-327.

Knowles, J. 1979. *Ohio Citizen Attitudes. A Survey of Public Opinion on Crime and Criminal Justice*. Columbus, Ohio: Office of Criminal Justice Services.

————. 1980. *Ohio Citizen Attitudes Concerning Criminal Justice*. 2nd ed. Columbus, Ohio: Department of Economic and Community Development.

————. 1982. *Ohio Citizen Attitudes Concerning Crime and Criminal Justice*. 3rd ed.Columbus, Ohio: Governor's Office of Criminal Justice Services.

————. 1984. *Ohio Citizen Attitudes Concerning Crime and Criminal Justice*. 4th ed. Columbus, Ohio: Governor's Office of Criminal Justice Services.

————. 1987. *Ohio Citizen Attitudes Concerning Crime and Criminal Justice*. 5th ed. Columbus, Ohio: Governor's Office of Criminal Justice Services.

Koenig, D. J. 1980. "The Effects of Criminal Victimization and Judicial or Police Contact on Public Attitudes Toward Local Police." *Journal of Criminal Justice* 8:243-249.

Krahe, B. 1988. "Victim and Observer Characteristics as Determinants of Responsibility Attributions to Victims of Rape." *Journal of Applied Social Psychology* 18:50-58.

Kramer, G. P., N. L. Kerr & J. S. Carroll. 1990. "Pretrial Publicity, Judicial Remedies, and Jury Bias.". *Law and Human Behavior* 14:409-438.

Kritzer, H. M. 1979. "Federal Judges and Their Political Environments: The Influence of Public Opinion." *American Journal of Political Science* 23:194-234.

Krosnick, J. A. 1988. "The Role of Attitude Importance in Social Evaluation: A Study of Policy Preferences, Presidential Candidate Evaluations, and Voting Behavior. *Journal of Personality and Social Psychology* 55(2):196-210.

Krosnick, J. A., & J. Schuman. 1988. "Attitude Intensity, Importance, and Certainty and Susceptibility to Response Effects." *Journal of Personality and Social Psychology* 54: 940-952.

Krueger, R. 1988. *Focus Groups: A Practical Guide for Applied Research*. Beverly Hills: Sage.

Krulewitz, J. E., & E. J. Payne. 1978. "Attributions About Rape: Effects of Rapist Force, Observer Sex and Sex Role Attitudes. *Journal of Applied Social Psychology* 8: 291-305.

Krulewitz, J. E., & J. E. Nash. 1979. Effects of Rape Victim Resistance, Assault Outcome, and Sex of Observer on Attributions About Rape. *Journal of Personality and Social Psychology* 47:557-574.

Lacayo, R. May, 1992. "Anatomy of an Acquittal." *Time.* 30-32.

Lafree, G. D., B. F. Reskin, & C. A. Visher. 1985. "Jurors' Responses to Victims' Behavior and Legal Issues in Sexual Assault Trials." *Social Problems* 32:389-407.

Langbein, J. H. 1995. "On the Myth of the Written Constitution: The Disappearance of Criminal Jury Trial." In G. L. Mays & P. R. Gregware (eds.), *Courts and Justice: A Reader.* Prospect Heights, IL: Waveland Press.

LaPierre, R. T. 1934. "Attitudes vs. Actions." *Social Forces* 13:230-237.

Leblanc, M. & M. Frechette. 1989. *Male Criminal Activity from Childhood Through Youth: Multilevel and Developmental Perspectives.* New York: Springer-Verlag.

Leesti, T. 1992. "Sentencing in Youth Courts, 1986-1991." *Juristat Service Bulletin,* 12(4).

Lefley, H.P, C.S. Scott, M. Liabre & Dorothy Hicks. 1993. "Cultural Beliefs About Rape and Victims' Response in Three Ethnic Groups." *American Journal of Orthopsychiatry* 63(4):623-632.

Lester, D. 1983. *Gun Control: Issues and Answers.* Springfield, IL: Charles C. Thomas, Publisher.

Levi, M. & S. Jones. 1985. "Public and Police Perceptions of Crime Seriousness in England and Wales." *British Journal of Criminology* 25(3):234-250.

Levin, C.J. 1966. "Toward a More Enlightened Sentencing Procedure." *Nebraska Law Review* 45:499-525.

Lewis, D. & G. Salem. 1986. *Fear of Crime: Incivility and the Production of a Social Problem.* New Brunswick, N.J.: Transaction Books.

Liberman, A., & S. Chaiken. 1991. "Value Conflict and Thought-Induced Attitude Change." *Journal of Experimental Social Psychology* 27:203-216.

Lind, E. A., J. Thibaut & L. Walker. 1973. "Discovery and Presentation of Evidence in Adversary and Nonadversary Proceedings." *Michigan Law Review* 71:1129-1144.

Lind, E. A., & T. R. Tyler. 1988. *The Social Psychology of Procedural Justice.* New York: Plenum Press.

Lind, E. A., J. Y. Huo & T. R. Tyler. 1994. "And Justice For All: Ethnicity, Gender, and Preferences For Dispute Resolution Procedures." *Law and Human Behavior* 18(3): 269-290.

Lind, E. A. 1994. "Procedural Justice and Culture: Evidence for the Ubigiotious Process Concerns." *Zeitschift fur Rechtssoziologie* 15:24-36.

Lind, E. A., R. J. MacCoun, P. E. Ebener, W.L.F. Felstiner, D. R. Hensler, J. Resnik & T. R. Tyler. 1990. In the Eye of the Beholder: Tort Litigants' Evaluations of Their Experiences in the Civil Justice System." *Law & Society Review* 24:953-996.

Lind, E. A., J. Thibaut & L. Walker. 1973. "Discovery and Presentation of Evidence in Adversary and Nonadversary Proceedings." *Michigan Law Review* 71:1129-1144.

Linden & M. LeBlanc (eds.), *Juvenile Justice in Canada. A Theoretical and Analytical Assessment.* Toronto: Butterworths.

Linsky, A. S. 1970. "The Changing Public Views of Alcoholism." *Quarterly Journal of Studies on Alcohol* 31:692-704.

Linville, P.W., G. W. Fischer & P. Salovey. 1989. "Perceived Distributions of the Characteristics of In-Group and Out-Group Members: Empirical Evidence and a Computer Simulation." *Journal of Personality and Social Psychology* 46(6):1254-1266.

Linz, D., E. Donnerstein, K.C. Land & P.L. McCall. 1991. "Estimating Community Standards: The Use of Social Science Evidence in an Obscenity Prosecution." *Public Opinion Quarterly* 55(1):80-112.

Linz, D., E. Donnerstein, B. J. Shafer, K. C. Land, P. L. McCall, A. C. Graesser. 1995. "Discrepancies Between the Legal Code and Community Standards for Sex and Violence: an Empirical Challenge to Traditional Assumptions in Obscenity Law." *Law & Society Review* 29(1):127-168.

Lippman, P. J. 1922. *Public Opinion.* New York: Harcourt, Brace.

Liss, M. B., N. J. Finkel & V. R. Moran. 1994. "Equal Justice for Accessories? Young Pearls of Proportionate Wisdom. Paper Presented at the American Psychology-Law Society's Mid Year Confrence," Santa Fe, NM.

Lord, C.G., L. Ross & M. R. Lepper. 1979. "Biased Assimilation and Attitude Polarization: The Effects of Prior Theories on Subsequently Considered Evidence." *Journal of Personality and Social Psychology* 37(11):2095-2109.

Lord, C. G., M. R. Lepper & E. Preston. 1984. "Considering the Opposite: A Corrective Strategy for Social Judgment." *Journal of Personality and Social Psychology* 47(6): 1231-1243.

Lord, C. G., D. M. Desforges, S. Fein, M. A. Pugh & Lepper, M. R. 1994. "Typicality Effects in Attitudes Toward Social Policies: A Concept Mapping Approach." *Journal of Personality and Social Psychology* 66(4):658-673.

Lord, C.G., M. R. Lepper & D. Mackie. 1984. "Attitude Prototypes as Determinants of Attitude-Behavior Consistency." *Journal of Personality and Social Psychology* 46: 1254-1266.

Lurigio, A. J., J. Carroll & L. J. Stalans. 1994. "Understanding Judges' Sentencing Decisions: Attribution of Responsibility and Story Construction." In L. Heath et al., (eds). *Application of Heuristics and Biases, Volume 3 of the Social Psychological Applications to Social Issues.* New York: Plenum Press.

Lurigio, A. J. & D. P. Rosenbaum. 1992. "The Travails of the Detroit Police-Victims Experiment: Assumptions and Important Lessons." *American Journal of Police* 11(3): 1-34.

MacCoun, R. J. & T. M. Tyler. 1988. "The Basis of Citizens' Perceptions of the Criminal Jury: Procedural Fairness, Accuracy, and Efficiency." *Law and Human Behavior* 12(3): 333-352.

Maclean's Magazine. 1995. *Crime. The Perception Gap.* January 2, 1995. 28-29.

Macrae, C. N., M. B. Milne & G. B. Bodenhausen. 1994. "Stereotypes as Energy-Saving Devices: A Peek Inside the Cognitive Toolbox." *Journal of Personality and Social Psychology* 66(1):37-47.

Maguire, M. 1984. "Meeting the Needs of Burglary Victims: Questions for the Police and the Criminal Justice System." In R. Clarke & T. Hope (eds.), *Coping with Burglary*, 219-232. England: Klumwer-Nigloff.

Maguire, K. & A. Pastore. 1995. *Sourcebook of Criminal Justice Statistics*. Washington, D.C.: U.S. Bureau of Justice Statistics.

Maguire, M., & T. Bennett. 1982. *Burglary in a Dwelling: The Offence, the Offender and the Victim*. London: Heinemann.

Maguire, K., & T. J. Flanagan. (eds.)., 1991. *Sourcebook of Criminal Justice Statistics 1990*. U. S. Department of Justice, Bureau of Justice Statistics. Washington, D.C.: USGPO.

Maguire, K., A. L. Pastore & T. J. Flanagan, (eds.), 1993. *Sourcebook of Criminal Justice Statistics -- 1992*, U. S. Department of Justice, Bureau of Justice Statistics. Washington, DC: USGPO.

Maguire, K., & A. L. Pastore. (eds.), 1994. *Sourcebook of Criminal Justice Statistics 1993*.

U.S. Department of Justice, Bureau of Justice Statistics, Washington, DC: USGPO.

Makela, K. 1966. "Public Sense of Justice and Judicial Practice." *Acta Sociologica* 10-11:42-67.

Mande, M. & P. Butler. 1982. *Crime in Colorado: A Survey of Citizens*. Colorado: Division of Criminal Justice.

Mande, M. & J. Crouch. 1984. *Crime in Colorado: 1984 Citizen Survey*. Colorado: Division of Public Safety, Division of Criminal Justice.

Mande, M. & K. English. 1989. *The Effect of Public Opinion on Correctional Policy: A Comparison of Opinions and Practice*. Colorado: Colorado Department of Public Safety, Division of Criminal Justice.

Mapp v. Ohio, 367 U.S. 643, 81 S.Ct. 1684, 6 L.Ed.2d. 1081 1961.

Margarita, M. & N. Parisi. 1979. *Public Opinion and Criminal Justice: Selected Issues and Trends*. Albany, N.Y.: Criminal Justice Research Centre.

Markwart, A. 1992. "Custodial Sanctions Under the Young Offenders Act". In: R. Corrado, N. Bala, R.

Marsh, J., A. Geist & N. Caplan. 1982 *Rape and the Limits of Law Reform*. Boston: Auburn House.

Mastrofski, S. 1981. "Surveying Clients to Assess Police Performance." *Evaluation Review* 5:397-408.

Mathews, T., M. Meyer, D. Foote, A. Mur, L. Wright, J. Hammer, M. Mabry, H. Manly, K. Springen & R. Crandall. 1992. "The Siege of L.A." *Newsweek*. May, 30-38.

Mauser, G. A. 1990. "A Comparison of Canadian and American Attitudes Toward Firearms." *Canadian Journal of Criminology* 32:573-589.

Mauser, G. A., & D. B. Kopel. 1992. "Sorry, Wrong Number": Why Media Polls on Gun Control are Often Unreliable." *Political Communication* 9:69-92.

Maxfield, M. G. 1988. "The London Metropolitan Police and Their Clients: Victim and Suspects Attitudes." *Journal of Crime and Delinquency* 25(2):188-206.

McFatter, R. M. 1978. "Sentencing Strategies and Justice: Effects of Punishment Philosophy on Sentencing Decisions." *Journal of Personality and Social Psychology* 36:1490-1500.

McGarrell, E. & T. Flanagan (eds.), 1985. *Sourcebook of Criminal Justice Statistics - 1984.* Washington: U.S. Department of Justice, Bureau of Justice Statistics.

Merton, R. 1987. "The Focussed Interview and Focus Groups: Continuities and Discontinuities." *Public Opinion Quarterly* 46:97-109.

Michigan Law Review. 1973. "Legal Knowledge of Michigan Citizens." *Michigan Law Review* 71:1463-1486.

Miethe, T. D. 1982. "Public Consensus on Crime Seriousness." *Criminology* 20:515-526.

Mihorean, S. & S. Lipinski. 1992. "International Incarceration Patterns," 1980-1990. *Juristat Service Bulletin* 12(3).

Miller, J.L., P. H. Rossi & J. E. Simpson. 1986. "Perceptions of Justice: Race and Gender Differences in Judgments of Appropriate Prison Sentences." *Law and Society Review* 20:313-334.

Moore, R. J. 1985. "Reflections of Canadians on the Law and the Legal System: Legal Research Institute Survey of Respondents in Montreal, Toronto and Winnipeg." In *Law in a Cynical Society? Opinion and Law in the 1980's,* D. Gibson & J. Baldwin. (ed.), Calgary: Carswell.

McAneny, L., & L. Saad. 1994. "On Eve of Jury Selection, Majority of Americans Still Think O. J. Probably Did It." *The Gallup Poll Monthly,* September, 7-10.

McAneny, L. April, 1993. "The Rodney King Case: Federal Trial's Split Verdicts Leave Black Americans Disheartened." *The Gallup Poll Monthly,* 27-29.

McAneny, L. February, 1993. The Rodney King Case: White and Black Biases -- Some Shared, Some Not -- Highlight Difficulties in Choosing Federal Jury." *The Gallup Poll Monthly,* 31-36.

McAneny, L. & L. Saad. 1993. "Strong Ties Between Religious Commitment and Abortion Views." *The Gallup Poll Monthly,* 35-42.

McCaghy, C. H., & S. A. Cernkovich. 1991. "Research Note: Polling the Public on Prostitution." *Justice Quarterly* 8(1):107-120.

McClosky, H., & A. Brill. 1983. *Dimensions of Tolerance What Americans Believe About Civil Liberties.* New York: Russell Sage Foundation.

McEwen, C. A., & R. J. Maiman. 1984. "Mediation in Small Claims Court: Achieving Compliance Through Consent." *Law & Society Review* 18:11-49.

McGarrell, E. F., & M. Sandys. 1996. "The Misperception of Public Opinion Toward Capital Punishment: Examining the Spuriousness Explanation of Death Penalty Support." *American Behavioral Scientist* 39(4):500-513.

Melton, G. B. 1983. "Minors and Privacy: Are Legal and Psychological Concepts Compatible?" *Nebraska Law Review* 62:455-493.

Memoirs v. Massachusetts, 383 U.S. 413 1966.

Midgley, J. 1974. "Public Opinion and the Death Penalty in South Africa." *British Journal of Criminology* 14(4):345-358.

Miethe, T. D. 1982. "Public Consensus on Crime Seriousness." *Criminology* 20:515-526.

Miethe, T. D. 1984. "Types of Consensus in Public Evaluations of Crime: An Illustration of Strategies for Measuring Consensus." *The Journal of Criminal Law and Criminology* 25:459-473.

McCaul, K.D., L. G. Veltum, V. Boyechko & J. J. Crawford. 1990. "Understanding Attributions of Victim Blame for Rape: Sex, Violence, and Foreseeability." *Journal of Applied Social Psychology* 20:1-26.

Miller v. U.S., 413 U.S. 153 1973.

Miller, D. T. & C. McFarland. 1986. "Counterfactual Thinking and Victim Compensation: A Test of Norm Theory." *Personality and Social Psychological Bulletin* 12:513-519.

Miller, D. T., W. Turnball & C. McFarland. 1989. "When a Coincidence is Suspicious: The Role of Mental Simulation." *Journal of Personality and Social Psychology* 57(4): 581-589.

Miller, D. T., W. Turnball. & C. McFarland. 1990. "Counterfactual Thinking and Social Perception: Thinking About What Might Have Been." 305-331. In M. Zanna (ed.), *Advances in Experimental Social Psychology*, 23.

Miller, D. T. & W. Turnball. 1990. "The Counterfactual Fallacy: Confusing What Might Have Been With What Ought to Have Been." *Social Justice Research* 4(1):1-19.

Mirande, A. 1980. "Fear of Crime and Fear of the Police in a Chicano Community." *Sociology and Social Research* 64(4):528-541.

Moore, D. W. 1994. "Majority Advocate Death Penalty for Teenage Killers." *Gallup Poll Monthly*, 2-6.

Moore, D. W., & F. Newport. 1994. "Public Strongly Favors Stricter Gun Control Laws." *The Gallup Poll Monthly*, 18-24.

Moran, G., & B. L. Cutler. 1991. "The Prejudicial Impact of Pretrial Publicity." *Journal of Applied Social Psychology* 21:345-367.

Morris, N. & M. Tonry. 1990. *Between Prison and Probation.* New York: Oxford University Press.

Mugford, J., S. K. Mugford & P. W. Easteal. 1989. "Social Justice, Public Perceptions, and Spouse Assault in Australia." *Social Justice* 3(37):103-123.

Mulford, H. A., & D. E. Miller. 1964. "Measuring Public Acceptance of the Alcoholic as a Sick Person." *Quarterly Journal of Studies on Alcohol* 25:314-323.

Munn, J.R. & K. E. Renner. 1978. "Perceptions of Police Work by the Police and by the Public." *Criminal Justice and Behavior* 5(2):165-180.

Murret, E. J., 1982. "Hear ye! Hear ye! Hear ye! The Courts Will Now Listen to the Public." *Judges' Journal* 21(2):4-7.

Murty, K. S., J. B. Roebuck & J. D. Smith. 1990. "The Image of the Police in Black Atlanta Communities." *Journal of Police Science and Administration* 17(4):250-257.

Myers, L. B. 1996. "Bring the Offender to the Heel: Views of the Criminal Court." In T. J. Flanagan and D. R. Longmire (eds.), *Americans View Crime and Justice: A National Public Opinion Survey*, 46-63. Thousand Oaks, CA: Sage Publications.

National Center for State Courts. (1978). *The Public Image of Courts.* Williamsburg, Virginia: National Center for State Courts.

Nesdale, A. R. 1980. "The Law and Social Attitudes: Effects of Proposed Changes in Drug Legislation on Attitudes Toward Drug Use." *Canadian Journal of Criminology* 22:176-187.

Newhart S., L. & G. Hill. 1991. "Victimization and Fear of Crime." *Justice and Behavior* 18:217-239.

Nisbett, R. E. & L. Ross. 1980. *Human Inference: Strategies and Shortcomings of Social Judgment*. Englewood Cliffs, N.J.: Prentice Hall.

Nisbett, R. E. & T. D. Wilson. 1977. "Telling More Than We Can Know: Verbal Reports on Mental Processes." *Psychological Review* 84:231-259.

Newman, G. R., & C. Trilling. 1975. "Public Perceptions of Criminal Behavior." *Criminal Justice and Behavior* 2:217-236.

Newman, G. R. 1976. *Comparative Deviance: Perception and Law in Six Cultures*. New York: Elsevier.

Newsday Crime Survey. July, 1989. Princeton, NJ: The Gallup Organization.

Newsweek. May, 1992. "The Siege of L.A." 30-38.

New York City Race Relations Survey March 6-11, 1987. The New York Time Poll. 1-18.

New York Newsday Stock Market Survey. Oct., 1988. Princeton, NJ: The Gallup Organization.

Nouwens, T., L. Motiuk, R. Boe. 1993. "So You Want to Know the Recidivism Rate." *Forum on Corrections Research* 5:22-26.

O'Brien, J. T. 1978. Public Attitudes Toward Police." *Journal of Police Science and Administration* 6(3):303-310.

O'Connnor, M. E. 1978. "A Community's Opinion on Crime: Some Preliminary Findings." *Australian and New Zealand Journal of Sociology* 14:61-64.

O'Connor, M. E. 1984. "The Perception of Crime and Criminality: The Violent Criminal and Swindler as Social Types." *Deviant Behavior* 5:255-274.

Ocqueteau, F. & Perez-Diaz. 1990. "Public Opinion, Crime and Criminal Justice Policies in France." *Penal Issues: Research in Crime and Criminal Justice in France*. 1:7-10.

Ogloff, J.R. 1987. "The Juvenile Death Penalty: A Frustrated Society's Attempt for Control." *Behavioral Sciences and the Law* 5(4):447-455.

Ogrodnik, L. 1994. "Homicide in Canada, 1992". *Juristat Service Bulletin* 14(4).

Opinion Research Corporation. 1982. *Public Attitudes Toward Youth Crime*. Chicago: Author.

Ouimet, M. 1990. "Profil d'une recherche appliquee sur le sentencing." *Canadian Journal of Criminology* 32:471-477.

Ouimet, M. 1990. "Underpunishing Offenders: Towards a Theory of Legal Tolerance." *Working Papers in Social Behaviour*. Montreal: Department of Sociology, McGill University.

Orcutt, J. D., 1976. "Ideological Variations in the Structure of Deviant Types: A Multivariate Comparison of Alcoholism and Heroin Addiction." *Social Forces* 55:419-437.

Padawer-Singer, A. M., & A. H. Barton. 1975. "The Impact of Pretrial Publicity on Jurors' Verdicts." In R. J. Simon (ed.), *The Jury System in America: A Critical Overview*, 123-129. Newbury Park, CA: Sage.

Palys, T. & S. Divorski. 1986. "Explaining Sentence Disparity." *Canadian Journal of Criminology* 32:471-77.

Paris Adult Theatre v. Slaton, 413 U.S. 49 1973.

Parisi, N., M. Gottfredson, M. Hindelang & T. Flanagan. 1979. *Sourcebook of Criminal Justice Statistics - 1978*. Washington: U.S. Department of Justice, Bureau of Justice Statistics.

Park, B. & R. Hastie. 1987. "Perception of Variability in Category Development: Instance Versus Abstraction-Based Stereotypes." *Journal of Personality and Social Psychology* 43:621-635.

Parker, H. 1970. "Juvenile Court Actions and Public Response." In *Becoming Delinquent*, P. Garabedian and D. Gibbons (eds.), Chicago: Aldine.

Pasework, R., D. Seidenzahl & M. Pantle. 1981. "Opinions Concerning Criminality among Mental Patients." *Journal of Community Psychology* 9:367-70.

Parton, D., M. Hansel & J. Stratton. 1991. "Measuring Crime Seriousness: Lessons from the National Crime Survey of Crime Severity." *British Journal of Criminology* 31: 72-85.

Pasework, R. A., & D. Seidenzahl. 1979. "Opinions Concerning the Insanity Plea and Criminality Among Mental Patients." *Bulletin of the American Academy of Psychiatry and Law* 7(2):199-202.

Pattison, E. M., L. A. Bishop & A. S. Linsky. 1968. "Changes in Public Attitudes on Narcotic Addiction." *American Journal of Psychiatry* 125:56-63.

Peek, C. W., G. D. Lowe & J. P. Alston. 1981. "Race and Attitudes Toward Local Police: Another Look." *Journal of Black Studies* 11(3):361-374.

Pennington, N., & R. Hastie. 1986. "Evidence Evaluation in Complex Decision-Making. *Journal of Personality and Social Psychology* 51:242-258.

Pennington, N., & R. Hastie. 1988. Explanation-Based Decision-Making: Effects of Memory Structure on Judgment." *Journal of Experimental Psychology: Learning, Memory, and Cognition* 14:521-533.

Penry v. Lynaugh, 45 Crl 3188 (1989).

Pepitone, A., & M. DiNubile. 1976. "Contrast Effects in Judgments of Crime Severity and the Punishment of Criminal Violators." *Journal of Personality and Social Psychology* 33(4):448-459.

Percy, S. L., 1980. "Response Time and Citizen Evaluation of Police." *Journal of Police Science and Administration* 8:75-86.

Peterson-Badali, M. & R. Abramovitch. 1992. "Children's Knowledge of the Legal System: Are they Competent to Instruct Counsel?" *Canadian Journal of Criminology* 34:139-160.

Podgorecki, A., W. Kaupen, J. Van Houtte, P. Vink & B. Kutchinsky. 1973. *Knowledge and Opinion about Law*. London: Robertson.

Poister, T.H. & J. C. McDavid. 1978. "Victims' Evaluations of Police Performance." *Journal of Criminal Justice* 6(2):133-149.

Primeau, C. C., J. A. Helton, J. C. Baxter & R. M. Rozelle. 1975. "An Examination of the Conception of the Police Officer Held by Several Social Groups." *Journal of Police Science and Administration* 3(2):189-196.

Pyszczynski & Wrightsman. 1981. "The Effects of Opening Statements on Mock Jurors' Verdicts in a Simulated Criminal Trial." *Journal of Applied Social Psychology*, 11:301.

Pyszczynski, Greenberg, Mack, & L. Wrightsman. 1981. "Opening Statements in a Jury Trial: The Effect of Promising More Than the Evidence Can Show." *Journal of Applied Social Psychology* 11:434-440.

Quinn, R., G. Barbara & J. Walsh. 1980. "Telephone Interviewing: A Reappraisal and a Field Experiment." *Basic and Applied Social Psychology* 1:127-153.

Quinney, R. 1973. *Critique of Legal Order: Crime Control in Capitalist Society*. Boston: Little Brown and Co.

——. 1975. "Public Conceptions of Crime." In *Perception in Criminology*. R. L. Henshel and R. A. Silverman. (eds.), Toronto: Methuen.

Rarick, D. L., J. E. Townsend & D. A. Boyd. 1973. "Adolescent Perceptions of Police: Actual and as Depicted in TV Drama." *Journalism Quarterly* 50(5):438-446.

Rauma, D. 1991. The Context of Normative Consensus: An Expansion of the Rossi/Berk Consensus Model, With an Application to Crime Seriousness." *Social Science Research* 20:1-28.

Ray, J. 1982. "Prison Sentences and Public Opinion." *Australian Quarterly* 54:435-443.

Redondo, S., E. Luque & J. Funes. 1996. "Social Beliefs About Crime." In G. Davies, S, Lloyd-Bostock, M. McMurran and C. Wilson (eds.), *Psychology, Law and Criminal Justice*. New York: Walter de Gruyter.

Reed, J. P. & R. S. Reed. 1973. "Status, Images and Consequence: Once a Criminal Always a Criminal." *Sociology and Social Research* 57:460-472.

Reitsma-Street, M. 1994. "Canadian Youth Charges and Dispositions for Females Before and After Implementation of the Young Offenders Act." *Canadian Journal of Criminology* 35:437-458.

Research and Forecasts, Inc. 1983. *America Afraid: How Fear of Crime Changes the Way We Live (The Figgie Reports)*. New York: NAL Books.

Riley, P. J. & V. M. Rose. 1980. "Public vs. Elite Opinion on Correctional Reform: Implications for Social Policy." *Journal of Criminal Justice* 8:345-356.

Reed, J. P., & R. S. Reed. 1972. "Status, Images and Consequences: Once a Criminal, Always a Criminal." In T. P. Thornberry & E. Sagarin, (eds.), *Images of Crime: Offenders and Victims*, 123-134. New York: Praeger Publishers.

Reed, E. F. 1993. *The Penry Penalty: Capital Punishment and Offenders with Mental Retardation*. Laham, Maryland: University Press of America.

Reming, G. C. 1988. "Personality Characteristics of Supercops and Habitual Criminals." *Journal of Police Science and Administration* 16(3):163-167.

Riedel, M. 1975. "Perceived Circumstances, Inferences of Intent and Judgments of Offense Seriousness." *Journal of Criminal Law and Criminology* 66:201-209.

Rist, R., L. Haggerty & D. Gibbons. 1974. "Public Perceptions of Sexual Deviance: A Study on the Interpretations of Knowledge and Values." *Western Sociological Review* 5:66-81.

Roberts, C. F., S. L. Golding & F. D. Fincham. 1987. "Implicit Theories of Criminal Responsibility: Decisionmaking and the Insanity Defense." *Law and Human Behavior* 11:207-232.

Roberts, C. F., & S. L. Golding. 1991. "The Social Construction of Criminal Responsibility and Insanity." *Law and Human Behavior* 15(4):349-376.

Roberts, J. V. 1984. "Public Opinion and Capital Punishment: The Effects of Attitudes Upon Memory." *Canadian Journal of Criminology* 26:283-291.

——. 1985. The Attitude-Memory Relationship After 40 Years." *Basic and Applied Social Psychology* 6:221-241.

——. 1988a. "Early Release From Prison: What Do the Canadian Public Really Think?" *Canadian Journal of Criminology* 30:231-249.

——. 1988b. "Public Opinion About Sentencing: Some Popular Myths." *Justice Report* 5:7-9.

———. 1988c. "Public Opinion and Sentencing: The Surveys of the Canadian Sentencing Commission." *Research Reports of the Canadian Sentencing Commission.* Ottawa: Department of Justice Canada.

———. 1988d. "Sentencing in the Media: A Content Analysis of English-Language Newspapers in Canada." *Research Reports of the Canadian Sentencing Commission.* Ottawa: Department of Justice Canada.

———. 1988e. *Empirical Research on Sentencing. Research Reports of the Canadian Sentencing Commission.* Ottawa: Department of Justice Canada.

———. 1990. *Sexual Assault Legislation in Canada: An Evaluation. An Analysis of National Statistics.* Ottawa: Department of Justice Canada.

———. 1992. "Public Opinion, Crime, and Criminal Justice." In M. Tonry (ed.), *Crime and Justice: A Review of Research,* 99-180. Chicago: University of Chicago Press.

———. 1996. "Public Opinion, Criminal Record and the Sentencing Process." *American Behavioral Scientist* 39:488-499.

———. 1997. "Paying for the Past: The Role of Criminal Record in the Sentencing Process." *In: M. Tonry (ed.), Crime and Justice. A Review of Research.* Chicago: University of Chicago Press.

Roberts, J. V., & A. N. Doob. 1989. "Sentencing and Public Opinion: Taking False Shadows for True Substances." *Osgoode Hall Law Journal* 27:491-515.

Roberts, J. V. & A. N. Doob. 1990. "News Media Influences on Public Views of Sentencing." *Law and Human Behavior* 14:451-468.

Roberts, J.V. & A. N. Doob. 1997. "Race, Crime and Criminal Justice in Canada." In: M. Tonry and R. Hood. (eds.), *Race, Ethnicity and Crime.* Chicago: University of Chicago Press.

Roberts, J. V., & D. Edwards. 1989. "Contextual Effects in Judgments of Crimes, Criminals and the Purposes of Sentencing." *Journal of Applied Social Psychology* 19: 902-917.

Roberts, J. V. & M. G. Grossman. 1990. "Crime Prevention and Public Opinion." *Canadian Journal of Criminology* 32:75-90.

Roberts, J. V. & M. Jackson. 1991. "Boats Against the Current: A Note on the Effects of Imprisonment". *Law and Human Behavior* 15:557-562.

Roberts, J. V. & R. M. Mohr. 1994. *Confronting Sexual Assault. A Decade of Social and Legal Change.* Toronto: University of Toronto Press.

Roberts, J. V., & N. R. White. 1986. "Public Estimates of Recidivism Rates: Consequences of a Criminal Stereotype." *Canadian Journal of Criminology* 28:229-241.

Roberts v. Louisiana, 428 U.S. 325 1976.

Roe, et al. v. Wade, 410 U.S. 113 1973.

Roese, N. J. (1994). The Functional Basis of Counterfactual Thinking." *Journal of Personality and Social Psychology* 66(5):805-818.

Rose, A. & A. Prell. 1955. "Does the Punishment Fit the Crime? A Study in Social Valuation." *American Journal of Sociology* 61:247-259.

Rossi, P. H. & A.B. Anderson. 1982. "The Factorial Survey Approach: An Introduction." In *Measuring Social Judgments: The Factorial Survey Approach.* P. Rossi and S. Nock. (eds.), Beverly Hills, California.: Sage.

Rossi. P., R. Berk & A. Campbell. 1995. *Popular Views of Sentencing Federal Criminals.* University of Massachusetts.

Robinson, P. H. & J. M. Darley. 1995. *Justice, Liability & Blame: Community Views and the Criminal Law.* Boulder, CO: Westview Press.

Rooney, E. & D. Gibbons. 1966. "Social Reactions to Crimes Without Victims." *Social Problems* 13:400-410.

Rossi. P. H. & A. Anderson. 1982. "The Factorial Survey Approach: An Introduction". In: P. Rossi and S. Nock (eds.), *Measuring Social Judgements: The Factorial Survey Approach.* Beverly Hills: Calif.: Sage.

Rossi, P. H. and S. Nock. (eds.), 1982 *Measuring Social Judgments: The Factorial Survey Approach.* Beverl Hills, Sage.

Rossi, P. H., E. Waite, C. E. Bose & R. A. Berk. 1974. "The Seriousness of Crimes: Normative Structure and Individual Differences." *American Sociological Review* 39: 224-237.

Rossi, P. H., & Henry, P. A. 1980. "Seriousness: A Measure for all Purposes?" In Malcolm W. Klein and Katherine S. Teilmann. (eds.), *Handbook of Criminal Justice Evaluation,* Beverly Hills, Calif: Sage.

Rossi, P. H., J. E. Simpson & J. L. Miller. 1985. "Beyond Crime Seriousness: Fitting the Punishment to the Crime." *Journal of Quantitative Criminology* 1:59-90.

Roth v. U.S., 354 U.S. 476 1957.

Rothbart, M. & S. Lewis 1988. "Inferring Category Attributes From Exemplar Attributes: Geometric Shapes and Social Categories." *Journal of Personality and Social Psychology* 55(6):861-872.

Rumelhart, D. E. & A. Ortony. 1977. "The Representation of Knowledge in Memory." In R.C. Anderson, R. J. Spiro, & W. E. Montaque (eds.), *Schooling and the Acquisition of Knowledge.* Lawrence Erlbaum Associates, Publishers: Hillsdale, New Jersey.

Rust v. Sullivan 111 S.CT. 1759 1991.

Ruttbush, R.L. 1989. "A Comparison of Androgynous, Masculine Sex-Typed and Undifferentiated Males in Dimensions of Attitudes Toward Rape." *Journal of Research in Personality* 23:318-342.

Ryan, M. 1983. *The Politics of Penal Reform.* London: Longman.

Ryckman, R. M., L. M. Kaczor, & B. Thornton. 1992. "Traditional and Nontraditional Women's Attributions of Responsibility to Physically Resistive and Nonresistive Rape Victims," *Journal of Applied Social Psychology* 22(18):1453-1463.

Saad, L., & McAneny 1995. "Black Americans See Little Justice For Themselves." *The Gallup Poll Monthly,* March, 32-35.

Sacco, V. & B. Fair. 1988. "Images of Legal Control. Crimes News and the Process of Organizational Legitimation." *Canadian Journal of Communication* 13:113-122.

Sacco, V. & H. Johnson. 1990. *Patterns of Criminal Victimization in Canada.* Ottawa: Ministry of Supply and Services.

Saladin, M., Z. Saper & L. Breen. 1988. "Perceived Attractiveness and Attributions of Criminality: What is Beautiful is Not Criminal." *Canadian Journal of Criminology* 30: 251-259.

Saliba v. State, 475 N.E. 2d 1181 (Ind. App. 2d 1985).

S., W. & E. Moulds. 1986. "The Effect of Crime Severity on Perceptions of Fair Punishment: A California Case Study." 77:931-947.

Sarat. A. 1975. Support for the Legal System: An Analysis of Knowledge, Attitudes, and Behavior." *American Politics Quarterly* 3(1):3-23.

Sarat, A. 1977. "Studying American Legal Culture: An Assessment of Survey Evidence." *Law & Society Review* 11:427-488.

Sarat, A. & N. Vidmar. 1976. "Public Opinion, the Death Penalty, and the Eighth Amendment: Testing the Marshall Hypothesis." *Wisconsin Law Review* 171-191.

Scaglion, R., & R. G. Condon. 1980. "Determinants of Attitudes Toward City Police." *Criminology* 17(4):485-494.

Scaglion, R., & R. G. Condon. 1985. "Determinants of Attitudes Toward City Police." In R.J. Homant & D.B. Kennedy (eds.), *Police and Law Enforcement* 3:107-114. New York: AMS Press.

Schell, B., H. Sherritt, J. Arthur, L., L. Beatty, L. Berry, L. Edmonds, J. Kaashoek & J. Kempny. 1987. "Development of a Pornography Community Standard: Questionnaire Results for Two Canadian Cities." *Canadian Journal of Criminology* 29(2):133-152.

Schneckloth v. Bustamonte, 412 U.S. 218 1973.

Schroot, D. G. & J. J. Knowles. 1990. *Ohio Citizens Attitudes Concerning Drug and Alcohol Use and Abuse: General Findings.* Columbus, Ohio: Governor's Office of Criminal Justice.

Schuman, H., & S. Presser. 1981. "The Attitude-Action Connection and the Issue of Gun Control." *Annuals of American Academy of Political Social Science* 455:40-47.

Schuman, H., & L. Gruenberg. 1972. Dissatisfaction With City Services: Is Race An Important Factor? *People and Political Urban Society* 386-387.

Schwartz, I., S. Guo & J. Kerbs. 1993. "The Impact of Demographic Variables on Public Opinion Regarding Juvenile Justice: Implications for Public Policy". *Crime and Delinquency* 39:5-28.

Schwartz, I. M. 1992. "Juvenile Crime-Fighting Policies: What the Public Really Wants." In I. M. Schwartz (ed.), *Juvenile Justice and Public Policy Toward a National Agenda* , 214-248. New York: Lexington.

Schwarz, N. & H. Bless. 1992. "Constructing Reality and Its Alternatives: An Inclusion/Exclusion Model of Assimilation and Contrast Effects in Social Judgment." 217-245. In L. L. Martin & A. Tesser (eds.), *The Construction of Social Judgments*, Lawrence Erlbaum Associates, Publishers: Hillsdale, New Jersey.

Scott, J. 1989. "Conflicting Beliefs About Abortion: Legal Approval and Moral Doubts." *Social Psychology Quarterly* 52(4):319-326.

Scott, J. E., & F. Al-Thakeb. 1977. "The Public's Perceptions of Crime: A Comparative Analysis of Scandinavia, Western Europe, the Middle East, and the United States." In C. R. Huff (ed.), *Contemporary Corrections: Social Control and Conflict*, 78-88. Beverly Hills, CA: Sage.

Scott, J. E., D. J. Eitle & S. E. Skovron. 1990. "Obscenity and the Law: Is it Possible for a Jury to Apply Contemporary Community Standards in Determining Obscenity?" *Law and Human Behavior* 14(2):139-150.

Scott, J. E. 1991. "What is Obscene? Social Science and the Contemporary Community Standard Test of Obscenity." *International Journal of Law and Psychiatry* 14(1-2):29-45.

Scott, W. A. 1969. "Structure of Natural Cognitions." *Journal of Personality and Social Psychology* 12:261-278.

Sebba, L. 1980. "Is Mens Rea a Component of Perceived Offense Seriousness?" *Journal of Criminal Law and Criminology* 71:124-35.

————. 1978. "Some Explorations in the Scaling of Penalties." *Journal of Research in Crime and Delinquency* 15:247-265.

————. 1983. "Attitudes of New Immigrants Toward White-collar Crime: A Cross-Cultural Exploration." *Human Relations* 36:1091-1110.

Secret, P. E. & J. B. Johnson. 1989. "Racial Differences in Attitudes Toward Crime Control." *Journal of Criminal Justice* 17:361-375.

Security. 1989. "Causes of Crime." 26:10.

Selby, J., L. Calhoun & T. Brock. 1977. "Sex Differences in the Social Perception of Rape Victims." *Personality and Social Psychology Bulletin* 3:412-415.

Sellin, T., & M. Wolfgang. 1964. *The Measurement of Delinquency*. New York: John Wiley.

Shaffer & Case 1982. "On the Decision Not to Testify in One's Own Behalf: Effects of Withheld Evidence, Defendant's Sexual Preferences, and Juror Dogmatism on Juridic Decisions." *Journal of Personality and Social Psychology*, 335-342.

Shapland, J., J. Willmore & P. Duff. 1985. *Victims in the Criminal Justice System*. Brookfield Vermont: Gower Publishing Company.

Sharp, F.C. & M. C. Otto. 1909. "A Study of the Popular Attitude Towards Retributive Punishment." *International Journal of Ethics* 20:341-357.

Sheley, J. F. 1980. "Crime Seriousness Ratings: The impact of Survey Questionnaire Form and Item Context." *British Journal of Criminology* 20:123-33.

Sheley, J. F. & C. D. Ashkins. 1981. "Crime, Crime News, and Crime Views." *Public Opinion Quarterly* 45:492-506.

Sheppard, B. H., & N. Vidmar. 1980. "Adversary Pretrial Procedures and Testimonial Evidence: Effects of Lawyer's Role and Machiavellianism." *Journal of Personality and Social Psychology* 39:320-332.

Sherman, R. C., & M. D. Dowdle. 1974. "The Perception of Crime and Punishment: A multidimensional Scaling Analysis." *Social Science Research* 3:109-126.

Shoemaker, D. J. & D. R. South. 1978. "Nonverbal Images of Criminality and Deviance: Existence and Consequence." *Criminal Justice Review* 25:65-80.

Shoemaker, D. J., D. R. South & J. Lowe. 1973. Facial Stereotypes of Deviants and Judgments of Guilt and Innocence." *Social Forces* 51:427-433.

Shotland, R. L., & L. Goodstein. 1983. "Just Because She Doesn't Want to Doesn't Mean it's Rape: An Experimentally Based Causal Model of the Perception of Rape in a Dating Situation." *Social Psychology Quarterly* 46(3):220-232.

Shotland, R.L. 1992. "A Theory of the Causes of Courtship Rape: Part 2." In J. W. White & S.B. Sorenson (eds.), "Adult Sexual Assault." *Journal of Social Issues* 48:127-143.

Sigler, R. T., & T. M. Dees. 1988. "Public Perception of Petty Corruption in Law Enforcement." *Journal of Police Science and Administration* 16(1):14-20.

Silver, E., C. Cirincione & H. J. Steadman. 1994. "Demythologizing Inaccurate Perceptions of the Insanity Defense." *Law and Human Behavior* 18(1):63-70.

Silvey, J. 1961. "The Criminal Law and Public Opinion." *Criminal Law Review* 25: 349-358.

Simmons, J. 1966. "Public Stereotypes of Deviants." *Social Problems* 13: 223-232.

Simon, R. J. 1967. *The Jury and the Insanity Defense.* Boston: Little, Brown.

Singer, M. S. & A. Jonas. 1985. "Attitudes Toward Actors in the Justice System: Police and Students in New Zealand." *Police Studies* 8(1):51-57.

Skogan, W. G. 1971. "Judicial Myth and Judicial Reality." *Washington University Law Quarterly* 25:309-371.

Skogan, W. G. 1989. *The Social Stratification of Procedural Justice.* Unpublished Manuscript.

Skogan, W. G., 1990. *Disorder and Decline: Crime and the Spiral of Decay in American Neighborhoods.* Berkeley: University of California Press.

Skogan, W. G. 1996. "The Police and Public Opinion in Britain." *American Behavioral Scientist* 39(4): 423-434.

Skolnick, J. H. & J. J. Frye. 1993. "Police Accountability II: The Public." In Jerome H. Skolnick & James Frye (eds.), *Above the Law,* 217-236. New York: Free Press.

Skovron, S. E., J. E. Scott, & F. T. Cullen 1988. "Prison Crowding: Public Attitudes Toward Strategies of Population Control." *Journal of Research in Crime and Delinquency* 25(2): 150-169.

Skovron, S. E., Scott, J. E. & F. T. Cullen. 1989. "The Death Penalty for Juveniles: An Assessment of Public Support." *Crime and Delinquency* 35(4):546-561.

Skowronski, J. J. & D. E. Carlston. 1987. "Social Judgment and Social Memory: The Role of Cue Diagnosticity in Negativity, Positivity, and Extremity Biases." *Journal of Personality and Social Psychology* 52(4):689-699.

Slobogin, C. & J. E. Schumacher. 1993a. "Rating the Intrusiveness of Law Enforcement Searches and Seizures." *Law and Human Behavior* 17(2):183-200.

Slobogin, C., & J. E. Schumacher. 1993b. "Reasonable Expectations of Privacy and Autonomy in Fourth Amendment Cases: An Empirical Look at "Understanding Recognized and Permitted by Society." *Duke Law Journal* 42(4):727-775.

Slovic, P., B. Fischhoff & S. Lichtenstein. 1982. "Facts Versus Fears: Understanding Perceived Risk." In D. Kahneman, P. Slovic, & A. Tversky (eds.), *Judgment Under Uncertainty: Heuristics and Biases,* 463-489. London: Cambridge University Press.

Smith, E. R. 1990. "Content and Process Specificity in the Effects of Prior Experiences." In T. K. Srull & R. S. Wyer, Jr. (eds.), *Advances in Social Cognition,* (3), Lawrence Hillsdale, New Jersey: Erlbaum Associates, Publishers.

Smith, P. E. & R. O. Hawkins. 1973. "Victimization, Types of Citizen-Police Contacts, and Attitudes Toward the Police." *Law & Society Review* 8(1): 135-172.

Smith, R. E., J. P. Keating, R. K. Hester & H. E. Mitchell. 1976. "Role and Justice Considerations in the Attribution of Responsibility to a Rape Victim." *Journal of Research in Personality* 10:346-357.

Smith, R. E., C. J. Pine & M. E. Hawley. 1988. "Social Cognitions About Adult Male Victims of Female Sexual Assault. *Journal of Sex Research* 24:101-112.

Smith, T. W. 1984. "Nonattitudes: A Review and Evaluation." In C. F. Turner & E. Martin (eds.), *Surveying Subjective Phenomena* 2:215-255. New York: Russell Sage Foundation.

Smith, V. L. 1991. "Prototypes in the Courtroom: Lay Representations of Legal Concepts." *Journal of Personality and Social Psychology* 61: 857-872.

Smith, V. L. 1993. "When Prior Knowledge and Law Collide: Helping Jurors Use the Law." *Law and Human Behavior* 17(5): 507-536.

Snyder, H. N., & M. Sickmund. 1995. *Juvenile Offenders and Victims: A Focus on Violence*. U. S. Department of Justice Office of Juvenile Justice and Delinquency Prevention. Pittsburg, PA: National Center for Juvenile Justice.

Solicitor General Canada. 1981. *Solicitor General's Study of Conditional Release*. Ottawa: Solicitor General Canada.

————. 1984a. *Selected Trends in Canadian Criminal Justice*. Ottawa: Canadian Government Publishing Centre.

————. 1984b. *Canadian Urban Victimization Survey: Reported and Unreported Offences*. Ottawa: Supply and Services Canada.

Sourcebook of Criminal Justice Statistics. 1977. Washington, D.C.: U.S. Department of Justice, Bureau of Justice Statistics.

Sprott, J. 1995. *Understanding Public Views of Youth Crime and the Youth Justice System*. Toronto: University of Toronto, Centre of Criminology.

Stalans, L.J. 1988. *Sentencing in Ambiguous Cases: Prototypes, Perceived Similarity, and Anchoring*. Unpublished Masters Thesis Department of Psychology University of Illinois at Chicago.

Stalans, L. J. & S.S. Diamond. 1990. "Formation and Change in Lay Evaluations of Criminal Sentencing: Misperception and Discontent." *Law and Human Behavior* 14:199-214.

Stalans, L. J. & A. J. Lurigio. 1990. "Lay and Professionals' Beliefs About Crime and Criminal Sentencing: A Need for Theory, Perhaps Schema Theory." *Criminal Justice and Behavior* 17(3):333-349.

Stalans, L. J. 1993. "Citizens' Crime Stereotypes, Biased Recall, and Lay Punishment Preferences in Abstract Cases: The Educative Role of Interpersonal Sources." *Law and Human Behavior* 17:451-470.

Stalans, L. J. 1994a. "Formation of Procedural Beliefs about Legal Arenas: Do People Generalize from Loosely Related Past Legal Experiences?" *Psychology, Crime & Law* 1: 39-57.

Stalans, L. J. 1994b.. "Lay Evaluations of Encounters With Governmental Officials: Do Expectations Serve as Filters and Standards?" In L. Heath et al., (eds.), *Applications of Heuristics and Biases, Volume 3 of the Social Psychological Applications to Social Issues Series*. New York: Plenum Press.

Stalans, L. J. & G. T. Henry. 1994. "Societal Views of Justice for Adolescents Accused of Murder: Inconsistency Between Community Sentiment and Automatic Legislative Transfers." *Law and Human Behavior* 18(6): 675-696.

Stalans, L. J. & M. A. Finn. 1995. "How Novice and Experienced Officers Interpret Wife Assaults: Normative and Efficiency Framing." *Law & Society Review* 29(2): 301-335.

Stalans, L. J. 1996. "Family Harmony or Individual Protection?: Public Recommendations About How Police Can Handle Domestic Violence Situations." *American Behavioral Scientist* 39(4):435-450.

Stalans, L. J. & Lurigio, A. J. 1996. Editor's Introduction: "Public Opinion about the Creation, Enforcement, and Punishment of Criminal Offenses." *American Behavioral Scientist*, 39(4):369-378.

Stanford v. Kentucky, 492 U.S. 361 1989.

Stangor, C., & D. McMillan. 1992. "Memory for Expectancy-Congruent and Expectancy-Incongruent Social Information: A Review of the Social and Social Developmental Literatures." *Psychological Bulletin* 111:42-61.

Steadman, H. J. & J. J. Cocozza. 1977-78. "Selective Reporting and the Public's Misconceptions of the Criminally Insane." *Public Opinion Quarterly* 41:521-533.

Steele, W. W., Jr., & E. G. Thornburg. 1995. "Jury Instructions: A Persistent Failure to Communicate." In G. L. Mays & P. R. Gregware (eds.), *Courts and Justice: A Reader.* Prospect Heights, IL: Waveland Press, Inc.

Steinhart, D. 1988. "California Opinion Poll: Public Attitudes on Youth Crime." *NCCD Focus*, December, 1-7.

Stephen, J. 1883. *A History of the Criminal Law of England.* London: MacMillan.

Stets, J. E., & R. K. Leik. 1993. "Attitudes About Abortion and Varying Attitude Structures." *Social Science Research* 22: 265-282.

Stinchcombe, A. L., R. Adams, C. A. Heimer, K. Scheppele, T. W. Smith and D. G. Taylor. 1980. *Crime and Punishment-Changing Attitudes in America.* San Francisco: Jossey-Bass.

Streib, V.L. 1988. "Imposing the Death Penalty on Children." In K. C. Haas, J. A. Inciardi (eds.), *Challenging Capital Punishment: Legal and Social Science Approaches*, 245-267, Newbury Park, CA: Sage Publications Inc.

Struckman-Johnson, C. & D. Struckman-Johnson. 1992. "Acceptance of Male Rape Myths Among College Men and Women." *Sex Roles* 27(3/4): 85-100.

Sue, S., R. Smith & C. Caldwell. 1973. "Effects of Inadmissable Evidence on the Decisions of Simulated Jurors: A Moral Dilemma." *Journal of Applied Social Psychology* 3:344-353.

Sue, S., R. Smith & R. Gilbert. 1974. "Biasing Effects of Pretrial Publicity on Judicial Decisions." *Journal of Criminal Justice* 2:163-171.

Sullivan, P. S., R. G. Dunham & G. P. Alpert. 1987. "Attitude Structures of Different Ethnic and Age Groups Concerning Police." *The Journal of Criminal Law & Criminology* 78(1):177-196.

Sumner, W. G. 1906. *Folkways: A Study of the Sociological Importance of Usages, Manners, Customs, Mores and Morals.* Boston: Ginn and Company.

Sunnafrank, M. & N. Fontes. 1981. "General and Crime-Related Racial Stereotypes and Influence on Juridic Decisions." *Cornell Journal of Social Relations* 17:1-15.

Surette, R. 1992. "The Media's Influence on Attitudes and Beliefs About Crime and Justice." In *Media Crime and Criminal Justice*, Pacific Grove, CA.

Surette, R. 1985. "Television Viewing and Support of Punitive Criminal Justice Policy." *Journalism Quarterly* 68(2):373-377.

Swann, W. B., Jr. 1984. "Quest for Accuracy in Person Perception: A Matter of Pragmatics." *Psychological Review* 91:457-477.

Sykes, R.E. & J. P. Clark. 1978. "A Theory of Deference Exchange in Police-Civilian Encounters." *American Journal of Sociology* 81(3):584-600.

Tanford, J. A., 1990. "The Law and Psychology of Jury Instructions." *Nebraska Law Review* 69:71-111.

Tanford, S., & S. Penrod. 1984. "Biases in Trials Involving Defendants Charged With Multiple Offenses." *Journal of Applied Social Psychology* 12:453-480.

Taylor, G. D., L. Scheppele, K. Scheppele & A. L. Stinchcombe. 1979. "Salience of Crime and Support for Harsher Criminal Sanctions." *Social Problems* 26:413-24.

Taylor, S. E. 1982. "The Availability Bias in Social Perception and Interaction." In D. Kahneman, P. Slovic, & A. Tversky (eds.), *Judgment Under Uncertainty: Heuristics and Biases,* 190-200. New York: Cambridge University Press.

Tennessee v. Garner, 471 U.S. 1 1985.

Tesser, A., & C. Leone. 1977. "Cognitive Schema and Thought as Determinants of Attitude Change." *Journal of Experimental Social Psychology* 13: 340-356.

Tesser, A., & D. Schaffer. 1990. "Attitudes and Attitude Change." *Annual Review of Psychology* 41:479-523.

Thatcher, M. 1985. Quoted in *The Economist,* July 20, .51.

Thibaut, J., & L. Walker. 1978. "A Theory of Procedure." *California Law Review* 66:541-566.

Thibaut, J., & L. Walker. 1975. *Procedural Justice: A psychological Analysis.* Hillsdale, NJ: Erlbaum.

Thibaut, J., L. Walker, S. LaTour & P. Houlden. 1974. "Procedural Justice as Fairness." *Stanford Law Review* 26:1271-1289.

Thomas, C. W., & R. J. Cage. 1976. "Correlates of Public Attitudes Toward Legal Sanctions." *International Journal of Criminology and Penology* 4:239-55.

Thomas, C. W., R. J. Cage & S. C. Foster. 1976. "Public Opinion and Criminal Law and Legal Sanctions." *International Journal of Criminology and Penology* 4:239-55.

Thomas, C. W., & J. M. Hyman. 1977. "Perceptions of Crime, Fear of Victimization, and Public Perceptions of Police Performance." *Journal of Police Science and Administration* 5(3):305-317.

Thomas, R.H. & J. D. Hutchinson. 1986. *Georgia Residents' Attitudes Toward the Death Penalty, the Disposition of Juvenile Offenders, and Related Issues.* Unpublished Manuscript.

Thompson v. Oklahoma, 487 U.S. 815 1988.

Thomson, D. R., & A. J. Ragona. 1987. "Popular Moderation Versus Govermental Authoritarianism: An Interactionist View of Public Sentiments Toward Criminal Sanctions." *Crime & Delinquency* 33(2):337-357.

Thornton, L. M. 1975. "People and the Police: An Analysis of Factors Associated With Police Evaluation and Support." *Canadian Journal of Sociology* 25:325-342.

Thurman, Q. C. 1989. "General Prevention of Tax Evasion: A Factorial Survey Approach." *Journal of Quantitative Criminology* 5:127-146.

Thurstone, L.L. 1927a. "Method of Paired Comparisons for Social Values." *Journal of Abnormal and Social Psychology* 21:384-400.

Thurstone, L. L. 1927b. "A Law of Comparative Judgment." *Psychological Review* 34:273-286.

Tison v. Arizona, 481 U.S. 137 1987.

Toch, H. 1972. "Cops and Blacks: Warring Minorities." In J.T. Curran, A. Fowler, & R.H. Ward (eds.), *Police and Law Enforcement* 3:243-247. New York: AMS Press.

Tonry, M. 1995. *Malign Neglect: Race, Crime and Punishment in America.* New York: Oxford University Press.

Tourangeau, R. & K. A. Rasinski. 1988. "Cognitive Processes Underlying Context Effects in Attitude Measurement." *Psychological Bulletin* 103(3):299-314.

Tourangeau, R., K. A. Rasinski, N. Bradburn & R. D'Andrade. 1989a. "Carryover Effects in Attitude Surveys." *Public Opinion Quarterly* 53:495-524.

Tourangeau, R., K. A. Rasinski & N. Bradburn. 1989b. "Belief Accessibility and Context Effects in Attitude Measurement." *Journal of Experimental Social Psychology* 25:401-421.

Traugott, M. W. 1986. *How Michigan Citizens View the Courts and Legal Systems: A Survey of Knowledge and Attitudes.* Ann Arbor: Institute for Social Research, University of Michigan.

Travis, L. F., F. T. Cullen, B. G. Link & J. F. Wozniak. 1986. "The Impact of Instructions on Seriousness Ratings." *Journal of Criminal Justice* 14:433-40.

Tremblay, P., G. Cordeau & M. Ouimet. 1994. "Underpunishing Offenders: Towards a Theory of Legal Tolerance." *Canadian Journal of Criminology* 25:407-434.

Trop v. Dulles, 356 U.S. 86 1958.

Turner, J. 1993. *Sentencing in Adult Criminal Provincial Courts. A Study of Six Canadian Jurisdictions.* Ottawa: Statistics Canada.

Turner, S. 1978. "Introduction to the Reprint Edition." In T. Sellin & M. Wolgang (eds.), *The Measurement of Delinquency.* Chicago: University of Chicago Press.

Tversky, A. & S. Sattath. 1979. "Preference Trees." *Psychological Review* 86: 542-573.

Tversky, A. & D. Kahneman 1973. "Availability: A Heuristic For Judging Frequency and Probability." *Cognitive Psychology* 4:207-232.

Tversky, A. & D. Kahneman. 1982a. "Judgment Under Uncertainty: Heuristics and Biases. In D. Kahneman, P. Slovic, & A. Tversky, (eds.), *Judgment Under Uncertainty:Heuristics and Biases,* 3-20. London: Cambridge University Press.

Tversky, A. & D. Kahneman. 1982b. "Belief in the Law of Small Numbers." In D. Kahneman, P. Slovic, & A. Tversky (eds.), *Judgment under uncertainty: Heuristics and Biases,* 23-31. London: Cambridge University Press.

Tversky, A. & D. Kahneman. 1982c. "Judgments of and by Representativeness." In D. Kahneman, P. Slovic, & A. Tversky (eds.), *Judgment Under Uncertainty: Heuristics and Biases.* 84-98. London: Cambridge University Press.

Tyler, T. R., & R. Folger. 1980. "Distributional and Procedural Aspects of Satisfaction With Citizen-Police Encounters." *Basic and Applied Social Psychology* 1:281-292.

Tyler, T. R., & P. J. Lavrakas. 1983. "Support for Gun Control: The Influence of Personal, Sociotropic, and Ideological Concerns." *Journal of Applied Social Psychology* 13(5): 392-405.

Tyler, T. R. & R. Weber. 1982. "Support for the Death Penalty: Instrumental Response to Crime or Symbolic Attitude?" *Law and Society Review* 17(1):21-45.

Tyler, T. R. 1984. "The Role of Perceived Injustice in Defendant's Evaluations of Their Courtroom Experience." *Law & Society Review* 18:51-74.

Tyler, T.R. 1987. "Conditions Leading to Value-Expressive Effects in Judgments of Procedural Justice: A Test of Four Models." *Journal of Personality and Social Psychology* 52(2):333-344.

Tyler, T.R. 1988. "What is Procedural Justice? Criteria Used by Citizens to Assess the Fairness of Legal Procedures." *Law & Society Review* 22(1):103-135.

Tyler, T. R., J. D. Casper & B. Fisher. 1989. "Maintaining Allegiance Toward Political Authorities: The Role of Prior Attitudes and the Use of Fair Procedures." *American Journal of Political Science* 33:629-652.

Tyler, T. R. 1990. *Why People Obey the Law: Procedural Justice, Legitimacy, and Compliance*. New Haven, CT: Yale University Press.

Tyler, T. R., & K. Rasinski. 1991. "Procedural Justice, Institutional Legitimacy, and the Acceptance of Unpopular U.S. Supreme Court Decisions: A Reply to Gibson." *Law & Society Review* 25(3):621-630.

United States v. Hendrix, 595 F.2d 883 (D.C. Cir. 1979).

United States v. Matlock, 415 U.S. 164 (1974).

Urschel, J. October, 1995. "Poll: A Nation More Divided." *USA Today*: 5-6a.

U.S. Department of Justice. 1987. *Federal Sentencing Guidelines: Answers to Some Questions*. NIJ Report No. 205. Washington, D.C.: U.S. Government Printing Office.

U.S. Department of Justice. 1987. *Criminal Victimization*. Washington, D.C.: Bureau of Justice Statistics.

Vala, J., M. Monteiro & J. Leyens. 1988. "Perception of Violence as a Function of Observer's Ideology and Actor's Group Membership." *British Journal of Social Psychology Society* 27(3):231-237.

Valez-Diaz, A., & E. Megargee. 1970. "An Investigation of Differences Between Youthful Offenders and Non-Offenders in Puerto Rico." *Journal of Criminal Law, Criminology, and Police Science* 61:549-553.

Van Dijk, J. 1978. *The Extent of Public Information and the Nature of Public Attitudes Towards Crime*. The Hague: Research and Documentation Centre, Ministry of Justice.

Veneziano, L. & C. Veneziano. 1993. "Are Victimless Crimes Actually Harmful?" *Journal of Contemporary Criminal Justice* 9(1):1-14.

Vidmar, N., & N. M. Laird. 1983. "Adversary Social Roles: Their Effects on Witnesses Communication of Evidence and the Assessment of Adjudicators." *Journal of Personality and Social Psychology* 44:888-898.

Vingilis, E., H. Blefgen, D. Colbourne, D. Reynolds & R. Solomon. 1986. "Police Enforcement Practices and Perceptions of Drinking-Driving Laws." *Canadian Journal of Criminology* 28(2):147-156.

Vidmar, N. 1974. "Retributive and Utilitarian Motives and Other Correlates of Canadian Attitudes Toward the Death Penalty." *The Canadian Psychologist* 15:337-356.

Vidmar, N. & T. Dittenhoffer. 1981. "Informed Public Opinion and Death Penalty Attitudes." *Canadian Journal of Criminology* 23:43-55.

Von Hirsch, A. 1985. *Past or Future Crimes: Deservedness and Dangerousness in the Sentencing of Criminals*. New Brunswick, New Jersey: Rutgers University Press.

Waddington, P.A.J. & Q. Braddock. 1991. "Guardians or Bullies?: Perceptions of the Police Amongst Adolescent Black, White and Asian Boys." *Police and Society* 2:31-45.

Waegel, W. B. 1984. "How Police Justify the Use of Deadly Force." *Social Problems* 32(2): 144-155.

Walker, J., M. Collins & P. Wilson. 1988. "How the Public Sees Sentencing: An Australian Survey." In *Public Attitudes to Sentencing: Surveys from Five Countries*, N. Walker & M. Hough. (eds.), Cambridge Studies in Criminology, LIX, Aldershot, England: Gower.

Walker, N. & M. Argyle. 1974. "Does the Law Affect Moral Judgements?" In *Perception in Criminology*, R. L. Henshel & R. A. Silverman. (eds.), Toronto: Methuen.

Walker, N. 1981. "The Ultimate Justification". In: C. Tapper (ed.), *Crime, Proof and Punishment: Essays in Memory of Sir Rupert Cross*. London: Butterworths.

Walker, N. 1985. *Sentencing: Theory, Law and Practice*. London: Butterworths.

Walker, M. A. 1978. "The Seriousness of Crimes." *British Journal of Criminology* 18: 348-364.

Walker, D. B. & P. C. Kratcoski. 1985. "A Cross Cultural Perspective on Police Values and Police-Community Relations." *Criminal Justice Review* 10(1):17-24.

Walker, D., R. J. Richardson, O. Williams, T. Denyer & S. McGaughey. 1972. "Contact and Support: An Empirical Assessment of Public Attitudes Toward the Police and the Courts." *North Carolina Law Review* 5:43-79.

Walker, D. B. & P. C. Kratcoski. 1985. "A Cross Cultural Perspective on Police Values and Police-Community Relations." *Criminal Justice Review* 10(1):17-24.

Walklate, S. 1992. "Jack and Jill Join Up at Sun Hill; Public Images of Police Officers." *Policing and Society* 2:219-232.

Wallace, D. H. 1973. "Obscenity and Contemporary Community Standards: A Survey. *Journal of Social Issues* 29(3):53-68.

Wallerstein, J. & C. Wyle. 1947. "Our Law-Abiding Law-Breakers". *Probation* 35:107-112.

Warr, M. 1989. "What is the perceived Seriousness of Crimes?" *Criminology* 20:185-204.

——. 1980. "The Accuracy of Public Beliefs About Crime." *Social Forces* 59:456-470.

——. 1982. "The Accuracy of Public Beliefs About Crime: Further Evidence." *Criminology* 20:185-204.

Warr, M., R. F. Meier & M. L. Erickson. 1983. "Norms, Theories of Punishment, and Publicly Preferred Penalties for Crimes." *Sociological Quarterly* 24:75-91.

Warr, M., J. P. Gibbs & M. L. Erickson. (19). *Contending Theories of Criminal Law: Statutory Penalties Versus Public Preferences*. 25-46.

Warr, M., R. Meier & M. L. Erickson. 1983. "Norms, Theories of Punishment and Publicly Preferred Penalities for Crimes." *Sociological Quarterly* 24:75-91.

Warr, M., 1980. The Accuracy of Public Beliefs About Crime." *Social Forces* 59:456-70.

Warr, M., 1982. "The Accuracy of Public Beliefs About Crime: Further Evidence." *Criminology* 20:185-204.

Washington State Guidelines Commission. 1992. *Implementation Manual*. Olympia: Washinton State Sentencing Guidelines Commission.

Webb, E., D. Campbell, R. Schwartz & L. Sechrest. 1981. *Unobtrusive Measures: Nonreactive Research in the Social Sciences*. Chicago: Rand McNally.

Webster v. Reproductive Health Services, 109 S. Ct. 3040 1989.

Weidner, G. & W. Griffitt. 1983. "Rape: A Sexual Stigma?" *Journal of Personality* 51: 152-166.

Weiner, R. L., & C. C. Pritchard. 1994. "Negligence Law and Mental Mutation: A Social Inference Model of Apportioning Fault." In L. Heath, R. S. Tindale, J. Edwards, E. J. Posavac, F. B. Bryant, E. Henderson-King, Y. Suarez-Balcazar &

J. Myers (eds.), *Applications of Heuristics and Biases to Social Issues.* New York: Plenum Press.

Wellford, C., & M. Wiatrowski. 1975. "On the Measurement of Delinquency." *Journal of Criminal Law and Criminology* 66:175-88.

Wells, Wrightsman, & Meine 1985. "The Timing of the Defense Opening Statement: Don't Wait Until the Evidence is In." *Journal of Applied Social Psychology* 15:758.

White, N. R., & J. V. Roberts. 1985. "Criminal Intent: The Public's View." *Canadian Journal of Criminology* 27(4):455-465.

White, M. F., & B. A. Menke. 1978. "A Critical Analysis of Surveys on Public Opinions Toward Police Agencies." *Journal of Police Science and Administration* 6(2):204-218.

White, M. F. & B. A. Menke. 1982. "On Assessing the Mood of the Public Toward the Police: Some Conceptual Issues." *Journal of Criminal Justice* 10(3):211-230.

White, G. F. 1975. "Public Responses to Hypothetical Crimes: Effect of Offender and Victim Status and Seriousness of the Offense on Punitive Reactions." *Social Forces* 53:411-419.

Williams, K. R., J. P. Gibbs & M. L. Erickson. 1980. "Public Knowledge of Statutory Penalties: The Extent and Basis of Accurate Perception." *Pacific Sociological Review* 23:105-128.

Williams, M. & J. Hall. 1972. "Knowledge of the Law in Texas: Socioeconomic and Ethnic Differences." *Law and Society Review* 7:99-118.

Wilbanks, W. 1987. *The Myth of a Racist Criminal Justice System.* Monterey, Calif.: Brooks/Cole.

Wilkins v. Missouri, 109 S. Ct. 2969 1989.

Williams, J.E. 1984. "Secondary Victimization: Confronting Public Attitudes About Rape." *Victimology* 9:66-81.

Williams, J.E. 1985. "Mexican-American and Anglo Attitudes About Sex Roles and Rape." *Free Inquiry in Creative Sociology* 13:15-20.

Williams, J.E., & K. A. Holmes. 1981. *The Second Assault: Rape and Public Attitudes.* Westport, CT: Greenwood Press.

Williams, K., J. P. Gibbs & M. L. Erickson. 1980. "Public Knowledge of Statutory Penalties: The Extent and Basis of Accurate Perceptions." *Pacific Sociological Review* 23:105-128.

Williams v. Florida 399 U.S. 78 1970. at 89-90.

Williams, J.S., C. W. Thoma & B. K. Singh. 1983. "Situational Use of Police Force: Public Reactions." *American Journal of Police* 3(1):37-50.

Willis, C.E. 1992. "The Effect of Sex Role Stereotype, Victim and Defendant Race, and Prior Relationship on Rape Culpability Attributions." *Sex Roles* 26(5-6):213-226.

Wilson, T. D., D. Kraft & D. S. Dunn. 1989. "The Disruptive Effects of Explaining Attitudes: The Moderating Effect of Knowledge About the Attitude Object." *Journal of Experimental Social Psychology* 25:379-400.

Wilson, P., J. Walker & S. Mukherjee. 1986. "How the Public Sees Crime: An Australian Survey." In *Trends and Issues in Criminal Justice*, P. Wilson. (ed.), Canberra: Australian Institute of Public Opinion.

Wissler, R. L., & M. Saks. 1985. "On the Inefficacy of Limiting Instructions: When Jurors Use Prior Conviction Evidence to Decide on Guilt." *Law and Human Behavior* 9:37-48.

Witherspoon v. Illinois, 391 U.S. 510 1968.

Wolfgang, M., R. Figlio, P. Tracy & S. Singer. 1985. *The National Survey of Crime Severity*. Washington, D.C.: U.S. Department of Justice.

Wolfgang, M & P. Tracy. 1982. *The 1945 and 1958. Birth Cohorts: A Comparison of the Prevalence, Incidence and Severity of Delinquent Behavior*. "Conference on Public Danger, Dangerous Offenders and the Criminal Justice System." Harvard University.

Woodson v. North Carolina, 428 U.S. 280 1976.

Wright, J. D., 1981. "Public Opinion and Gun Control: A Comparison of Results From Two Recent National Surveys." *Annals*, 455:24-39.

Wu, B. & C. H. McCaghy. 1993. "Attitudinal Determinants of Public Opinions Toward Legalized Pornography." *Journal of Criminal Justice* 21:13-27.

Yankelovich, D. 1991. *Coming to Public Judgment*. Syracuse, N.Y.: Syracuse University Press.

Yankelovich, Skelly & White, Inc. 1978. *The Public Image of Courts*. Williamsburg, VA: National Center For State Courts (publication no. SC001).

Yarmey, D. A. 1982. "Eyewitness Identification and Stereotypes of Criminals. In A. Trankell (ed.), *Reconstructing the Past: The Role of Psychologists in Criminal Trials*, 205-225. Stockholm, Sweden: P.A. Norstedt & Soners Forlag.

Yarmey, A. D. 1993. Stereotypes and Recognition Memory For Faces and Voices of Good Guys and Bad Guys." *Applied Cognitive Psychology* 7:419-431.

Yarmey, D. A., & S. Kruschenske. 1995. "Facial Stereotypes of Battered Women and Battered Women Who Kill." *Journal of Applied Social Psychology* 25(4):338-352.

Yarmey, A. D. & S. R. Rosenstein. 1988. "Parental Predictions of Their Children's Knowledge About Dangerous Sitiuations." *Child Abuse & Neglect* 12(3):355-361.

Yarmey, A. D. 1991. "Retrospective Perceptions of Police Following Victimization." *Canadian Police College Journal* 15(2):137-143.

Young, J., C. J. Thomsen, E. Borgida & J. L. Sullivan. 1991. "When Self-interest Makes a Difference: The Role of Construct Accessibility in Political Reasoning." *Journal of Experimental Social Psychology* 27:271-296.

Young, R.L. 1991. "Race, Conceptions of Crime and Justice, and Support for the Death Penalty." *Social Psychology Quarterly* 54(1):67-75.

Young, R.L. 1992. "Religious Orientation, Race and Support for the Death Penalty." *Journal of the Scientific Study of Religion* 31(1):76-87.

Zamble, E. 1990. "Public Support for Criminal Justice Policies: Some Specific Findings." *Forum on Corrections Research* 2:14-19.

Zamble, E. & K. Kalm. 1990. "General and Specific Measures of Public Attitudes Toward Sentencing." *Canadian Journal of Behavioural Science* 22:327-337.

Zamble, E., & P. Annesley. 1987. "Some Determinants of Public Attitudes Toward the Police." *Journal of Police Science and Administration* 15(4):285-290.

Zanna, M. P., E. C. Klosson & J. M. Darley. 1976. "How Television News Viewers Deal with Facts that Contradict Their Beliefs: A Consistency and Attribution Analysis." *Journal of Applied Social Psychology* 6:159-176.

Zeisel, H. & A. Gallup. 1989. "Death Penalty Sentiment in the United States." *Journal of Quantitative Criminology* 5:285-296.

Zemans, F. K. 1995. "In the Eye of the Beholder: The Relationship Between the Public and the Courts." In G. L. Mays & P. R. Gregware (eds.), *Courts and Justice: A Reader*, 7-24. Prospect Heights, IL: Waveland Press, Inc.

Zevitz, R. G. & R. J. Rettammel. 1990. "Elderly Attitudes About Police Service." *American Journal of Police* 9(2):25-39.

Zimmerman, E., D. Jeangros, D. Hausser & P. Zeugin. 1991. "La drogue dans l'opinion publique suisse: Perception du probleme et des mesures a prendre." *Deviance et Societe* 15:157-173.

Zimmerman, S., D. J. Van Alstyne & C. S. Dunn. 1988. "The National Punishment Survey and Public Policy Consequences." *Journal of Research in Crime and Delinquency* 25:120-149.

Zimring, F. & G. Hawkins. 1986. *Capital Punishment and the American Agenda*. Cambridge: Cambridge University Press.

Zuckerman, D., & L. Rosenthal. 1981. "Verbal and Nonverbal Communication of Deception." *Advances in Experimental Social Psychology* 14(1):38-40.

About the Book and Author

Taking on one of the most popular issues of the day—crime and the way we make sense of it—Julian Roberts and Loretta Stalans reveal the mismatch between the public perception of crime and the reality of crime statistics. Discussing such issues as public knowledge of crime, sources of crime information, information processing by the public, public attitudes about crime, and the effectiveness of punishment, this book considers the role that public opinion plays in the politics of criminal justice issues. Based on extensive data from the United States, with comparisons with Canada and the United Kingdom, Roberts and Stalans reveal the truth behind how the public perceives crime and how this perception compares to actual criminal activity.

Julian V. Roberts is a professor in the Department of Criminology at the University of Ottawa. **Loretta J. Stalans** is an associate professor of criminal justice at Loyola University of Chicago.

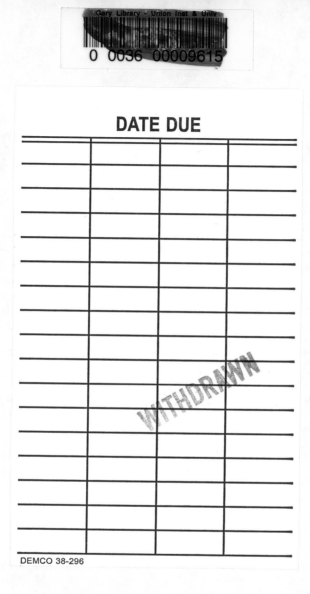

DATE DUE

DEMCO 38-296

Printed in the United States
78369LV00003B/46

9 780813 367934